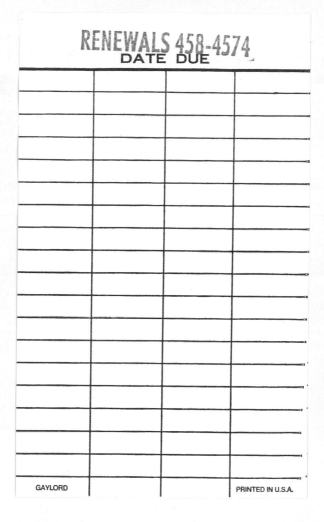

RENEWALS 458-4574

DATE DUE

GAYLORD			PRINTED IN U.S.A.

*The publisher gratefully acknowledges
the generous contribution to this book
provided by The S. Mark Taper Foundation.*

Booking Passage

CONTRAVERSIONS

Critical Studies in Jewish Literature, Culture, and Society

Daniel Boyarin and Chana Kronfeld, General Editors

Booking Passage

*Exile and Homecoming
in the Modern Jewish Imagination*

Sidra DeKoven Ezrahi

UNIVERSITY OF CALIFORNIA PRESS
Berkeley · Los Angeles · London

University of California Press
Berkeley and Los Angeles, California

University of California Press, Ltd.
London, England

© 2000 by the Regents of the
University of California

Library of Congress Cataloging-in-Publication Data

Ezrahi, Sidra DeKoven.

Booking passage : exile and homecoming in the modern Jewish imagination / Sidra
    DeKoven Ezrahi.
        p.   cm. — (Contraversions; 12)
    Includes bibliographical references and index.
    ISBN 0-520-20645-2 (alk. paper).
    1. Jewish literature—History and criticism.   2. Jewish diaspora in literature.
    3. Palestine—In literature.   4. Zionism in literature.   5. Israel—In
    literature.   I. Title.   II. Series.

PN842.E87   2000
892.4'09—dc21   99-14018
                                                 CIP

Manufactured in the United States of America

08   07   06   05   04   03   02   01   00   99

    10   9   8   7   6   5   4   3   2   1

The paper used in this publication meets the
minimum requirements of ANSI/NISO Z39.48-
1992 (R 1997) (*Permanence of Paper*).

The following chapters are revised versions of materials published elsewhere: introduction, as "Our Homeland the Text . . . Our Text the Homeland: Exile and Homecoming
in the Modern Jewish Imagination," in *Michigan Quarterly Review*, special issue on the
Middle East, ed. Anton Shammas, vol. 31, no. 4 (fall 1992): 463–97; chapter 5, as "The
Grave in the Air: Unbound Metaphors in Post-Holocaust Poetry," in *Probing the Limits
of Representation: Nazism and the Final Solution*, ed. Saul Friedländer (Cambridge,
Mass.: Harvard University Press, 1992), pp. 259–76, copyright ©1992 by the President
and Fellows of Harvard College and reprinted by permission of Harvard University
Press; chapter 6, as "Dan Pagis and the Prosaics of Memory," in *Holocaust Remem-
brance: The Shapes of Memory*, ed. Geoffrey Hartman (Oxford: Blackwell, 1994),
pp. 121–33; chapter 9, as "The Grapes of Roth: 'Diasporism' between Portnoy and
Shylock," in *Studies in Contemporary Jewry* 12, Literary Strategies: Jewish Texts and
Contexts, ed. Ezra Mendelsohn (winter 1996–97): 148–58, copyright ©1997 by Oxford
University Press, Inc., and used by permission of Oxford University Press, Inc.

For Talya, Ariel, and Tehila
ha-yahalomim she-ba-keter

A barren land, bare waste. Vulcanic lake, the dead sea: no fish, weedless, sunk deep in the earth. No wind would lift those waves, grey metal, poisonous foggy waters. Brimstone they called it raining down: the cities of the plain: Sodom, Gomorrah, Edom. All dead names. A dead sea in a dead land, grey and old. Old now. It bore the oldest, the first race. . . . The oldest people. Wandered far away over all the earth, captivity to captivity, multiplying, dying, being born everywhere. It lay there now. Now it could bear no more. Dead: an old woman's: the grey sunken cunt of the world.

James Joyce, Ulysses

Often around 5 or 6 o'clock I see an elderly woman on the kibbutz sitting on a bench, singing to herself, and I don't know what she sings, because it's Polish. And I think to myself: That woman 45 years ago must have been a romantic girl with braids sitting by a stream some-where in Poland singing a Hebrew song about Jerusalem . . .

Amos Oz, "After the Sound and the Fury: An Interview"

Contents

Acknowledgments

Parts of this book were written at the Hebrew University and in the cafés of Jerusalem, at the Yaddo Artists' and Writers' Colony in Saratoga Springs, at the Humanities Institute of the University of Michigan, and at Princeton University. I wish to thank my colleagues and friends in all those places for stimulating conversation: Anton Shammas, James Winn, Thomas Pavel, David Shulman, Froma Zeitlin, Daniel Boyarin, Richard Cohen, Robert Alter, Andras Hamori, Carl Schorske, Avrom Udovitch, T. Carmi, Amnon Raz-Karkotzkin, Gabriel Levin, Eva Katz, Molly Myerowitz Levine, Lily Galili, and Nomi Chazan. A National Endowment of the Humanities grant launched the project and a number of publications housed earlier versions of several chapters: *Probing the Limits of Representation*, edited by Saul Friedländer; *Shapes of Memory*, edited by Geoffrey Hartman; *Michigan Quarterly Review* (fall 1992), special issue, edited by Anton Shammas; and *Studies in Contemporary Jewry* 12 (1996–97).

Like any project that takes more than a decade to complete, this book represents a very personal journey and its fellow travelers have been many. It is with great joy and pride that I acknowledge certain of them and it is with great sadness and sense of loss that I mention others. Three readers— Vera Solomon, Kalman Bland, and Chana Kronfeld—contributed their wisdom, their knowledge, and their companionship to every page of this book, but bear no responsibility for its errors. There were times when, in editing the manuscript with Vera, we seemed to be afloat on a lifeboat in the middle of the ocean; once I overcame my seasickness, I realized it was the most exciting adventure of my life. Kal combed every chapter with the dedication and intelligence of a medieval scholar and the loving-kindness of a lifelong friend. Chana's comments delayed the publication date of the book by introducing caveats and questions; I cannot think of a more compelling reason for procrastinating or of a more perfect reader. The final draft was read by Alfred Kazin just months before his death. For twenty years his conversation punctuated my life, and I miss him dearly. Saul Friedländer's nuanced understanding of cultural contradictions and confluences have contributed to my own sense of place more than I can say; several of the chapters were written under his watchful eye. Anita Norich's insightful support has always been crucial to my understanding of the world that produced the great works of Yiddish literature. Bernard Avishai helped to shepherd this book through its final stages with intelligence, good humor, and love; I dedicate the next, unwritten, chapter to him. When the manuscript came to resemble a detective story more than a critical study, Joel Weiss, my research assistant, was there with his indefatigable cheer and resourcefulness. I could not have done this without him.

I would like, finally, to acknowledge my gratitude to Yaron Ezrahi, who was my partner for over three decades, for all the shared ideas and acts of kindness along the way. He read the entire manuscript and offered both support for flagging spirits and solutions for critical conundrums. The signposts of the path we traveled together are scattered throughout the pages of this book.

My parents have navigated between Israel and America with as much finesse as any travelers represented in these chapters; I hope that this travelogue of my own spiritual and physical journey is worthy of their trust.

Booking Passage is dedicated to my precious children.

Booking Passage

Jewish Don Quixote, Russian translation of *The Travels of Benjamin the Third,* by S. Y. Abramovitsh. Translated by Klemens Iunosha. Kazan, Russia: V. F. Borodaich, 1899.

Introduction

A Poetics of Exile and Return

This book was conceived in Jerusalem but has a tendency, as the Jews have, to wander off. In reclaiming sacred space as habitable territory, a people who were on the road for two thousand years had to renegotiate in the twentieth century what had been an epic Jewish journey and a portable Jewish geography. The radical shift inscribed in modern Jewish letters between the path and the goal, between journey and destination, is one of the most telling signs of the cultural upheaval that has accompanied the historical upheavals in our time. In the various places to which it takes us, this process evolves as an ongoing dialectic between the temporal and the spatial, between the "imaginary" and the "real," the mimetic and the original, desire and fulfillment.

"Wenn ihr vollt, Ist es kein Märchen" is the motto of Theodor Herzl's utopian novel, *Altneuland* (1902). If you will it, it is not a dream. If you desire it, it is not a fairy tale. Im tirtzu, ein zo aggada. Oyb ihr vilt, is dos nit keyn bobe-mayse.[1] The many translations of what would become the clarion call of political Zionism acknowledge the tendency of people in exile to invest their desires in stories and, implicitly, the danger to storytelling—and to life itself?—that comes from the fulfillment of desire, the actualization of imaginary worlds.

The struggle to realize the utopian vision of a sovereign Jewish place under the sun gives rise to a new chapter in the poetics of exile and return. Evolving out of an inherited model of Homecoming that was essentially ahistorical, it describes a zigzag pattern across the borders between real and imagined spaces. The deep structure of *provisionality*, of an exile theologically constructed between the ancient memory of domicile and the messianic vision of an endlessly deferred return, once introduced into political, "historical" time and place, generates more than one set of grammars. For Jews who had developed a culture of *substitution* in all the lands of their dispersion, reconnecting with Zion, or Jerusalem, meant an intoxicating—and toxic—encounter with the only place that had the status of *the real*. Repudiating mimetic culture in favor of a reclamation of "original space" also activates, at the deepest level, a mechanism for renouncing the workings of the imagination, the invention of alternative worlds, to replace them with the recovery of what is perceived as the bedrock of the collective self.

In drawing connections between poetic and narrative texts written over the last century, I am attempting to elucidate what I see both as the aesthetic manifestations and ideological implications of a paradigm of return and as the critical potential of alternative paradigms. I am tracing a Zionist discourse that emerged along an Eastern European–American axis;[2] it was fairly oblivious to Jews from the countries of the Near East and effaced the Arab by a peculiar act of incorporation. Drawing on male-dominated languages of representation, ancient and modern, it figures the woman as "home" in both its conjugal, personal and its mythic, territorial dimensions. In exploring these powerful forms and counterforms, I also hope to bring the deeper currents of the Jewish imagination to bear on the critical discussion that locates the Zionist enterprise primarily within the precincts of Western nationalism and colonialism.

This book was not only conceived in but is also largely about Jerusalem, yet its stories, even when they are situated in Jerusalem, are nearly always located elsewhere. The people who live here and who are trying to preserve their sanity, their humanity, and their passion for life learn that she is a city on which to touch down gingerly, tentatively, so as to avoid being suffocated by her deadly embrace.

RECOVERY OR *DISCOVERY*?

"Recovery" is an interpretive strategy that assigns special meaning in the present to an act or event of the past. The drama of the recovery— or reinvention—of ancient Rome by the Italian painters, sculptors, and philosophers of the sixteenth century has been described as a kind of spontaneous eruption of relics of the lost self: the seemingly random resurfacing of the *Laocoön*, the *Tiber*, and scores of other works of art from the buried substrata of the city. At a safe distance from both Renaissance Rome and the ancient city whose ghosts and statuary constitute Rome's "other population,"[3] today's art historian can provide a meditation on the function of relics as signs of the hidden sources of a regenerating civilization. Without the benefit of such distance from the object of inquiry, without the dispassion that only distance can grant to the struggles of any city perched so recklessly close to heaven, I venture some tentative analogies between Rome in the sixteenth and Jerusalem in the twentieth century as major sites in the recovery of symbolic space. "Apart from a very brief time, the history of Rome is a history of the idea of a city that used to be. Through a quite simple mechanism, the more depressed the reality of Rome, the more potent the symbolization," writes Leonard Barkan. "Just as real power recedes from Rome, so the graven images of that power become increasingly pure symbols."[4]

The transformation of graven images into symbols as power and territory recede, and their recovery some two thousand years later, is one of the major themes of this book. In the Holy Land, depressed for centuries and suspended in her ruined state—"captive of her dream," in the words of a popular Israeli song—scrolls tend to replace graven images as primary authenticating artifacts. The members of Zion's "other population" (its ancient dead) have become so present in the lives of its latter-day inhabitants that the manuscripts they read and wrote in this region two millennia ago are front-page items in today's newspapers. There is no emblem of the complex connections between texts and territory and the disputed claims for hegemony in the Holy Land more dramatic than the Dead Sea Scrolls, buried in the hillsides of Qumran for nearly two thousand years, discovered—randomly, of course, like the *Laocoön*—by Bedouin shepherds tending their flocks, and the struggle over access to them being waged among different hermeneutic communities. There are no letters delivered in today's mailboxes more urgent than those bearing Bar Kokhba's signature. There is no speech more politically loaded in contemporary Israel than the one that Elazar ben Yair "delivered" in 73 C.E. to the would-be filicides, homicides, and suicides of Massada, as "reported" by Josephus and "confirmed" by Yigal Yadin some nineteen hundred years later. As fragmented as they might appear, these parchments and protocols become the early chapters in what must emerge as a continuous narrative.

But what is it these ancient scrolls remember? What is the memory sought in the crumbling parchment that lay buried for nearly two millennia near the Dead Sea? Yadin was one of the chief architects of the symbolic link binding the Dead Sea Scrolls—which, he said, had been "waiting in caves for two thousand years, ever since the destruction of Israel's independence"—and the moment when "the people of Israel had returned to their home and regained their freedom."[5] What is being excavated is the narrative that, grounded in the past, grants the present its meaning. In other words, archaeology retrieves the factual, tangible evidence, the script that upholds and validates the entire enterprise. The scroll becomes here both object and signifier. But because the scroll is the *thing itself*, it is less important for those who have "returned" to actually *read* the story it tells; it may even be such a dangerous venture that the slow progress of reassembling, deciphering, and publishing the scrolls defers the process of collective self-analysis that such an exposé of "original narratives" could provoke. (Certain prophets have intimated that ingesting the scrolls is a form of incorporation more effective than attempts to decipher them.)

This is a dramatic instance of the distinctions between *discovery* and *recovery* as constructs of the conquest and settlement of territory: between, for example, the "discovery" (or invention) of America as terra incognita (Nuovo Mundo)—with all of its implications for self-invention, innocence, and rebirth as fundamental paradigms of American self-representation—and the Jewish return to sacred space as a recapitulation of origins and a reconnection with the material as well as the spiritual sources of being.[6] In the one case, the land itself was conventionally represented as pristine, with an infinity of images reflected in its surfaces—a relatively benign state of nature sparsely populated by "savage" beings; in the other, the land was represented as lying in ruins, the terrain harsh and barren with an infinity of secrets concealed in its depths. To a degree even more pronounced than in the sixteenth-century recovery of ancient Rome, the prevailing cultural tropes in latter-day Palestine are those of *excavation* and *closure*.

The quest for origins that proceeded over centuries throughout Europe linked both America and Palestine, at one time or another, to the lost continent of Atlantis. Yet beyond regular attempts to historicize it, as Pierre Vidal-Naquet has shown, Atlantis maintained its mythic status as the "fabled land" of origin.[7] It sinks, one might say, into the watery depths of the unconscious as primary reference, not as destination. Palestine in ruins, however, retained its physical presence—and its promise of recovery. Whatever the revolutionary fervor of the early Zionists, and their claim for discontinuity vis-à-vis the Jewish past, the force of a reconnection with *original* space seems if anything to foster over the years an enhanced sense of teleology and of closure. "As always," writes Jacques Derrida, "archaeology is also a teleology and an eschatology; the dream of a full and immediate presence closing history . . . "[8] Identifying, deciphering, and interpreting the scrolls take on the urgency of a reconstitutive act within a community that never recoiled from anachronism as an organizing principle.

JEWISH JOURNEYS

. . . Keep Ithaka always in your mind.

Arriving there is what you're destined for.

But don't hurry the journey at all. . . .

Ithaka gave you the marvelous journey.

Without her you wouldn't have set out[.]

    C. P. Cavafy, "Ithaka"

Consistently, for most of two millennia, the Holy Land remained a *ruined* landscape in the minds of its rememberers, *Judea capta*, a dusty relic. Maurice Halbwachs explores the disjunction between the testimony of witnesses and the formulas of collective memory as, from the first century on, they construct and reconstruct the topography of the Holy Land, the competing and overlapping sites of Jewish and Christian reference: "The collective memories that are attached to a place coalesce, divide, become attached to one another, or scatter, as the case may be."[9] Such orientations toward Palestine, in which the yearning for ultimate homecoming is compatible with the most radical form of homelessness and the most protean notion of home, can be traced not only to a fascination with ruins and the picturesque, culminating in nineteenth-century European romanticism, but, in the Jewish imagination, to a preservation of the desolated homeland as appropriate correlative of the ongoing, indefinite exile of its original inhabitants. Hebrew poets of the Middle Ages such as Yehuda Halevi yearned expressly for the ruined shrines. In the next chapter I will trace the voyage this twelfth-century poet actually undertook; but as he did not survive to tell its end, every succeeding writer is left to try to do so. Yehuda Halevi's own ill-fated vessel gives rise to a fleet of ships, generations of "Zionides" that hold the shore in a state of suspense. Those who do arrive are greeted, predictably, by ruins that evoke a sense of déjà vu. As late as the mid–nineteenth century, the Hebrew geographies maintain a quasi-scientific tone—until they

reach the foothills of Jerusalem, when the scientific tour yields to a holy
pilgrimage—replete with ruins, tears, and the pilgrim's acute sense of
being a stranger on "native" ground.[10]

Jewish journeys fill the second millennium after the destruction of the
Second Temple and the first half of this book. From Yehuda Halevi
through S. Y. Agnon, Jerusalem is the destination that determines the epic
dimensions of the journey. And the Jew-on-the-Road acquires correlative status as liminal presence in the Christian imagination. But in our
century, experienced and conceptualized by "the homeless mind,"[11] writing the exile carries an authority beyond the specific myths of banishment that define the origins, the odyssey, and the theodicy of Jews and
Christians. Within a more generalized, universalized narrative of exile,
the figure of Wandering Jew is reabsorbed—no longer the boundary figure, when boundaries shift so regularly; no longer the stranger, in the
"global village" where no one is at home; no longer the lone weary traveler, in a world in which everyone is a tourist. After Joyce, whose *Ulysses*
synthesized and domesticated into a modern urban myth the Jewish and
Greek paradigms of exile, one might legitimately argue that certain literary traditions have exhausted their privilege and then ask what there
is in the Jewish story that warrants particular attention.

In arguing for a specifically Jewish poetics of exile and return, I am
defining a revolution in self-representation mandated in manifest ways
by the experience of migration, dislocation, and extermination of masses
of Jews in the twentieth century and by the reinvention and settlement
of the ancient Jewish homeland—but it is a revolution informed by a
complex of largely unspoken axioms. The exploration of these axioms
constitutes the first part of this book and offers a map to the subterranean pathways through which Jewish culture travels in our time and
a means to decipher some of the most seductive and perplexing of its external signs.

The *epic* of return is, then, the implicit paradigm of the Jewish journey that will be traced in the coming pages; the *anti-epic* follows the epic
like a rudderless sailboat in the wake of a steamship, describing in its el-
lipses a skeptical parody of the redemptive itinerary. S. Y. Abramovitsh's
Travels of Benjamin the Third rewrites the religious pilgrimage as a
quixotic adventure at the very moment in modern Jewish history when
it is issuing in a political platform. The course is righted in *In the Heart
of the Seas*, S. Y. Agnon's unerring journey to and settlement in the Holy
Land. In *Tevye the Dairyman* and *The Railroad Stories*, Sholem Aleichem
provides a running commentary on both schemes, but in *Motl the Can-*

tor's Son he elaborates a third itinerary: the "discovery" of America and the exchange of wandering as a Jewish curse for mobility as an American opportunity. These journeys reinvent some of the most ancient reflexes in the Jewish imagination bred on the experience and the theodicy of exile.

The modern, not unlike the romantic, discourse on home, exile, and return captures the intensified longing for a place of origin as ultimate reference or antecedent—the presumption of a paradise whose loss or absence preserves it in a kind of negative space. The categories and strategies of reading may have changed radically, but the theme of exile and homecoming is as old as literature itself—and has become nearly synonymous with our understanding of the psychogenesis of literary practice. As the source of a long intertextual journey, Psalm 137 generates the poetic vocabulary of exile: "By the waters of Babylon, *there* we sat and cried as we remembered Zion." The pleonastic "there," repeated in the third verse, calls attention to itself by its very redundancy; syntactically superfluous, "there" defines exile as the place that is always *elsewhere*. Being elsewhere, being far from Zion, is the pre-text for poetry. Goaded into song, the exiles' first response is demurral: "How can we sing God's song in a foreign land?" And then, after no more than the space of a breath, the speaking voice moves from first-person plural to first-person singular and the song of exile begins: "If I forget thee, O Jerusalem, let my right hand forget its cunning, let my tongue cleave to my palate . . . " The malfunctioning writing hand and singing tongue are both the signs of *and* the punishment for amnesia. Singing becomes mnemonic compensation for absence—and eventually the Temple becomes a memory palace, located for this remembering community in the pages of its Talmud.[12]

But what is "remembered" is of course also imagined, as mimesis takes on the authority and license of memory and memory becomes an article of faith. In its most radical form, memory and imagination describe a circularity that promotes an aesthetics of the whole. The postmodern critique of romantic notions of homecoming invokes the culture of exile as a response to the dangers of circularity and closure. If the banishment from the garden is the "moment" when myth becomes history, so *histoire*—both history and story, as challenged by Edmond Jabès, Jacques Derrida, and other theorists of the postmodern—is in its most reductive form represented as the narrative of creation, exile and redemption. "It has a beginning (Once upon a time), a middle (. . .), and an end (happily ever after)," writes Mark Taylor. "The history of the West unfolds between limits set by the garden and the kingdom . . . [between the] felicity of the beginning and the perfection of the end."[13] Resisting both felicity and perfection, both beginnings and endings, this is a sensibility that privileges the *middle* as an errant, meandering, endlessly deferred, never-ending story. Writing the exile thus becomes more than a response to displacement (and in its generic form does not depend on physical dislocation at all); it becomes in itself a form of repatriation, of alternative sovereignty. It is what makes Kafka both the quintessential modernist and the prophet of the postmodern; it is the "elsewhere" to which such prophets go when they are "excluded from Canaan. . . . Cast out of the world, into the error of infinite migration, [Kafka] . . . had to struggle ceaselessly to make of this outside another world and of this error the principle, the origin of a new freedom."[14] As an exile he can never, by definition, reach backward or forward to the "place itself."

In exploring the Jewish poetics of exile, I am arguing that the imaginative enterprise in *galut* was subsumed under the struggle to construct the future as projected image of the lost past—but that within such an apparently rigid teleological structure it remained a remarkably open-ended adventure. The forms of textual repatriation, of alternative sovereignty, were *conceptually* one remove from the "thing itself" or the "place itself." As Franz Rosenzweig was to define it in his polemic with Zionism, the land that is deemed holy is also unpossessable, that is, generates its own diasporic force field of desire.[15] In its most radical form, this is an imaginative license that has no geographical coordinates: it is an affirmation and reconfiguration of the Jewish word as nomadic exercise and Jewish exile as a kind of *literary* privilege. Each of the writers and their vast and scattered community of readers are bound by a commitment to provisional, imagined (or remembered) worlds, to desire as the principle of fiction, and to a lack of closure as the truest guarantee of continuity.

"OUR HOMELAND, THE TEXT"

("The road sucks us in and thus disappears. . . . Ink shrinks
space down to the letter. You will print the earth in its split
attention. You will print the sky in its diffuse impossibility.
Rectangles of grass or sand, or blue or clouds. The rays of
the sun are penholders which night gorges with ink."—Reb
Adal)

                                    Edmond Jabès, Le Retour au livre

Edmond Jabès is one of the modern architects and exemplars of text-centeredness as an exilic priority: "Gradually I realized that the Jew's real place is the book. In the book he questions himself, in the book he has his freedom, which has been forbidden him everywhere. . . . Moses, in the act of breaking the tablets, gave the word a human origin."[16]

But after 1948, the book has once again to compete with the soil as center of gravity. Those who continue to dwell in the book when an earthly home has become available to the Jews cannot, according to this reading, partake of its materiality: their wandering consists in keeping their distance from the Land, in remaining loyal to the ever-deferred promise.

George Steiner carries this argument to its logical extreme in his polemic with the "territorial imperative"; he has become the most contentious postwar exponent of exile as both the necessary condition of and the catalyst for that particular Jewish prerogative of being "unhoused" in the world and "at home in the word." Arguing for "our homeland, the text," Steiner writes:

> Heine's phrase is exactly right: "das aufgeschriebene Vaterland." The "land of his fathers," the *patrimoine*, is the script. In its doomed immanence, in its attempt to immobilize the text in a substantive, architectural space, the Davidic and Solomonic Temple may have been an erratum, a misreading of the transcendent mobility of the text. . . . The deeper truth of unhousedness, of an at-homeness in the word, . . . are the legacy of the Prophets and of the keepers of the text. . . . When the text *is* the homeland, even when it is rooted only in the exact remembrance and seeking of a handful of wanderers, nomads of the word, it cannot be extinguished.[17]

Steiner does not limit the Jewish "homeland" to canonic Jewish texts or to texts housed in Jewish languages. "Each seeking out of a moral, philosophic, positive verity, each text rightly established and expounded is an *aliyah*, a homecoming of Judaism to itself and to its keeping of the books," he says. Invoking the highly charged language of *'aliyah* to the Torah while blocking its modern Zionist connotations, Steiner is polemically affirming the primacy of rites of reading over rites of pilgrimage and settlement on holy land. He regards Mandelstam, Kafka, and Celan as latter-day prophets and any place where there is a library as an "'Israel' of truth-seeking."[18]

The literacy of the exile becomes, by these lights, a kind of semiotic privilege through which the library as sacred center and reading as an act of devotion and deciphering can be extended infinitely. It is not only specific books, and not only books, that are read, but the world itself.

The metaphor of nature as a book and of wandering as the way to "read" it is at least as old as the Latin Middle Ages; from Paracelsus, for whom the "whole earth is a book or a library in which the pages are turned with our feet, which must be used 'pilgrimly,'" it reappears in every age with its emphasis and premise of legibility slightly different.[19] In many border crossings, the exile claims to comprehend the book of nature as well as the social contract with a different intelligence. Learning to read the inscriptions of nature, rather than of the self into nature, to "spell the landscape" as an intelligible text,[20] would then be *a deciphering but not a proprietary or political act*. The travelers on the road, like the fingers on the page, trace in their meanderings the imprints of a universally accessible universe.

When the journey across space is a pilgrimage to a holy site, however, then the sentence constructed or construed is more likely to resonate with that *other* book, the Good Book, whose inscriptions of natural phenomena are infused with specific, culturally tendentious meanings.[21] The religious imagination reconciles Scriptures with the Book of Nature, while creating in the very idea of the book room for a third—*human*—form of imagining, of authorship, and of authority.[22]

Granted, in its Jewish versions that license implies the diminished or derivative status of local landscapes as well as the diminished status of human authors. The generalization that postbiblical Jews knew more about the flora and fauna of Palestine than about their immediate diasporic environs, that the world in Yiddish literature was "almost devoid of trees" and the "skies practically empty of birds," belongs to the hyperbolic language of the maskilic (Enlightenment) and the Zionist polemic with Jewish culture-in-exile.[23] But while the vernacular worlds are not quite as denatured as such polemicists would have it, the Jewish calendar and classical vocabulary do reflect the relative weight ascribed over time to Palestine as the "real" place, the only place where topography and climate *matter*.

The assignment of status to the Holy Land as center of the earth's blessing and the Bible as its map does not, however, limit God's dwelling to a specific shrine. The Jews living within the broad confines of a postrabbinic monotheism were in "God's country" anywhere. One could even argue that monotheism evolved into a strategy for making the world one's home; the God whose glory fills the earth is simply not to be confined. As *HA*-makom, God is not only *THE* place, but place itself. A rabbinic midrash on "Jacob's pillow" relates to the rock under Jacob's head at Bethel (Gen. 28) as metonymy for the entire Land of Israel—arguably a proprietary, Palestine-centered reading. But Rabbi Shimeon refines this by suggesting that God folded the rock like a notebook or ledger (*pinkas*) and put it under Jacob's head.[24] This reductive image (Eretz Yisrael as text) is striking as a sign of the rabbinic project of creating a viable, portable Jewish civilization in exile through its signifying practices.

In his discussion of Jewish aesthetics, Kalman Bland explores the plastic dimensions of the sacred text through its late medieval sources, a tradition in which "Scripture formally recapitulates sacred, architectural space," in which the Hebrew Bible's tripartite division is "isomorphic" with the Temple itself.[25] In traditions culminating in the Kabbala, time and space become conflated so that the sanctity of place is projected not only onto texts but also onto the rhythm of weekly ritual: the Sabbath becomes a sacred center, analogous to Jerusalem and the Garden of Eden, and the synagogue a miniature temple (*mikdash m'at*), allowing for a regular re-creation of cosmos out of chaos. Time carved out of the quotidian and sanctified as sacred space provides a nonmaterial as well as an ahistorical accommodation or provisional resolution to exile.[26]

So the parameters of the religious Jewish imagination as it developed over the centuries became emancipated from dependence on sovereignty conceived within any geographically specific boundaries. In fact, the position of the Jew as citizen of the cosmopolis, articulated most provocatively in recent times by Steiner and Jabès, becomes a curiosity only when measured against very ancient or very new forms of sedentary life. The idea of *galut* or *golus* as a viable condition in an unredeemed world made it possible over many centuries to establish social and cultural connections that were nonterritorial and nonproprietary. The terms of group survival, the principles of exclusion and inclusion, would be renegotiated at every crisis point in the early development of Jewish collective existence, and the status of major variables—territory and ritual space, genealogy, and faith—would vary as the historical conditions changed.[27] The centrality of "the Book" entails a wide culture of substitution for or imitation of the territorial dimension; in its devotional procedure and performative substitute for Temple rites, it created the rationale and the instruments for a mobile civilization—incorporating, spiritualizing, temporarily superseding, but never entirely effacing the memory and the promise of "Yerushalayim shel mata," of terrestrial Jerusalem as linchpin of the *axis mundi*.

And yet in late-twentieth-century constructions of Jewish memory and imagination, the elevation of textuality or even of temporality as a diasporic privilege based on the traditional Jewish valuation of the book

and the calendar tends to camouflage a major shift in the value of means
relative to ends, the value of the now-time and this-place relative to the
End-of-Time and Ultimacy-of-Place. By turning necessity into a virtue,
as it were, latter-day Diasporism challenges the very premise of provisionality as the key to Jewish theodicy and destabilizes the mimetic imagination as a nonabsolute marker of place. Steiner's metaphoric Talmud
is a text signifying the *vacancy of place* (not the *vacated place*). From a
modern point of view, this appears compatible with the character of a
religious culture that, in its portable ritual spaces, designates holiness as
a systemic (i.e., referentially arbitrary) category:[28] a culture that delin-
eates diaspora in its most fundamental function as the place of replica
and imitation—as *imaginative* space. But presented as a kind of textual
essentialism, unmoored from specific sources of authority and codes of
faith, Jewish textuality is reduced to a set of gestures or postures, and
the Jew becomes simply a generic social or moral critic, a "reader" of
culture. A barricade of books and poststructuralist claims to life "in the
text" may be a good hedge against the territorialization and fetishiza-
tion of the Jewish word, but they often invoke a language that signifies
the vacancy of content and displays the cultural valorization of signifiers
without the specific and stable, if distant, referents that licensed cultural
mobility.

With the (re)territorialization of the Jewish imagination in the twentieth century, a radical shift takes place in the relative position of ends
and means, of original and mimetic space, of holy and profane, of ownership and tenancy. If exile is narrative, then to historicize the end of the
narrative is to invite a form of epic closure that threatens the storytelling
enterprise itself—an enterprise that remained alive, like Scheherazade,
by suspending endings. Conversely, to claim an absolute place for the
exilic imagination is to privilege *the story* as the *thing itself*; the map for
the territory, language without referent;[29] and to regard "nomadic writing" as the inherently Jewish vocation. The danger of turning scrolls into
sacraments by which to consecrate the soil is matched by the danger of
dissociation, of dissolution, that has afflicted generations of emancipated
Jewish Quixotes.

The relative value of places to the Place as both territorial and divine
locus maintained a tension and an ambiguity throughout a long history
of Jewish journeys, and it is that ambiguity and the new forms it has generated, especially over the last century, that will shape the chapters of
this book. If Land was transfigured into texts-in-exile, then we are examining how in one context it has begun to come back and "reanimate"

the texts—as if the words were so many custodians or shelters that allowed the elements of a world in ruins to be preserved until such time as it could be reclaimed—and how, in another context, it retains its status as sacred center, unpossessable, elusive, and generative of an infinity of possible worlds.

JEWISH GEOGRAPHY

Jews constructed not only memory temples and Sabbaths out of the ruins of their material existence but also stories out of the relics of hearths that were abandoned along the way and were, by definition, remote from the sacred center. Rahel carried her *teraphim*, her household gods, from place to place, even when admonished that holiness could not be confined in local icons and lowercase homelands. But the safest and most enduring hiding places for the lares and penates of deserted homes were the stories that contained and superseded them.

In the modern Yiddish and Hebrew fiction that began to appear in the late nineteenth century, the changing status of lowercase and uppercase homelands helped to launch a new constellation of imaginary and actual worlds—encompassing both a fictional universe that more freely experiments with the laws of narrative conventions and an ancient Jewish territory subjecting its returnees to the laws of gravity. The prospect of a resettled Jewish homeland, as it took on political dimensions, also regenerated a notion of original space to which the text culture could return. In the implicit dialectic that ensued between Hebrew and the other Jewish languages, this return, a secularized reflection of the religious vision of reunification with sacred space, would eventually embolden the diasporic imagination of writers from S. Y. Abramovitsh and Sholem Aleichem to Philip Roth to pursue fictional alternatives, mimetic counterparts to the very idea of original, unduplicable space.

By the early twentieth century, the shtetl had become the specific locus of Eastern European Jewish life and imagination; its viability was a function of its presumed ubiquity. The small-town, small-minded Jews in S. Y. Abramovitsh's Yiddish and Hebrew prose compose a static picture animated by the lively narrational skills of Mendele the Bookpeddler, whose mobility is his passport to the future. His Kabtzielites, remote descendants of the Babylonian and Roman exiles, forced by a great "conflagration" to leave their shtetl, hang their rags on a willow or two.[30] No lyres, no songs of Jerusalem, and just enough memory for self-debasement: yet in those very tatters and fragments of royal clothes and royal texts lie the domesticated dimensions of a modern replay of exile and desire.

Sholem Aleichem, in his later Yiddish prose, decontextualizes Kasrilevke, his invented town in the Russian pale of settlement; now weightless like a figure on a Chagall canvas, Kasrilevke reappears on the train, in London, and finally in America. Traveling by train, by ship, by foot, Motl the cantor's son lands with both feet on American soil; only the death of the author would eventually arrest his progress. Over the course of our century, the diasporist cultural paradigm reshuffles old forms and shifts its locus westward. America emerges as a different kind of homeland, as a continent that houses the wayward imagination and the liberal invention of counterlives. America is the site of Sholem Aleichem's most forward-looking, self-created character and the licensing bureau for Philip Roth's most zany diasporist plots.

Most of the Jews of Eastern Europe were, however, headed for another destination. As in so many accounts of the Jewish experience in the twentieth century, the blank page that separates the two sections of this book signifies the black hole that may or may not be considered a "location" on the Jewish map. Is Auschwitz a Jewish place? Is there a symbolic vocabulary that belongs there? German Jewish poet Paul Celan wrote "Todesfuge" [Deathsfugue] just after he was released from labor camps in Transnistria and probably before the war had ended. In that poem, which was to become the site of both the most reverential and the most incriminatory readings, the Jews are commanded to "shovel a grave in the air there you won't lie too cramped." His compatriot from Bukovina, Dan Pagis, who survived the war to become one of Israel's foremost scholars and poets, writes in the "posthumous" first person: "Against my will / I was continued by this cloud" ("Footprints").[31] Are Celan's "grave in the air" and Pagis's "cloud" the most authentic postwar signifiers of the awful portability of Jewish geography? The struggle between the centripetal and centrifugal forces is also a struggle between materialization and dematerialization in twentieth-century reconfigurations of Jewish culture in the wake of Jewish history.

The simultaneous effacement of homelands in Europe and creation of a central Homeland in Palestine forms the primary metanarrative of modern Jewish culture; its most powerful counternarratives represent "home" as overdetermined by the ideology and enactment of a collective repatriation in Israel while at the very same time, for the majority of Jews of European extraction, even an *imagined* return to native grounds is preempted by devastation. In modern Hebrew literature, this paradox is ex-

pressed most powerfully by Dan Pagis in his forgetful poetry and his remembering prose and by Aharon Appelfeld in his displaced fictions.

In their very status as "nonoriginal" ground of reference, Jewish spaces
outside of the Land of Israel were always emblematic of a very particular, elastic state of mind. But after the physical destruction of Jewish Europe, can such places be contained even within the vast open borders of
postwar poetry? Why do *we go* to such places in search of palpable traces
of the past? Should we read what Pierre Nora might call "les lieux de mémoire juive" not as new memory palaces but as *reliquaries*, constructed
outside of the Holy Land by a modern imagination increasingly intoxicated by the sanctification of *place*? Founded belatedly on nostalgia and
on incomplete mourning, the diasporic imagination will eventually generate a postwar Europe without walls as a site of pilgrimage—literary at
first and then literal, a substitution for Jerusalem as the ruined shrine.[32]
I. B. Singer will reinvent Jewish Eastern Europe and Paul Celan will pre-
side as high priest of the scattered relics of Jewish Central Europe.

While it is still too early to draw any conclusions regarding the relative impact on the imagination of the destruction of Jewish spaces in the
ancient Holy Land and in modern Europe, a pattern does begin to suggest itself: what was destroyed becomes over time an authentic original
that can be represented but not recaptured; it becomes accessible to the
pilgrim/tourist only as an unredeemed ruin, subject to a nonproprietary
gaze. Hence the Holocaust may have turned the European exile from a
place in which Home is imagined to a "real" home that can only be re-
called from somewhere else and reconstructed from its shards; retrospectively, that is, the destruction seems to have territorialized exile as a
lost home.

What is the fate of specific Jewish languages that inhered in specific
places outside the sacred center? Do Yiddish and the other "secret" languages of the Jews, like their secret places, persist as primary points of
reference and reverence long after—or because—they have been effaced?[33] Is there a subtle exchange, over the years, between Yiddish and
Hebrew as the locus of mystery and ruin, if not of authenticity? And the
Hebrew that has been lost in Europe and found in Zion—how does it
resonate through the echo chambers of the one and the crowded mar-
ketplaces of the other? As two German-speaking compatriots from Romania, Paul Celan comes to Hebrew (and to Zion) as pilgrim, Dan Pagis
as immigrant. For Pagis, Hebrew is the material of a new social grammar, and his poetry is located in the interplay of its deep and its surface
structures. For Celan, Hebrew appears as the only authentic, and still-

undeciphered, ur-language of the Jew—as both marker of a vanished civilization and utopian pledge to some idea of a deferred future. In his totemic images Hebrew words survive as incantatory fragments of a liturgical, scriptural lexicon.

The return to the Land, perceived simultaneously (by different interpretive communities) as the *beginning* and the *end* of history, has the potential to undermine the power of its own metaphors and to demonstrate the dangers of literalization. Pagis's poetry exemplifies a radical skepticism directed at the heart of the utopian/messianic enterprise; through a series of defamiliarizations, it calls attention to the implications of the encounter between Jewish modes of imagining homecoming as part of the narrative of exile and that homecoming as actualized in history. Emanating from the chaotic matter of his destroyed world and suspended just above the newly created cosmos that would absorb them, these poetic fragments enact the tensions between the myth of perfection and the messy actualities of any homecoming in real time.

Whether the cultural phenomenon we are examining is utopian or messianic in its political or religious manifestations,[34] whether it is an apocalyptic modernism that takes refuge in the autonomy of the imagination[35] or a theodicy that culminates in a place and time perceived as *athalta de-ge'ula*, the opening bars in the symphony of redemption, what struggles to emerge—even (especially?) in a civilization that had for so long managed successfully to resist its own "sense of an ending"—is an aesthetics of total perfection, of the perfection of totality. Utopian desire is the very fire of fiction; utopia "realized" threatens to consume the fictive by subsuming all alternative worlds.[36] Banishing the poets from the new republic is an act that the architects and guardians of Hebrew culture would not have countenanced; but even as only a logical, hypothetical extension of the utopian project, such exclusion signals the dangers of any all-encompassing cultural vision.

Utopias take up a lot of room. The correspondence—or distance—between what Israeli anthropologists Zali Gurevitch and Gideon Aran call *makom katan* and *makom gadol*, place and Place[37]—between physical locatedness or nativism as a natural human state (and a "normal" Jewish state) and "Eretz" as the idea of sacred, redemptive territory—is a measure of the struggle between quotidian and utopian negotiations with place in modern Israel: and this struggle assumes a wide spectrum of cultural expressions. Different literary strategies replace the deferred, *u-topian* imagination of place with the topos of an actual, physical pres-

ence. The appeal of the visual, the original, and the palpable as opposed
to the verbal and the mimetic reconnects the modern Jewish imagination
with deep, archaic forms of relating to divinity.

The question at the center of this book is how the reacquisition of the
spatial dimension has affected the Jewish literary imagination in the twentieth century; more specifically, it asks whether (particular) space as the
manifestation of holiness replaces the text that has served as its surrogate.

Probably the purest representation of "return" and repossession in
contemporary Hebrew literature—the one that comes closest to a perfect fit between places "Large" and "small"—can be found in the writings of S. Y. Agnon, whose prose incorporates most of the layers of Hebrew memory. His novella *In the Heart of the Seas* (1934) is our only
exemplum of a modern triumphal epic; in this slim but fully articulated
narrative of return we can see how the enactment of both journey and
arrival gives a different resonance to the biblical verses that, having served
as place markers for thousands of years, are now reinscribed as landmarks. While much of Agnon's fiction comes as close as any modern
Hebrew text to opening a stable passage between cosmic planes, a yearning for place that is so much greater than arrival could possibly satisfy
makes any nonironic encounter with the shrine a studied act of piety
saturated with pathos. Gravitational forces have to work overtime in
order to keep ingathered a people so used to wandering and to invest-
ing every way station with temporary holiness and provisional value;
confining the deity to the geopolitical borders of a modern state becomes
then an urgent task, fraught with consequence. (Will the Green Line, re-
drawn, keep Him in—or set Him free?)[38] Divinity in postrabbinic Judaism was not localized, and current attempts to localize it inevitably
involve a move toward interdicted forms of idol worship. A modern replay of the conflict between priestly and prophetic orientations moves
between localized and mobile concepts of the godhead. Efforts to rescue Diasporism are also efforts to preserve the God-in-Exile as the truest
form of monotheism.

For Jews during the centuries of their exile, pilgrimage to the Land of
Israel was not confined to any single structure or ruin; the soil itself had
the properties of holiness that had once inhered in specific edifices. But
if for the Jewish pilgrim the sacred territory was always a place to visit
and then to leave, a different kind of coming and going would have to
evolve in order to secure life in the place where divinity had been localized in habitations of earth and stone only in its earliest monotheistic

phases. The unself-conscious paganism that begins to reinform Jewish culture in Israel ensues in a tension between myth and fiction, between the stable, unchanging "real" and the forces that refuse to be held down. The Wailing Wall—for ages a pilgrimage site, ground zero, the very *axis mundi*—not only is the final resting place of all the writing, of all the petitions deposited in its cracks, but also becomes a kind of bulwark against any threat (or promise) of flight: "the last stop of history . . . a blank wall with no open-sesames or hidden crypts . . . the ultimate dam, built to hold back the Jews in their restless proclivity to return to their past. 'Halt!' it says. 'No Passage Allowed Beyond This Point.'"[39] Where, then, is the restless Jewish spirit to go?

As modern Hebrew literature attempted to "spatialize" or stabilize the Jewish imagination while the Arab-Israeli conflict confined that space to a claustrophobic, hermetic sphere,[40] time could be rescued only in the interstices where the unquenched desire of the not-yet-arrived continually invaded sacred space to make room for narrative. In his most pious or nostalgic stories, Agnon represents the possibility of a close fit between Place and place; his nightmarish tales represent the misfits. Yehuda Amichai provides the most elastic poetic representations of the *im*perfect fit between the spaces—the very seas on which the Temple Mount can set sail from what is otherwise the most landlocked city in the world.[41] Amichai's verses hover over the chapters of this book as an ongoing commentary on the sentences that preceded him. He reengraves the psalm of exile, Psalm 137, back into the native landscape through ironic reversals and the intrusion of private, even unspoken, sentences into the formulas of collective memory:

> If I forget thee, Jerusalem,
> Then let my right be forgotten.
> Let my right be forgotten, and my left remember.
> Let my left remember, and your right close
> And your mouth open near the gate.
>
> I shall remember Jerusalem
> And forget the forest—my love will remember,
> Will open her hair, will close my window,
> Will forget my right,
> Will forget my left[.][42]

The poet-in-Jerusalem rescues the human beloved, the woman *in* Jerusalem, from the suffocating grasp of the metaphoric woman who *is* Jerusalem. The literalizing occasion allows this poet to ground, but also to undermine and to personalize, biblical texts—to inscribe on the private body what has been inscribed on the landscape in ways that do not denature either.

The whimsy of a poetry that can play wantonly in its own backyard can also be a response to the dangers of reconnecting a long-preserved memory with its source—memory that, looping back on its own epic beginnings, would stubbornly refuse the blessings of a forgetting that is always also a forgiving.[43] The second half of the psalm that began the journey, the half that is rarely quoted, reveals the potentially vindictive horrors of total recall:

> Remember, O Lord, against the Edomites
> The day of Jerusalem's fall
> How they cried, "Strip her, strip her
> To her very foundations."
> Fair Babylon, you predator,
> A blessing on him
> Who repays you in kind
> What you have afflicted on us.
> A blessing on him who seizes your babies
> And dashes them against the rocks.

This is memory with a vengeance, against which the imagination wages a desperate battle. The danger of total recall matches the seduction of ultimate arrival. It gives rise to what I call the "denaturing" of Jerusalem in such texts as Uri Zvi Greenberg's poem "Bizkhut em u-vena viyirushalayim" [For the Sake of a Mother and Her Son and Jerusalem], written during the Israeli War of Independence. Appropriating biblical imagery and medieval poetic cadences such as those we will encounter in the verses of Yehuda Halevi, Greenberg realizes the sacramental potential in the literalizing and grounding of metaphor. The keening mother yields up her private grief to the consecrating soil, "knowing" that her son is no longer in his grave, that his "small body" has been utterly incorporated into the place of sacrifice. Personified as mother earth, as lover, and as "wife," absorbing into the soil the sacrificed body of the young soldier, Jerusalem takes on a kind of mystical materiality that supersedes and therefore denies its status as poetic symbol.[44]

Beneath the apparently benign surfaces of an idea of total homecoming lie the impulse to literalize, the pledge to vengeance, and the death wish inevitably associated with arrival. Israel's first real-estate transaction in ancient Canaan was the purchase of the burial cave of Machpelah. As Arnold Eisen has argued, "one can live in the land, 'sojourn' there . . . without possessing it. To die in it, however, one needs a . . . holding. So when Sarah dies, Abraham must negotiate the purchase of a grave property."[45] Throughout the Jewish literature that spans our century, the shore of the Mediterranean is also life's final shore.[46] Exile and narrative, the time or *durée* of life itself, can yield only to homecoming, closure, and the place of (the place that is) death.

Once cursed with eternal life, the Wandering Jew could celebrate an end to wandering by trading his immortality for a simple grave. But it is the simple grave that is hardest to gain in a society intoxicated by the idea of staying put for eternity. As ancient burial sites are turned up almost daily by tractors with other agendas, Israel appears as one vast cemetery for the ancient dead whose unearthed skeletons provide bones of contention among archaeologists, ultra-orthodox burial societies, and the still quick who want only to compete for some of the *real estate*.

The ancient graves and the ancient caves are believed to carry the "answer" to the riddles of this people's beginning and destination. The dry bones and scrolls are the secret rememberers; they make the act of arrival an act of return and the act of discovery an act of recovery. But *recovery* and *return* both territorialize the Jewish imagination through closure. Their ultimate expression—death and the "necrophoria"[47] that has always been a part of the imagination of arrival, of the ultimate reunion and consummation with the beloved—has possessed the Hebrew imagination from its earliest manifestations in medieval love poems to Jerusalem to its most recent forms of grave worship in the Holy Land.

Where return and recovery are the prevailing political and aesthetic gestures and the biblical text both a code of memory and a travel guide, the Arab becomes the romantic embodiment of the self through a paradox of identification. In literary and visual representations that run through the early decades of this century, the Arab, as Bedouin, is at the same time the native, autochthonous man in an organic, preindustrialized connection to the land *and* the aboriginal Semite, the ancestral Jew moving naturally in his surroundings next to the predatory and mechanized locutions of the Jewish pioneer.[48] The Arab woman appears as more than reincarnation of the exotic and dangerous female other; she is the primordial Rebecca, still drawing water from the well after all these years. Like the Dead Sea Scrolls, they surface as relics of an authentic past, of the lost self. But the Arab who is thus claimed as ancestral self is in danger of becoming invisible as *other*—not by being overlooked but by being so totally incorporated.

Leah Goldberg's "Songs of Zion" (1955) lament what could be benignly defined as a deficit of attention:

Sing us from the Songs of Zion!
How shall we sing a song of Zion in the land of Zion
if we have not begun to listen?[49]

Back in the land of Zion, the first act should be to put one's ear to the ground. To the chorus of this land's "other population"—its ancient dead—come the voices of Palestine's other, *live* population. Asserting their claims as narrating subjects with stakes in geopolitical as well as sacred space in Palestine, the Arab voices that have begun to be heard resonate with the silenced voices of Jewish exile.

The pledge to memory, to vengeance, and to the autism that insulates them should not, then, outlast the longing or the journey; as a compass to help the community of the faithful navigate through the uncharted paths of exile, memory has performed its office. Even the dead, who have finally received proper burial, can stay safe in the ground where graves belong; their remembering dust can relieve the poet of the memory that, like Joseph's mummified bones carried through the forty years in the desert, is the burden—and the story—of exile.[50] Back "home," a different kind of transference can be restored between objects and memory, between things and language, between material and spirit—and between different rememberers. The celebratory can replace the mnemonic. Amichai in Jerusalem can, finally, begin to *forget*:

Let the memorial hill remember instead of me,
that's what it's here for.
. . . .
Let the beasts of the field and the birds of the heavens eat
     and remember.
Let all of them remember so that I can rest.[51]

The ultimate challenge to the Israeli writer is how to keep images from becoming icons, archaeology from becoming eschatology, "arrival" from becoming the terminus of a vengeful excess of memory, the eros of an unconsummated journey from being extinguished in the killing fields of exclusive visions—how to *reopen* the narrative so that narrative itself can continue and one can hear the suppressed, the silenced, the restless and unpatriated voices.

PART ONE

Jewish Journeys

Jewish journeys originate either in the biblical myths of punishment or quest or in the historic memories and legends of the destruction of the Temples in Jerusalem. Adam and Eve as prototypes of the mortal condition, Cain as exemplum of the workings of conscience, and Abraham and Moses as architects of the covenantal charter yield to the personifications of Jerusalem as wanton lover and grieving widow and of Israel as her scattered progeny.

Distance, coded as exile, will generate as many poetic as pragmatic forms of return to the place of banishment. In its earliest phase, return was enacted as pilgrimage to the sacred center and then to the ruins of the sacred center. Over time, the Jewish Diaspora developed both lamentational and mimetic practices to signal the loss of the Temple and a peculiar narrative of defeat to accommodate the covenantal theodicy.

In *Epic and Empire*, a study of the narratives that emerged in the ancient world in response to the triumph and defeat of large collectives, David Quint argues that

> the *Aeneid* ascribes to political power the capacity to fashion human history into narrative; drawing on the two narrative models offered to it by the *Iliad* and the *Odyssey*, Virgil's poem attached political meaning to narrative form itself. To the victors belongs epic, with its linear teleology; to the losers belongs romance, with its random or circular wandering. Put another way, the victors experience history as a coherent, end-directed story told by their own power; the losers experience a contingency that they are powerless to shape to their own ends.[1]

In a similar vein, Leopold Zunz wrote in his essay on "Jewish geography" in 1841, "great voyages, enterprises of importance, could of course not be expected from the excluded, the persecuted."[2] The story of the "loser," the "excluded," the "persecuted" captures the yearning, the unconsummated love, and the endlessly deferred end that gives the story of exile its particular strength.

In the twelfth century, Yehuda Halevi established both a personal and a poetic model for "return" based on not only pilgrimage to but also settlement in the Holy Land. Nevertheless, the privileged descriptions of his native Andalusia and the mysterious circumstances surrounding his disappearance after arriving in Palestine inscribed themselves as the unresolved tensions that would inform Jewish journeys for the next millennium.

As the imagination of "Zion redeemed" took on the aspect of an anticipated triumph in the century that began with mass migration from Eastern Europe and the first Zionist congresses, travel narratives grew epic in their structure and scope, becoming linear and "end-directed." In contrast, those stories still located in the poetic realm that had accommodated a culture of "losers" were structured as romances or mock-epics, characterized by "random or circular wandering." While the epic narratives are one-way tickets to utopia, the diversionary tales are round-trips that return to their point of origin: though based on the model of pilgrimage, they are suffused with a modern skepticism and a form of critical thinking that refuses to take refuge in the promise of collective social or religious redemption.

The linear or teleological stories I will explore in the following chapters are central to the narrative of *galut,* which, in its Zionist resolution, takes on a material aspect and destination. The diversionary stories, impeded by an infinite series of detours and ostensibly authorized by hermeneutic procedures rather than by the dynamic of an inner-directed, autonomous narrative, ultimately describe a subversive circularity in their return to an exilic point of departure.

In 1878, several hundred years after the odes and itineraries of the most illustrious medieval Hebrew pilgrims to the Holy Land, S. Y. Abramovitsh introduces his traveler Benjamin to the Yiddish-speaking world in one of the first modern Jewish novels, *The Travels of Benjamin the Third*. Benjamin arrives on the scene as belated explorer, as pilgrim to an ever-deferred site (the Mountains of Darkness, the Sambatyon River, and the lost tribes of Israel)—but most explicitly as quixotic wandering Jew. His peregrinations are a parody of exile as a viable condition in an unredeemed world. The inherently teleological dynamic of an entire community in suspended animation between banishment and redemption is the declared itinerary of this narrative. But Benjamin not only proves incapable of propelling himself forward into heroic space; his sluggish movement through the stagnant waters of the neighboring shtetls leads back, eventually, to his hometown, describing a countertrajectory to the linear thrust of the Jew-in-exile as eternal pilgrim oriented toward final acts of salvation. Contextualized both by the fin de siècle in which it was written and the fin de siècle in which we reencounter it, this narrative resonates as a skeptical gesture vis-à-vis the utopian imagination.

Movement based on the model of pilgrimage to the Holy Land is inherently invested in what Jonathan Z. Smith calls a "locative view of the cosmos": that is, sacred things have their place and in their very placement maintain the order of the universe.[3] The counterdynamic to both the epic and the mock-epic—that of the Jewish wanderer with no clear teleological direction, the penitential *na' va-nad* patterned after Cain, or the existential wanderer or explorer—will, eventually, create a place of perpetual motion in America. By the close of the nineteenth century, Eastern European Jewish civilization had begun to move its center of gravity westward, in what would eventually amount to a continental drift, evolving narrative forms that could accommodate such movement and give it new legitimacy within the old, but infinitely expandable, rubric of exile. The Jewish idea of place in America is a variation on the American ethos of vastness, of expansive, imaginative spaces and the ever-deferred frontier: the ultimate, detoxified—and eventually, perhaps, self-destructing— expression of *galut*. And, at the very farthest edge of the West, Hollywood, the miniaturized, parodic expression both of America and of an alternative Jewish utopia, becomes the embodiment of place as movement or movement-in-place (*motion pictures*), as fantasy and simulacrum.

The (re)settlement of the Land of Israel, its reclaiming of sacred spaces, enacts the "centripetal" (ingathering)—the search for stability and placement to resolve the condition of exile; settlement in the United States enacts the "centrifugal," a continent-embracing diffusion that requires and privileges mobility and evolves as the most sanguine accommodation to the diasporic condition.

For an entire people on the move from Eastern Europe, the place or placement of the abandoned Jewish town would become no less crucial as primary locus for renegotiating points of departure and reference than the Spanish homeland had been for the medieval poet.[4] The contours of the useable past would be determined for the Yiddish-speaking world largely by their perceived distance from this referent; where the shtetl is regarded as portable and therefore interiorized, the mobility and plasticity of diasporic culture are affirmed; where the shtetl is regarded as fixed point of origin and matrix of identity, distance and loss are the prevailing articulations of the past. The maverick literary critic David Frishman, who died in 1922, claimed that if the shtetl were to be destroyed (!), it could be reconstructed from the stories of S. Y. Abramovitsh;[5] still, probably the most durable and referenceable, if not strictly mimetic, reinventions of the shtetl, its psychic structures, idioms, and landscapes, are to be found in Sholem Aleichem's prose. Site of the most circumscribed form of Jewish life, the shtetl lived on in many of these stories as a familiar but economically nonviable space that the forward-looking Jews left behind with little regret. For all their built-up defenses against sen-

timentality, these stories would, in turn, prompt in their expatriated readers a potent mixture of nostalgia and relief. Something of this posture
is mimicked in the postwar stories of Isaac Bashevis Singer and in their
reception—with a measure of magical realism to mark the distance between naive and ironic, between proximate and belated evocations of the
Jewish town. Later still, when geopolitical changes facilitated it, pilgrimages to places of origin would begin to rescue fading memories and personalize mythic references.

In his study of the literary image of the shtetl, Dan Miron identifies
central metaphoric clusters that dominate Yiddish and Hebrew fiction
around the turn of the century; the one that foregrounds conflagration,
banishment, and wandering might be called the "exile" paradigm; its counterpart, based on the exodus from Egypt and the constitution of nation-
hood and a new social and legal system, could be called the "exodus"
paradigm.[6] For Miron, these clusters both establish the connection—by
diminution—of small-town Jews to the events that signal their epic birth
and establish the ephemeral nature of those small towns when measured
by the magnitude of Jewish origin and destiny. Taking this argument even
further, one might explore the epistemological assumptions in the two
paradigms that shape the representations of the shtetl itself as well as the
departure from it. One crucial difference is the absence or presence of
free will in each of the models. As we will see, an epistemology of freedom leads to a skeptical gesture on the part of Abramovitsh in *The Travels of Benjamin the Third* and a celebratory gesture on the part of Sholem
Aleichem in *Motl Pesye dem Khasans* [Motl the Cantor's Son]. As a corol-
lary of the shift in the relative place of place, the postromantic, democratic language of personal quest and the role of personal alienation
within the general condition of collective exile will evolve into a peculiarly American diasporic agenda.

Even as Yiddish worlds are dismantled, transported to, and reconstructed in America, a parallel process unfolds in those linguistic precincts
that will someday become the material space of Israeli culture. Hebrew
language and literature begin to take on a constitutive role in the building of a vision of political, national sovereignty, effecting a shift in the
center of gravity from the *inter*textual to the *con*textual. For a short while,
then, both Yiddish and Hebrew resided in a new tension between the
word and the world. The rapidly changing circumstances can be measured in the different valence assigned to the same or similar texts in different languages. The Hebrew version of *The Travels of Benjamin the
Third* (1896), which Abramovitsh wrote some twenty years after the Yid-

dish original, can be read as a consequential response to historical events; between the Yiddish and the Hebrew versions, a full-fledged nationalism had radically changed the blueprint of Jewish expectations. Several decades later, with the Yishuv (Jewish community) in Palestine already a reality, S. Y. Agnon's *Bilvav yamim* [In the Heart of the Seas] (1934) realizes the ever-deferred narrative of return through the actual arrival of the pilgrims; the language of miracle and the language of history become mutually reinforcing, and the eternal wanderer is replaced and redeemed by the repatriated *mortal* Jew.

Closure has always been rare and dangerous in these narratives. Yehuda Halevi, whose end is never recorded, pursues his journey for centuries like a kind of Ancient Mariner in the precincts of the Hebrew imagination; intimations of further travel problematize the final pages of the Hebrew version of *Benjamin the Third*; and yet another, unfinished, chapter of *Motl* is found on Sholem Aleichem's deathbed. Of all the characters we will consider in the following chapters, only one, Agnon's Hananiah, is allowed to arrive—and, having arrived, to die. The formal connection between death and closure is never more dramatically demonstrated than in the juxtaposition of these figures. If it had not been for the cataclysmic death that awaited all of these wandering Jews, this book could easily have concluded with an argument for the inherent openendedness of the exilic condition. As it is, the reappearance of such figures at the end of the twentieth century occurs self-consciously in the name of the continuation of a story that has been interrupted by catastrophe; they represent the exigencies of the imagination as diasporic privilege, in the name of mimesis or simulation as competing with original space or the implacability of "the real."

The Poetics of Pilgrimage

Yehuda Halevi and the Uncompleted Journey

Pilgrimage is the ritual performance of a "way back" that is predicated on a diaspora located at a distance from the sacred center. Pilgrimage to Jerusalem (*'aliyah la-regel*) in the time of the Second Temple, as the Jewish Diaspora continued to grow and Jewish proselytizing began to yield many converts, must have been an impressive sight: "No one land can contain all the Jews, for they are very numerous," writes Philo of Alexandria. "They dwell in thriving places in Europe and Asia, on islands and on the mainland. They view the holy city as their mother city (*metropolis*), for there stands the holy Temple of the Most High God. The cities that they inherited from their ancestors of previous generations they view as their homeland (*patris*), for there they were born and raised."[1]

The distinction between Zion as Motherland and one's native country as Fatherland will reverberate throughout centuries of Jewish longing.

LAMENTATION VERSUS MIMESIS: THE KARAITES

As an act that would touch but not dwell in the desolated shrines, pilgrimage to Jerusalem after the destruction of the Second Temple (beginning around the fourth century) becomes a function of the different terrain of holiness and the different rituals of encounter that each of the monotheistic religions maps out.[2] With the passage of time, earthly Jerusalem would become for Moslems one of three holy pilgrim sites and for Christians the imitable trail of the footsteps of Jesus as well as protean blueprint for the Heavenly Jerusalem. While both made attempts to repossess the Land through crusades and conquests, the Jews alone could not seek repossession, maintaining in unresolved tension over twenty centuries the collective memory of spiritual and physical exile, with its promise of redemption and return, and a distant and unpossessable geographic referent.

For this reason, the very term "pilgrim" should be used advisedly in the Jewish context: its Hebrew equivalent, 'oleh la-regel, which carries the double connotation of the peregrine who "walks" and the worshipper who ascends to the holy shrine on appointed feast days, captures the specific temporality and topography connected with the Temple service in Jerusalem as it is preserved in Jewish memory. (In its modern reincarnation, 'aliyah or "ascension" relates not to pilgrimage to but to settlement on the land.) In the absence of the Temple, the Jewish practice of pilgrimage for the sake of sacrifice was superseded by two modes of approach to the ruined shrine: the one a form of mimesis of the temple cult and the other a form of lamentation over its absence. These will become competing aesthetic as well as existential options for living in exile.

Lamentation fuels the messianic imagination. One of the most curious of the medieval groups to have taken on pilgrimage and settlement as an early form of political messianism were the Karaites, who attempted in the late ninth and early tenth centuries to reestablish Jerusalem as spiritual center, as proving ground for the redemptive promises of Scriptures.[3] Their rejection of the legitimacy of the Talmud and the rabbinic institutions was a refusal to grant ontological status to galut and to synagogal representations of the Temple and the Ark of the Covenant. By insisting on the irreproduceability of the original site of revelation, they rejected those forms of mimesis and reproduction that facilitated the mobility of Jews separated from their cultic center: "And know that if you designate any place as a sanctuary other than the one so sanctified by the Lord, it is the same as an act of worshipping other gods." An intensification of the language of exile characterizes their writing: "wandering to and fro, wandering hither and thither in the Dispersion, crying and weeping (mitnoded na' va-nad ba-galut)," Israel is portrayed as seeking to return to its source.[4]

Appropriating the role of chief "mourners" for the devastated city (avelei tzion), the Karaites who came to Jerusalem contributed to the iconicization of the Holy City as female figure of desolation and ruin; the dominant image that recurs in the rhetoric of this group is that of Jerusalem as mother.[5] At the same time, their performative enactment of such passages as Psalm 69 tends to literalize or concretize the biblical texts: "When I wept and fasted, I was reviled for it. / I made sackcloth my garment; I became a byword among them." They provide a very early form of what would eventually constitute, in the poetics of return to Zion, a reification of the symbolic language of exile and closure of its open-ended narrative.

MEDIEVAL ITINERARIES

But the Sephardic Jewish communities ranging from Spain to Babylon would also generate other patterns of travel and pilgrimage documented in lively reports and itineraries, and eventually other aesthetic possibilities as well.[6] S. D. Goitein has shown that a particular form of "popular messianism" prevailed in the cultures that can be reconstructed from the Cairo Geniza, a messianism that was not apocalyptic and that viewed Jerusalem as a proximate place that would facilitate not only the eventual ingathering of the exiles from the far corners of the earth but also the more imminent reunion of family members and business partners scattered in different countries. What emerges from the evidence of ordinary, mundane transactions are the pragmatic, domestic dimensions of a messianism in which Jerusalem figures both as the ruined shrine and sacred center and as a reference for the rearticulation of dispersed parts of the community, a kind of grand convention center.[7] And many of the travel narratives of the time encompass more than the trip to the Holy Land. Over the years, as I noted in the introduction, a kind of "rhetoric of ruins" comes to pervade nearly all of the reports from the Holy Land. But the Jewish journey also becomes increasingly prosaic as it becomes more pragmatic. From the ninth through the twelfth centuries, from the writings of Eldad the Danite through the memoirs of Benjamin of Tudela, the records of travel feed the curiosity and the commercial interests as well as the messianic projections of generations of Jews—long before the Spanish Inquisition would provide the exilic imagination with new points of departure.

The texture of the medieval Hebrew *récits de voyage* is a marvelous blend of observation, empirical authenticity, and the aggadic imagination. Eldad the Danite (Eldad Ha-dani), a mysterious figure who appeared late in the ninth century claiming to have hailed from the lost tribe of Dan—which was said to be located in Havilah, near Ethiopia—traveled extensively throughout Africa, Spain, and Egypt. He established in his writings the coordinates of an imaginary geography that would, when fully mapped out, embrace the Ten Lost Tribes (or the "Red Jews") who live just beyond the Sambatyon River—a river that in its various representations either flows only on the Sabbath or reduces its tempestuous current on the seventh day, justifying in any case its name, the "Sabbath River." This river, which first surfaced in the writings of Josephus and appeared in Greek and midrashic sources as well, is a signifier of the movable boundary of the known world and the inaccessible but somehow "familiar" status of the unknown. Eldad Ha-dani's travelogue relegates both unclassified and fantastic species to a place on the other side of that border.[8] The ongoing search for the Ten Lost Tribes and the miraculous river located at the very edge of the known world can be viewed as one of the topographical expressions of the status of holy land as unpossessable.[9]

The complex relation between the original and its simulacra in the (*as the*) state of exile, the status of the mythical as protecting the borders of an ultimate but elusive reality, may account in part for what Leopold Zunz, in his 1841 essay on the geographical literature of the Jews, laments as "unconnected sentences on the structure of the world, the seventy nations, the fables of the depths of the sea, of the river Sambatjon, of the dark mountains, etc."[10] This essay, which appeared with a new English translation of the *Itinerary* of Benjamin of Tudela, provides a fascinating study of Jewish geography from the Babylonian Talmud through the medieval travelogues, while revealing attempts of nineteenth-century German-Jewish *Wissenschaft* historiography to reconcile Jewish imaginative and scientific understandings of space.

Benjamin of Tudela, who hailed from the northern Spanish province of Navarra, traversed some three hundred cities and towns in the late twelfth century and described the Jewish communities of Europe and the Mediterranean basin. His lively eye for the colors, sights, and shapes of this world and his clear commercial interest offset the more fanciful elements of his ostensible search for the Lost Tribes informed by stories gleaned from Eldad the Danite. It is significant for the future imagination of voyages not consumed in the vortex of the sacred center that the record of Benjamin's voyage culminates but does not end in the Holy Land. The realism of his prose, which is more characteristic of travel narratives than of pilgrimage tales, has a leveling effect on the mythic imagination, so that sites of biblical drama like the Tower of Babel are naturalized into a landscape dotted with more easily verifiable landmarks.[11]

The itineraries of both Eldad the Danite and Benjamin will provide landmarks and language for the travel narratives that evolve into fictions of Jews on the move in the nineteenth century. If the modern novel was born of the convergence of narratives of pilgrimage and exploration, as first expressed in *Don Quixote*,[12] the medieval Hebrew travelogues constitute early models for what will become, in a parallel if anachronistic literature that developed out of the Jewish Haskalah (Enlightenment), the ground of a full fictional universe.

The voyages of exploration not only revealed "the wonder of the new world," as Stephen Greenblatt calls it,[13] but, for Jews, promised a reconnection with lost origins. They reinforced certain cyclical patterns that I have defined as gestures of *re*covery rather than *dis*covery. Because even the strangest of beings could be identified with some archaic version of the Jewish self (the "lost" tribes), it is not "wonder" and the representation of alien forms of life as wholly other but rather *recognition* that emerges as the dominant cognitive category. In a study of what he calls the "rediscovery" of the Holy Land in the nineteenth and early twentieth centuries, Yehoshua Ben-Arieh rather naively maintains that the explorers shared a sense of déjà vu as they took the measure of a land that had been suspended in time: "Exploring the Holy Land was unlike the penetration of Africa or the discovery of other unknown regions. Here, even the unknown was somehow familiar. The Bible, Josephus, the writings of the church fathers, Crusader chronicles—all seemed *to come alive out of the dusty ruins and the forsaken landscape*. To this day, archaeological discoveries in Israel have this familiar quality about them."[14]

Zion, then, is not an "unknown" colony of the mind to be "penetrated" like Africa or America; rather, it is a land *in suspension*. Jerusalem's image as quintessential woman, omphalos of the world, and quintessential ruin could easily be incorporated into the romantic imagination that connects ruins with the female self and with death.[15] Yet some of the more "irreverent pilgrims" of the last century, especially Americans notoriously unimpressed by antiquity and unburdened by a sense of the past or a veneration of relics, saw only the barrenness, the stoniness, and a terrain that had not been dusted off for millennia. In 1868, Mark Twain said of Palestine that "every hundred acres of arable land is protected by three mountains on each side and a desert at each end to keep it from bolting for want of company." In 1857, Herman Melville referred to Judea as "one accumulation of stones—Stony mountains & stony plains; stony torrents & stony roads; stony walls & stony fields, stony houses & stony tombs, stony eyes & stony hearts." As late as 1916, a *National Geographic* reporter referred to the Holy Land as a collection of "old cities, old ruins, old roads, old men and old women."[16]

However tempered by the skeptical mind, these poetically charged images of eternal ruin as a kind of suspended animation, with its potential reconnection with the matrix of life, are carefully preserved for centuries along with the premise that no rebuilding could take place before the return of the Jews.[17] These are the images, perhaps, that enabled Zionists to envision Palestine as a "land without people" waiting to be redeemed by a "people without land." Jerusalem as the *ruined shrine* continued to reverberate in the religious imagination at least until the middle of the nineteenth century, when scientific, political, and economic interests began to activate a more present-oriented, dynamic encounter with the Holy Land.[18] While round-trips characterize the dynamic of pilgrimages to the Holy Land in other religious traditions, Jerusalem persists, in the sectarian behaviors of the Karaites and the travelogues of medieval explorers—and, as we will see shortly, in the poetry of Yehuda Halevi—as a *place waiting to be redeemed* and not only as a shrine that facilitates the redemption of the individual pilgrim.

YEHUDA HALEVI AND THE UNCOMPLETED JOURNEY

This year I traveled a long way
to view the silence of my city.
A baby calms down when you rock it, a city calms down
from the distance. I dwelled in longing. I played the hopscotch
of the four strict squares of Yehuda Ha-Levi:
My heart. Myself. East. West.

I heard bells ringing in the religions of time,
but the wailing that I heard inside me
has always been from my Yehudean desert.

                                        Yehuda Amichai, Jerusalem 1967

It is with Yehuda Halevi that I have chosen to launch this study of the journey back, for he provides its earliest and most enduring model. His life and writing capture the tensions between desire and fulfillment as they begin to play themselves out in a poetics of exile and return. Composed in the Moslem and Christian cultures of Andalusia and northern Spain (ca. 1075–1141), his late Hebrew poetry became a crossroads of the metaphysics and erotics of longing for the ruined shrine and the physical and mental anguish of the journey toward the object of desire. In privileging and interrogating Spain as his point of departure, Yehuda Halevi creates one of the most powerful expressions of "nonoriginal" space as the negotiable domestic realm of the diasporic imagination; his uncompleted pilgrimage to Jerusalem activated both the erotic language of unconsummated desire and what became the concretizing and reifying gestures of the Zionist imagination. Once introduced through a bold actualization of the metaphors of displacement and desire, the oscillation between symbolic-mythic and empirical-historical language—corresponding, in some degree, to the oscillation between conventional and individualized form—reverberated throughout the literature in which Jewish journeys were imagined. A critical reading of these constructions can, therefore, expose the sources of anxiety and conflict in the entire discourse on exile.

Some of what came to be known as Yehuda Halevi's "Songs of Zion" were written on the high seas, during his fatal voyage to Palestine via Egypt. The motifs and images of these poems, which evoke the familiar landscape of the poet's country of origin, the visions of Judea as a devastated, legendary landscape (time suspended over the Holy Land as a convention of exilic desire), and the discomforts and adventures of the voyage itself, would resonate in Hebrew texts for centuries as a rhetoric that shifts almost imperceptibly between the mimetic, the metaphoric, and the sacramental.

In his Judeo-Arabic treatise *Kitab al Khazari* (ca. 1130–40), translated into Hebrew thirty years after its composition and widely circulated as *Sefer ha-kuzari*, Yehuda Halevi became arguably the first Jewish thinker to introduce material and historical as well as spiritual categories into the vocabulary of exile. The book is a simulated dialogue between the King of the Khazars who converted to Judaism in the eighth century and the "Haver" who represents a scholar or rabbinic authority. The almost stark realism of certain passages in Yehuda Halevi's late poems might be read as a poetic correlative of the political imagination that focuses in the *Kuzari* on the place of exile and of Jerusalem in Jewish memory and destiny. Yehuda Halevi's own journey took place shortly after he had completed the *Kuzari*; recently discovered and deciphered evidence of the polemic between the poet and his admirers and patrons in both Spain and Egypt over his declared vow to undertake a pilgrimage to the Holy Land enriches our modern encounter with both the prose and the poetry.

In the context of the projected and then the actual voyage, the convention of Time personified, a common feature of the medieval Hebrew lyric, becomes intensified and problematized as a property of exile.[19] Entropy as the fate of nature and of human beings in their unredeemed state is the very definition of exile, of life lived in historical time. Pales-

tine contains the two other time zones: Time *suspended* is the condition
of the Holy Land in ruins; Time *fulfilled* is the condition of the Holy
Land redeemed.

> . . . If only I could roam through those
> places where God was revealed to your
> prophets and heralds!
> . . . I
> would weep, as I stood by my ancestors'
> graves, I would grieve, in Hebron, over
> the choicest of burial places!
> . . . It
> would delight my heart to walk naked
> and barefoot among the desolate ruins
> where your shrines once stood; where
> your Ark was hidden away, where your
> cherubim once dwelled in the inner-
> most chamber. I shall cut off my
> glorious hair and throw it away, I shall
> curse Time that has defiled your pure
> ones in the polluted lands [of exile].[20]

The messianic resolution to entropy begins as a symbolic projection
within the created universe:

> Rid yourself of Time,
> as birds ruffle their feathers of last
> night's dew.[21]

For the most part, however, in the imagined topography of the Holy
Land—the sites of the biblical drama of revelation, of monarchy, of
conquest—time is frozen in the moment of its devastation, like Pompeii,
with apparently no real claim on the present.

But the potential suspension or demotion of the temporal only serves
to mask the essential struggle between Yehuda Halevi's privileging of the
prophetic and messianic moment (his impatience with the unfulfilled
promise of redemption) and his immersion in the phenomenology of his
own historical moment and vision of a resolution of the anomaly of exile by reclaiming the Land in historical time. Such contextualization radically transforms the otherwise conventional personification of Time. Although in many poems typological references signal specific historical
developments such as the Crusader invasions and despoliations, a kind
of historical *consciousness* suffuses the "Songs of Zion" and competes
with the image of Time either as fatally entropic or as static and suspended.

The conflict was to have been proleptically reconciled and poetically

inscribed in the poet's own act of migration. Twentieth-century appro-
priations of his last writings as either a proto-Zionist manifesto or a spiritual renunciation of all this-worldly properties tend to be reductionist
interpretations of an inherently conflictual state of mind:[22]

> Hard-pressed for the living God, driven
> to search out the thrones of my anointed ones;
> denying myself a parting kiss for my child,
> family, companions; not even shedding
> a tear over my orchard planted, watered
> and pruned to blossom in abundance,
> nor letting myself dwell on the memory
> of Yehuda and Azariel, two lovely
> flowers, the pick of the lot, or Isaac—
> sun-ripened fruit, lunar yield—
> fancied as my own son. I have all but
>
> forgotten the house of prayer and its study,
> my retreat; have ceased
> caring for the Sabbath's pleasures,
> the charm of my festivals and glory
> of Passover. Let others—mere stick figures—
> bandy about my high station
> and good name. I've swapped my home
> for the shadow of a shrub; the bolted security
> of my gates, for a low-lying thicket.
> Choicest spices sated my palate—now
> I reek of thornbush. I'm through
> with scraping and bowing, for I've cut
>
> a path in the heart of the sea. My sights
> are set on the Lord's sanctum.[23]

The rhetorical figure (litotes) that exposes profound anxiety by
affirmation through denial ("denying myself a parting kiss . . . not even
shedding a tear . . . nor letting myself dwell . . .") holds in uneasy balance the existential weight of the present moment—the pleasures of the
life of a courtier poet in Andalusia, the domain of the private—and the
normative value ascribed to the act of pilgrimage.[24] The ambivalence is
resolved only if one embraces what Ross Brann calls "the conversion
theory," which posits that a moment of "mystical rebirth" redefined not
only Yehuda Halevi's itinerary and religious journey but his poetics as
well, the autonomy of the poetic genius becoming harnessed to and transformed by the spiritual quest. Brann goes on to show that this theory
does not take account of the poetry written even as the poet was en route
to the Holy Land, his "poems to Egyptian Jewish notables . . . conspic-

uous for their mundane panegyric and . . . celebration of the beauties of this world."[25]

Yehuda Halevi's poetry remains a strong presence as it embraces and refashions the inherently unresolvable conflicts of pilgrimage, resisting the ongoing attempts at co-optation by apologists for one ideological position or another. The mysteries of an incomplete conversion give legitimacy to a millennium of journeys that never fully renounce their point of origin. In "Ha-tirdof na'arut ahar hamishim" [Past Fifty, Still Hot on the Heels of Juvenile Pastimes], the voyage itself is articulated in a portrait of both cosmic and social chaos and an anthropomorphized seascape that glitters with the detritus of exile: the stars are reflected in the sea "like / strangers (*ke-gerim*) expelled from their homes."[26] This seventy-eight-line poem contains numerous biblical intertexts, illustrating the technique of *shibbutz*, or tesselation, that creates a "shadow text" to underpin the most original or empirical utterances. The effect in several of these seafaring poems is of a poetic syncretism that embraces biblical and apocalyptic conventions of return and redemption along with the specific and very mundane mechanics of the journey and personalized expressions of struggle and yearning. In one Halevi asks, "Has a flood washed the world to waste? / . . . Leviathan whitens the surf with age in its churning."[27] And in another he investigates the full range of physical discomfort and mental anguish:

> Greetings ladies, kith and kin,
> brothers and sisters, from hope's
> captive. Purchased by the high seas,
> he's placed himself in the hands
> of rival winds: the west wind
> steers the ship forward, the levant
> whips it back. Between him and death—
> a step, a plank. He's trapped
> alive in a wooden casket, without earth,
> not even a bare four cubits.
> He squats to keep his balance,
> lies, but cannot stretch his legs,
> is sickly, suspicious of strangers,
> of pirates and the spookish winds.
> Helmsman and crew—mere striplings—
> are the pashas and deputies here.
> The wise and learned, unless they can swim,
> have neither honor nor grace.
> The thought for a moment clouds my face over
> but heart and core thrill, for soon,
> at the site of ark and altar,

> I'll pour out my soul and render to you,
> Lord, who bestows favors on the unworthy,
> the pick of my songs and praise.[28]

Even in its oscillation between biblical-eschatological and actual land-scapes and modes of travel, in its ongoing resistance to the logic of narrative (which is exile) and the spaces of human history, this poetry takes on a distinct chronotopic quality as the journey itself proceeds, providing "space" for all future journeys.

Yehuda Halevi's "Songs of Zion" constitute a major development in the Jewish journey as the site of literary experiment and innovation. Dan Pagis singles them out as examples of the individuality and "genuine self-expression" of the medieval poet.[29] The poets of the "Golden Age," in their self-representation as literary heirs to the Hebrew Bible, imitating biblical style and incorporating biblical intertexts while continuing to use Arabic-Andalusian meter, stanzaic forms, and imagery,[30] were making a highly charged ideological statement—and not entirely an unequivocal one—in the Moslem culture into which they had become so fully assimilated. Especially in light of their claim that the legacy of biblical Hebrew had been dissipated in the course of exile,[31] such acts of "retrieval" take on additional significance in the pilgrimage poems. The authorizing power of scriptural references, accumulated as ballast on dangerous trips through the heart of the seas, will accompany travel literature into its most modern phase.[32] This process recalls the psalmist's exhortation against forgetting (Ps. 137); it is the chain that connects travel, poetry, and collective memory and, at the same time, reflects the ongoing tension between porousness and hermeticism in the diasporic encounter with host cultures.

Given the proliferation of sources that makes these poems a kind of echo chamber of quotations and typological scenes, their individuality is even more striking. The elements of experiential or psychological specificity both reinforce the authority of the individual poetic voice and add linear, historical modes of representation to cyclical, archetypal forms. Yehuda Halevi's poem "Ha-tirdof na'arut ahar hamishim" begins in the same conflictual state that we begin to see as characterizing the enterprise throughout:

> Past fifty, still hot on the heels of juvenile
> pastimes, your days primed for flight?
> Will you flee from serving Elohim
> just to please every man's whim,
> and seek comfort of many

> while ignoring the one to whom all desire's
> laid bare? Don't hem and haw
> when going to sea is mentioned;
> don't muff your future the minute
> your stomach rumbles for food
> (imagine selling out for a plate of lentils).[33]

The images of aging and nostalgia for lost youth, together with the juxtaposition of the rumblings of the poet's particular stomach and the biblical transaction over a plate of lentils, concretize and give a signature to
the process of leave-taking; they also create a language of approach to
the Holy Land, the physical and metaphysical source of all quotations.

> . . . Suddenly the waves calm down, and
> are like flocks spread out over the fields.
> And the night—once the sun has gone
> down the stairway of the heavenly hosts,
> who are commanded by the
> moon—is like a Negress dressed in
> gold embroidery, or like a violet robe
> spangled with crystal. The stars are
> astray in the heart of the sea, like
> strangers expelled from their homes.
> And in the heart of the sea they cast
> a light, in their image and likeness,
> that glows like fire. Now the sea and
> the sky are pure, glittering ornaments
> upon the night. The sea is the colour of
> the sky—they are two seas bound
> together. And between these two, my
> heart is a third sea, as the new waves of
> my praise surge on high![34]

Andras Hamori argues that as this poem unfolds, it moves, like the
Kuzari, from the philosophical to a more "historically oriented ethics
and metaphysics, . . . providing the intellectual exhilaration of a sudden shift from shadow to substance."[35] In the very substantiation of the
shadow world, in the personal voyage that incorporates and supersedes
the Platonic voyage of the soul, in the reinvention of conventional images lie the peculiar power of this poetry and of the poetic act itself. The
merging of shadow and substance, of self and cosmic order, is effected
through an eclecticism that embraces a total geography of land and ocean,
of mythical and historical memory. The visual vocabulary contains elements of biblical memory and poetic possibility; Jonah's tenure in the
whale and the parting of the Red Sea, a vision of the Holy of Holies and

the Jordan River, give way to exotic catalogues of worlds forfeited or not yet discovered ("And the night . . . is like a Negress dressed in / gold embroidery, or like a violet robe / spangled with crystal") and then to private associations. Landlocked similes ("Suddenly the waves calm down, and / are like flocks spread out over the fields") serve both to soothe the queasy stomach and to refamiliarize and domesticate the topography of the beloved country. That Zion is the center that spatially orients the poet whose "heart is in the East [while he is] at the edge of the West" is demonstrated in a poem like "Tzion ha-lo tishali" [Ode to Zion]:

> O Zion, will you not ask how your
> captives are—the exiles who seek your
> welfare, who are the remnant of your
> flocks? From west and east, north and
> south, from every side, accept the
> greetings of those near and far, and the
> blessings of this captive of desire.[36]

Addressing Zion as the female beloved (reinforced by the gendered noun), exhorting her to "accept the greetings of those near and far" (*rahok ve-karov*; Isa. 67:19), the speaker situates himself both *at a distance from* and *in the very midst of* the longed-for place by invoking a Palestine-centered poetic geography in which *yam* (sea) is west and *Teman* (Yemen) is south. Fixed within such a particular map of expectations, *yam*, the very medium of the journey eastward, is thus semantically and symbolically a marker of both Being-in-the-West and Being-on-the-Way. The inherent contradictions within this poetry are illustrated by the more neutral compass invoked in "Kiru 'alei vanot" [Greetings Ladies, Kith and Kin], presumably written during the impatient days before conditions allowed the poet to set sail for Palestine from Alexandria; in this poem, local navigational considerations prevail over the spiritual/poetic geography and a battle ensues between the "west" wind (*ma'arav*) and "east" wind (*mizrah*).[37]

The Crusader expeditions in Yehuda Halevi's lifetime not only added to the urgency of his own pilgrimage and sense of collective endangerment at the hands of the Church militant; it may also have enhanced the accessibility of the Holy Land to the Jewish imagination—through the dialectic of competing or overlapping religious claims. The medieval Christian cartography that placed Jerusalem at the center of the universe was consonant with the midrashic (and later Kabbalistic) Jewish notion that the material world conforms to its spiritual geography. But the Crusaders may also have contributed to the dimension of travel and conquest that begins to unfold in historical time. "Sabbath begins in China eighteen hours later than in Palestine," explains the Rabbi in the *Kuzari*, "since the latter lies in the centre of the world."[38]

As the voyage itself takes on substance, its telos becomes more intensely imagined—still invisible but palpably proximate. Imagining arrival entails acts of concretization that seem to interrogate the very status of metaphor. As the center and ground zero of the imagination, Jerusalem cannot be likened to anything but herself—but in so saying we already acknowledge a primary poetic transaction in the gendered designation of the city. Jeremiah's and Isaiah's personification of Jerusalem as a woman and as an emblematic dweller in the city, as well as Micah's image of Zion as a woman who can also *leave* the city and go into exile, transmutes the convention of city-as-woman, diffused throughout the ancient Near East, into a more mystical and more portable element in the relationship between the people of Israel and the sources of the sacred.[39] Eventually, the "spirit of Jerusalem" that attaches itself to the people in its exile takes on the identity of the *shekhinah*, the female aspect of Divinity. That is, the city becomes at the same time both absolutely fixed and static in its suspended state of ruin and strikingly mobile and dynamic in its gesture of dispersal and eventual return.

This condition, emblematic of the exile itself, is meant to be temporary; the parts will reunite when the people are ingathered. Ingathering, therefore, signals a new aesthetic principle. Already imaged in the earliest scriptural sources as a woman both static and mobile, then allegorized, reified, and grounded in Talmudic exegesis, the city invoked by the medieval poet undergoes yet another kind of transformation. Johan Huizinga's argument on the centrality of symbolic thinking in the High Middle Ages may point to a further stage enacted by the Hebrew pilgrim: "the Middle Ages never forgot that all things would be absurd if their meaning were exhausted in their function and their place in the phenomenal world, if by their essence they did not reach into a world beyond this."[40] When Yehuda Halevi sets out for the Holy Land, does not the image that pointed to that place "beyond," now about to be fully realized *as itself*, render the "beyond" palpable and concrete, entailing a shift in poetic sensibility as the symbolic connection is materialized— and thus effectively annihilated? Within a poetic tradition that is highly elaborate in its conceits, its similes, and its metaphors, symbolic language per se is not what is relinquished in Halevi's late vision of Jerusalem; rather, the poet's anticipation of a kind of union with or incorporation into the female beloved seems at some fundamental level to subvert the

metaphoric premise of separation, exchanging the poetic symbol for visions of mystical or sacramental acts:

> . . . I'd soar on eagle-wings
> if only to mix my tears with your dust.
> . . . I shall kiss
> and cherish your stones. Your earth
> will be sweeter than honey to my lips.[41]

Or in another poem:

> . . . Greetings
> from a captive of desire,
> who sheds tears like the dew of Hermon and longs
> for them to streak your slopes. . . .
>
> Who will give me wings to flee far off,
> bearing the shreds of my torn heart
> to your cleft mountains? Falling on my knees,
> I would delight in your stones
> and be stirred to pity
> by your dust. . . .
> How I would delight to walk naked and barefoot
> among the rubble
> where your shrines once stood.[42]

As the poetic hovers at the edge of the mystical imagination, the anticipation of mingling through the act of pilgrimage threatens to anni-
hilate the distance inherent in procedures of similitude and mimesis. Paradoxically, that is, the imagination of arrival projected erotically onto the
territorial plain comes close to substituting sacrament for symbol; "bearing the shreds of [his] torn heart," "delight[ing] to walk naked and bare-
foot among the rubble / where your shrines once stood," the poet-turned-
pilgrim would reconcretize sacred space through ritual performance.
Implicitly, I am suggesting, the exilic license to imagine poetic substitu-
tions is revoked as the Holy Land is reclaimed.

> . . . The flock
> of your people—exiled, scattered,
> from mountain range to hillside—have not forgotten
> your borders; they cling to the edge
> of your cloak and strive
> to climb up into your palm
> to grasp its fronds.[43]

The image of the "flock of your people . . . cling[ing] to the edge of
your cloak" resonates with figures from the Song of Songs and Lamen-

tations. Yehuda Halevi's reappropriation of these metaphors can be seen against the background of rabbinic literalization of the biblical imagination: the "filthiness . . . in her skirts" (Lam. 1:9) is re-placed in *Eikha rabba* as the more topographically literal "outskirts" of the city (Lam. R. 1:36); such interpretive acts tend to de-eroticize (by concretizing) and to limit the resonances of the trope.[44] Reconnecting to the object of desire, the medieval poet both re-eroticizes the journey and anticipates its consummation. In enhancing the romantic underpinnings of the voyage, Heinrich Heine would, some seven centuries later, name Jerusalem explicitly as the poet's beloved: "Jene, die der Rabbi liebte / . . . sie hieß Jerusalem."[45]

It seems natural that more or less contemporaneously with the early Kabbalists, the poets of Andalusia who had reconnected with the biblical imagination would reflect some of the imagery of concrete possession that comes to be articulated in the Kabbalistic notion of *yihud* or "binding": conceived in its sexual and sacrificial aspects, physical return from exile is associated with the renewal of concrete cultic acts that can be performed only in (and on) the Holy Land—recalling the sacramental orientation of the Karaites. Moshe Idel argues that ancient figurations of Eretz Yisrael as female that had been repressed in rabbinic sources may in fact have been preserved in non-Jewish texts, to resurface in early Kabbalistic texts of the twelfth and thirteenth centuries; what he calls the "theosophical brand of Kabbalah," which "sexualiz[ed] . . . the relationship between the Land of Israel and its Jewish inhabitants," focused on the concrete properties of and behaviors in the Holy Land as not only a reflection but also an instrument of supernal harmony:

> The [theosophical school of] Kabbalists were interested not only in *imitatio Dei*; beyond their own imitative role, they strove for a certain participation ("*participation mystique*") in the supernal processes which they understood to be intrinsically linked to their own behavior as a sort of *imitatio* in reverse. This is the reason why they conceive of the habitation of the Land of Israel as meaning more than a mere reflection of the divine in the realm of the material. According to them, actual historical "possession" of the Land of Israel by righteous Jews has theurgical overtones: the supernal processes can be influenced by means of sympathetic corresponding actions performed below. In other words, the divine dynamic union between *Tiferet* and *Malkhut* [the male power and the female power] can, and must, be reinforced by religious acts performed in the Land of Israel.

Idel goes on to say that the "theosophical brand of Kabbalah" was countered and eventually supplanted by the "prophetic" or "ecstatic" brand that posited the human body as the "true analogue of the Land of Israel."

Expounded by R. Abraham Abulafia and R. Isaac of Acre, the focus shifts from a geographical locus to the mobile body of the Jew, leading to later Kabbalistic and eventually Hassidic notions of individual salvation and symbolic rather than concrete connections with a sacred center.[46]

The struggle between the metaphorizing and the concretizing imagination, and between body and territory, undertaken in the service of a reclamation of political-historical or mystical access to holiness, will reverberate dialogically throughout the long history of Jewish journeys. The poem "Ha-fashat ha-zman bigdei haradot ve-lavash et begadav ha-hamudot" [In Alexandria], written in Alexandria and replete with the rich imagery that characterizes some of the most sensuous secular poems that Yehuda Halevi composed in Spain and Andalusia, is remarkably eroticized, suggesting both the abandon of one who is fast approaching his beloved and the sheer delight in imaginative constructs still predicated on distance from the object of desire:

> The earth is decked in gold-shot silk.
> The seeded banks of the Nile are a checkered quilt
> . . . .
> while the fields of Goshen resemble straps of a breastplate.[47]

But as the focus of yearning for ecstatic union, the sacred center remains a dangerous place for the pilgrim living in an unredeemed hour and determined not just to visit but to abide in its domain. "All roads lead up to Palestine, but none from it," says the Rabbi in the *Kuzari*, ironically foretelling the death of the author.[48] Yehuda Halevi's traces are lost after his reported departure from Egypt on a ship bound for Palestine, though legend relates his unconfirmed death as taking place at the gates of the Old City of Jerusalem, where he is trampled by an Arab horseman while reciting his "Ode to Zion." The most famous of the legend-mongers, again, was Heinrich Heine, who lavishly embellished the rumor that Yehuda Halevi found his death midsong in the ruins of Jerusalem:

> Auch Jehuda ben Halevy
> Starb zu Füßen seiner Liebsten,
> Und sein sterbend Haupt, es ruhte
> Auf de Knien Jerusalems.[49]

While in the series of travel poems that never reach their destination there is an obvious structural absence of closure, the poet enacts in his *person* the danger of arrival as final gesture. Delaying by at least fifteen years his departure from Spain, and then by at least eight months his departure from Egypt, Yehuda Halevi seems to confirm the psychological and poetic as well as the theological function of deferral. The poet's vision of arrival incorporates a hike among the ruins and a poetic offering that merges with the language of sacrifice, issuing in death:

> . . . Soon I will enter
> your gates with thanksgiving
> and there will I dwell
> counting my heart as an offering
> on your altar. I'll raise
> my headstone in your land—
> proof of my passing.[50]

> . . . I would pour out
> my life on the very site where the spirit
> of Elohim once drenched
> your chosen ones.[51]

One is tempted to go so far as to argue that as the poet inscribes his yearning on the body of the beloved—Zion's map as female beloved—so he enacts in his death the inevitable consequence of union with the loved one. The swan song that heralds the annihilation of the self, sacrifice and death in Jerusalem, and the projection of one's own tombstone on the landscape of death where love is consummated all constitute a return to a primordial, material, concrete encounter with the sacred center. Death in the Holy Land, like messianic redemption, is an imagined end that gives meaning to life as a journey through exile.

It is possible, then, to resolve the conflicts in Yehuda Halevi's poetry through the engulfing of human *eros* in the divine *thanatos* that Michael Fishbane designates the "kiss of God." "For Halevi and similar seekers, life in this world is a torment of false desire, a web of entanglements in which the face of pleasure is the receding image of God," writes Fishbane. "Only the death of these drives, by the grace of God, will give life. . . . The desire for death torments the God-intoxicated soul; for only in death (spiritual or physical) is there release from the earthly *yetzer* and absolute devotion to God."[52] I have argued, however, that notwithstanding the poetry saturated with images of ecstatic death, the poet's own mysterious death, and the legends that attend it, the conflict is never resolved. Rather, life with its earthly desires holds the same value throughout the poet's career, even as it is repeatedly challenged in the rhetoric of renunciation; the concretization of the metaphors of Zion as the desired woman and the plethora of details delineating the mechanics of the journey itself serve to ground the vision in a Jerusalem that is quite earthly and not at all inconsistent with the idea of redemption in "real"—that is, human—time.

The belief that reunion with the object of desire leads necessarily to self-annihilation may be at the center of what would become, at various points in Jewish history, a death-intoxicated, sacramental, or self-sacrificial culture, but it continues to compete with the force of reunion as generative and life-affirming. Viewed heuristically as a "poetic site" where notions of unity with the godhead intersect with messianic expressions of impatience and yearning, Yehuda Halevi's poetry is also a prototype of acts of *concretization* that transform and problematize inherited visions of Jerusalem as a ruined, distant shrine and a desolate, absent woman. In "The Last Benjamin of Todela," Yehuda Amichai inscribes the ironies of Jerusalem's embrace and Israel's belated return in the undulating landscape of the female body:

> . . . [*Turn around now.*] Ladies and gentlemen, observe the hollow
> passing down the back and deepening between the buttocks. Who
> can say where these begin and where
> the thighs end; here are the bold buttresses
> of the pelvis, columns of legs,
> and the curlicues of a Hellenistic gate
> above the vagina. The Gothic arch that reaches
> toward the heart and like a reddish Byzantine flame between
> her legs. [*Bend down into a perfect arabesque.*]
> A Crusader influence is evident in the hard jawbones,
> in the prominent chin. She touches the earth with both palms
> without bending her knees, she touches
> the earth that I didn't kiss when I was brought to it
> as a child. Come again, ladies and gentlemen, visit
> the promised land, visit my tears and the east wind,
> which is the true Western Wall. It's made of
> huge wind-stones, and the weeping is the wind's, and the papers
> whirling in the air are the supplications that I stuck between
> the cracks. Visit the land[.][53]

CHAPTER TWO

Lost in Space

S. Y. Abramovitsh and the Skeptical Voyage

In the twelfth century, Yehuda Halevi became the poet-in-the poem who never arrived. The Land of Israel and its people, imagined in a state of temporary alienation, generated a poignant, erotic tension between the promise of arrival and the poetics of longing. Seven hundred years later, as Zionists attempted to resolve that tension, Yehuda Halevi's writings came to seem a foreshadowing of the pragmatic reclamation of the sacred as political space.

What few readers realize today is that one of the first and most enduring nineteenth-century meditations on recovery of the Holy Land was not a Zionist work of imminently realizable dreams—not Herzl's *Altneuland* or Bialik's "El ha-tzipor" [To the Bird]—but a mock-epic that gently subverted desire itself: a satire of travel in which the ironies and urgencies of the mundane "real" quickly supersede the manifestly naive longings of the heroes. *Kitzur Masoes binyomin hashlishi* [The Travels of Benjamin the Third], by S. Y. Abramovitsh, is a text that, remarkably, more nearly anticipates the post-Zionist critique of the 1990s than the Zionist writings of the 1890s.

Abramovitsh (1836–1917) published *The Travels of Benjamin the Third* in 1878. In the novel, one of the first in Yiddish literature, he invited his readers to examine snapshots of exile and scenarios of redemption together, through the stereopticon of a pretend pilgrimage to the Holy Land. In their search for the Dark Mountains, the Sambatyon River, and the Ten Lost Tribes of Israel, two benighted shlemiels grope their way through a number of townlets in the Russian Pale of Settlement. The diasporic itinerary is reduced in this narrative to its two basic elements: the figure of the Jew as solitary soul lost in mythic space and the topos of a journey authorized by both aggadic sources and medieval conventions of pilgrimage.

At the end of the novel, the two protagonists return to their homes and their wives. This was read, at first, as a satire of the limited capacity of the shtetl Jew in the world of affairs. But by the time Abramovitsh's Hebrew translation was published, some twenty years after the Yiddish, changes in the historical climate and subtle changes in the text conspired to target a different object of satire: the epic Jewish journey itself, enacted in real space and real time. The round-trip that returns these shlemiels to their point of origin released a profound skepticism toward one-way, utopian resolutions to the condition of exile—and toward the erotic desire that fuels the journey.

Between 1878 and 1896, when the author published his Hebrew version (*Kitzur mas'ot Binyamin ha-shlishi*), major upheavals—the pogroms of the 1880s and the initial settlement of pioneers in Palestine—had launched the Jewish masses of Europe on a series of migrations that would radically alter the map of the Jewish future and all of its cultural forms. The Yiddish text was written largely in response to challenges to the stagnant life of the Eastern European Jew, challenges represented in the maskilic mind by Western storehouses of knowledge and power and by voyages of discovery, expansionism, and imperialism; the Hebrew text entered very different space.

Placing the textual variations within their changing historical context, I will also argue that the Hebrew translation of *Benjamin the Third*—which appeared, along with Theodor Herzl's *Der Judenstaat*, within a year of the First Zionist Congress in Basel (1896–97)—would outlive its historical moment. The enduring power of this text lies in its potential to destabilize both contemporary complacencies and utopian desires. The Hebrew translation became a subtle but scathing superscription on the Zionist blueprint, a counternarrative to the translation of messianic dreams into the language of nineteenth-century nationalism and of return to "original" space. The same text, only slightly emended, was utterly transformed by the shift in the political context in which this narrative traveled; the reading I am proposing exemplifies the interpretive possibilities inherent in the correspondence between such linguistic and historical shifts. Whereas the mock-heroic effect is achieved in the Yiddish text by a juxtaposition of Jewish languages, in the Hebrew text a *dystopic* effect is achieved less by interlinguistic or intertextual than by *con*textual juxta-positions. In both versions the transgressing of boundaries occurs not in the geography that is the declared space of the novel but in linguistic zeugmas, in sexual and social reconfigurations, and in political satire.

The structure of this journey is determined by the myth of redemption rather than of banishment. If "exodus" as a choice is opposed to "exile" as a punitive condition, then whatever freedom inheres in this narrative, which is severely circumscribed in its geographical reach, is a function of the initial free choice of the main protagonists. Benjamin is a book-intoxicated shtetl Jew who convinces his friend Sender to accompany him in searching for traces of the Red Jews with the purpose of (re)establishing an independent kingdom in the Holy Land. Their aborted pilgrimage to foreign lands actually takes them only as far as the neighboring towns. Eventually, they are hoodwinked and abducted into the czar's army, trading the freedoms of the road and spiritual self-delusion for physical incarceration and spiritual enlightenment.

From the very outset, an ironic relationship is established between two distinct narratives: the adventures of Benjamin and Sender as recorded by Benjamin on the one hand and as framed by the voice of Mendele Moykher-Sforim (Mendele the Bookpeddler) on the other. Mendele here, as in most of the texts that bear his imprimatur, functions as mediator and redactor; he is also, in a complex way, the primary ventriloquized voice and alter ego of the author. His is the liminal figure that combines folksy presence with intellectual distance, blunting the satirical edge of Abramovitsh's prose while deflating the pathos of the shtetl Jew's lofty and futile ambitions.[1] The prologue, presented in Mendele's name, is introduced by a third authorial voice, a thundering, off-stage impresario: "Omar Mendele Moykher-Sforim"—"Thus spake Mendele Moykher-Sforim." As parody both of the conventional apostrophe that opens a religious text and of the official subtext—the twelfth-century *Itinerary* of Benjamin of Tudela, which begins: "'Amar rabi binyamin bar yona z'l"—the prologue establishes the explicit ironic distance between Mendele and the community of the faithful to which Benjamin belongs:

Mendele Moykher-Sforim (the Book Peddler) says:
"Praised be the Creator who marks the course of the spheres in the heavens above and the course of all His creatures on the earth below. Not even a blade of grass can creep out from the ground unless an angel strike it and say: 'Grow now! Come forth!' And how much more so a human being, he most certainly has an angel who strikes him and says: 'Come, come, come forth!' And even more so, our fine people, our praiseworthy little Jews. No fool can blurt out a word among us Jews, no moron can give advice, no ignoramus

can become a Hassid, no ruffian an enlightened gentleman—unless he be struck by his angel, who thereby goads him to become what he becomes. The angels also strike our paupers, saying: 'Grow, ye paupers, beggars, schnorrers, rag-pickers, native poor, nouveau poor, open, hidden: Sprout, grow, like grass, like nettles! go, ye sons of Israel, go—go a-begging!'"

(Y 3–4; E 179; H 5)[2]

After such an invocation, incorporating fragments of midrashic material as well as topical allusions, in which the angelic forces authorizing the text allocate a few square kilometers for the foolish antics of two of their less distinguished wards, the narrative proceeds by alternating "quotes" from Benjamin's travelogue with Mendele's third-person narration and commentary. Benjamin, a good citizen of the small town of Moochville, "used to be like a chick in its egg, or a worm in horseradish . . . [thinking] that the world ended on the other side of Moochville [Tuneyadevke; Batalon]" (Y 11; E 185; H 11); nevertheless, he becomes intoxicated by stories told in the local bathhouse about the adventures of Eldad the Danite, of the First and Second Benjamins and other Jewish explorers,[3] and about enchanted places and lost tribes waiting to be rediscovered and redeemed. Still something of a coward, Benjamin manages to summon up the courage to set out on his own journey—"just like a chick starting to peck and creep its way out of the egg into the bright world" (Y 13; E 186; H 13). He is, after some coaxing, accompanied by Sender, whose namesake is none other than Alexander the Great and who, running away from his own "missus," becomes Benjamin's "housewife."

"RECOVERY" AS REFAMILIARIZATION IN AN ENCHANTED UNIVERSE

The retrograde progress of these two unlikely pilgrims is charted by the cognitive defects manifest in their every encounter with reality beyond the borders of their circumscribed lives; they do not read the maps or speak the languages or fathom the customs of the world around them, and they demonstrate a total blindness to any semiotic system outside their own. If, however, as I have been arguing, it is not wonder but recognition, not discovery but *recovery* that is the key to Jewish journeys through a universe that is intelligible and divinely supervised from the moment of its creation—a universe whose sacred center is waiting in suspended animation to be redeemed—then the familiarization of the unfamiliar, culminating in the expectation that the messiah will surely come

any day now, is built into their perceptual apparatus. Each twist of the
road, therefore, promises to open to the miraculous panorama of the
Mountains of Darkness and the Sambatyon River beyond which dwell
the Red Jews. Benjamin and Sender practice reciting the *Akdamot* prayer
for Shavuoth as preparation for speaking the ancient Jewish Aramaic vernacular to the Sons of Moses, who "certainly don't know a word of Yiddish" (Y 44; E 209; H 38).

The linguistic imagination that goes as far as liturgical border crossings into Aramaic is a semiserious allusion to the medieval *Itinerary* of
Benjamin of Tudela, in which the mythical and the quasi-ethnographic
blend almost imperceptibly; it is also an acknowledgment of the non-
Ashkenazi communities and languages that are still to be recovered and
incorporated. But in serving the myth of *recovery*, the primary function
of this border crossing, I submit, lies in linking the latter-day mission of
redemption to the constitutive moment in Jewish memory when the Temple was destroyed and the (Aramaic-speaking) Jews were exiled from the
Holy Land.[4]

Living entirely in an enchanted, divinely countenanced universe inscribed in and deciphered through selected texts, Benjamin and Sender
refuse to recognize any animal or plant whose existence is not validated
by the appropriate blessing or scriptural reference. Exotic and mythical
flora and fauna share equal status in the "intelligible" primordial landscape of the biblical and apocalyptic imagination: dates and carobs, drag-
ons and lindworms (of the sort presumably used by Solomon to cut stones
for the Temple). On a boat in the stagnant Puddlemud River in Dumbsville [Heb., the Sirahon or Stink River in Kisalon], the captain tells the
travelers that what they had thought was an island was in fact "the blos-
soms that bloom on the river surface every year."

"But I," Benjamin writes, "would not be convinced that that was blossom-
ing vegetation. To be sure, it did have a fragrance (Heb., *reah meshuneh*), but
I have never heard in all my life or read in any of my books that water can
blossom. If it did blossom, then it would have to bear some sort of fruit, over
which one could say a benediction: 'Blessed be He who createth the fruit of
the water!' But no such benediction exists! I am of the opinion that the green
phenomenon was the gigantic oceanic fish, the khileyno, of which there is a
very lovely description in the book *Image of the World*." . . .
    Once, when Benjamin peered into the river, he saw some kind of creatures
deep in the water, they looked just like women. "Long before that day," writes
Benjamin, "I had read in the books that mermaids live in water, and the author of *Image of the World* testifies as follows: 'A Sea-Nymph's Head, Body,
and Breasts look like those of a Maiden, and she singeth very beautifully, and

she is known as a *Shreyno.*' . . . [T]oday I saw some with my own eyes. I pointed the maidens out with great astonishment to the captain, but he pointed at some washerwomen who were doing laundry on the shore. And since neither of us could understand the other's language, he did not know what I was showing him, and I did not know what he was showing me, and so I was unable to get any precise information from him about the mermaids."

(Y 92–93; E 246–47; H 80–81)

This of course parodies not just the divine economy but all economies ruled by a single principle—whether it be that of holy texts or class wars or the marketplace. Our two explorers are rescued from their own provincialism by the boundaries of the province itself: the great distances they believe they have covered in fact embrace only a few versts in the Pale of Settlement and a few small Jewish towns, where they experience familiar forms of discourse and negotiable if not identical landscapes. After some time (several days? weeks?) on the road, they have gotten only as far as Snoresville [Teterivke; Tsalmona], where they are nearly overtaken on a rickety bridge by none other than Sender's wife. A narrow escape is negotiated by rearguard action, and they proceed on the dusty road to the Mountains of Darkness and the Sambatyon River.

Each of the towns encountered along the way has a specific contour and the travelers (designated in Hebrew as *tayarenu*—"our sojourners" or "our tourists") expose the governing conceits through their entrances and exits and their instruments of surveillance. In Snoresville they participate in a shadow-play reenactment of the Crimean War. Approaching the town of Dumbsville [Glupsk, Kisalon], they follow the flow of nutrients into (and out of) the collective digestive system. But it is there, in Glupsk, that another connection is established between the Holy Land and the Jews of the Ukrainian shtetl, as the town's legendary ancestors are identified with descendants of the town of Ophir, which was founded by King Solomon. Ancient historical memory becomes mythical while myth becomes historicized. In the telling, the link between the monarchical, sovereign Jewish past in the Holy Land and the present-day Pale of Settlement appears no more or less absurd than the link between the Pale of Settlement and the vision of a reinstated Jewish sovereignty in the Holy Land. However, while such connections, expressed in the language of archaeology, anticipate latter-day claims to surfaces in the name of the depths of the past, another myth is also developing here—one of the antiquity and duplicability of derivative spaces, which presents a kind of diasporic alternative to the centrality and authenticity of sacred space in the Holy Land.[5]

When the pair finally arrive in Dnieprovitz [Pardiona], they meet up with two men who are the first to validate their mission and their heroic reading of Jewish geography, going so far as to offer to expedite their journey along the Dnieper River to the Great Ocean. After a pleasant interlude they are led to the Dnieprovitz bathhouse—the ultimate site of Jewish daydreams, of projected commerce with and schemes for mending the world.[6] A bit more ornate in appearance than what these country bumpkins are used to, the building to which they are taken turns out to be a military induction center (not the last time that what promises to be a Jewish bath turns out to be something else altogether . . .); our heroes discover that the two solicitous Jews were in fact *khappers*, or collaborators, and that they have been conscripted into the czar's army.[7]

At this point all the veils of delusion are removed and the dilemmas are redefined in terms of specific historical imperatives. Mythic topography gives way to real space (the confines of a military barracks) and the narrative collapses toward its denouement. The two hapless soldiers manage to screw up enough courage to attempt an escape. As they sneak out of their barracks, Sender makes a little speech about his grandfather's unfulfilled dream of reaching the Holy Land; on his deathbed, he had expressed the hope that one of his progeny would realize that dream. "My heart tells me now," adds Sender, "that he meant me." At this point Mendele Moykher-Sforim, who has been a less-than-compassionate narrator and (invisible) fellow traveler, interjects with some empathy that "Sender's prayers were heard by someone else!"—and a Russian soldier materializes to clap them in jail (Y 113; E 261; H 99–100). Thus utterly reduced in circumstance, the two await their court-martial.

The final act is an astounding verbal performance by Benjamin, who seems to talk his way out of the army. His speech has less of the delusionary—bombastic, bathetic, inflated—rhetoric that hitherto characterized his language and, though still bound by its own circumlocutions and internal diglossia, it appears more efficacious than anything he has declaimed to that point:

> "Your highness," Benjamin blurted out. "Grabbing people in broad daylight and selling them like chickens in the marketplace—that's permitted; and when those poor people try to save themselves, that's called a crime! If that's the way things are, then the world is lawless, and I swear I don't understand what 'permitted' and 'not permitted' mean! But nevertheless, let's ask the people here, let them say who the guilty party is. For instance, what if someone captured you somewhere on the road and shoved you into a sack. Would you, God forbid, be guilty of a crime if you did all you could to get out of the sack? I tell you plainly: We were forced from the very beginning, we were taken

in. . . . We swear to you that we knew absolutely nothing about military strategy, we don't know anything about it, and we don't want to know anything
about it. We have wives, thank the Lord, and we have future plans of our
own, and we absolutely can't have anything to do with such stuff, our minds
just couldn't take them in. So why do you need us? I think you ought to get
rid of us yourselves."

(Y 117; E 263–64; H 102)

Not quite Ivan Karamazov—yet Benjamin, in his references to the social
implications of "what is permitted," nevertheless enhances his stature
and sense of agency in the real world. His speech acts are interpreted in
his own mind as an open sesame to get two military misfits released from
service—even if, as Mendele informs us, they only provide the military
officers with a welcome excuse to do so. Their story concludes in the
Yiddish as "Benjamin very cordially took his leave with a bow and began striding off. Sender raised his legs like a soldier and marched right
after him" (Y 118; E 264).

TRANSLATING BENJAMIN

In locating the subversive weight of this text in its transformation from
Yiddish into Hebrew, I am not claiming that this translation is unique.
Nor is it my purpose to examine the linguistic and structural parallels
and changes in the two versions; these have been studied elsewhere.[8]
Much critical attention has been paid to the "internal bilingualism" of
Jewish writers in the modern period generally and to Abramovitsh in
particular. Modern Hebrew and Yiddish were siblings that had been
farmed out to different, though neighboring, foster homes. Abramovitsh,
who was fluent in several languages in addition to Hebrew and Yiddish
and who was largely if not uncritically committed to the maskilic program that endorsed a widespread change in cultural horizons and forms
of representation, had, by the time he wrote the Yiddish original of *Benjamin the Third*, abandoned his early Hebrew endeavors to devote himself to developing a language and a literary form that would carry Yiddish prose into the next century.[9] His eventual return to Hebrew in the
form of an invented *nusah*, a more inclusive prose that incorporated Talmudic and folkloristic as well as biblical layers of linguistic memory,
would become for generations of Hebrew writers a major source of
influence—and of anxiety. Even if this linguistic mobility was the norm
among transitional figures of the turn of the century—Benjamin Harshav
reiterates the argument that "to a large extent, Hebrew and Yiddish were

one literature, with the same writers and the same readers often shifting from one language to the other"[10]—certain texts were key in constituting different interpretive communities out of that common reservoir of readers. In what would come to be known as the "battle of the tongues," reflecting the larger struggle between conflicting visions of cultural boundaries and autonomy, Hebrew maintained a minority status in Europe and a privileged status among the polyglots in the Jewish Yishuv in Palestine. Yiddish, in contrast, gained temporary ascendancy in Europe and America—to be fatally defeated by the forces that eliminated its readers along with its writers. A figure like Abramovitsh who engaged in his last years in self-translations from Yiddish to Hebrew is generally agreed to have "tried to emulate the achievements" of the first language in the second.[11] But arguing from the context in which each of his texts appeared, as well as from internal evidence, one can make a case for a significant difference between the two: the Hebrew resonates as a political satire of far greater consequence than that of its Yiddish older sibling.

The translation of 1896 is not the first occasion on which the Yiddish text is ferried over to those more respectable precincts where Hebrew is spoken. In fact, the opening pages of the Yiddish version of this narrative set up not only an ironic relationship between Mendele the editor and Benjamin the official "author" of the text, as we have seen, but one between the two languages in which Benjamin writes.

Following the prologue in Mendele's voice, the narrative itself opens with a quote from Benjamin's own composition, which establishes the interlinguistic dialectic: "'*All my days*,' writes Benjamin the Third (he starts his book off in Hebrew but is kind enough to explain everything in Yiddish), '*All my days did I dwell in Moochville*, I mean, I spent my whole life in Moochville until my great voyage. I was born there, I was raised there, and there I married the *wife of my bosom*, my missus, *that pious spouse*, Zelda—*long may she live*'" (Y 7; E 181; H 7). Benjamin's mission is conceived in an elevated biblical diction, which is clearly the only "appropriate" language for a voyage of such epic proportions. The Hebrew (italicized) enters as a patchwork of citations from the Bible that serve to authorize the Yiddish text both by invoking the heroic scale associated with the Jewish memory of sovereignty and power and by mimicking the practices of rabbinic discourse.[12]

The ratifying or satirizing potential of scriptural passages, their proper and "malaprop-er" application, is one of the leitmotifs of the Jewish journey; as we have seen in the poetry of Yehuda Halevi and will see again in the prose of S. Y. Agnon, scriptural memory is both the weightiest and most elastic item of luggage carried by the Jews on their long sojourn in *galut*. The biblical text, embedded in the Talmud and surfacing during periods of biblical recuperation, is reinvoked in this source-ridden fiction through strategies inherent to a journey constructed alternately as pilgrimage or as mock-pilgrimage.

While the Hebrew passages in the original version of *Benjamin the Third* establish the epic reach, the Yiddish narrative continually subverts the heroic rhetoric and cuts Benjamin and his travels down to actual size. (Joachim Neugroschel's struggle to simulate in English translation the linguistic anxiety choreographed as a pas de deux between the Hebrew prince and the Yiddish ragpicker is partly resolved by rendering the biblical passages in italics.) Mendele's Yiddish is in fact "meant" to be only a place saver until the great poets of the age get around to writing the Hebrew epic worthy of its theme. He confides to his readers that "before the Jewish authors, whose little finger is thicker than my loins, before the Jewish authors get around to publishing their tomes on Benjamin's voyage in Hebrew, I will, in the meantime, try to put out at least a digest in plain Yiddish" (Y 5; E 180–81; H 6). The Hebrew Bible as the locus of God's word confers authenticity on the language itself and everything written in it. Just as the sojourn in *golus* has no normative value but functions as a provisional marker of the authentic place, so the Yiddish is always an ersatz, incomplete text beside the real, the primary, totalizing "Hebrew original."

Ruth Wisse compares the effect of the "Hebrew-Yiddish cross movement" with Alexander Pope's use of epic language and imagery to "inflate the style and inevitably deflate events so described." As she and other readers have shown, Yiddish lends itself to satiric acts of self-diminution.[13] The juxtaposition of languages in this text sets the present condition of the Jews in exile against the deep structure of primordial memories. Yiddish is the language of exile *as it is lived*. And yet, at the linguistic level, the passage from one language to another reflects the premise of mobility as well as its obstacles. In its commerce with its surroundings, Yiddish became the language that was porous, inclusive—the language that wandered and incorporated alien worlds as it went. Hebrew remained the lingua franca, the universal referent, the conduit for a dispersed civilization precisely *because of* its relative immobility, its stasis and boundedness, its grounding in both a corpus and a place.[14] As Jewish civilization refashioned itself at the turn of the century, a process of concretizing or reifying that tended to immobilize and stabilize the object world may have been a desired by-product of the self-translations from Yiddish to Hebrew. Yet paradoxically, certain writers—including Abramovitsh, U. N. Gnessin, M. Y. Berdichevski, and, a generation later, David Fogel—followed the same premise to the opposite conclusions: Hebrew was considered so inextricably associated with territory that it could furnish *in itself* the material base for an imagined world.

This process can be traced in the Hebrew version of *Benjamin the Third*, both in the ways it reflects the Yiddish text and in the ways it incorporates biblical Hebrew. A kind of literalization takes place through concretizing the idioms of the one culture and resurrecting the dead metaphors of the other. In a structural analysis of *Benjamin the Third*, Menakhem Perry, who argues that the Yiddish is not only the original text but also the *sub*text of the Hebrew, demonstrates that in many places the Hebrew narrative implicitly *enacts* the Yiddish idiom for which it provides no explicit verbal translation.[15] The effect is to expose the underlying structures and hierarchies of the culture that are embedded in its idioms, clichés, and curses. The strategy of literalizing biblical metaphor, though similar, has different import: it not only establishes the epic reference for mock-epic effect but restores the suspended referent, via demythification, to earthly dimensions.

While in the Yiddish text the social criticism is located in the play between the two languages, in the Hebrew translation the irony is not interlinguistic but semantic and intralinguistic; it emerges not in the gap between two languages—one the language of ambition/memory and the other the language of life in the present—but rather in the gap between exalted language and a *diminished life that can have no legitimate linguistic correlative*. Because it is theologically always the point of departure, the ur-text, Hebrew can hardly stand any gaps at all. Yiddish, by contrast, is never the "real" text but always its substitute, as exile is a substitute for the Land of Israel, the rhinestones that stand in for the diamonds on a Jewish matron's Sabbath headpiece; as a worthless simulacrum, it can easily be made the writer's plaything.

Although Aramaic is introduced to attempt to reproduce the Hebrew-Yiddish diglossia, and a vernacular of stuttered Slavicisms provides the line of communication between Benjamin and Sender and the world of peasants and draymen in which they travel, the comedy arises from the attempt to make Hebrew a more elastic language in the present tense— a language in which a nose is not only an anthropomorphic quality of the Almighty but a prominent and sonorous appendage to a Jewish face.[16]

As the medium of Scriptures and tales of collective sovereignty, Hebrew was always loaded with prowess—hence the Kabbalistic faith in the powers that can be unleashed by the proper combinations of its letters and words. Once Hebrew moves from the status of archaic heroic text to the status of actor-in-history, the ironies no longer inhere in the interlinguistic or intertextual space but rather in the diminishing and barely legitimate space between the actual world and its re-presentations. As the linguistic matrix of a utopian vision, the power of Hebrew is now measured not only by its reference to the point of departure but also by its proximity to the absolute value of the world-as-it-should-be. The translation of *Benjamin the Third* into Hebrew is, by this logic, an alchemical process that automatically converts the story from a satire of the shtetl into a satire of pilgrimage to utopia.

The gap between Yiddish and Hebrew (Hebrew in the broadest sense as the Hebraic mandate, code, and canon), the real and the ideal, surface and deep memory, is the birthplace and primary dwelling of the shlemiel. By the same token, in the utopian place where the real and the ideal become conflated—rendering the gap between them impossible— the shlemiel necessarily dies. As I will argue later, the climate of the Land of Israel will prove utterly inhospitable to the figure who adapted so well to the climes and the landscapes of Eastern Europe. To "translate" Benjamin into an idiom that cannot ultimately accommodate him is, in effect, to sound the first notes of his arrival as pilgrim and of his death knell as shlemiel.

THE JEWISH DON QUIXOTE

The narrative declares itself to be a journey modeled after the voyages of the two Benjamins. But while allusions to the literature of pilgrimage include extensive intertexts from the medieval itineraries of Eldad the Danite as well as of Benjamins the First and Second, and extend to modern voyages of exploration and colonization, it is as a "Jewish Don Quixote" that Benjamin the Third undermines (though only, in the end, to under*write*) the inherited vocabulary of exile.[17] As a narrative of random encounters in the search for an impossible dream, as a parodic romance featuring a benighted picaro and his pragmatic sidekick, as a journey authorized by the mythical texts at the foundation of the cultural tradition under attack, *Benjamin the Third* reproduces the generic, structural, and epistemological qualities of *Don Quixote* and its iconoclastic status.

With so many available prototypes of the Jewish traveler, from the itinerant biblical forefathers to Yehuda Halevi, the decision to model the heroic vision and mission of Benjamin the Third on the seventeenth-century Spanish knight at the least reflects the maskilic notion of permeability at the borders of Jewish consciousness. In the process, the Quixote figure from the European canon—who is destined to a kind of aimless wandering (and is ruled by the authority of texts) yet is burdened with neither the mission nor the guilt of Ahasuerus, the Wandering Jew, whom he resembles but in crucial ways remains different from—adds another dimension and a new cast of characters to the Jewish discourse on exile.[18]

Don Quixote, arguably the first modern novel in the Western tradition, furnishes a paradigm for diverse and often contradictory clusters of meaning: the quest for justice, the endurance of practical jokes and self-delusion, the allegory of life as a journey, the narratological possibilities of writing-as-travel.[19] The last are consistent with modern readings of both Cervantes and the "nomadic" character of the Jew. The Promethean figure of Ahasuerus in Shelley's *Queen Mab*, as well as other representations in the romantic tradition that began to locate the Jew at the outer limits of the human rather than in the netherlands of the demonic or the subhuman, eventually generated an image of the Jewish itinerary as the most mobile of all cultural agendas. That emphasis on nomadism has, as we have seen, persisted to this day in various post-structuralist and postcolonial forms.[20] In making wandering the Jew's *nature* rather than his punishment, this version of the myth is as challenging as the more traditional attribution of both the rootlessness and the "immortality" of the Jews to a primordial curse; it denies their distinction as a people "truly longing to return home," substituting instead the image of the "wanderings of a nomadic people such as the Gypsies."[21]

Michel Butor's "science of *iterology*" helped to shape another conceptual vocabulary; with a minimum of gravity, as is appropriate for such expeditions, it treats Reading as Travel, Travel as Reading, Travel as Writing and Writing as Travel. Perhaps the paradigmatic instance of the "iterological" experience is the act of reading *while* traveling:

> A trip is, for our contemporaries, a privileged place for reading; how many read only in the subway, the train, the plane? [And consider further that] within the moving train, I can change cars between two chapters; furthermore, all the immobility upon the earth's surface is also only an illusion: we need enlarge only slightly our frame of reference to perceive that we are always moving in relation to other celestial bodies; we need merely apply time to space

(travel is an illustration of this) to arrive at that traditional, and inexhaustible, metaphor of the individual life, or even all of history, as a journey from birth to death.[22]

Narratives such as those by Cervantes—and Abramovitsh—that not only are *récits de voyage* but also contain characters who themselves are reading *récits de voyage* create, if read en route, a dizzying infinitude of moving mirrors. In the ten days on board a ship bound for "New Amsterdam," Thomas Mann, who has brought along *Don Quixote* as shipboard reading, intends to "come to the rim of this ocean of a book, at the same time as we come to the other rim of the Atlantic." (Moreover, in this case, Mann himself is transported between the realms of experience and of his own fiction when he claims to be reading *Don Quixote* while sitting in his deck chair, a "transmogrification of Hans Castorp's excellent reclining-chair.")[23]

For Mikhail Bakhtin, *Don Quixote* is the "parodied hybridization of the 'alien, miraculous world' chronotope of chivalric romances, with the 'high road winding through one's native land' chronotope that is typical of the picaresque novel"; it is, additionally, one of the earliest exemplars of a genre in which the "literary, novelistic discourse [is] being tested by life, by reality." But for Michel Foucault, it is the site at which "language breaks off its old kinship with things and enters into that lonely sovereignty from which it will reappear, in its separated state, only as literature."[24] Whether one reads this narrative as affirming or as undermining the "old kinship with things," it is that kinship which is surely at the heart of the quixotic quest.

In the text before us, inherited visions of redemption replace chivalric romances as sources of delusion; but, as we will see, it also contains more than a hint of the contemporary practical strategies to bring near what is far and to make the eschaton secular, historical, and even banal so that the high road of the miraculous and the alien may someday wind through one's native land. For a culture such as that of the Jews of late-nineteenth-century Eastern Europe, in which the struggle between literature and "the world" was about to redefine an ancient historical condition, for a people about to move from "map" to "territory," the Cervantean model—with its invitation to a rich ambiguity of possible readings—would have been most attractive.[25]

The move from map to territory recalls the colonial moments that are captured in each of these texts. Reflections of the "discovery" of the "New World" in *Quixote* have their analogue, as I have already suggested, in the tropes of "recovery" of the "Old/New Land" in *Benjamin the Third*.

The argument that the "discovery of the New World charged the air around Cervantes with the energies and the mirages of utopias"[26] can most certainly be applied to the pervasive atmosphere in the Jewish Pale of Settlement in the late nineteenth century. It appears fairly certain that had Cervantes been granted his wish to emigrate to the New World, *Don Quixote* would never have been written[27]—and it is equally likely that had Abramovitsh joined the Hovevei Zion who were forming the first Zionist settlements in Palestine in the early 1880s, the Hebrew version of *Benjamin the Third* would never have seen the light of day.

The episodic structure of the picaresque novel both privileges the different stations at the expense of the final destination and constitutes a loose unity of divergences, contingencies, and detours. As "belated" readers, we need not join earlier critics of *Benjamin the Third* in regarding the absence of the propelling forces of external causality or psychological development as a failure of form.[28] Our concern here is rather how this picaresque structure relates to the deeper structures of a community whose millennial journey of infinite detours was being radically rerouted.

As Benjamin sets out on his Hebrew journey, his egress is so encoded in speech that he is understood to be as besotted as was his Spanish predecessor; "hu halakh 'al pi ha-dibur" (H 5), says Mendele of Benjamin, which loosely translates as "he went by the book." (This phrase, which literally means that he went "by speech," or "as commanded," does not appear in the original Yiddish.) The Hebrew books that furnish the language of grandeur and the sources of inspiration are revealed at the end to be sources of self-delusion. But the consequences are far greater than those suffered by Quixote on discovering the delusive nature of chivalric romance. Benjamin's bombastic rhetoric and ambitious design cannot be repudiated without repudiating the entire project of repatriation—a project that was designed to supersede a verbal, passive, "book" culture. His ultimate return to his point of origin thus is as much a return to the logocentric culture of the European Diaspora as it is an eschewal of political activism or religious messianism.

Benjamin's voyage is conceived, admittedly, out of a quixotic intoxication with pseudo-scientific texts and mythical geographies and is suffused with the rhetoric of pilgrimage to the Holy Land. Nevertheless, its true motivating force and its ultimate, domestic reference is the henpecked condition of the two central characters, Benjamin and Sender. The changing image of domestic "bliss" is located in a series of doubled references to exile: "'ol galuta shel zugatkha ha-mirsha'at" (H 28; see Y 60; E 200), or the "exile of [which is] your wicked spouse,"[29] cited as the impetus for departure, will be reconfigured at the end of the narrative as an act of return to the equivalent of "wife in [as] house." As we will see, it is in the identical gestures of departure and return that the implicit power of the narrative resides.

GOING HOME AS CRITICAL GESTURE

In his study of "travel as metaphor" in French philosophical literature from the late Renaissance through the Enlightenment, Georges Van Den Abbeele investigates the critical implication of travel in relation to "entrapment" and "radical innovation." Because the theme of the voyage is so ubiquitous in literature, he argues, it interrogates the very "status of the literary discourse itself": "The voyage . . . has a powerful ability to dislodge the framework in which it is placed or understood, to subject it to critical displacement—although that displacement is not always to where one expects, nor is its criticism necessarily what one expects to find. The voyage, in other words, always takes us somewhere."[30] Whereas forms of dislodgement and displacement characterize recorded and imagined journeys from the Babylonian *Gilgamesh* through the Irish *Ulysses*, the period on which Abbeele focuses is peculiar in its rather "remarkable conjunction between the vogue of exoticism and imaginary voyages, on the one hand, and the philosophical trends of skepticism, relativism, and *libertinage*, on the other."[31] Swift and Voltaire are two of many eighteenth-century writers whose parody of travel literature serves the purposes of satire. In each case, the parody mocks the excesses of both the romance *and* the travel-narrative.[32] By the same token, *The Travels of Benjamin the Third* can be read as a parody both of a text culture— a culture grounded in mythic texts whose relation to observable, scientifically certifiable reality is as remote as that of the romances Quixote read—and of the teleological journey that is the very self-definition of a civilization in *galut*. Drawing on the same epistemology that conceives mobility of thought to be the truest form of travel, S. Y. Abramovitsh, like Gogol and other Russian satirists of his century, shares with the French writers of the sixteenth through the eighteenth centuries a commitment to the critical gesture trained back on points of origin. In 1870, eight years before the first publication of *Benjamin the Third*, Abramovitsh wrote:

The more accomplished man has become in theoretical and practical knowledge, the more the world opens and expands around him and the more capable he is of communicating his own interests to all people of different countries, and of moving freely to whatever and wherever he likes. This is because
spatial movement is in direct ratio to intellectual movement. To the very extent that a person becomes more accomplished in his intellect, talents, and
language his movement in the world is made possible and his capability of
going to different places grows. . . . However, the ignoramus is fettered; he
cannot secure even the necessities of life and, like the primitive savage, he depends on chance and coincidence for everything. He engages in transactions
only with a few people who are like him and the circumference of his movement is very limited precisely as his knowledge is limited.[33]

Yet because the very condition of *galut* that defines the Jew is coded *as*
a journey, the critical posture in this case adheres not in either the trope
or the actuality of travel but in the redundancies of the very return to
the point of departure. In the narrative's Hebrew version such a conclusion becomes even more consequential, given the new historical options available to the Jewish traveler.

What makes Benjamin's travels in both languages less a pilgrimage
and more a speculative voyage, in spite of its declared telos, is the nature of his return to the source, to what Abbeele calls "an *oikos*, a same,
to which everything and anything can be referred back."[34] Pilgrimage
presupposes travel within the known and "complete" world to a previously established site of revelation; the subject's point of departure is
measured by its distance from the sacred center. In the Jewish vocabulary, the point of departure is, by definition, not home but exile. For
Catholics and especially for Jews, pilgrimage remains a primary official
justification for travel, but that was not true for everyone; "with pilgrimages to the Holy Land and to Rome less important for Protestant
England, Englishmen found other reasons for going to the Continent—
for study, for trade, for picking up new languages and fashions, for diplo-
matic service. In fact, the great scholars of the period all traveled."[35]

Although the pilgrimage is often recounted as a combination of spiritual quest and guidebook to exotic places, there remains a profound distinction between the travel narratives defined as pilgrimage and those
defined as voyages of discovery, commerce, education, or speculation.
As the narrative of pilgrimage and return to sacred space is transformed
or superseded first by the narrative of adventure and exploration, of
ethnographic and existential quest, and then, in turn, by the secular quest
for a collective homecoming, its flexibility enables it to contain all the
possible resonances of the modern Jewish journey.

Because the Jewish pilgrimage to the Holy Land was being redefined at the end of the nineteenth century as a mission of reclamation and settlement, the return to the (profane) diasporic source takes on added valence as a skeptical gesture, as a refusal to find anchorage in that dream and in the aesthetic it generated. Claude Lévi-Strauss isolates the "crucial moment in modern thought when, thanks to the great voyages of discovery, a human community which had believed itself to be complete and in its final form suddenly learned . . . that it was not alone, that it was part of a greater whole, and that, in order to achieve self-knowledge, it must first of all contemplate its unrecognizable image in this mirror."[36] Voyages of speculation both issue from and return home; the reflected image of one who returns from such a journey may be unrecognizable until he has incorporated all that has been encountered along the way—but the mirror itself remains fixed in place on the wall of the house. After the requisite trip to Italy, Montaigne returns to "Montaigne," which, Abbeele reminds us, is as much his "proper name as it is the name of his property. 'Moy' is difficult to distinguish from 'chez moy.'" The wife, like the mirror, remains—and represents—home. Even the mobility of Montesquieu's Persian traveler, so perceptive about the culture of France from his distant perspective, "finds its correlative in the veiled and immobilized status of the women kept back home."[37] By the same token, Benjamin and Sender return to their respective wives—"chez soi," as it were—as to the mirror on the wall waiting to reflect their altered selves.

If Benjamin is like Gulliver in encountering each of the towns he visits in its own peculiar shape and form (though it is debatable whether any of these encounters significantly challenges or dislodges his perspective), in the end he is like Candide, abandoning philosophical or ideological optimism to return to cultivate his garden: "mir zenen, barukh-hashem, bavaybte" ("we have wives, thank God"—more literally rendered as "we are bewived"; Y117; E 162). The Hebrew, in contrast, signifies the male hegemony that already pervades Zionist discourse: "anu, barukh ha-shem, ba'alei nashim"—a phrase whose connotation is "our wives are, thank God, husbanded" (H 102). Both the passive construction in the Yiddish and the reincorporation of the domestic in the very person whom the men's journey was devoted to putting at a distance invite speculation on the protean space of the feminine as place of both departure and possible border crossing. But it is in the homoerotic descriptions of the relationship between Benjamin and Sender that we find the most dramatic manifestation of that crossing.

SEXUAL BOUNDARY CROSSINGS

We have already seen that Sender is from the very outset described as a housewife, first the henpecked husband of his generic wife (*ployniste*; *plonit*) and later the acquiescent feminine partner of Benjamin. "'Sender, my dearest friend, let me kiss you,' cried Benjamin, [overjoyed at Sender's consenting to accompany him on his journey,] and he lovingly threw his arms around Sender the Housewife." Throughout the journey, in both versions, the two are referred to in the language of biblical eros as "love-birds" (*ha-ne'ehavim ve-ha-ne'imim*), a "ravishing bride in the eyes of the groom" (*ke-khalah na'ah be-'eynei dodah*), "like a loving couple right after the wedding" (*ve-hayu domim be-ota sha'a le-hatan ve-khalah be-shiv'at yemei ha-mishteh*). The process culminates in Sender's dream of childbirth: "I wasn't Sender, I was—a woman, if you please, no sign of a beard, I had a woman's jacket on, and my belly, my belly . . . I had a horrible stomachache—may all Jews be spared! 'Don't worry!' someone shouted, 'the first baby's always the hardest'" (E 200, 202, 204, 247, 251; H 28, 30, 33, 82, 87).

Critics have not overlooked the transgressive sexual language, though for the most part they have regarded it is symptomatic of something else. Menakhem Perry reads the "pseudo-marriage" theme as a comic diversion devoid of the status of the real.[38] Gershon Shaked reads manifestations of sexual "deviance" as a sign of the distractions caused by economic deprivation.[39] Dan Miron and Anita Norich view the homoerotic (or "pseudohomosexual") passages as part of the political satire; the conquest of Palestine and liberation of the Red Jews are framed within a "grotesque" love affair that resonates with the language of the sentimental romance. In this reading, the "game is [more than] . . . that of planting a mock romance into the framework of a mock epic," going so far as to mimic the messianic/Kabbalistic language of a mystical union of the male and female elements. It thereby becomes a parody unparalleled in Jewish literature of the Kabbalistic version of messianism—and, by extension, of all redemptive schemes. Essentially, Miron and Norich argue, through the union of Benjamin, the savior, and Sender, the passive subject-in-exile, Abramovitsh was expressing his sense of despair at the likelihood that any such schemes would radically alter the political status of the Jews. "If a political vision of change (represented by Benjamin) had to find its 'practical' correlative, its physical embodiment, in a Senderl, then the volition which such a vision carries with it must be frittered away and debased."[40]

By recontextualizing those very passages that would have raised contemporary Jewish eyebrows, Miron and Norich underscore the power
of the political allegory with its anti-Zionist message. But other readers
of the late twentieth century seeking early signs of transfiguration in inherited patterns of representation are more inclined to take these passages on their own terms. Jeffrey Fleck argues that the relationship between Benjamin and Sender is one of the manifestations of the contested
taboos of a society in transition.[41] Similar "transgressions" occur in other
fictions by this author and his contemporaries, suggesting that within a
more self-reflexive context, both the culture of Westernizing Jews of the
fin de siècle and representations of the feminine become potential sites
for radical or subversive shifts in self-definition.

As part of a larger study of constructions of sexuality in postrabbinic
culture and its transformations in the modern period, Daniel Boyarin
quarrels with the conventional reading of European Jewish civilization
as feminized, debased, and self-loathing: "One way that the negative aspect of Freud's fin-de-siècle thought can be redeemed is . . . by retrieving and transvaluing the delineation of male Jews as female, arguing that
historically Jewish men were indeed differently gendered from the general European ideal."[42] He is here exploring the language of gender belonging at that time to the culture of Western Europe, especially Germany and Austria. The vocabulary of masculinization in the Zionist
enterprise can provide both a hermeneutic code for those reading the literature of the late nineteenth century and a code of differentiation for
those attempting to rebuild a competing diasporic sensibility at the end
of the twentieth century by reclaiming subordinated images and disinherited patterns of cultural self-presentation.

Yiddish is an appropriate conduit for such experiments both as what
Sander Gilman calls the "secret language of the Jews"—that is, the safe
arena of an internal discourse—and as the Jewish language that, unburdened by the exalted status of Hebrew, could license acts of experi-
mentation. Naomi Seidman's lively exploration of the "transsexual
imagination" of Abramovitsh and other writers considers how Yiddish
itself is defined by its own writers as the territory of illicit encounters and
implicitly sexual boundary crossings.[43] As such, it may have been the only
place where these writers could engage in transgressive acts, especially
since women were ostensibly the primary (and only legitimate) targets
of this literature.[44] As Hebrew becomes the instrument of the masculinization of Jewish culture, the language of Jewish power—initially of
theurgy and its derivatives, prayer and Kabbala, and finally of the phys-

ical power of Zionism—Yiddish becomes increasingly associated with
the female. Although the sexual innuendos are translated faithfully into
the Hebrew version of *Benjamin the Third* and indeed rendered even more
explicit there, the homoerotic element intensifies the quality of unfulfilled
desire, of the voyage to the Holy Land as an impossible romance; the
eventual return home is, perforce, a return to woman, which is exile—
which is *Yiddish*.

LINGUISTIC BOUNDARY CROSSINGS

All such approaches enhance the sense of Abramovitsh's narrative as disruptive of both the old and the new orders and as one of the pivotal texts
in an ongoing redefinition of Jewish culture. Its effect in displacing the
norms of social discourse is almost inversely proportional to its geographical reach. That is, the critical posture is structured not by the voyage itself but by the forms and norms of mobility—including the gesture
of return—articulated within the immobility defining the condition of
the shtetl Jew. Language takes flight where people are earthbound. The
instruments of distancing in this text are the lenses of the microscope
and of the telescope. One set of tropes that recurs in Abramovitsh's fiction
establishes analogues between human actors and varieties of animals and
insects, adapting Darwinian language to a maskilic worldview and re-
ducing the Jews to specimens in a laboratory. The dream of a heroic hand-
shake between Benjamin and Alexander the Great becomes, as dreamscapes give way to the harsh light of day, something else altogether:
"'Your Majesty,' I cried, grabbed his hand, and squeezed and squeezed
it. But then suddenly my nose was filled with a horrible stench, it made
me sick. I woke up and in my hand I felt a squashed up bedbug" (Y 98–99;
E 250; H 85–86). Criticized by a coachman for "crawling along like
crabs," Benjamin and Sender "scurry off in different directions like poi-
soned mice" (Y 57; E 219; H 50). Benjamin, as we have already seen, is
repeatedly compared to a chicken just before or in the act of hatching;
the metaphor is reified when he appears in the town square with egg on
his face.[45]

Another group of metaphors moves in quite the opposite direction,
enacting the journey that can take place only in language: "Going off
without Sender would have been strange and unnatural *like a ship without a helm, a state without a prime minister*" (Y 36; E 204; H 32). "Our
friends strode off and tramped at a smart pace; . . . their broad coattails
billowing in the wind made them look *like a ship scudding along with*

full sails" (Y 40; E 206; H 35). "Because Benjamin's legs were still aching, and because the handfuls of straw were so soft to lie on, he remained in Leechville for the rest of the day. He was *like a ship at sea, which has foundered on a sandbar, and there is no good wind to drive it away*" (Y 52; E 215; H 44–45). The similes (emphasized by my italics) that abound in this text, in Mendele's voice, help establish not only a ridiculous contrast between the stated and the actual position of these pilgrims but also an autonomous sphere of linguistic freedom.

What is the relationship, then, between the books that Benjamin reads, which becloud his mind with the exotic imaginary, and the truly liberating domain of metaphor? And what of the dreamscapes that punctuate the two other landscapes, that of the backwater shtetl and that of the mythic imagination? Dreams explicitly function throughout the text as a stage for illicit sexual transactions, but toward the end they take on additional import. Mendele himself questions as he comments on the "messages" Sender receives from his grandfather while in prison awaiting trial: "A good dream is a fine thing. Isn't the world a dream?" (Heb., *ve-khi kol ha-'olam kulo lav halom hu?*) (Y 114; E 262; H 100). In this casual aside, flung out as the narrative gathers momentum and nears its conclusion, Mendele elevates the dreams from being sources of illicit drama or hermeneutic code to providing a kind of radical skepticism that will counter the ontological claims of Zionism—an enterprise based on Herzl's assurance to a dream-prone people that "if you will it, it is not a dream." Are dreams the blueprints for alternative realities, or simply the magic of the imagination? And does all this mean that in the final analysis Mendele himself also "holekh 'al pi ha-dibur"—goes by the book? What, that is, are the legitimate uses of the imagination? And how, ultimately, does the skeptical gesture confirm or undercut the creative gesture?

The wanderings of the picaro, unlike those of the exile or the pilgrim— or the exile who is by definition *always a pilgrim*—are not teleological: they are the aimless wanderings of a free spirit or the reflexive movement of the returning spirit. While Benjamin and Sender are going around in circles looking for that unattainable utopian/messianic place, Mendele, whom Dan Miron has labeled the "eiron," the truly "free spirit," a "traveler disguised,"[46] is exploring his true freedom, which is in imagination, in metaphors that take flight, in liberation from the shackles of social and sexual convention. What I call the movement in perception, from viewing wandering as curse to seeing mobility as blessing, begins with Mendele and can be traced through the writing that travels through Europe and lands eventually on American shores.

To be sure, in the text before us it is not Mendele but Benjamin who represents the quixotic figure. Because their two voices collapse into one at the end of the narrative, we sense that while the misguided travels of the benighted soul were the primary object of satire, the resolution in favor of a return home is endorsed by *both* narrators, Benjamin and Mendele. Mendele remains a free spirit even when, or especially when, he "frees" Benjamin to assert the privilege and obligation of returning home. One might even argue that the last speech before the military tribunal, when the narrative voices implode into one voice, reflects the nostalgic (Benjamin) and the skeptical (Mendele) at a rare moment of amalgamation. As with other maskilic satire, and most pointedly in the versions of autobiography that Abramovitsh himself published during the last decades of his life,[47] bitter critique was becoming something of a nostalgic recall of what was already passing: by the time the Hebrew version was being composed, another handwriting was already visible on the crumbling walls of the shtetl.

ON THE ROAD, AGAIN . . .

As it is in the nature of satire when thwarted by nostalgia to turn its venom toward a new target, its iconoclastic hammer toward newly minted idols, so *The Travels of Benjamin the Third* in its final Hebrew edition can be read as a summons to *épater les sionistes* through an affirmation of the *journey itself*. Ever ambivalent about political Zionism, closer in many ways to the cultural Zionist position of Ahad Ha-am than to any other thinker in his intellectual milieu,[48] Abramovitsh makes increasingly explicit in subsequent versions whatever may have been left ambiguous in the Yiddish original. The two framing passages in the Hebrew edition of 1911 are encrusted with the rhetoric of the Zionist project. Mendele's mimicking in the Yiddish prologue of the condescending voice of the Jewish angel who prods his people—"geyt, yidishe kinder, geyt,—iber di hayzer!" (go, ye sons of Israel, go—go a-begging!)—becomes through a subtle change in the Hebrew version a highly subversive parody of the clarion call that marks the secular messianism of the age: "*Beit ya'akov, lekhu—ve*-hizru al hapetahim" (House of Jacob, go—a-begging from door to door). Whereas the primary intertext is the vision in Isaiah 2 of the great ingathering at the end of days, the more proximate subtext is the source of the acronym of the "Bilu" pioneers of the First Aliyah (*beit ya'akov lekhu ve-nelkha*); the summons to the House of Jacob to rise up and "walk in the light of the Lord" becomes here a meek sendoff to

nowhere for a nation of beggars. By the same token, at the conclusion
of the Hebrew narrative, when Sender proudly turns to follow Benjamin
into the next (unwritten) chapter of their lives, he is portrayed in the 1911
Hebrew version, which was added to the original version published in
1896, as "ve-holekh aharav *komemiut*" (H 103). *Komemiut*, translated
literally as "upright," is co-opted into the Jewish nationalist lexicon from
biblical and liturgical sources and connotes the rise in stature that collective repatriation in Zion will bring. Half a century later, it will be used
to designate the 1948 War of Independence.[49]

But it is in the Hebrew epilogue, titled "Acknowledgments and Revelations" (*lehitvadea' ve-lehigalot*; H 104) and missing in the Yiddish and
in the first Hebrew version, that the Zionist script is most seriously undermined. *Lehigalot* can mean both "to acknowledge," or "to be revealed," *and* "to be exiled." Recovering his own voice, Mendele declares
that while he was busy preparing the text of Benjamin's travelogue for
publication, word came of Benjamin's next venture as the head of a group
of *tayarim* (tourists) to the very same "Mountains of Darkness" that he
had previously "visited." This episode begins with a public proclama-
tion: "Since the Holy One, Blessed be His Name, has revealed to us the
mouth of the Sambatyon River," it was decided, lest any brazen souls
begin to doubt the words of the rabbis, to found the Society for the Preservation of the Honor of the Scholars of the Torah and to "travel there
and back." All God-fearing Jews are asked either to join the pilgrims or
to contribute to the expenses of their journey. Benjamin hears this an-
nouncement and immediately collects "Senderl the Woman, his tallit and
tefillin, his staff and his sack" and presents himself before the honorable
public servants (*'askanim nekiyei ha-da'at*). And now, continues Mendele,
Benjamin "is leading them like a horse in the great desert. . . . And I wish
him well from the bottom of my heart: may God bless his way and *return* him to us in good health, and I will attempt to inform the tribes of
Israel also about his second trip" (H 104; emphases mine).

If we read from within the precincts of a Zionist discourse, it is hard
to miss the mocking allusions to the early pioneers, to the Hovevei Zion,
and to *Benyamin* Zeev Herzl—particularly in the epilogue.[50] Some of the
language of Herzl's scientific utopia enters into the discussions held in
the synagogue, in the lodgings, in the public square, in the bathhouse. A
Jew in a bathhouse—which, as we have seen, is both a microcosm of the
Jewish sphere and the sign of its diminutive status in the world's affairs—
is described in the Yiddish as "vi in a foterland, vi in a frayer medine"
(as if he were entering a Fatherland and a realm of freedom, i.e., a place

where all people have the same rights; Y 103; E 254). The twin images
of Zion as the distant Motherland and one's diasporic place of birth as
the Fatherland are, as noted in chapter 1, at least as old as Philo; here
the language of civic emancipation (*in a frayer medine*) evolves in the
Hebrew of late-nineteenth-century Jewish nationalism into "eretz moledet u-medina hofshit" (a homeland and a free state; H 91). Written at
a time when Zionist utopias were proliferating as a literary genre that
both reflected and nourished the blueprints of political Zionism, the later
versions of the Hebrew narrative become satires of the genre in the name
of a more traditional and mythic—that is, implausible—messianism.[51]
Menakhem Perry points to the image of the bird that recurs in this text
(Y 109, 114; E 258, 262; H 95, 101) as alluding to the imagery that pervades the poetry and songs of the Hibat Zion pioneers.[52] But even when
acknowledging the polemic with Zionism that grows increasingly transparent as one continues to contextualize the publishing history of this
book, such readings tend to overlook what remains to my mind the most
salient point: namely, that—to stay with the migratory bird for a moment—
this symbol of freedom and flight is also the bird *who returns* unerringly
to its point of origin. (After all, even the bird in Bialik's earliest published
poem, "El ha-tzipor" [To the Bird, 1892], who brings greetings to the
poet from the warmth of distant lands, is returning to their common home
in the cold northern regions of Volozhin.) Redundancy makes the reflexive gesture explicit in the Hebrew epilogue to *Benjamin the Third*. The
reference to a group of religious pilgrims (*tayarim*, or tourists) invokes
both Habad Hassidim and a journey that by definition includes a *return
trip*.

   "We swear to you that we knew absolutely nothing about military
strategy, we don't know anything about it, and we don't want to know
anything about it," Benjamin tells his military captors (Y 117; E 264; H
102). Having finally become an autonomous subject, he shows no desire
to translate his new stature into political capital. Dan Miron and Anita
Norich have argued that he "treats the concept of military prowess as
something beneath contempt":

> But one cannot slight the military concept without renouncing politics alto-
> gether since the army with its hierarchy, discipline and ethos of organized vi-
> olence is the very essence and basis of political power. Without even noticing
> it Benjamin is renouncing his own vision of Jewish independence to be achieved
> through the military prowess of the ten lost tribes. Allowing for all possible
> differences, a Jewish army would not be basically different from the Czarist
> Russian army. . . . Yet if the concept of a Jewish army is discarded that of an

independent Jewish state cannot be maintained. Furthermore, politics as such must be proclaimed a matter extraneous to whatever is important to human experience.

By this interpretation, it is not only Benjamin but also Abramovitsh himself who ends up contradicting the very premises with which he set out: "starting with a criticism of Jewish political impotence in the imperialist world he now arrives at a position which implies a critique of politics per se."[53] Miron and Norich appear to be telescoping the process through which a call for Jewish participation in the affairs of the world yields to a call for Jewish self-empowerment. Their argument can be strengthened by tracing its course beyond the confines of the Yiddish narrative to the final edition of the Hebrew narrative—a process that covers a period of over three decades—and perhaps into its long afterlife beyond that.

Although Abramovitsh apparently intended to write a sequel to *Benjamin the Third*—so both internal evidence in the Hebrew version and external evidence in letters he wrote suggest—he did not. That failure has been attributed, in recent rereadings, to the collapse of the original norms of the text and their replacement by an exposé of the excesses and absurdities of political power. But I wonder whether one might not view the epilogue and the promise of untold adventures and stories rather as, in structural terms, presenting the open-ended narrative as a generic form of resistance to the Quixote model of sequels or second halves that grant their characters death as well as disenchantment: "Congratulate me, good sirs, for I am Don Quixote de la Mancha no longer, but Alonso Quixano, called for my way of life the Good. . . . Now all profane histories of knight errantry are odious to me. I know my folly now, and the peril I have incurred from the reading of them . . . stop your fooling, and bring me a priest to confess me."[54]

Denied both death and the full measure of disenchantment, Benjamin becomes in the Hebrew epilogue the explorer, the storyteller, and the Jewish wanderer as self-appointed loser in the military-political universe. As he takes up "his staff and his sack" and goes off on further adventures, he comes to resemble the discarded figure of the Jew whose itinerary is circular and whose position is, once again, set precariously at the critical margins of the social discourse. If we read the narrative *as* a journey no less perilous than the journey *in* the narrative, we can see in both Abramovitsh and Mendele not the self-destructing source of their own premises so much as the skeptical voice that circles back upon itself and thus affirms its critical position.

THE AFTERLIFE OF *BENJAMIN THE THIRD*

Beyond simply recasting a scorned convention, the self-reflexive gesture takes on critical status in whatever ideological context it travels. *Benjamin the Third* was deleted from the Israeli school curriculum in the 1980s, presumably because it was thought to portray too negative a picture of provincial Jewish life in the nineteenth-century Pale of Settlement,[55] but its true dangers to the students lay elsewhere—in its subversive invalidation of utopian worlds and epic tales of victory and power. While David Quint reminds us, in his study of the narrations of empire, that "to the victors belongs epic, with its linear teleology; to the losers belongs romance, with its random or circular wandering," he suggests as well that the representations of the "loser" can also be construed as "a resistance to form." The romance need not appear only by default: it can be understood to be a rejection of the dominant form, as structural repetition represents the nonending ending of the "repeatedly defeated, but unconquerable."[56]

In Hebrew fiction written in the decades straddling the two centuries, Abramovitsh underscored this possibility by reinforcing the cyclical and then the mythic pattern of the Jewish journey—or both. The short story "Biyemey ha-ra'ash" [In a Tumultuous Time], published in Hebrew in 1894, follows the first strategy. It enacts the round-trip in more condensed and explicit terms as a thwarted pilgrimage to the Holy Land: here Mendele becomes a fully realized character and not just a transmitter or redactor of another's story—indeed, he actually contemplates relinquishing his trade altogether and becoming a pioneer in Palestine (in order to beat words into plowshares, as it were). But the romantic gesture that brings the hero back to his point of origin also brings Mendele back to Kabtziel/Kisalon, to his old trade, his people, and even his old horse.[57]

The other strategy reinforces the journey as critical movement by returning it to the realm of the mythic, thereby divesting it of its historicizing temptations. In the story "Ha-nisrafim" [Burned Out], the aimless itinerary of Mendele's townspeople of Kabtziel is a cameo reenactment of the inexorable paradigm of Jewish life: settlement, conflagration, exile, dispersal, and universal poverty.[58] The historical challenge embedded in the original text fades before the mythic status of life lived in a suspended, eternally recurrent state of exile. "Aggadot ha-admonim" [Legends of the Reds] (1902–1903) incorporates Benjamin's travels into the legendary cycle of pilgrimage tales as a latter-day midrash, while irony withdraws to the remote region of a bemused but detached consciousness.[59] Benjamin is credited here with having accomplished his journey by outwitting a gryphon who acted as his guide—and even with having brought back material evidence of his encounter with the Red Jews: sand and pebbles from the Sambatyon River that now reside in reliquaries of the British Empire and continue to display their miraculous qualities by agitating for six days and resting on the seventh. And he has brought examples of the oral tradition of the "Reds": unabashedly fictitious documents (*aggadot*) that conflate Benjamin's exploits with those of Eldad the Danite, and an elaborate scholastic apparatus that approximates the erudition and the self-enclosed language of Jewish hermeneutics. Benjamin's own travelogue has thus becomes an intertext enjoying the same status as the specious books by which his original journey was shaped.

Such texts do more than resist or counter the material realization of the utopian-messianic imagination. The encroachment of the mythic on historical geography without being undercut by satire can perhaps be seen as a kind of reclaiming of folkloric elements in the imagination of the Jewish writer at the turn of the century. In this context, invented scientific evidence works to corroborate fantasy and the geographical-historical reference functions as a rhetoric of evidence within the mythic imagination.

Dan Miron draws a distinction between Mendele, a performer before an audience of readers, and Sholem Aleichem's Tevye, whose audience—Sholem Aleichem in the persona of storyteller—is an internal part of his world.[60] This reading can perhaps lead us to understand the fate of the two bodies of fiction. As we will see in chapter 4, Tevye's audience is, necessarily, always the same; his drama remains safely in the past, acquiring the patina of nostalgia as time and catastrophe do their work—but Mendele's audience, appealed to with the urgency of direct performance, changes over time. It is always *us*.

To observe Benjamin over the decades, as he is elevated by his readers from the status of fool to that of shlemiel or hero (or shlemiel-as-hero) and then to that of skeptic, is to trace the process by which Jewish society reinvents itself and then rehabilitates its characters. In 1912 the critic Shmuel Niger, Abramovitsh's younger contemporary, found Quixote's advantage over Benjamin to be in the former's position as a fearless innocent standing up to falsehood; for him, the latter remains a cowardly fool outwitted by cleverness.[61] Some sixty years later, Ruth Wisse redefined such cowardice as a form of heroic inner faith in the face of insuperable external forces.[62] And in 1980, Dan Miron and Anita Norich suggested a reading that renders "Benjamin the madman as a being of higher sanity."[63] My own reading sees in the act of return home a profoundly critical, skeptical gesture. Clearly, whether one regards Benjamin as helpless fool or as sane nay-sayer and Jewish Quaker, speaking justice to power, has everything to do with one's own cultural vantage point; late-twentieth-century readings rest equally on the advantage of a secure but vigilant distance from the horrors of genocide and on the destabilizing precincts of a self-critical discourse both safeguarded and constantly challenged by the existence of sovereign Jewish power.

Dissonant against the utopian voices of one fin de siècle but perhaps more in harmony with the dystopic voices of another, the "Jewish Don Quixote" can now receive a new kind of attention, and alternative readings can be seen as alternative cultural strategies. As silly in their uniforms as Moses E. Herzog will be some seventy years later with his father's rusty pistol, Benjamin and Sender become the forerunners of the old/new diasporists who eschew military power; as gullible in their faith as Gimpl the Fool will appear some five decades later, they stand at the head of a line of shlemiels who will reclaim their status as part of a post-martyrological and postheroic reinvention of discarded sensibilities. But viewed against the background of an empowered Jewish community, Benjamin may come closer to his model, namely the Man of La Mancha as dreamer and idealist.

In Israel the literary imagination is now moving from being constitutive of a world that did not yet exist to acting more conventionally as counterpoint to the real. If Benjamin and Sender's induction into the Gentile army meant they were being used as a source of power attached to an alien narrative, and if the czarist army reminds the reader of who it is that wrote the "real" story in this area, then once having "arrived" in Zion—through the agency of their Hebrew readers—the pair could almost be imagined as two conscientious objectors in an Israeli army. In this sense, they move from being objects in a universe in which the only power behind what happens is "other"—whether Russian or divine—to embracing self-disempowerment as a kind of hard-won humility before all claims of power. In such belated readings, Benjamin can relinquish his metonymic status as quintessential Jew-in-Exile, subjugated by both the forces of his own foolishness and the unrestrained power of the Gentiles, and acquire instead a status more compatible with the Western paradigm of the hero as seeker embattled with his own society.

In the Heart of the Seas

S. Y. Agnon and the Epic of Return

"In that Empire, the Art of Cartography reached such Perfection that the map of a single Province occupied a whole City, and the map of the Empire, a whole Province. In time those Enormous Maps no longer sufficed and the Colleges of Cartographers raised a Map of the Empire that was the size of the Empire and coincided with it exactly. Less Addicted to the Study of Cartography, the Following Generations understood that that expanded Map was Useless, and not without Impiety they relinquished it to the Inclemencies of the Sun and of the Winters. Disintegrated Ruins of the Map remain in the Western deserts, inhabited by Animals and Beggars; in the whole Country there endures no other relic of the Geographic Disciplines." Suárez Miranda: *Viajes de varones prudentes*, fourth book, chapter XLV, Lérida, 1658.

Jorge Luis Borges, "Museo"

The pilgrim's uncompleted journey toward the Holy Land is open to infinite sequels, holding the map to scale, preserving the object of desire at an insurmountable distance. But the stony surfaces of early-twentieth-century Palestine, disenchanted by Zionist pioneers with pickaxes, yielded to the "Art of Cartography" and became inhospitable to the stardust that had bewitched Yehuda Halevi and blinded Benjamin the Third. The old maps, tattered by wear and then dusty from disuse, could still glitter with faint traces of the miraculous and the unpossessable. S. Y. Agnon was enough of an alchemist to illuminate those traces and enough of a modernist to mark the gaps. In his Hebrew fictions, he enlists the inherent contradictions between mythic and political forms to reclaim the future in the name of the past.

Nowhere are the contradictions more dramatically demonstrated than in his novella *Bilvav yamim* [In the Heart of the Seas], and nowhere are

they more dramatically reconciled. The pilgrim who appears at port in
Bilvav yamim is equipped with both a magic handkerchief and a compass to navigate between heavenly promises and earthly geographies. Relying on the narrative of homecoming that loops back to its epic point
of origin, his journey to and arrival in the Holy Land enact a metaphysics
of return and an aesthetics of the whole. Begun shortly after Agnon's
own round-trips between Palestine and Germany were being resolved in
favor of settlement in Jerusalem, the story bears the traces of that journey as well. It incorporates the pilgrimage to Zion, as charted in Yehuda
Halevi's poetry of yearning for the beloved object, and a utopian resolution of the condition (and the comedy) of exile, as parodied in the prose
of S. Y. Abramovitsh.

Satire is utopia in its degraded form. Reading *The Travels of Benjamin
the Third* (1878) and *In the Heart of the Seas* (1934) in sequence forms
a kind of reconstructive pattern, as Abramovitsh's abortive, circular,
satiric pilgrimage reclaims its ideal, linear form in Agnon's novella. The
messianic epic of return is rescued here in the narrative's embrace of the
materiality of Zion: now become a political destination, it no longer animates the myth of deferral.

The fictions of Shmuel Yosef Agnon (1888–1970), Israel's Nobel lau-
reate and most enduring literary presence, spanned much of the twentieth century, and have continued after his death in the posthumous publications overseen by his daughter. *Bilvav yamim*, written in midcareer,
is one of those narratives that seems to live in the shallows, displaying
a deceptive naïveté. Posing like an innocent fellow traveler beside every
misguided pilgrim, it becomes both one of the few articulations of the
master narrative of the Zionist century and one of Agnon's few stories
self-consciously impervious to his own penetrating irony and skepticism.[1] In enacting the perfect arrival and the perfection of form, it books
passage not only for the people but for the verses that were set loose
in the universe when the Temple was destroyed and all its elements
dispersed.

AUTHORIZATIONS

The narrative opens with the protagonist's appearance before a group
of pilgrims from Galicia who are about to depart for the Holy Land.

> Just before the first of the Hassidim went up to the Land of Israel, a certain
> man named Hananiah found his way to their House of Study. His clothes
> were torn, rags were wound around his legs, and he wore no boots on his

feet; his hair and beard were covered with the dust of the roads, and all his worldly goods were tied up in a little bundle that he carried with him in his kerchief. . . .

It can clearly be seen, said the comrades to Hananiah, that you have walked far.

True indeed, said he to them. It is not a short distance I have come.

Where were you? they asked.

Where was I? he answered. And where was I not?

Whereupon they began to question him on every side, until at last he recounted all his travels.

At first, said Hananiah, I went from my town to another town, and from that town to yet another.[2]

The substantiality and specificity of the travelers or pilgrims contrast starkly with the protean contours of this newcomer. Continuing throughout to inhabit a geographical and temporal twilight zone, Hananiah bears the trappings of the Jew as eternal wanderer or *geyer*, as impecunious tzaddik, or as *meshulah* or emissary. What is otherwise a localized, meticulously recounted journey of limited duration is displaced repeatedly by his untimely exits and entrances. While the group of pilgrims, who are designated within the Hassidic code as *anshei shlomeinu* (our folk), embody the flesh-and-blood dimension of Hassidism, Hananiah represents its status as an ideal construct. The nonspecific, potentially infinite, metaphysical space of his journey and the specific, finite physical space of theirs are represented structurally in the chronology and chronotopes of the narrative. The chapter headings are the signposts of that double itinerary: "Avak derakhim," "Ha-muzmanim," "Yetziah," "Nisayon shel satan," "Yeridah va-'aliyah," "Derekh eretz polin u-moldava," "Mayim rabim," "Be-tokh ha-yam," "Razei 'olam," "Stambul," "Sa'ar gadol ba-yam," "Admat kodesh," "Nimtzaim 'omdim bi-yerushalayim," "Shkhenim la-shekhinah" [Dust of the Roads, The Summoned, Departure, Satan's Temptation, Descending and Ascending, Through Poland and Moldavia, Many Waters, In the Sea, Secrets of the Universe, Istanbul, A Great Storm at Sea, The Holy Land, Standing in Jerusalem, The Shekhinah's Neighbors].

The temporal range is equally unstable. Internal references to the "first of the Hassidim" and to Napoleon would place the *fabula* in the eighteenth century;[3] but figures from the ancient, largely legendary past and from the author's own life (including himself, Shmuel Yosef, and his wife, Esther) anchor both the tale of miraculous delivery and the prosaic travelogue in an anachronistic, mobile center of consciousness.[4] For most of the journey, *Bilvav yamim* behaves as what Gérard Genette would call

a "pure case of heterodiegetic autobiography, where the author attributes
the narrative of his life to a non-witness biographer and, for safety's sake,
to one a few centuries posterior to himself."[5] But at the very last moment the autobiographical character—who, as one of the travelers, lives
a few centuries anterior to the author—merges with the narrator. Suddenly he has stabilized both his own position as scribe and the fluidities
of a text that has now congealed as a canonic, fully authorized source:
"The sages and rabbis of Jerusalem have long desired that all that befell
Hananiah should be put on record in a book, [but this matter was] deferred from day to day and from year to year; until I came and wrote all
the adventures of Hananiah in a book which I have called 'In the Heart
of the Seas'" (E 126; H 550).

    This "homodiegetic" mode, in which the author manifests "himself"
at the end as narrator, receptor, and transmitter of the story, is characteristic of many of Agnon's narratives.[6] Both self-reference and anachronism are typical of Yiddish satire and parody; in the emergent Hebrew
literature such embedded strands of autobiographical reference are, additionally, reminiscent of the transition from the reality of *nouvelles* to
the realism and license of the "novel" in English and American fiction of
the eighteenth and nineteenth centuries. They thus serve to authenticate
and adjudicate as well as define the perspective of the world through
which the narrator travels. But they also conform to another paradigm:
the "received" text, modeled on the transmission of Scriptures, which
remains for Agnon the competing prototype of the artistic enterprise, its
metaphysical status always threatening to overshadow its mimetic value.
The autobiographical voice confers the kind of authority that recorders
of the miraculous in medieval travelogues and in modern Hassidic tales
confer on their subjects. The role of the storyteller as eyewitness, a convention of Western pilgrimages and *récits de voyage* from *The Canter-
bury Tales* through *Tales of the Wayside Inn*, is compounded here by the
multiple authorizations of the literary imagination and its conflicted status as exilic privilege and burden. The miracles for which the human author does not claim responsibility—narrated by an undramatized voice—
alternate with the deeds attributed to human agency and authorship. By
the end of *Bilvav yamim*, this process has resolved into a thick layer of
sedimentation that absorbs and domesticates all magical properties. And
when the "sages and rabbis of Jerusalem" put their seal on Hananiah's
story, they grant a (not entirely tongue-in-cheek) imprimatur to the human act and time of creation.

ANSHEI SHLOMEINU

In addition to Reb Shmuel Yosef the storyteller, other travelers—such as old Reb Alter the "slaughterer and inspector"—are differentiated by name, occupation, and their practical role in facilitating the journey. Others, through bold acts of reification, make valuable contributions to redeeming the Land of Israel from its metaphoric status. Rabbi Shelomo, a "Cohen" and businessman, had "finally given up the estates of this world and set his heart on going up to the Land of Israel" (that is, not only exchanging a commercial estate for a spiritual one but potentially *grounding* the one in the other). Young Reb Alter the teacher, while studying the Talmudic tractate *Ketubot*, which deals with marriage contracts, had been struck by the thought that "after all the Land of Israel is a marriage contract between Israel and the Holy One, blessed be He; and it is an accepted principle that a man must never be without his marriage contract. Whereupon he felt that as long as he continued to dwell outside the Land he would have no rest" (E 14, 16; H 489).

By literalizing what had been held in trust in a language of suspended signifiers, these travelers participate in the redemption of the land of Israel from its dormant state. Indeed, in its various manifestations this principle of literalization, reification, or realization is the dominant aesthetic of what might be considered the consummate Hebrew novel. All of the characters are individuated just enough within the economy of the folktale to save them from their generic status, rendering them candidates for the fictive imagination and implicitly inviting more conflictual, dialogical readings. But despite its reach, the narrative falls just short of what Robert Alter calls thinking "novelistically."[7]

The women, though even less differentiated both by name and function, and largely identified by affiliation with their husbands, are allowed some agency in deciding their fate and in expressing their ongoing ambivalence about the journey. They privilege domestic space and security above the dangers of the voyage and the elusiveness of its destination: "When day broke and the sea could be seen, the women began crying, O, we are afraid to set out on the sea." (E 55; H 511).

The apposition of wife and home is familiar from *Benjamin the Third*; one can hardly help noticing that in all the travelogues we are considering it is not the women who signify the voyage. "What stories indeed could a woman possibly have to tell?" asks Nancy Huston mischievously in analyzing a basic incongruity between the conventionally nurturing position of the woman and the narrating position of the novelist. "Did women go on expeditions to the North Pole?"[8] They are the ones who wait, descendants of Sarah in her *ohel* and of Penelope in her *oikos*; if forced to travel, they endure at best—or, by carrying their household gods with them, they actively impede the journey. The wives in Agnon's narrative make up their collective mind to return to Buczacz and are divorced from their husbands. Immediately, however, they recant: "The women remembered how folk buried outside the Holy Land must suffer by having to roll their corpses through caves and tunnels underground to reach the Holy Land" (E 55; H 512). They cajole their husbands into taking them back, demonstrating their primary concern with personal and material comfort (both in this world and the next), as well as the popular association of the Holy Land with death and the end of days.

Hananiah remains the only irregular traveler in this group. It is not only his reported geographical reach ("Where was I? . . . And where was I not?") that marks him as both wandering Jew and tzaddik and threatens to undermine the mimetic status of the narrative, but also his rather unconventional form of behavior and travel. The other pilgrims (including the autobiographical Shmuel Yosef), a collective unit of specialized parts, are journeying from Galicia through Turkey to Jaffa by means of stagecoach and ship. Hananiah, by contrast, has been engaged to resolve the mysterious disappearance of the husband of a woman identified only as an *'aguna* (abandoned wife); this mission brings him into the murky, liminal realm of brigands and thieves and takes the story into the realm of adventure, danger, and the carnivalesque. As a result, Hananiah literally misses the boat. He consoles himself at the port by spreading his kerchief, sitting on it, and effecting, with some divine assistance, what would qualify in the Hassidic lexicon of small miracles as a *kefitzat derekh* (a literal "leap of faith," or "leap of the faithful").[9] As the ship slowly wends its storm-tossed way toward Palestine, Hananiah, who was counted as missing, appears to the passengers as an unidentified flying object ("a kind of light shining on the sea") and finally as "the likeness of a man on the sea." A dispute arises among them as to the identity of this apparition:

> And what did the Gentiles say when they saw a man sitting on his kerchief and floating in the sea? Some of them said, Such things are often seen by seafarers and desert-farers. Others said, *Whoever he is, he has a curse hanging over him so that nevermore can he rest.* That is why he wanders from place to place, appearing yesterday on the dry land and today on the sea.
>
> On that ship there were representatives of each of the seventy nations of

the world, and each of them was overwhelmed and terrified at this apparition. So Israel stood on one side and the nations of the world on the other, fearful and staring, until their eyelashes became scorched by the sun. Then Rabbi Shmuel Yosef, the son of Rabbi Shalom Mordekhai ha-Levi, said, *It is the Divine Presence, which is bringing back the people of Israel to their own place.*

(E 59, 64–65; H 514, 517; emphases mine)

At this point the tug between the gravitational and the divine forces is resolved in favor of the latter; for the duration of the trip, or so it appears, the Hassidic, mystical imagination precedes and supersedes the utopian-historical vision. But a subtle shift is already taking place; the narrative, which previously seemed to mediate almost even-handedly between the language of deferred arrival and the language of repatriation in historical time, begins to incorporate the one into the other. At the same time, the polemic mimicry between the Wandering Jew in Christian theodicy and the Eternal Jew in Jewish theodicy is resolved, as *wandering* is redefined as *return*. In appearing to the passengers through the interpretive strategies of Reb Shmuel Yosef as none other than the *shekhina* navigating the ship that carries the "people of Israel [back] . . . to their own place," Hananiah becomes the composite figure of Israel-on-the-road: nimble tzaddik, "eternal" Jew, semidivine conductor. The Wandering Jew—a character implicated in the guilt of Jesus' passion and assigned a rather dubious place in the Christian pageant of the Second Coming—resurfaces here as a diaphanous agent of Jewish redemption.

Floating just above and not quite embedded in the thickness of a real journey, Hananiah manages to transform all of its properties.[10] Floating just above and increasingly impervious to the ironic readings that would deflate his aeronautic kerchief, he achieves an iconic status that threatens to iconicize the story itself. As a kind of jack-of-all-trades in the union of Kabbalistic workers, he engages in "repairing" the vessels that were shattered in the dim days of creation. Hillel Barzel regards Hananiah as an example of the "redemptive" recasting of received archetypes in Agnon's fiction; taking pity (*hanan-iah*) on the wanderer, God returns him to his land where settlement (*hishtak'ut*) replaces wandering and the blessing of a long but mortal life replaces the curse of immortality and rootlessness.[11] But this *hishtak'ut*, taken literally as a consummated union of the mythical and the material, is also a self-consuming process. Literal repair—of anomalous situations and even of physical vessels such as shoes and trunks to be used on the journey—replaces the metaphoric status of mystical and messianic language, anticipating the substantiation of images of redemption in their "original"—that is, in real—space.

FINAL STATION: THE HOLY LAND

While Hananiah as a character is differentiated from the other pilgrims by his quasimythical status, his fate is also differentiated from that of the group, who more or less die a collective death when the exigencies of form dictate that the story be brought to a close. It is particularly significant for the literary representation of the idea of fulfillment that death enters this narrative not just as a necessary index of the return of the footloose Jew, to "mortalize" the eternal wanderings of the eternal Jew, but equally as prelude to the messianic chapter that will begin with the resurrection. That is, in order to gain "Eternal Life," the "eternal Jew" must first die.[12] The journey was, like *galut* itself, a state of suspension; no one died or got sick on the voyage. It is only after their arrival that the physicality of their lives is allowed full expression.

Death itself becomes an affirmation, even a celebration, of the material world; for unlike the Golah, where a Jew is buried with a metonymic sack of earth from the Holy Land, these pilgrims have the privilege of being buried in the soil itself. Every rhetorical resource is marshaled for this final act. The collective appellation of the group changes from the mildly ironic mark of fraternization, *ha-nilbavim, anshei shlomeinu*— "our comrades" or "our comrades in peace"—to the highly charged *anshei ge'ulateinu*, "our *redeemed* brethren"; and the reference to their death is couched in maternal images of reincorporation:

> "And so our redeemed brethren dwelled together within the Holy Congregation of the Holy City, joyously fulfilling the commandment to dwell in the Land of Israel; until their end came and they passed away, *returning their souls unto Him to whom all souls belong, and leaving their bodies to the bosom of their mother*; for they were found worthy to be buried in the soil of the Holy Land on the Mount of Olives at Jerusalem, facing the Temple of the Lord, at the feet of the Holy One, blessed be He; until the time comes for them to awaken to everlasting life, on the day of which it is written: 'And His feet shall stand in that day upon the Mount of Olives.'"
>
> (E 124; H 549; emphasis mine)

Once again, Eretz Yisrael is the motherland to which the physical evidence and remains of life are entrusted. The story of the wanderer who has no place, like the myth of the restless souls who have no burial and the vision of the dry bones rolling in the subterranean passages to their final destination, becomes rearticulated. Here the "Art of Cartography" reaches such a high level of correlation with the ground of which it is the measure that it briefly effects a cosmic realignment.

Hananiah, unlike his fellow travelers, "lived many long years," growing stronger by the year so that "when he was a hundred years old, he was like a lad of twenty" (that is, like a lad only in the fulfillment of the commandments and the performance of good deeds; E 124; H 549), exemplifying the folk version of the traditional blessing for longevity ('ad mea ke'esrim). Hananiah is a patently artificial assemblage of the properties that accrued to the Messiah over centuries of Jewish folktales: his versatile kerchief originates in Talmudic stories of the messianic figure who binds his wounds among the beggars of Rome;[13] his acts of reparation are among the few unadulterated instances of successful *tikkun* in Agnon's always-decomposing universe; and his longevity is of the kind reserved for saintly individuals identified with Moses.

The *na' va-nad*, the penitential wanderer who reappears from time to time in Agnon's fiction, performs an existential quest within the general context of exile.[14] However, as an unblemished synthesis of the figures of wandering Jew, tzaddik, and messiah, Hananiah is an incarnation of the ideal type to which many of Agnon's protagonists aspire, as their stories aspire to scriptural status and as their reality refers back to an edenic past. The retrograde movement of romantic desire, the gesture of recovery or nostalgia for the past and for the messianic future that is its mirror image, saturates much of Agnon's prose with a kind of melancholy; it is redirected in this story into the linear trajectory of historical possibility. More than in his other pious or pseudo-pious tales, the story of miraculous delivery is here harmonized with or subsumed under the story of human agency. The dispersal of persons and of legends, represented by divine and human storytellers collaborating in fantastic narratives, gives way to a new dynamic of ingathering. Agnon achieves a kind of continuity by treating real geographical place as corroborating and incorporating the legendary and the fantastic rather than as disenchanting the imaginary. Though Hananiah and *anshei shlomeinu* operate within different geographical and temporal schemes, they all end up in that Jerusalem where the schemes collapse into one axis that realigns the upper and the lower spheres.

Agnon succeeds in redeeming not only such scorned archetypes as the Eternal Jew but also the spiritual pilgrimage itself from its fallen status in modern Jewish literature. If, as I have suggested, we read the two travel narratives by Abramovitsh and Agnon as intertexts in a discourse in which a parodic pilgrimage rehabilitated becomes, by default, a "naive" tale of ascension, then *Bilvav yamim* recovers the ur-text of which *Benjamin the Third* is the parody, or the epic that the earlier work mocks.[15]

That is, its own parodic subtexts are embraced in the grand sweep of in-corporation. Within the competing itineraries that constitute the Jewish Journey, the circular route of the "losers" is supplanted by a triumphal linear movement crowned by arrival. The voyage is no longer impeded by the delays and digressions of endless deferral; even the associative dis-course of storytelling, a discourse of infinite detours, takes place on but does not impede the journey itself. This is a voyage of consequence more radical than the arrival (and inevitable departure) of the pilgrim at the holy center. As Hananiah's journey proceeds, it is transformed from the random pattern of the peregrine (*na' va-nad*), through the circumambu-lation of the pilgrim (*'oleh regel*), to the unerring homing pattern of the "repatriate" (*'oleh*). The footloose Jew, the shlemiel, is transformed into a subject whose efforts are measured not only by his faith but also by the concrete results of his actions.

KINUS: INGATHERING OF THE STORIES

It became evident to many writers as the nineteenth century drew to a close that a whole treasury of stories and folktales was being jeopar-dized in the intoxicating moment of collective redefinition. As the map comes closer than ever before to approximating the territory it repre-sents, acts recuperating mythic geographies reflect both an urgency and a profound ambiguity. On the road for so many centuries, the Jews had created a wealth of literary signposts and simulacra. Now the road and the languages were shifting to accommodate a new enterprise that, like a Borgesian narrative, would conflate the highways and the story lines, the visible and invisible structures, of a reinvented Jewish civilization. If the Jews had perfected over the centuries what Georges Van Den Abbeele calls the "topological theories of language in which the utterance becomes a question of choosing the right 'route,'" they were now discovering, be-latedly, the form of "travel [that] requires the ability to 'read' a map."[16] The challenge would be to avoid the temptation to stretch the *territory* so that it coincided exactly with the map.

Shmuel Werses has traced the language of Agnon's *nilbavim* to sources both in the Mishnah and in the travel narratives of the Middle Ages and the seventeenth to eighteenth centuries. The mishnaic literature of pil-grimage, with its emphasis on the round-trip dynamic of cultic acts such as the three-day trip from Jaffa to Jerusalem and back, and the aggadic incorporation of underground caves, the Ten Tribes, and the Sambatyon River provide the quasi-historical and quasi-mythological cartographic elements in this approach to the Holy Land. The medieval and early modern texts supply prototypes for the infinitely expandable episodic structure, for the delays and impediments arising from inimical natural or human sources, for the uneven calibration—contraction and expansion—of time and topography, and for the ethnographically inspired encounters with scattered Jewish communities (encounters whose anachronism in this text lend them some levity).[17] The projection of utopian spaces into the recounting of the (often uncomfortable) daily routine of travel furnishes the narrative with a point of ultimate reference much like that which a specific destination furnishes the process of navigation.[18]

But the most radical change in the diasporic orientation to the physical world finds its expression in a *metamorphic* landscape that replaces both metaphor and metonymy. The language of miracles in *Bilvav yamim* fulfills in its hypostases the incomplete process we traced in the poetry of Yehuda Halevi, which became more intense and more substantial as he drew closer to the shores of the beloved country. It may also signify a dimension of the revolutionary shift in the relation of fictional and actual worlds. The Hebrew literature emerging both in Europe at the turn of the century and in the Yishuv of the early twentieth century was conceived by its writers and readers as an autonomous enterprise, but what came to be called the Hebrew "republic of letters" also had a constitutive role in creating a material culture;[19] this is what makes Hebrew literature such an interesting example of the links between modernism and nationalism. Herzl's "if you will it, it is not a dream," the emblem of the Zionist emergence from the "dream-state" of the aggadically minded, reflects a cultural challenge of the highest order. Those forms of the Jewish imagination that were inherently nonrevolutionary because they were, in some fundamental sense, nonreferential are being mobilized to perform a revolutionary task; "*will*," the fuel that empowers the imagination, is meant eventually to supersede it.

Benjamin Harshav observes of the European diasporic culture at the end of the nineteenth century: "In their everyday awareness—as Jews—they were connected to a *universe of discourse*, a 'fictional world' outside of history and geography, based on a library of texts and their interpretations. . . . Hence the centrality of discourse (rather than love of the land) for their self-understanding. When this universe of discourse lost its moorings . . . the anchoring of a universe of discourse vis-à-vis the 'real,' historical world became the most important existential question for any alternative, any mode of Jewish culture, and for every individual."[20] In the analysis of the crucial relation of text to territory that is our explicit theme, this argument may have been overstated, even if it has been the guiding wisdom for at least two generations of scholars. But it provides a useful transition to a very different epistemology. Like the journey itself, this development appeared to be one-way: Robert Alter writes that only "after writers had succeeded in creating an 'as if' reality in Hebrew" had certain prerequisites of consciousness been met that would facilitate the construction of an "actual Hebrew reality," with all its concomitant physical and social structures in the "real geography of this world."[21] But the logic that guided the movement of modern Hebrew literature toward referentiality a century ago eventually will prove to have been only one phase in an *ongoing* dialectic; as our own century wanes, new reconstructions of diasporic culture privilege speech acts and texts once again. That was hardly foreseeable, however, at the moment of revolutionary fervor we are now examining.

The role played by the *kinus*, or collection of traditional literary material, as a proleptic act of the ingathering of the people is an important component in the construction of the republic of letters.[22] The neoromantic incorporation of mythic and folk elements into Hebrew poetry and prose beginning at the end of the nineteenth century will eventually signal a more complex encounter with the past. Within the space of a few years, H. N. Bialik begins working with Y. H. Ravnitzki to compile aggadic folklore in what will become *Sefer ha-aggada*; Martin Buber launches a lifelong engagement in the translation, interpretation, and adaptation of tales of the Hassidic masters; and Mikha Yosef Berdichevski collects and publishes Hassidic and aggadic legends in German, Hebrew, and Yiddish. I. L. Peretz, whose cultural appeal is to the secularizing, modernizing Jew in Poland, begins incorporating folk motifs, particularly Hassidic and Kabbalistic elements, into his fiction.[23] Sh. Ansky, the former Narodnik revolutionary, spends his last decades gathering "ethnographic" fragments of the Jewish spirit to be placed in a museum dedicated to the renewal of Jewish creativity.[24] The process as a whole, like acts of literary recuperation in the creation of modern national cultures generally (especially in older civilizations such as those of Greece and Ireland), involves both collecting and reinventing folk traditions.[25]

This phenomenon is articulated in all its complexity in the fiction of S. Y. Agnon. Jewish writers of the turn of the century, depending on how radically they separated from the past, felt varying degrees of guilt and nostalgia as well as revulsion and denial, expressed as much in acts of suppression as in acts of rescue; for some the encounter with the past generated and for others it impeded their own creative enterprise.[26] In the case of Agnon, who began the project of compiling the "corpus ha-sidicum" with Buber in the early twenties but abandoned it in 1924, when the fire that destroyed his Homburg home destroyed the nearly completed volume, some of the conservationist impulse was rechanneled into his fictions, most saliently into those that acquired the status of pious or pseudo-pious folktales.[27]

In *Bilvav yamim*, Agnon adds a new dynamic to the intertextuality that had become, in its many forms, a means of rescuing the endangered past. The delusionary authority of the pseudo-scientific, semimythical sources that clouded the cognitive faculties of Benjamin the Third, not unlike the romances that had clouded Don Quixote's vision, are rein-vested with authority as a revalorized wellspring of Jewish spirituality. The wealth of legendary material from biblical, Talmudic, and medieval literature that appears in this novella as strands woven into a tale of both miraculous and mundane travel to the Holy Land recapitulates the Journey that is Exile and the stories gathered along the way—including Agnon's own earlier narratives. The stories, sometimes recounted by Shmuel Yosef the storyteller, sometimes incorporated into the visual ex-perience of the pilgrims as minidramas enacted along the way, are con-jured from the deepest layers of the collective consciousness.[28]

At what was to prove the midpoint in Agnon's career, the act of re-casting, through a kind of grace, elements and characters from his own stories may be as significant as the grounding of the metaphoric and ag-gadic imagination. The intricate ways in which he incorporates earlier figures, or their descendants, from his fictions into a given narrative con-tribute to the sense that he is writing the ongoing epic of an entire civi-lization; we see this even in his last writings, when the horrible prophecy about the future of the Jewish people from the novel *Ore'ah nata la-lun* [A Guest for the Night], made on the eve of World War II, is recorded as *fact* in the postwar, posthumously published story "Kisui ha-dam" [Covering the Blood].[29] The strategy, which often highlights continuities, also underscores ironies in the intergenerational unfolding of the drama of Jewish life. A *mitnaged* in one story ("Ha-nidah" [The Outcast]) gives birth to one who appears in *Bilvav yamim* as a Hassid. The "kerchief" that will be recycled in *Bilvav yamim* appears not only in the story by that name ("Ha-mitpahat") but also in the early story "'Agunot" [Aban-doned Wives] (1908) that gave the writer his own name. From that short narrative, the first of many in which a heedless human act creates a cos-mic rift that leads lost souls to wander throughout life seeking to make amends, the image of a penitent rabbi floating aimlessly on the great seas *on a kerchief,* seeking to redeem *'agunot,* is reincorporated in *Bilvav yamim* in the figure of Hananiah—whose direction is clear and who *succeeds* in fulfilling those tasks the rabbi only set out to perform.

The ontological fluidity of characters who appear here and there in previous fictions as they vacillate between aggadic landscapes and real geographies establishes the kind of "discursive unity" defined by Thomas Pavel as inherent in the open (or openly negotiated) boundaries between fiction and nonfiction "*from an internal point of view*": "In *War and Peace* is Natasha less actual than Napoleon? . . . Fictional texts enjoy a certain discursive unity; for their readers, the worlds they describe are not necessarily fractured along a fictive/actual line."[30] Here, too, Hananiah is no less "actual" than Napoleon or, for that matter, than "Shmuel Yosef."

The poignancy of ingathering the scriptural and aggadic sources along with the community who preserved them, and of incorporating the writer's own earlier work, climaxes in the final chapters when the biblical verses are not only invoked but *repatriated.* Having finally reached the Wailing Wall in Jerusalem, the group of pilgrims recites the Song of Songs and "Rabbi Moshe lean[s] his head against the wall and remember[s] that he [is] standing at a spot from which the Divine presence itself had never moved." In this reconsecrated sacred center he recites the very verses—"The King hath brought me into his chambers" (Song of Songs 1:4)—that his brother Gershom had begun to recite (in another place and another story) at the moment of his death.[31] But unlike his brother, Rabbi Moshe is able to complete the verse as "the joy of the Land of Israel" fills him. Agnon here presents another resolution to his own narrative dilemma (which is, after all, the dilemma of exile), rewriting his own story in the moment of grace, with the end in sight (E 116; H 545). There may be no more powerful confluence of text and territory, or absorption of text *in* territory, in all of modern Hebrew literature.

Throughout his long writing career, Agnon's peculiar and often elusive synthesis of (or vacillation between) poetic alternatives endeared him both to traditionalists, who regarded him as a scribe of orthodox civilization and Hassidic folklore, and to modernists, who hailed him as Kafka's Hebrew voice representing lonely individuals lost in an absurd universe. Agnon's fictions provide unique and daring examples of the recombination of modes of prophetic writing that enter as fragments into the universe of authority within which the modern poet operates. By assuming a prophetic modality, the author makes possible a selective, self-conscious anachronism in retrieving poetic options from the ruins of past (or passing) traditions.

Comparative studies of Abramovitsh and Agnon usually attribute the difference in tone to the satiric agenda of the one and the recuperative or even romantic enterprise of the other. Abramovitsh, in any event, is living through the revolutionary moment of Hebrew (and Yiddish) creation while Agnon, whose youth corresponds with Abramovitsh's last decades, is witness to and participant in the accomplished revolution, followed by the denial and then the destruction of the Eastern European culture of origin. Regardless of a writer's particular agenda, nostalgia succeeded by a deep pessimism are natural stages in the long period of mourning over the violent death of a community. In the narrative that we have been considering, the romantic/nostalgic attitude toward a past that has been largely disinherited but not yet destroyed is manifest in characters like Hananiah and in the tales of piety and its reward. Just a few years later—on the very eve of World War II, as the struggle for material survival becomes paramount—little trace of the mythical remains in a text like *A Guest for the Night* (1939). Tropes that recur in Agnon's narratives, such as the kerchief in *Bilvav yamim*, are neither personal nor entirely public but rather *rescued* figures; as the reality of Jewish life becomes more harsh, the rescue efforts become more desperate and unconventional. The metonymic key that would have opened the doors to innumerable, replicable houses of prayer and endless stories in the European Diaspora is saved at the last minute and brought "back" to the Land of Israel in the baggage of the narrator of *A Guest for the Night*, returning from his decimated and soon-to-be-eradicated hometown in Galicia.[32] It is as strong an acknowledgment of the death throes of a form of Jewish imagination as any we will encounter.

MUCH LATER: JUST YESTERDAY

Under the shadow of genocide, the tales of pious pilgrimage and arrival undergo a kind of self-mutilation that comes increasingly to characterize the writing of Agnon's last decades: *Tmol shilshom* [Just Yesterday], written during the war years and published in 1945 but set in the Second Aliyah period (1905–14), begins, as does *Bilvav yamim*, in a promissory language that could become either epic or mock-epic.

The novel opens with a highly conventionalized representation of modern rites of ascent in which the biblical allusions can be read as either

authenticating or undermining (by their very seniority) the Zionist vocabulary: "Like the rest of our brethren, candidates for redemption, sons
of the Second Aliyah, Yitzhak Kummer left his land and his native home
(*artzo . . . u-moladeto*) and his city and went up to Eretz Yisrael to rebuild it from its ruins and to be rebuilt in it."[33] Kummer's youth has been
spent yearning for the Holy Land; his vision of the Land is condensed
into a string of biblical verbs enacted by disembodied automatons, as if
the Scriptures could be somehow literalized without human agency: these
generic figures sow and plant and reap during the daytime and sit under
vine and fig tree by evening (p. 7). Kummer's daydreaming impairs his
judgment in the family business to such an extent that his father decides
to send him to Palestine "so that he may see with his own eyes that the
whole Eretz Yisrael business is a fiction (*davar badui hu*) that was invented by the Zionists and so that he will rid his heart of it" (p. 9). Yitzhak
never returns, suggesting once again that Eretz Yisrael is not only not a
fiction or a dream but is in fact *so real* that it kills him.

As a down-to-earth transfiguration of Hananiah the pilgrim,[34] this
dream-intoxicated Yitzhak should have been entitled to at least minimal
attention from the heavenly spheres. But it is stated quite explicitly that
"no miracle was performed" (p. 100); the money for the journey had to
be borrowed—at a hefty interest rate—and the journey itself had to be
endured with no mediation from higher quarters. It becomes clear, in the
context of the divine summons and the theodicy that suffuse the master
narratives of Israel's wanderings and Agnon's own pilgrimage narratives,
that Yitzhak Kummer's story takes place in a *disenchanted* world. Indeed, the book has often been read as acerbic social commentary.[35] But
circular movement takes on particular poignancy when the venue is
Jerusalem, a poignancy that may be the most disruptive aspect of this
story of thwarted pilgrimage to and thwarted settlement in Eretz Yisrael.
The subverted expectations of utopian or messianic salvation are represented in the aimless and hopeless wanderings through the Holy City of
the mad dog Balak in an era that is described as having the face of a dog.
The most desperate gesture of all is the re-creation of exilic circumam-
bulation within the utopian space where exile was to have been resolved.[36]

Even though only twelve years separate the publication of the one text
from the other, and at least one chapter of *Tmol shilshom* was written
during the same period as *Bilvav yamim*,[37] the tension between the world
of faith inhabited by Hananiah and the pragmatic world of the *nilbavim*—
maintained throughout the sixty-five-page novella and resolved largely
in Hananiah's favor—could hardly have been sustained over the course

of an entire novel, particularly a novel written during World War II.[38]
Incompatibility between the kind of epic perspective that includes an unmediated proximity to the Divine and the modernist novel, between divinely authorized and self-authored texts, leads to a tension that we have
already identified as running throughout much of Agnon's work. But a
more radical interpretation of forms of closure and the relation of parts
to the whole should be offered: a text like *Bilvav yamim* should, I submit, only be read in light of its conclusion and can therefore hardly be
represented synecdochically in any of its parts—precisely because any
fragment would naturally invoke the convention of the Jewish journey
toward an endlessly deferred end. It is, therefore, *arrival itself* that re-
contextualizes the entire journey, not only giving it a particularly topical, contemporary twist but reframing the entire narrative of exile and
return.

A FRAGMENT FOR FRANZ

The issue of framing the narrative is dramatized by the publishing history of the text, which demonstrates that, as we saw in the case of *Benjamin the Third*, changing contexts evoke entirely different interpretations. The first known appearance of *Bilvav yamim* is as a fragment
consisting of eleven handwritten lines sent to Franz Rosenzweig, part of
the 1926 "gift-text" (*Die Gabe*) to which Buber, Scholem, and others
also contributed in honor of the ailing philosopher's fortieth birthday.[39]
In its entirety, the collective tribute to Rosenzweig affords a glimpse into
the rich and varied spiritual life of the far-flung Jews of the interbellum
period. Anne Golomb Hoffman refers to the fragment in concluding her
poststructuralist interpretation of Agnon's fiction. She considers it briefly
as conveying a peculiar kind of hermeticism:

> Unlike virtually every other gift offering in the collection, Agnon's is enclosed
> within itself; the simple presence of its Hebrew script appears to lack exter-
> nal reference beyond its opening dedication and its closing signature with place
> and date of writing: "The old city of Jerusalem, may it be built and estab-
> lished, *Vayechi,* 5687 S. Y. Agnon." . . . This signature is a small text of its
> own that invokes the temporal scheme of redemption. It sums up the iden-
> tity of the writer by joining his name to the restoration of a Jerusalem that is
> as much the heavenly *Yerushalayim shel ma'alah,* as it is the writer's earthly
> dwelling place.[40]

In its fragmented, or what I would call its *pre*contextualized, state, this
passage does seem to conform to the diasporic "temporal scheme of re-

demption" encapsulated in the signature. That Agnon sends his little text back across the seas to Germany from that heavenly/earthly dwelling place, from the place to which the pilgrims in the text are migrating, bears less significance in Hoffman's scheme than the journey through what she calls "the text that is reading" itself.[41]

But it is worth taking a close look at the passage in light of its subsequent history. The lines that Agnon chose as his offering to Rosenzweig describe a ship sailing on calm seas while the passengers engage in reading psalms, followed by other verses from the Bible:

> A man is driven from home, and wanders to distant places; he opens his sack and removes a vessel that he had used at home with his wife and children— How he rejoices in this vessel! All the more so with a book, which he would read, study, and pore over. There is not one word in it that he has not uttered a hundred times or more, each time finding new meanings, new connotations. Instantly, his face lights up, his eyes well up with tears, and his voice quivers within his throat. This may be likened to a man exiled, who on his journey encounters dear friends who greet him with embraces, hugging and kissing him; he rejoices in them as they rejoice in him; and when he speaks his speech emerges choked from the tears and the joy of finding his friends who now accompany him. So they would sit with their books in hand reading in the Pentateuch, the Prophets, and the Writings. The holy city of Jerusalem, may it be built and established, Vayechi, 5687 [1926] S. Y. Agnon.[42]

Hoffman's argument that the journey to the Land of Israel is actually "displaced by the metaphors of reading" embedded in this passage is meant to substantiate her claim that "for Agnon, the direction through the text remains the primary journey" and that "any place outside the text of Scripture is, in effect, an exile, from which one returns through the act of reading." It is this movement she sees as "ceaselessly acted out in Agnon's writing"; sacred space continues to be conflated with text *even as* the drama of return unfolds in the text itself. In an evocative chapter, Hoffman argues that both "Edmond Jabès and S. Y. Agnon are 'autochthons of the Book' in Jacques Derrida's phrase, [that is, they] take their identity as writers from the rootedness of the Jews, displaced people, in the Book."[43] That claim is further supported by the aborted journey of the gift-text itself, which was sent to Palestine from Germany after Rosenzweig's death along with the rest of his library on a ship that was waylaid and arrived instead in Tunis; the manuscript bound for Palestine then made its way to the Leo Baeck Institute in New York.

Although both reading and writing as acts of reappropriating and rearranging the sacred sources are major gestures toward homecoming, reinforced in the published version of our story by the image of Hananiah skimming the waves on his kerchief while *reading a book*, this argument overlooks the tensions inherent in Agnon's writing (and his profound doubts about the enterprise of writing itself); more specifically, it fails to take account of the unique *resolution* of those tensions in the full text of *Bilvav yamim*. But the approach may well be justified as a reading of the *fragment* itself, contextualized only as a loose leaf in a volume of disparate writings.

Only seven years after the fragment appeared, the entire narrative was published in Berlin in *Sefer Bialik*, the anthology that honored Bialik's sixtieth birthday. The earliest known mention of this story, outside of the fragment sent to Rosenzweig, is in a letter written by Agnon to his publisher S. Z. Schocken in 1931, referring to the manuscript-in-progress as "among the best of my stories."[44] What is interesting here, for our purposes, is that only the first eight lines of the passage in *Die Gabe* appear in the published versions of the story. In Agnon's gift offering, which may be read in its precontextualized form as a significant gesture toward Rosenzweig, the man who had so forcefully reconceptualized the idea of *galut* as a viable spiritual condition, the destination of the trip is not specified; were it not for the title that Agnon appended to this passage— "On the Way to the Land of Israel: A Few Lines from My Story 'In the Heart of the Seas'"—it could appear to be simply another of the endless journeys of a people in exile. The redundant images of banishment, the very doubling of exile in the compounded simile or *mashal*, without teleological reference ("a man is driven from his home . . ."; "this may be likened to a man exiled . . . "), *which are then expunged from the various published editions of the story*, prepare the ground for interpreting the passage as an instance of aimless wandering against which only reading can provide refuge and linear structure.

What is missing, then, in this early fragment of the story, and in a view of it as an expatriate or a synecdoche of the larger narrative that is exile, is precisely the ecstasy of arrival offered in the final chapters of *Bilvav yamim*. Its counterpart in *Tmol shilshom* is the despair of the unrealized dream; but arrival here not only provides closure for what Gustav Krojanker calls the "journey of a people in its eternal road toward the desired object, the harvest of its faith," but also points to something outside of or beyond what Hoffman calls the "capacity of language to evoke a variety of meanings simultaneously, summoning up sources and subjecting them to a playfulness that both negates and affirms their prior references."[45] In 1926, when he presumably began writing the story, Agnon himself had just resettled in Jerusalem after a sojourn of eleven years in Germany; by 1934, when the story was published, many of the ambiguities in the text had hardened into a one-way voyage with a nostalgic gaze at the past, demonstrating that the polyphony and playfulness that are the prerogative of the diasporic text have given way, for the moment at least, to fixed meanings and clear forms of closure. In a universe in which men travel and women wait, in which the return to wife describes a circular motion or a round-trip, the redemption of 'agunot, of the women whose men are lost and whose narratives have no direction, also in effect resurrects the linearity of the journey *and* the narrative.

By focusing exclusively on texts and the soteriological act of writing, Hoffman downgrades *con*texts in Agnon's fictions and the tension between them, as if she would place him in the company of the exiles in the desert or with the inhabitants of the house that exists primarily as a *bayit* in a poem.[46] But the published version of *In the Heart of the Seas* ends with an admonition that can also be taken as a hermeneutic clue, as self-reflexive or "hermetic" readings are relegated to a distinctly inferior position in the spectrum of possible readers' responses: "Some will read my book as a man reads legends, while others will read it and derive benefit for themselves. With regard to the former I quote the words of the book of Proverbs; 'But a good word maketh the heart glad'; a good word maketh the soul to rejoice and delivereth from care. But of the latter I say in the words of the Psalmist: 'But those who wait for [lit., "hope for" or "trust in"] the Lord, they shall inherit the land'" (E 126; H 550).

If the religious pilgrimage is inherently a round-trip to the Center and back, and if the messianic trip is inherently deferred, then the religious Zionist trip is inherently a one-way trip with a destination that revalorizes the material world and the referential vis-à-vis the sacred. Even the short paragraph quoted is textured and authorized by scriptural references; yet the preferred second reading is that which points beyond the text: "A *good word* maketh the heart glad" and sustains the Jews throughout their years of exile, but those who "will read it *and derive benefit* for themselves" will inherit the earth. "Benefit for themselves" (*to'elet le-'atzmam*), a phrase with a curiously pragmatic resonance, locates the fictive text in both a didactic or utopian/messianic *and* a referential space; the promise of reward for the faithful in the form of *territorial* inheritance (*ve-kovei ha-shem hema yirshu aretz*) is implicitly withdrawn from its deferred eschatological context (that is, to judge by Hananiah's fate, the "waiting period" is over) and inserted into a new political and ideological semantic. The whimsical or ironic interweaving of the political/historical and the legendary/pious, making the utopian novel a unique forerunner of magical realism in the Hebrew narrative, boldly manipulates the given archetypes of the Jewish journey to incorporate them into the space of historical possibility.

Where irony is withdrawn, such acts resemble sacraments more than self-reflexive fictions; and, as we saw in the poetry of Yehuda Halevi, the oscillation between the two possibilities illuminates the proximity of the symbolic and the sacramental as alternative modes of approaching holiness. Just as one can make an argument for return *through* the text, so one can argue for the repatriation *of* the text. The story "Tehila," published some ten years before *Bilvav yamim*, is similarly a pseudo-pious folktale with a saintly figure at its center. It is set in the Mandate period, and though much of the story wends its way through the Old City of Jerusalem, it is global in its reference. Positioned at the Wailing Wall, the very *axis mundi*, the narrator invokes HA-makom (Place) in all its possibility and paradox: "From Jaffa Gate as far as the Western Wall, men and women from all the communities of Jerusalem moved in a steady stream, together with those newcomers whom The Place had restored to their place, although they had not yet found their place" (*she-heviam ha-makom limekomam va-'adayin lo matzu et mekomam*).[47] There is a ritual aspect to this passage and to the story as a whole, as if a rite of reconsecration were being performed by the community of the faithful after an absence of many years—a repossession that would realign the vertical planes to include iconographic space. "The irruption of the sacred does not only project a fixed point into the formless fluidity of profane space, a center into chaos," writes Mircea Eliade; "it also effects a break in plane, that is, it opens communication between the cosmic planes (between earth and heaven) and makes possible ontological passage from one mode of being to another."[48] The eponymous Tehila, who inhabits a place that is both of and between spaces (Jerusalem and Galicia) and spiritual planes (the Old City of Jerusalem and the ancient cemetery on the Mount of Olives), carries to her grave the "letter" (the story itself) that repairs an act of sundering that took place nearly a century before and many thousands of miles away. Reparation here consists of quite literally grounding the text in sacred soil.[49]

An ancient journey that had begun "in the heart of the seas" when the prophet Jonah floated the verse that would carry him to dry dock (2:4), and that moved through the last documented poem of Yehuda Halevi, written aboard a ship in Alexandria waiting to depart for the Holy Land through "the heart of the seas," comes to its epic and pragmatic conclusion in Agnon's story by that name. Those who "read it and derive benefit for themselves" are admonished to go beyond the "good word" to "inherit the land," delivered from the "heart of the seas" (*bilvav yamim*) unto a place that might be designated as the "heart of days" (*bilvav yamim*), the quotidian. Such a resolution was temporary, as we have seen, undermined in Agnon's own work in the postwar period by a despair nearly as great as the hope that had animated triumphal forms of closure; the dark shadow of dystopia always accompanies utopia.

But my argument, that the narratives of arrival refuse the diasporic comfort of exile in the word or repatriation in the text, does not account for the absolutely *literary* quality of the enterprise, the consummation of a form that had sought and resisted closure for so many centuries. The text at hand is a flawless exemplum of an aesthetics of perfection and a remarkable enactment of messianism in historical time. It does more than explicitly perform the master narrative of the Zionist century, for it proceeds by incorporating and superseding its own subversive subtexts. The writer who "finds" and "relates" the story becomes its first commentator. It is not only arrival but death on holy soil that grants the closure that the narrative of exile lacked, making the language of the real even more absorbent. The return that is death achieves perfection of form as it renders the past perfect and the future perfect. This most aesthetic gesture lives not in the "text" but in the *book*, which has become a kind of sacrament, its verses no longer substituting for but grounded or literally incorporated in the soil. Of course soil that is so consecrated can hardly be abandoned or negotiated. It demonstrates both the seduction and the danger of literalizing the word and abolishing metaphor from the new republic. The truncated verse from Song of Songs reaches completion at the Wailing Wall, at the very "spot from which the Divine presence itself had never moved"; Tehila's letter buried in the ground of the Mount of Olives, like Bar Kokhba's letters exhumed from the ground, contains characters that insist on traveling between and therefore canceling out the boundaries that partition this world from all the others.

CHAPTER FOUR

By Train, by Ship, by Subway

Sholem Aleichem and the
American Voyage of Self-Invention

The Jewish journey, as we've traced it from the end of the nineteenth century, assumes two alternative and dialectically related poetic forms. When the primary epic is articulated as a pattern of "return" (*shivat Zion*), its reference is to the earliest, sacred memory-places and pilgrimage narratives and to a vision of their reinscription in "political time"— a downscaled version of messianic time. Its parody, the picaresque voyage, though ostensibly linear, is episodic in form and circular in direction. Mired in the stagnancy of *galut* culture, but propelled by the skepticism of a return to the profane point of departure and the reflexive aesthetic of the romance, it issues in an implicit rejection of any utopian or epic resolution.

Mass migration westward from the homelands of Eastern Europe issued in another paradigm. As a kind of sanguine rewrite of both the epic, utopian and the anti-epic, satiric narrative of Israel's sojourn among the nations, it constitutes a third, *non*-epic model. The quotidian in this model is neither redeemed nor purgatorial time, but simply the time of our lives; neither time fulfilled nor time suspended, but time spent; neither Zion nor Galut but Diaspora. Although examples of the journey to (and in) America abound, and many of the writers from the "other Europe" have celebrated the haven they found there over a century of mass immigration,[1] it is Sholem Aleichem's last, unfinished novel, *Motl Peyse dem Khazns* [Motl the Cantor's Son], that comes from the same workshop as and therefore furnishes the best commentary on Abramovitsh's anti-epic; from our perspective, it can also furnish an "innocent" and there-fore subversive commentary on Agnon's epic. The story of the journey to America is the most affirmative of Sholem Aleichem's writings and in many ways the most mobile and open-ended of the fictions of his gen-eration. It comes at the end of his series of travel narratives, which we will examine briefly; their cumulative effect is to reinvent and finally to relinquish the world of the shtetl as the Jewish imaginary.

KASRILEVKE: A MOVABLE FEAST?

Dov Sadan argued in 1959 that Sholem Aleichem (b. Shalom Rabinowitz, 1859; d. 1916) had not received the critical attention he deserved, an oversight attributable to his position as the middle element in the "clas-sic triad" that also included Mendele (S. Y. Abramovitsh) and I. L. Peretz; Sadan then went on to assert that Sholem Aleichem had achieved in his work a true measure of mobility while the other two remained essen-tially chained to the society that nourished their nostalgia as well as their disdain. The "travels" of Benjamin the Third are predicated on imagin-ing remote places and are enacted within the narrow confines of a few versts in the Pale of Settlement, creating a "satire of the desire to trans-form Jewish destiny" through movement. I. L. Peretz extends the time line of the Jewish spirit while remaining within the physical bounds of Poland and its environs. Though Sholem Aleichem's narratives are time bound, many of them move spatially along "the most dynamic lines of Jewish existence during the past generations, namely, along the routes of Jewish migration." Rooted in the Ukraine, his fictions reach out to the most remote lands of the European and even as far as the American Diaspora: "The Jewish migratory course throughout time and place is the very essence of Yiddish prose, but anyone desiring to find its outline in the works of the classic triad will be led only to Sholem Aleichem. The fact that none of them ever set eyes on Jerusalem, the oldest among them dying in Odessa, the next in line in Warsaw, and the youngest in New York, is more than mere biographical data."[2]

Jerusalem, the place on which "none of them ever set eyes," will re-main a protean reference, the motherland that beckons her children home and also impedes their arrival, making other itineraries possible. Sholem Aleichem, the one who died in New York, had in the last of his narra-tives incorporated the American city into a viable extension of Jewish geography; these fictions initiated a process that substitutes mobility as a Jewish opportunity for wandering as a Jewish curse. In each of the stories I will consider, distancing from the point of origin is a function both of a specific form of mobility and of the narrative's implicit recipient or addressee, a subtle acknowledgment of the global village as a Jewish echo chamber for the Yiddish storyteller.

The epistolary travelogue of *Menakhem-Mendl* (1892–1913) expresses both the wanderlust and the essentially domesticated orientation of the shlemiel. As traveler and would-be entrepreneur in the affairs of an indifferent and exploitative world, Menakhem Mendl ventures as far away as New York, only to return. Even as he leaves the shtetl behind for the metropolises of Europe and America, his wife Sheyne Shendl remains the lodestone that draws him back to the fictive Ukrainian town of Kasrilevke; within the rubric of Jewish exile, once again, it is the wife at home, the wife *as* home, that allows the male to wander.[3] By contrast, the narratives that constitute the cycle of *Tevye der milkhiker* [Tevye the Dairyman], written between 1894 and 1916, maintain Kasrilevke as their proving ground and Tevye-in-Kasrilevke as center of gravity; Tevye's agon is primarily with his Creator,[4] and even Kasrilevke is large enough to accommodate dramas enacted on the vertical plane.

The majority of the stories that came to be known as *Ayznban geshikhtes: ksovim fun a komivoyazher* [The Railroad Stories: Tales of a Commercial Traveler] were written between 1909 and 1911,[5] when Sholem Aleichem himself was on the road in Eastern Europe, giving readings to adoring crowds but already ill with the tuberculosis that would shorten his life. He had essentially been en route since 1905, when his first attempt at settling in and transplanting his literary center to America (1906–1907) had ended in defeat. (His second attempt, in 1914, was more successful—or at least irreversible; he died and was buried in New York in 1916.) The *Railroad Stories* are confined to a space that is both a microcosm of the shtetl and the site of its deconstruction; the oral exchanges in the railway cars that progress sluggishly from one nondestination to another do not even gesture toward incorporating the romantic or skeptical act of return.

The serial novel *Motl* overlaps in part with the composition of the *Railroad Stories*, as it was begun in 1907 and was still being written on the author's deathbed in 1916. The forward thrust that distances the characters from Kasrilevke, their point of departure, also allows them to incorporate it as portable luggage in this narrative. Here there are no personal, geographical, or even linguistic impediments to the assimilation of the wonders of the New World.

TEVYE: DEFERRING THE LAST JOURNEY

Neither interior spaces nor vast outdoor panoramas contain the saga of
Tevye the dairyman and his daughters; the country roads, the courtyards,
and the forests provide the settings for his ongoing monologue with/at
God. But in his dotage a new geographical possibility seems to unfold
before him. The final chapters of *Tevye der milkhiker* plot what is meant
to be Tevye's last journey—to the Land of Israel. A scheme by the petit-
bourgeois husband of Tevye's youngest daughter Beylke to be rid of his
impoverished father-in-law focuses on sending the old man to the farthest corner of the world; as he explains unabashedly, "With a business
like mine, a reputation like mine, a public position like mine, I can't af-
ford to have a cheesemonger for a father-in-law. . . . How about Palestine? *Isn't that where all the old Jews like you go to die?* . . . You take
the express train to Odessa . . . and from there a ship sails to Jaffa" (emphasis mine).[6] Tevye recounts this episode to his interlocutor, Sholem Aleichem, adding: "don't ask me what I'll do in the Land of Israel if I get
there safely, God willing." In attempting to answer the (unasked) question, he reveals that like his son-in-law, he views the Land of Israel on a
par with Heaven itself, where the dead (including his own wife) spend
their time interceding for the living.[7] The only thing he knows "for sure"
at the end of the story titled "Tevye Leaves for the Land of Israel" (1909)
is that as soon as he arrives, "right off, I plan to visit Mother Rachel in
her grave. I'll pray there for the daughters I'll probably never see again"
(E 116; Y 195). Despite all the intervening years and changing sensibilities, it is a dream not unlike Yehuda Halevi's death-saturated vision of
worship at ancestral shrines.

Sholem Aleichem's relationship with Tevye was described by his son-
in-law as an intensely empathic one. In reminiscences of the author's last
years, Y. D. Berkovitz relates that Sholem Aleichem had taken to writing a new installment of the Tevye saga each year; during the nearly two
decades in which his story unfolded, Tevye aged and changed along with
his creator. "Tevye Leaves for the Land of Israel" was written while
Sholem Aleichem was recovering from a serious bout of tuberculosis. The
writer, who remained a Zionist in principle throughout his life, had been
informed by Zionists in Kiev that they were close to realizing their plan
to build a house for him in Palestine: a delegation leaving for Jaffa to
buy agricultural land would include some property for him in their purchase. In anticipation of this, explains Berkovitz disarmingly, "he would
dispatch Tevye the dairyman ahead of him to Palestine, and if he should

follow him and settle there, Tevye could be his mouthpiece and intercessor." Berkovitz assures us that whenever Sholem Aleichem returned
to writing Tevye, he did so with great gaiety; while the actual work of
composition exhausted him, he positively shone with the joy of creation.[8]
Holding on for a moment to the charming conceit of Tevye as his creator's fellow traveler, I want to argue that the decision to "send" Tevye
to the Holy Land, corresponding with Sholem Aleichem's own battle with
the Angel of Death, is more complex than it at first appears.

The next and penultimate story in the final version of the *Tevye* cycle, "Lekh-lekho," is dated 1914; written in America, it follows the
thread that had been introduced in the previous story but weaves it into
a very different tapestry. "Lekh-lekha," the biblical account of the divine summons to Abraham to leave his fatherland and travel to the land
of promise, and Abraham's alacritous response (Gen. 12), comes near
the beginning of the annual lectionary cycle and constitutes the most fundamental reference for the theodicy of exile and homecoming. The actual effect of the intertext here, however, is not to inspire Tevye to settle
in Palestine as part of either an ancient religious injunction or a modern
historical-political strategy for changing Jewish fate. On the contrary, it
reinforces *wandering* as mythic Jewish behavior grounded in the ancient
sources and the vision of the Land of Israel as the "other side": "I had
one foot on the *other side* (*yener zayt*), that is, in the Holy Land" (E 117;
Y 200).[9] Tevye gives Sholem Aleichem a lesson based on his own inim-
itable, and proprietary, reading of the Bible:

> *Lekh-lekho*—get thee out, Tevye—*meyartsekho*—from your land—*umimoy-
> ladetkho*—and from the village you were born in and lived in your whole life—
> *el ha'orets asher arekko*—to wherever your legs will carry you. . . . And when
> did it occur to the powers-that-be to tell me that? Not a minute before I'm so
> old, weak and lonely that I'm a real *al tashlikheynu le'eys ziknoh*, as it says
> in the Rosh Hashanah prayer. . . . Only I'm getting ahead of myself, because
> I was telling you about my trip and what's new in the Land of Israel. Well,
> what should be new there, my dear friend? It's a land flowing with milk and
> honey—if you don't believe me, you can read up on it in the Bible. There's
> only one thing the matter with it, which is that it's there and I'm here . . . and
> not only am I still here in Russia, I'm still a schlimazel in Russia, and a schli-
> mazel I'll be till I die![10]

> (E 117; Y 200)

What was it that subverted this scheme at (as) the very last moment?
Why is it that Sholem Aleichem, old and ailing in America, deprived his
equally aged and frail Tevye of the moment of arrival in the Land of Israel? Why, in 1914, is there no "news" from the Old/New Land? Why is

the historical option, tentatively entertained in "Tevye Leaves for the Land of Israel," superseded by a resounding return to the sanctuary of the *text*? Is it an interrogative, reflexive gesture similar to that which released Benjamin the Third both from the czarist army and from his fantasies of rescue and redemption in the Holy Land?

At the level of the *fabula*, the scheming son-in-law goes bankrupt and flees to America; another son-in-law dies suddenly and his widow Tsaytl and their children move in with Tevye: "How could I even think of a pilgrimage to the Holy Land when I had a house full of little pilgrims myself?" (E 118; Y 201).[11] At this point the true meaning of *lekh-lekho* reveals itself: the authorities prepare a little "pogrom" for the Jewish townspeople (in which they are invited to smash their own windows) and then expel them. Finally, Chava, the beloved daughter excommunicated for having married out of the faith, is reunited with her family and elects to share their fate. The structural function of this reconciliation as closure for the family saga is revealed by Tevye himself, who interrupts his tale at the moment Chava appears in order to assure his interlocutor that "it was just like in one of your books" (E 129; Y 219).[12] But however self-reflexive or contrived its presentation, this is only a provisional ending, which is inevitably undermined by the biblical scaffolding that authorizes the narrative and demands a resolution of a different order. I am proposing that we shift our attention from the romantic theme, which is certainly dominant throughout all the stories, to the migration theme and examine its relation to forms of narration and closure.

In the context of the pogrom that is a cameo version of the original scenario of banishment and exile, Tevye once more cites the injunction to Abraham, this time explaining it to Tsaytl as a decree devolving on him and "all the Jews": "*lekh-lekho meyartsekho*, get thee out of thy land, did Abraham ask Him where to? God told him exactly where to, *el ha'orets asher arekko*—which means in plain language, hit the road! We'll go where all the other Jews go—that is, where our two feet take us" (E 126; Y 213).

So making his "trip to Israel" turns out to be nothing more—nor less—than divesting himself of all forms of private aggrandizement (even the old horse has been sold) and preparing for the proverbial crossing to the Other Side. But since Sholem Aleichem in his infinite mercy will not allow Tevye to die, he cannot admit him to the Holy Land; foreclosing Tevye's *'aliyah* to the Holy Land is, in a way, foreclosing closure itself, endowing him with the eternal life that guarantees the continuation of his narrative and a complicating or doubling of exile as the primary condition of Jewish storytelling.[13] In the chapter published just before Sholem Aleichem's death (1916), which provides the coda for the entire Tevye cycle, "arrival" is relegated to the messianic future; every practical option for the Jewish journey is entertained except that which would bring the journey itself to an end:

> "You see, ever since I was given that lesson in Lekh-Lekho, I've been on the go; there hasn't been a place I could point to and say, 'Tevye, we're here; now sit down and relax.' But Tevye asks no questions; if he's told to keep moving, he does. Today, Pani Sholem Aleichem, we met on the train, but tomorrow may find us in Yehupetz, and next year in Odessa, or in Warsaw, or maybe even in America . . . unless, that is, the Almighty looks down on us and says, 'Guess what, children! I've decided to send you my Messiah!' I don't even care if He does it just to spite us, as long as He's quick about it, that old God of ours! And in the meantime, be well and have a good trip."[14]
>
> (E 131)

Tevye takes up his staff and goes off into an undetermined afterlife. The Land of Israel reverts to a place in a text, a place identified with the arrival that is death—with the shrines to the dead patriarchs or with one's own death or messianic high drama. When it comes to living, and making a living (meager as it is), one stays here, on this side, in Yehupetz or Odessa or even . . . America.

THE RAILROAD STORIES: GETTING NOWHERE, SLOWLY

Admittedly, it seems rather perverse to argue that just a few decades before the mass extermination of the Jews of Europe and the establishment of the State of Israel, Odessa or Warsaw retains a position in the Jewish imagination as the place of the living and Jerusalem as the domain of death; as early as 1907, after all, writers like S. Y. Agnon were referring to the shtetl as 'ir ha-metim (city of the dead).[15] I am nonetheless arguing here for the value of a self-consciously naive reading, especially of the Railroad Stories. Trains shuttled Jews back and forth in the Pale of Settlement and provided the locus for their stories and jokes for several decades before becoming the metonymy of their collective doom. For the post-Holocaust reader, spending even a few moments cooped up with these third-class passengers without reference to their extratextual fate is a self-limiting gesture, an act of resistance to the "backshadowing" or anachronism that inevitably informs belated encounters.[16] Not only does such a strategy help reconstruct the "pres-

entness of the past," but it also preserves the profiles of those characters for whom the trains were crowded enough without adding ghostly
presences from the future. As we saw, the last story in the *Tevye* cycle
is recited in the train. If wandering is reaffirmed here as Jewish destiny,
it is in the *Railroad Stories* and finally in *Motl the Cantor's Son* that the
journey itself becomes primary.

The train, the most palpable and ubiquitous embodiment of the in-
dustrial revolution, has informed the imagination of every society
through which it has passed.[17] The forms of complex pastoralism that
characterize both the American and the European reception of the railroad are, for the most part, represented in late-nineteenth-and early-
twentieth-century art and literature by views of the serene landscape
marked (or pockmarked, as the case may be) by the steam engine and
its snaky appendage. The view we get of the train in many Yiddish and
Hebrew fictions is not the gaze from the outside, the gaze of a society
in charge of its natural environment, but the nervous report from within
the overpopulated third-class compartment. Such compartments become,
in their literary representations, the cultural compensation for a kind
of mobile proletariat in a state of profound socioeconomic alienation.
Reflecting the absence of a proprietary relationship to the surroundings,
the view *from the inside* reinforces both the intimacy and the hermetic
quality of this space; the train stories by Yiddish and Hebrew writers
in fact constitute a uniquely intermediate imaginary space at the turn
of the century.[18]

In his reconstruction of "everyday" spaces for the "ordinary man,"
Michel de Certeau invokes the immobility of both inner and outer spaces
that is belied by the *experience* of railway travel between two points. The
"order" within the railway car is at once fixed and provisional, based
on the anonymity and randomness of the encounters:

> There is something at once incarcerational and navigational about railroad
> travel. . . . Between the immobility of the inside and that of the outside a cer-
> tain *quid pro quo* is introduced, a slender blade that inverts their stability.
> The chiasm is produced by the windowpane and the rail. . . . The window-
> pane is what allows us to *see*, and the rail, what allows us to *move through*.
> The first creates the spectator's distance: You shall not touch; the more you
> see, the less you hold—a dispossession of the hand in favor of a greater tra-
> jectory for the eye. The second inscribes, indefinitely, the injunction to pass
> on; it is its order written in a single but endless line: go, leave, this is not your
> country, and neither is that—an imperative of separation which obliges one
> to pay for an abstract ocular domination of space by leaving behind any proper
> place, by losing one's footing.[19]

Lekh-lekho. Go, leave, this is not your country. . . . We might argue that unlike one who is rooted to a place and observes from a stable position on the outside a train cutting through the landscape—or, for that matter, a *picture* of a train slicing the landscape[20]—the traveler enacts the "imperative of separation" from the land she or he traverses. This separation, experienced through the agency of the machine, mimics for the duration of the journey the essential condition of the *golus* Jew whose cultural ambassador is the storyteller. The "silence of these things put at a distance," of "object[s] without discourse" beyond the windowpane that in de Certeau's scheme separates interior from exterior space, "makes our memories speak or draws out of the shadows the dreams of our secrets."[21] It thus becomes the perfect venue for telling stories. Silence holds the pageant enacted on the outside; speech is inside. The speech-intoxicated Jews hardly have time to look out the window at scenery to which they can never lay claim anyway. These stories rarely have any relation to the landscapes through which the train travels, except for occasional references to stations that function as terminals or watering holes. The coach promotes the illusion both of being away from home and of having a "roof over your head" (E 143; Y 25)—an interior space whose physical boundaries are the dimensions of the railway car, but whose cultural boundaries are defined by the Yiddish speech within and the goyish landscape without.[22]

S. Y. Abramovitsh's Hebrew story "Shem and Japheth on the Train" (1890) moves between stations in a railway coach filled with Jews whose destinations seem determined by the exigencies of their hungry stomachs. Jewish exile is confirmed here as an inexorable pattern of the universe; even the comets (Japheth as Polish cobbler) that stray into this (third-class) galaxy learn to conform to its physical laws.[23] Such narratives, which tease their passengers with a whiff of westward, forward motion, are but journeys into the recesses of the Pale of Settlement. As mobile echo chambers for storytelling, trains will also furnish Sholem Aleichem with the perfect venue for practicing his craft.

The absence of destination in Sholem Aleichem's narrative cycle defines the aimless movement of Jews through a space measured only as the distance between neighboring stations. Even the pretense of direction offered in Abramovitsh's tales has been relinquished in the *Railroad Stories* in favor of the narratological function of local stations as the terminal points of a story. One of the lines, the Slowpoke Express (*Der leydikgeyer*), moves so slowly that "you needn't ever worry about missing it: whenever you arrive at the station, it's still there" (E 184; Y 105). What verbal compensations are there for such sluggish movement through space? The Jews confined in crowded railway cars consider the same subjects that were aired in that other claustrophobic place, the bathhouse, in *Benjamin the Third*—but with a keener edge: the discussion of the "recent harvest" gives way to a heated negotiation of the war with Japan, the Revolution of 1905, the Constitution, the "pogroms, the massacres of Jews, the new anti-Semitic legislation, the expulsion from the villages, the mass flight to America . . ." ("Baranovich Station," E 152; Y 41–42). (The causal connection between the pogroms and the mass migration to America was elevated to the status of theodicy in Sholem Aleichem's writing as early as 1906; we will see later how it became an animating force in *Motl*.)

The *Railroad Stories* are vignettes of life in the shtetl as captured from a distance without preserving them for future reference in the formaldehyde of nostalgia, as did Sholem Aleichem's more popular fiction, but instead recording the moment of the breakup of the society—the economic, social, and psychological upheaval that is a response to threats from within and without. Dan Miron argues persuasively that they are *not*, as I. I. Trunk suggested, "Kasrilevke on wheels,"[24] but rather a gesture of *distancing* from the shtetl as the matrix of an innocent, pristine existence and point of reference for the alienated traveler. Miron goes so far as to define these stories as "anti-Kasrilevke" and sees in their deviation from what had come to be understood and adored as Sholem Aleichem's style the reason for the relative lack of critical attention paid them. But the more popular Kasrilevke stories have, after all, been filtered through the roseate lenses of their American reception and Sholem Aleichem's benedictory presence in them. The railroad stories lack the unifying "comic-pathetic" narrative voice of a folk hero such as Tevye or Menakhem Mendl or Motl, or the mediating presence of a "Sholem Aleichem," and thus the words are a more flimsy barrier against the destructive forces undermining shtetl life from the outside. The motifs of "immigration, displacement, separation and alienation," which run throughout Sholem Aleichem's fiction, appear here without the "grace and the innocence" of the small-town context; it is, Miron argues, the story of the road as opposed to the home, of the transitory as opposed to the permanent, of passing as opposed to ongoing human encounters, of cognitive dissonance or systematic misunderstandings in place of the subtle mutuality of intimates, of the anonymity that provides not only a context for the revelation of sordid human behavior but also a smoke screen against the consequences of such revelations.[25] On this reading, the crowded third-class coach imposes the forced, ephemeral intimacy of strangers who convene as a "community" only for the purpose of hearing a story: "My three Jews had parted company," says the narrator after relating a tale of mutual misunderstanding between a storyteller and his listeners; "the brief friendship was over. . . . It was curious how the three had become total strangers" ("Eighteen from Pereshchepena," E 166; Y 68).[26]

This is one of the moments in which the modern representation of exile as alienation and anomie adds an entirely new existential layer to the inherited meanings of *golus*. True to the monologic form (in a sense its very distillation, produced in the laboratory of a railway coach), nothing really happens in narrative time except for *narration itself*; granted, people eat and sleep and pray, and a few peddlers even manage to peddle their wares . . . but mostly what people do in these coaches is to tell stories. Many of their stories are narrated acts of suicide, extortion, and embezzlement and assorted reports of hard-heartedness. They are stories from which the softness of Sholem Aleichem's benevolent and gentle sensitivity has been withdrawn—and it is not coincidental that he "himself" does not appear as either the narrator or addressee of the stories. That this is perhaps the most sinister of Sholem Aleichem's fictions is evidenced by the absence of the compassionate intervention of the narrator-qua-author. Instead, the mediating voice is that of an anonymous self-styled "commercial traveler" (*komi-voyazher*)—not exactly a writer and most certainly not Sholem Aleichem. The passengers are in some profound sense truly lost, abandoned even by the gently chiding humor of their creator, who joins Stephen Dedalus's God-as-artist—refined out of existence, indifferent, paring his fingernails.

And yet something urgently personal or even self-consciously autobiographical in these stories is paradoxically signified by the author's withdrawal as persona; on the road since 1905, Sholem Aleichem refers to himself in correspondence from the sanatorium as a "reizender, a komi-voyazher be-khol tefutzot Yisrael" (a voyager, a commercial traveler in all the diasporas of Israel).[27] The stories are artifacts from the shtetl as well as evidence of its disintegration and of the author's remove from it. The circumstances of their composition, as related by Berkovitz, add another dimension to the narratives themselves and to the representation of the life of the author as fellow traveler in his constructed universe. By his own account, Sholem Aleichem was "incarcerated" in the sanatorium at St. Blasien in the company of the moribund ("hatzi-metim," in Berkovitz's words); on one of his regular walks in the rain-drenched

Schwartzwald, his encounter with a young yeshiva student who had come there expressly to meet the great writer produced a unique "collaboration" that issued in four of the *Railroad Stories*. The student was, naturally, curious to hear stories from the mouth of the literary eminence— but Sholem Aleichem was interested only in listening to the "facts" his interlocutor had to convey from his backwater shtetl in Podolia. It is the same appeal that the ailing writer makes in the above-mentioned letter, asking a journalist friend in White Russia for "raw material from Homel, from Vitebsk, from Bialystok, from wherever you care to, as long as it is subject matter that I can use in my 'Railroad Stories.'. . . Please keep one thing in mind, though," he adds: "I don't want anything imaginary, just facts, the more the better!"[28]

Of particular interest here is the emphasis Sholem Aleichem places on "factuality," insisting that both the student and his correspondent relay true and not invented stories.[29] Berkovitz points out that his father-in-law, on the road for some time, was separated from the sources of his creativity and languishing among the sick and dying; a healthy young man full of stories from the homeland acted as a catalyst for his imagination. It is tempting to argue, nevertheless, that Sholem Aleichem is concerned with something far more subtle and consequential than mere accuracy in transmitting these stories—though they do reproduce the diction of the region and other local colors, the raw material has clearly gone through the alchemy of Sholem Aleichem's pen. The very insistence on facts is not only a well-worn literary convention for authorizing flights of the literary imagination but also a refusal of the digressions from the press of history that Sholem Aleichem's humor had provided in the stories that had endeared him to his readers; at the same time, it marks his distance from the source. The author here makes a testimonial or conservationist gesture vis-à-vis an endangered culture not unlike that which motivated Agnon or Buber or Berdichevski, each fashioning a specific form of intertextual or "documentary" response to the passing traditions whose very passing they had encouraged. David Roskies argues that storytelling filled the vacuum created in the process of transition, becoming a kind of "politics of rescue"—a form of displacement or "creative betrayal" by which the culture could reincorporate its own oral traditions.[30]

The storytelling performed on a train follows certain external constraints peculiar to its context. Sholem Aleichem, writing from St. Blasien, creates a third-class, claustrophobic version of the sanatoria, spas, hotels, and inns that so frequently provide the venues for random encounters in twentieth-century fiction. But what is most striking in these mobile talking chambers is that their destination is absent or insignificant except as a structural element. Unlike *Benjamin the Third*, the train stories do not trace a skeptical pattern of return. Where there is no teleological orientation, there is also no antiteleological or dystopic disorientation. The Jews may not be going anywhere on the train, but they're not going back to the shtetl either (except for a visit or to "buy" a kosher wife).[31]

The ultimate consolation for the breakdown of social cohesion is the perfection of form. The short story is as protective of its parts as the train is of its cars; when it reaches the station, the "terminal" that signals that the story has ended and history has begun—halting the "incarceration-vacation," the "Robinson Crusoe adventure of the travelling noble soul that could believe itself *intact* because it was surrounded by glass and iron"—then narrative must end and "history begin again."[32] The generic advantage of the short story, which can capture the life it tells in a frozen cross-section, is doubled here within the context of the railroad. Virtually all of these stories are structured by the intervals between stations, marking the entrances and exits of the players; a few of them, like "Baranovich Station," which tells an excruciating tale of extortion practiced by a villager who had been saved by his fellow townspeople from a flogging, are abruptly discontinued when the train reaches the storyteller's point of disembarkation: "Hey there! You can't do this to us! We won't let you go. You have to tell us the end of the story!" (E 163; Y 58)

Many of the other stories do reach closure—but it is the provisional closure of life captured in a moment, *in medias res*, between stations. In "Happiest Man in All Kodny," a storyteller accompanies a medical specialist to his home to examine his tubercular son; the story relates the father's successful adventure in persuading the good doctor to pay the poor Jew a house call. He is indeed the "happiest man"—enjoying temporary respite in what is sure to unfold *beyond the confines of the train and the story* as a tragedy.

The reader and Sholem Aleichem "himself" do not belong inside the railway coach; like distant relatives or curious onlookers, they are relegated to the other side of the window, peering in. The pane of glass that separates the voyagers from the reader is an alienating device that is utterly shattered in *Motl*. That novel directly addresses a large second-person audience, as the young narrator brings with him to America not only all the inhabitants of the shtetl but all of its readers as well.

AMERICA: DETOXIFYING THE EUROPEAN STORY

That the most affirmative of Sholem Aleichem's writings is a narrative of
the journey to (and in) America can be understood largely in terms of a
common thread binding a host of European writers and their American
readers. The perennial rediscovery of America as an inherently optimistic
construct illuminates some of the darkest corners of the European imagination. As unlikely as the comparison between Sholem Aleichem and
Franz Kafka may appear at first,[33] even Kafka's *Amerika* can reveal the
transformative power of the ethos of immigration.

In the American cartography of Europe, both Sholem Aleichem and
Kafka are identified with remote places: the small Jewish towns of Eastern Europe and the urban remnants of the Austro-Hungarian Empire. Each
of these writers was imported into America as the expression of a different aspect of the European imagination and Jewish fate: the one representing innocuous Jewish humor (identified eventually with fiddlers on
roofs), the other a sense of the absurd and the alienated (associated ultimately with Jews in gas chambers). But in the European cartography of
America, neither would be viewed as a creator or recorder of American
landscapes. It is true that whereas Sholem Aleichem spent the last years
of his life in New York and was buried there, Kafka, who hardly ever ven-
tured outside Prague, seems barely to have dreamed of America.[34]

Yet Motl's New York has the same pride of place in the Yiddish narrative as Karl's "Nature Theatre of Oklahoma" in the German. Both *Motl
Peyse dem Khazns* and *Amerika*, written during the same years and left
unfinished at the time of their authors' deaths,[35] represent not only versions of the American immigrant saga, and the story of childhood or
youth whose innocence is assaulted but never completely undermined,
but also a major recasting of the topos and telos of the Jewish journey—
as the curse of wandering yields to the blessings of mobility.

Kafka's America, the target not of celebration but of mild scorn, would
nonetheless become the place where his imagination could play with relative safety: where the innocent are exploited *but not killed*;[36] where wide
open spaces replace the confinement of the "European prison";[37] where
aphasia replaces the burden of knowledge and memory;[38] where modern technology and architecture are restricting and possibly enslaving but
not lethal;[39] where the insidious forces that stalk their victims everywhere
in this godless universe are somehow *interrupted* in their work;[40] and
where, finally, tinsel and apocalypse come together to produce a version
of Hollywood's never-never land as directed from Prague.

It was the darker side of Kafka's imagination that was imported to America in the 1940s when the American mind needed a European language to speak of European forms of alienation and finally of European atrocities;[41] *Amerika*, the sunniest of Kafka's long fictions, never quite received the attention lavished on *The Castle* or *The Trial*. To be sure, one can overstate the sunny disposition of this narrative. Some among Kafka's readers offer powerful counterarguments that from the very first glimpse of the teeming immigrants on the boat and Miss Liberty with a sword in place of a torch, *Amerika* is a scathing indictment of *Zivilization* without *Kultur*, a transposition onto the American imaginary of Kafka's "Mitteleuropa decadence"—or even that it is the quintessential modern representation of the Jewish condition of exile.[42] Nevertheless, in America the elements of Kafka's imaginative universe undergo detoxification. In the case of Sholem Aleichem, as I will show, the journey to and arrival in America are more akin to alchemy—not so much dispelling the fear as transforming the dross of one's European baggage into the gold of American opportunity. The writings of both are related to the American discovery narrative and the primary myth of self-invention. "In its simplest, archetypal form, the myth affirms that Europeans experience a regeneration in the New World," observes Leo Marx. "They become new, better, happier men—they are reborn."[43]

Rebirth is predicated on a forgetting and an "oceanic feeling" that in Kafka's and Sholem Aleichem's narratives are initiated by crossing the ocean itself. *Motl Peyse dem Khazns* moves deliberately from the invented town of Kasrilevke through several of the stations that make up the actual geography of the European migration (Brod, Cracow, Lemberg, Vienna, Antwerp, London), with New York as its terminus. They describe a tangent that brushes and then moves resolutely away from the circular geometry of the Pale of Settlement, away from the stations of the train that, laden with Jewish passengers in its third-class compartments, snaked its way aimlessly through the Eastern European landscape. This story is narrated in the first person by Motl, the young son of the ailing Cantor Peyse. The father's illness and death precipitate the divestment that ends in the family's emigration to and settlement in America.

When first published as a whole, posthumously, in 1920, the narrative was divided into two volumes: the first brings the group of *emigrantn* to England, the site of embarkation for America; the stories of the second, which remains unfinished, are located onboard the ocean liner, on Ellis Island, and finally in the streets and tenements of New York. Consistent with their theme, the publishing history of these stories also embraces the entire range of Jewish geography; the first story was published in *Der Amerikaner* in New York in May 1907; others appeared in Yiddish journals in Vilna and Petersburg as well as New York. The earliest story of the second part appeared in 1914, but the outbreak of World War I postponed until 1916 the publication of the other "American" chapters.[44]

Serialization was common in contemporary Yiddish and Hebrew fiction; but the publication of this text as a series of relatively autonomous narratives distributed over time and space becomes significant as thematically and even formally emblematic of its expansive spatial purchase. Although the first story, published as an occasional piece in honor of Shavuoth, does not give any indication of a larger conceptual framework, the open-ended narrative, read as structurally inherent rather than as a defect, elides questions of artistic intent and control as well as closure. The open-ended story also proves functional in generating interpretive communities.[45] Discussing immigrant journalism in the United States at the turn of the century, Werner Sollors argues that "serialized fiction intensified the sense of community between writer and audience as well as among the readers themselves."[46] Still, there is something quite extraordinary in the ingathering of Sholem Aleichem's readers, scattered as they are over the globe. His status as a storyteller was reinforced in the public readings he gave during the decade of his peregrinations in Europe—and his funeral, attended by as many as a quarter of a million people, was a public rite testifying not only to the affection with which he was regarded but also to the value accorded to both the storyteller's performance of literature and the audience's act of witnessing.[47]

And yet by giving both the *Train Stories* and *Motl* the label *ksovim* (writings), Sholem Aleichem may be acknowledging another direction in which this storytelling tradition is moving. The presumed transition from "oral" to "written" culture implies the very mobility that is being enacted in his narrative. The act of writing is a form of *editing* reality, and "reality" includes the orally transmitted folk wisdom no less than the events being related. The cozy boundaries of the storytelling circle are canceled here, as Motl in his monologue appeals directly to an explicit but nonspecific, extratextual reader without the mediation of "Sholem Aleichem" or the crowd of familiar strangers of the sort that traveled through the train stories. The second-person formal pronoun, which incorporates both singular and plural addressees, is as essential to the progress of the narrative as it is undefined: "I spend the whole day at the river fishing and swimming. I learned how to fish all by myself. If you wish (*az ir vilt*), I can teach you. You take your shirt off . . ."; "Before I start telling you (*eyder ikh gey aykh dertseyln*) how one makes a living in the new country . . . "[48] It is as if Sholem Aleichem en route to and in America had opened his storehouse to an unbounded world of readers; by taking his (expandable) audience with him, he manages to leave his native ground without relinquishing his ties to posterity.

Many critics have noted the contrast between the events of the first, "European," part of *Motl*, encoded in the adult mind as a series of catastrophes, and their redefinition in the child's narrative; Motl's "forgetting," or inappropriate response, one might say, takes on the weight of a radical reformulation of cultural, social, and eventually linguistic categories. The boy as tabula rasa is the site of negotiable realities. Other consciousnesses, recorded faithfully by Motl, mediate the related events: that of "our friend Pini," the local prophet and know-it-all; that of "our brother Eliahu," the bane of Motl's young existence; those of the teary-eyed mother and her multiple-chinned friend Pessie. But Motl's voice is not only the most persistent; it is also the loudest and most outrageous. The first chapters, located in Kasrilevke, narrate the process by which the family's chattel is sold to purchase medication for Motl's sick father— a dispossession celebrated by the nine-year-old son as a form of liberation.[49] Orphanhood signals the initial deliverance from authority; "Mir iz gut—ikh bin a yosem!" (It's grand to be an orphan) (E 23; Y 1:33) are the words by which he announces to his readers that his father has died.[50]

The chapters located in the shtetl and on the journey itself are thus under the sign of a massive negation, a rewriting of the world. Dan Miron reads *Motl* as a mythic story of death and regeneration, in which "death is not only a convenient point of departure, but a necessary one. Implied is that one cannot begin a new life without laying the old one to rest." Death is the place where "comedy and tragedy fuse: the myth of the old father, king or god, who dies in order to fertilize a wasteland for its eventual flowering under the spirit of the young divinity."[51]

Insistence on the primordial, and therefore inexorable, nature of the myth holds particular comfort for those of us who survey, from the end of this bloody century, the waves of immigrants who left their "fatherlands" to embrace a new order in Palestine or in America (each a world of sons and daughters) and reflect on the great conflagration that utterly consumed what was left of the "world of the fathers." *Motl*, however, conceived at the more innocent end of our century, reconstructs this myth out of local, more lightweight materials: the American theater of self-invention provides the stage and the narrative privilege of Purim furnishes the script by which Jewish worlds are abandoned and then reinvented.

PURIM: CASTING OF LOTS AND RECASTING OF PLOTS

The acts of exaggeration or masking and of repression or transformation are transparently connected in this narrative with theatricality or the carnivalesque and with language as a medium for restructuring reality.[52] Though the holiday that Jews celebrate is explicitly referred to as an instance of self-empowerment and deliverance, the Purim principle of inversion or *nahafokh-hu* is manifest in this narrative more as a series of compositional strategies. Cognitive dissonance marks Motl's monologues, as we have seen ("It's grand to be an orphan"); systematic misunderstanding marks his dialogues. In exchanges between Motl and Kopl, another young emigrant traveling from Kasrilevke to London, the inevitable subject of pogroms arises:

> I ask him what is a pogrom? All the emigrants keep talking about "pogroms" but I don't know what they are. Kopl says, "Don't you know what a pogrom is? Then you're just a baby! A pogrom is something that you find everywhere nowadays. It starts out of nothing, and once it starts it lasts for three days."
> "Is it like a fair?"
> "A fair? Some fair! They break windows, they bust up furniture, rip pillows, feathers fly like snow. . . . And they beat and kill and murder."
> "Whom?"
> "What do you mean, *whom*? The Jews!"
> "What for?"
> "What a question! It's a pogrom, isn't it?"
> "And so it's a pogrom. What's that?"
> "Go away, you're a fool. It's like talking to a calf."
>   (E 147–18; Y 1:213–14)

The circular reasoning that loops back on the initial question keeps the threat contained—but also exposes the sinister underpinnings of Yiddish idioms in which a fair (*yarid*) can yield up its original meaning to signify a pogrom. The next time the subject comes up, Motl is ready with a more aggressive form of defense that self-consciously edits out the gloomier aspects of Jewish memory: "Once upon a time, when I heard people tell about pogroms, I was all eyes and ears," admits Motl. "Now, when I hear the word *pogrom*, I run. I prefer jolly stories."[53] Compare the epistemological effects of such denial here with Isaac Babel's short Russian story "The Story of My Dovecot" (1925), in which the slow evolution of a child's consciousness of evil culminates in the invocation of the sinister word. By the time he can admit the term "pogrom" into his own lexicon, Babel's young narrator has endured a rite de passage into the adult world where evil and violence prevail.[54] Motl's passage is to a world that refuses to accommodate evil—or, for that matter, adults.

In a universe perceived as having been created with an answer for every conundrum, a balm for every plague, a cure for every disease, America is represented as the remedy prepared in anticipation of the pogroms that would drive the Jews there. In the chapters written in and about America, composed shortly before the author's death, this is an article of faith enunciated by "our friend" Pini with all the pomposity of one who has just passed the Statue of Liberty: "You forget that God created America in order to shelter and protect the meek and the poor, the offended and the persecuted, and the ones who are hounded from all parts of the world" (E 252; Y 2:64).[55]

Patterned after such a divine model, the license to rewrite a sinister plot can be an invitation to a Purim carnival; Miecke Bal has pointed to the analogous acts of casting lots (*purim*) and recasting *plots*.[56] Motl's "revisionism" becomes a form of masquerade that borders on the grotesque. In the leave-taking passage, as his family departs for America, the egregious deformities of each of the characters serve to undermine the conventional pathos of the situation by suggesting to the unsentimental narrator a form of *teater* (theater); as players in a melodrama, they act their roles to the hilt: "All of a sudden everybody starts to sniff and to cry. Mother cries harder than anyone. She falls into Pessie's arms, wailing, 'You've been a sister to me! You've been more than a sister!' Our neighbor Pessie doesn't cry, but her triple chin trembles and tears, as large as peas, roll down her fat glistening cheeks. Everybody has done his share of kissing except Pini. To see Pini kiss is a spectacle (*zen Pinyen kushn zikh—darf men nisht keyn teater*). He kisses the middle of somebody's beard, the tip of somebody's nose, or else he bumps into somebody's forehead" (E 112; Y 1:163). The significance of Motl's chosen "vocation" as cartoonist is nowhere more pronounced than in this scene.[57] His métier takes the place of satire, which he is too young and nonreflective to enact, serving as a distancing device from the culture of origin. The connection between caricature, theater, and the masking or rewriting of reality is maintained as long as it is functional and necessary—that is, through the shtetl chapters and the voyage to America.

The journey itself, fraught with the terrors of the unknown, exacts extraordinary editorial feats. The escape from Europe and the ocean voyage are recorded and edited with Puccini-like realism so that the intolerable lies fully disclosed—a corpse on the stage about which Motl tiptoes in madcap denial. Mama's tears wash over the narrative like a tidal wave over an ocean liner, leaving the threat of both maudlin sentimentalism and trachoma in their wake. Seasickness, bedbugs, the inequities of the immigrant aid societies, missing luggage, and missing persons submit, one by one, to the spirit of Purim.

The Purim spirit is an inebriated state in which one confuses the saintly Mordecai with the villainous Haman. It is a ritual reenactment of the effect of a contravening narrative on the "original" story of genocide, a performative interpretation of a royal decree that empowered the would-be victims to commit preemptive acts of self-defense against the edict that had authorized their murder. The "revision" converts the outcome from a funeral into a masked ball. Recent studies of Purim as exemplifying the "cultural poetics of Judaism" stress the acts of writing and reading that are central to the scroll of Esther itself and the observance of the holiday, the inherently "diasporic" nature of the event and of the forms of its commemoration, and the more obvious principles of inversion and masquerade.[58] The sinister aspects of the holiday as licensing vengeance, which have also been explored in the less-apologetic historiography of the late twentieth century,[59] reveal the desperate undercurrents that run through a chronically disabled culture. In *Motl*, these undercurrents are suppressed by the abiding presence of the child who keeps the tale within the safe precincts and innocence of make-believe. The acts of violence transfigured through magical writing can include even the "killing" of the father at the beginning of the narrative (and the "killing off" of the whole community at the end, as we will see below).[60] Defined as a defense against the fear of annihilation in the Esther story, a defense against the fear of the death of the father and the journey to the unknown in *Motl*, the act of writing becomes utterly consequential.[61]

AMERICA IS FOR CHILDREN

Purim is for children, and so is America. At the beginning of the century, the idea of America as a place of rebirth meant, symbolically, that it was a place for the young. "Amerike—a naye velt far yiddishe *kinder*," wrote Sholem Aleichem in a letter to Bialik and in Motl's monologue—a comment that can be loosely paraphrased, with a nod to Yeats, as "that is no country for old people."[62] The romantic and midrashic notions of the child who comes into the world trailing clouds of glory, close to the source but amnesiac, represent the American moment captured in this narrative. Motl's redefinition of old-world reality is a very active form of amnesia. The inconsistencies of presenting as the author of "writings" a boy who, as it turns out, is preliterate, who has the literalizing mind of a child but the vocabulary and occasionally the syntax of a sophisticated adult, who does not grow up or mature over the nine years in which the chapters of his journey are being composed and disseminated, render this story something other than a historical novel or bildungsroman.[63]

Though Motl doesn't grow, he *moves*, ultimately acting out his capacious dreams in New York's streets. In the economy of this narrative, change is located not in time or character development but in geographic venues, each with a different social value. The first chapter is marked by emergence from the darkness of winter, the cellar, and the lugubrious sickroom where Peyse the Cantor lies dying; the second celebrates the space gained when the furniture is sold to buy medicine and food for the sick man; the middle chapters are laid out across the expanse of the voyage; and the final chapters chart urban and domestic spaces in America. But space in urban America is not empty; discarding the old creates room for acquisition, for grounding in the world of *things*. The child as site of a Purim sensibility and as a miniature shlemiel, editor of an intolerable reality, performs what may be the ultimate act of alchemy in modern Jewish letters. But no less significant, though seldom remarked, is that it is followed by its antithesis: the embrace of an alternative reality, of America as the space of unlimited possibility. Preoccupied with the child's redefinition of reality, critics often fail to note that this principle is no longer operative in the second section of the novel: American reality as configured in these chapters does not require a radical act of rewriting in order to fit Motl's yea-saying disposition.

The Purim privilege is renounced as superfluous in a country in which every day is Purim. As the gang who once swarmed over the dirt paths of the shtetl in the hopelessness of their poverty populate the streets of New York in the first flush of their success, Motl's friend Hershl, who had been nicknamed "Vashti" in Kasrilevke (after the unfortunate first wife of King Ahasuerus in the Book of Esther), is renamed "Harry":

> This is Vashti, who in the old country never saw a coin, even in a dream. Except on Purim in return for delivering Purim sweets for others. But Purim comes only once a year—while here, every weekday is Purim for Vashti. He earns money every single day.
>
> "Columbus, who can compare with you!" our friend Pini is moved to exclaim when he strolls along Rivington Street and with his own eyes sees Vashti working at the stand. He goes up to him, buys three cents' worth of carobs, and gives Vashti one cent, *na tshayock*, or a "tip," as they say here, in America.[64] (Words appearing in English in the original are underscored here.)

With the help of Pini's ideological slogans, we can trace the process by which the world of the shtetl is replaced by the world of America: "Vashti" is exchanged for "Harry" and Purim for Columbus, the coinage of Russian poverty for American capitalism and Yiddish for English.

Granted, a sweatshop is not a textile factory, and Brother Eliyahu's salary doesn't quite match Rothschild's; but role-playing is so much a function of the fluidity of the American economy that every day is carnival day. Like a quick-change artist, Eliyahu moves from sweatshop to entrepreneurship as waiter, as "collector," and ultimately as petty businessman with a newspaper stand. America has become the incarnation of Motl's optimism, rendering it unnecessary to recast the world in language. If conditions are bad, if the "fumes of gas in the pressers' shop are so strong that it weakens the workers, and many of them even faint," then the remedy is not a verbal rewrite but remedial action: "No, this can't go on any longer. We'll have to call a strike," writes the young capitalist with a socialist consciousness (E 284; Y 2:113).

The reality of America is affirmed as the realia of America penetrate the language of the narrator with an abandon that precludes the need for further acts of magical thinking. Although Motl begins his life in the Golden Land with the desire to turn a somersault, he acts less to turn the world over than to explicitly renounce such *luftgesheftn*; he celebrates the ground beneath his feet in a chapter titled "With Both Feet on the Ground" or "Down to Earth" (E 244; Y 2:57). Even the items in the family's little stand are enumerated with a celebration of their *thingness* that is the antithesis of the process of *divestment* and creation of empty spaces in the first part of the novel: "One sells cigarettes, writing implements, candy and soda water. And newspapers too. . . . We sell ice cream in sandwiches . . . [and] 'cider.' . . . People who have tasted champagne wine say it tastes like real champagne. And even though cider is an American drink, who do you suppose manufactures it? My brother Eli! . . . Later on, in mid-summer, when watermelons appear on the market, we make even better business" (E 322–25; Y 2:173–77).

While the language is not altogether different from that of Menakhem Mendl in his business ventures, or even from the get-rich-quick schemes of Motl and his brother in Kasrilevke, in the American chapters words do not invert but only exaggerate reality. Seeking, like so many city people before and after him, to be absorbed into what Philip Fisher defines as the "magical life of . . . things, the vitality of objects in the city [and] what Walter Benjamin called the 'sex-appeal' of objects," Motl remains undeveloped and revels in the projection of his desires onto the object world that surrounds him in New York. Like characters in Zola or Dickens, he lacks the consciousness of a private self and discovers instead the "maps for the empire of the self within the city."[65]

In addition to the public areas of the street, the train station, the subway, and the candy stand, there are new interior spaces—such as the "kitchen" (in English in the original) or the bedroom—that signify the private forum of the family and the self. In the shtetl stories the interiors were represented either as too confining for dialogues with one's Creator, in the case of Tevye, or as too undifferentiated, serving simultaneously as sites of cooking, sleeping, and (in the case of Motl's father) dying; but here they are affirmed as part of the differentiation of space that allows for exploration of "new" worlds. This process is of a piece both with the comic view that reconstitutes the material fragments of a world in dissolution and with the modernist view that embraces profane space as the site of primary encounters.[66]

THE ALCHEMY OF WORDS

In Motl's world the borders of language become as porous as the physical boundaries. For even if movement through space seems to be the primary form of mobility and the physical environment more definitive than the linguistic, the acoustic aspects of this narrative are no less salient here than elsewhere in Sholem Aleichem. But the narrative privilege that defines the world of the shlemiel, caught as he is in *discourse* itself,[67] culminates in this, the last of Sholem Aleichem's narratives—and then self-destructs in the wide-open spaces of America. Language has not lost its magical properties nor the Diaspora its narrative privilege; but America emerges as a world in which *words* come into alignment with the *object world*.

The presence of foreign phrases in the Yiddish of Sholem Aleichem is one of the most striking components of his polyphonic universe. Miron presents the linguistic corruption in the *Railroad Stories* as emblematic of the existential condition of the travelers themselves, arguing that the frequency of words and phrases in Russian, Ukrainian, and Polish marks the decline or "twilight" of the culture and a deviation from Sholem Aleichem's own former standards of authenticity. The babel of languages reflects, in this instance, "a socio-linguistic reality of people who are no longer within their intimate world of the community of origin. . . . They go so far as to introduce the linguistic estrangement into their souls. . . . These are people whose fortified boundaries of their cultural territory have been infiltrated. . . . The language confusion . . . reflects the larger collective condition of spiritual and cultural confusion."[68]

Miron sees both the more sinister manifestations of that process in the *Railroad Stories* and its more humorous manifestations in *Motl* as part of the evolution of an aesthetics of cacophony or disharmony. I am arguing here that the fragmentation of language that signals the cultural breakdown in one text may signal cultural formation in another. In *Motl* the increasing porousness of the Yiddish in the "American" section (nearly every chapter title contains an English word)[69] is made more conspicuous by the absence of the scriptural or liturgical intertexts that pepper Tevye's speech. Motl has very few texts in his head; the rare allusions to holiday liturgy or to the *parshat ha-shavu'a* biblical readings represent the limited repertory of a child of the Eastern European shtetl. Their presence or absence relates to the authorizing forces behind the novel, reflecting how the concept of narrative itself is changing: rather than proceeding as commentary on another text, it becomes a self-authorizing process. The source of authority is no longer hermeneutic but experiential. Motl doesn't read; he exists, he observes, he listens. What he hears and experiences does not refer to other worlds, to private or collective memory. This form of retrenchment serves the trope of rebirth and signals the oceanic feeling that will become, in the next generation, the pervasive amnesia of a transplanted culture lost in the embrace of its host.

If the *Railroad Stories* can be said to have been written by the last rays of a culture's twilight, it was by the dawn's early light over a new continent that *Motl* was composed. In the former, the confusion of languages is a function of profound levels of miscommunication and dispossession; in the latter it is a celebration of new forms of aggrandizement—spatial, material, linguistic. The porousness at the borders of language signals an aesthetics of fragmentation that is fundamentally compatible with American democratic aesthetics.[70]

The parallel processes of a massive forgetting and a massive recall of Scriptures that unfold simultaneously on two continents are anticipated in the respective monologues of Motl and Tevye. Y. D. Berkovitz suggests that when Tevye "arrives" in Palestine, he'll find "a whole new world with new *pesukim* [biblical quotations] and midrashim—the real *pesukim* that float there wherever you turn."[71] Since he lives by the book, as it were, transporting him to the place of that book's original enactment would realign Tevye with the very ground of his being. Like that of Benjamin the Third, Tevye's shtetl world is a self-enclosed, hermetic reality, reflected in a textual prism; Motl's world, in contrast, is full of objects undergoing constant interrogation and renaming. The Holy Land as the place where "original" speech can be reactivated, the place where ancient memory animates the present, is the alternative to America as the land of amnesia and self-re-creation.

As I have already noted, however, Tevye never made it to the Holy Land, an arrival that would have been equivalent to his being transported to the Other Side. One might say that as the locus of a true diaspora, America is not a place for the dead; Motl's mother puts it best, with a sigh and a backward glance at her dear departed husband; "he who lives, comes; he who lies in the ground, comes not" (*ver es lebt, der kumt. Kumen kumt nit nor der, vos ligt in der erd*; Y 2:58).[72] The last chapter that Sholem Aleichem was working on at the time of his own death was called, appropriately enough, "Mir mufn" [We Move]—leaving open the possibility of another chapter and another station, of movement itself as the principle of this new universe. Sholem Aleichem's final act of grace is to grant Motl, Tevye, and himself the option of moving on to keep the story going and to resist the seductions of the Other Side.

The tendency to regard the final words that are squeezed from a dying writer's pen as his last literary will and testament is reinforced in this final novel by the polemic culture that informed Hebrew and Yiddish literature and that defined Jewish life as a set of specific alternatives. Somehow Sholem Aleichem managed to embrace *all* of the three possible routes followed by Jews that nearly every other writer found mutually exclusive: the "old home," Zion, *and* America. Although the manifestations changed over the years, *golus* remained largely a positive but increasingly remote reference; Zion was an ideal but not an existential imperative. Unlike Abramovitsh, Sholem Aleichem ideologically embraced Hibat Zion and then Herzlian political Zionism. In his polemical writing he argued that "the Jews need a land of their own."[73] But it remained for him and his characters, as for so many of the writers of the preceding eight centuries, the Other Side, the place of ultimate arrival—and death.

Sholem Aleichem's global reach and his irrepressible mobility are ironically underscored by his fate after death. Though he was buried with great fanfare in New York, the family had planned to remove his body and give it permanent burial in Kiev, Russia; even though he lived his last years and died in America, he continued to be regarded as a Russian writer. And he remained in the minds of his Yiddish readers always the storyteller from the shtetl.[74] In 1912, in the New York Yiddish paper *Dos yidishes tageblatt*, Sholem Aleichem had written: "The power of

'home'! Time doesn't weaken it. The ocean can't obliterate it. Freedom
won't make you forget it. On the contrary—the further away you are,
the more you want to know what's going on over there in our unfortunate home. How are our unlucky brothers and sisters doing? How are
they managing to bear the yoke of exile? What makes them laugh, what
makes them cry, and what do their writers have to tell us?"[75]

He seems to be implying that the "yoke of exile" does not extend to
America. The paradoxes of Jewish life in the early twentieth century are
highlighted when we recognize that the American Diaspora is the place
to which the Jews of Eastern Europe are *self-exiled* from their home in
golus. As a voluntary condition, the American exile will provide the
launching pad for imaginary rearticulations of the European *golus* in the
second half of the century in the fictions of such writers as I. B. Singer
and Philip Roth. Notwithstanding all his—and his readers'—emphasis
on the "factuality" of his portraits of the shtetl Jews, Sholem Aleichem
evokes a "home" that is captured entirely in the imagination, embalmed
in accessible forms later mined by other writers in the years of devastation and partial recovery. Burning Kasrilevke near the end of Motl's story
dramatically enacts the effacement of the past that is the fundamental
premise of this forward-looking narrative.[76]

This is not the only fictional narrative of its time in which the Jewish
town is burned as a sign of its moribund, anachronistic state—or of its
future reference as a ruined shrine; Sholem Aleichem's own story, "Ha-
nisrafim shel Kasrilevke" [Kasrilevke in Flames] and Abramovitsh's "Ha-
nisrafim" [Burned Out] partake of the mock-epic paradigm that is
difficult for post-Holocaust readers to approach without, once again,
superimposing the epic dimensions forced by historical hindsight.[77] In
1943, when Maurice Samuel published his whimsical *World of Sholem
Aleichem*, he introduced the book as "a sort of pilgrimage among the
cities and inhabitants of a world which only yesterday—as history goes—
harboured the grandfathers and grandmothers of some millions of American citizens. As a pilgrimage it is an act of piety; on the other hand it is
an exercise in necromancy, or calling up of the dead. . . . For that world
is no more. . . . Fragments of it remain *in situ*; other fragments, still recognizable but slowly losing their shape in the wastage of time, are lodged
in America."[78] Unable to fully anticipate, from his vantage point in the
midst of the war, either the extent of the destruction then occurring or
the acts of pilgrimage to and "necromancy" in the burned cities, towns,
and concentration camps that would follow several decades later, Samuel
nevertheless provided an early model for the forms of return and senti-

mental reappropriation of the shtetl through the writings of Sholem Aleichem and then through fragments of its physical culture.

The figure of the shlemiel in general and Motl in particular presented
a challenge that postwar Israeli culture would resist in subtle ways. In
Palestine in 1945, Hebrew poet Natan Alterman wrote an elegy to the
Jews of Europe in the form of a last letter from Menakhem Mendl to his
wife Sheyne Shendl; moribund himself, Menakhem Mendl uses his last
breath to describe the death of all the inhabitants of Sholem Aleichem's
house of fiction, including Motl.[79] This poetic eulogy acts as a form of
compassionate exclusion, effectively preempting any acts of the imagination that would bring Motl and his fellows closer to the shores of Palestine. For that very reason, perhaps, the nine-year-old child continues to
haunt the recesses of Hebrew memory, reappearing some forty years later
in a radical rewrite of the history of catastrophe, David Grossman's novel
'Ayen 'erekh: ahava [See Under: Love] (1986). Living in Israel in the 1950s
among Holocaust survivors, the child narrator, Momik, begins reading
Sholem Aleichem and eventually finds in Motl a companion and kindred
spirit. What explains Momik's fascination with Motl is the latter's un-
qualified success in rewriting unacceptable scenarios. Momik's revisionist
attempt to glorify obscure figures like "Sonder from the Commando" as
the head of a fighting unit in Europe can be seen as a latter-day version
of "It's grand to be an orphan."

Motl's naïveté and negative capability are his passport into an American future, whereas those very same qualities lead Momik in Israel to a
form of madness: the difference has everything to do with the time and
place of telling and the consequentiality of speech acts. After World War
I, Walter Benjamin proclaimed the loss of the capacity to tell stories: "the
art of storytelling is coming to an end. . . . A generation that had gone
to school on a horse-drawn streetcar now stood under the open sky in a
countryside in which nothing remained unchanged but the clouds, and
beneath these clouds, in a field of force of destructive torrents and ex-
plosions, was the tiny, fragile human body."[80] Whatever remained of the
revising potential of the fictive imagination after World War I barely survived Auschwitz; even Momik's youthful inventions cannot release him
from his parents' untold story. But by engaging in a major act of reinventing the past, Momik reassumes some of the prerogative and burden
of the Diaspora and challenges the limits of narrative as they had developed in Hebrew literature.[81] As we will see below, it is post-Holocaust
writers from Europe such as Dan Pagis and Aharon Appelfeld who introduce new centrifugal forces into Israeli culture.

Celebrating the theatricality of everyday life, the richness and variety of the object world, and the street as the venue of urban experience, Motl is one of the first of a series of Jewish Walkers in the City. As Jews acquire new spaces in their journeys across the globe, the distinctions between the appropriation of object space in Palestine and in America will go through numerous transformations before the century is out. At the same time it was being slowly and then brutally divested of its tenancy in Europe, the Jewish imagination was becoming intoxicated with ownership and realia in two alternative dimensions: as sacred, original space in Zion, signified by the reclaiming of "territory" and acts reifying and realizing the text culture of Exile; and as a fascination with the material world in America, with "real" estate, and with the *thingness* that signifies not original but duplicatable space—and, eventually, with its mechanical reproductions and simulacra.

PART TWO

Jewish Geographies

With the twelfth century as designated point of origin and the twentieth as point of entry, the Jewish journey was represented in the first part of this book as the pursuit of utopian space in its epic and anti-epic dimensions. Six years and six million deaths changed all that. For the survivors of the *Shoah*, the Jewish journey would become a more urgent exercise in the recovery of a lost continent. Acts of recall, fueled by grief, despair, or nostalgia, are the broken echoes at the end of our century of the utopian yearnings at its beginning.

Hovering lightly over the forsaken but indelible landscapes of Bukovina, one of the former enclaves of the German-speaking Jews of Central Europe, are the different homing patterns of her native sons. Paul Celan, Dan Pagis, and Aharon Appelfeld survived the war to become major writers in the elsewheres of the Jewish story. Celan remained a quintessential *galut* Jew, a polyglot citizen of the world yet lost at sea, positing his poetry as a message sent out in a bottle—potentially consequential but hardly hopeful of destination, and eventually carrying his watery death as its ultimate signature. The other two writers washed ashore, in Palestine, into a reterritorialized language urgently carving its epic story on hillsides and coastal plains, on rocks and valleys and ancient caves.

In "Conversation in the Mountain," Celan's rare foray into prose, the poet recapitulates the mythical rhetoric of the wandering Jew: "One evening, when the sun had set and not only the sun, the Jew—Jew and son of a Jew—went off, left his house and went off . . . went under clouds, went in the shadow, his own and not his own—because the Jew, you know, what does he have that is really his own."[1] In taking his language with him into exile as the only thing that was really his own, Celan was performing a profoundly Jewish act.[2] But it was not the only option available to a young survivor of Hitler's scourge in the middle of this century. The wandering Jew, a weary, battered Peter Pan, regains his shadow when he regains his "mortality" and the confines of an obligatory material world; Celan's compatriots struggled with the force—and the claustrophobia—of a collective homecoming, with its allure of sunrise and its burden of shadow.

Indeed, I argue that by relinquishing their native language as well as their native soil and by adopting Hebrew as their literary medium, both Pagis and Appelfeld, in different idioms, blocked access to the conversation that had been so abruptly suspended in the land of their birth.

Celan, however, living in radical isolation in a German idiolect in Paris, over the years increasingly became locked in a self-referential, autonomous universe. Judged by its distance from their common point of departure, the writing of these three men illuminates the evolution of discourse in the postwar world, its poetic, existential, and cultural boundaries. The position each represents within the global conversation among Jewish writers or between Jewish writers and their audiences defines their different roles as authors—and authorizers—of the past. In the following three chapters, I will explore the poetry and prose of Paul Celan and Dan Pagis and the narratives of Aharon Appelfeld as acts of necromancy and levitation in the endless search for the lost conversation and the lost continent.

Appelfeld expresses the nightmare of dislocation and its narrative possibilities more fully than does any other Jewish storyteller. His early writing inhabits that no-man's-land between adopted and native landscapes and languages, between the collective story of repatriation and regeneration and the individual experience of loss and struggle to retrieve a remembering self to narrate the past. Even those of his fictions ostensibly set in postwar Israel in effect follow the contours and recesses, the haunted byways and vast emptinesses, of Central Europe. As the backdrop for the only story Appelfeld could tell, these protean vistas accommodate every postwar scenario. Europe is the inevitable point of origin, the site of whatever warm memories of home can be retrieved through the dark glass of time and loss—and the only place where one can still reenact the condition of the Jew as a traveler in space. The physical world of childhood remains a frozen, unchanging point of reference; to the native son who returns to that world many years later, the potted geraniums, standing in the shops and homes where the Jews once lived, "at exactly the same angle as before, perfectly preserved," witness their owners' absence more eloquently than do the gaps in his own memory.[3]

The survivor who immigrates to Palestine in an Appelfeld narrative does not find a home there—and that is both the underlying source of this writer's power and the quality of his displacement in Hebrew fiction. The epic landscape, thick with matter and with things that matter, forms a palimpsest with the minimalist lines of Appelfeld's prose. There is always a remainder, a surplus of unusable data—or an absence of referent—to remind us of what cannot be redressed within the precincts of the postwar Israeli "redemptive" culture. His characters are never fully (re)patriated in the ancestral homeland and his gaze returns to Europe, not only because it is the ruined fatherland but because it provides space itself. And as a sense of destiny overwhelms any notion of the fortuitousness of Jewish experience, the landscapes of Central Europe become a more authentic and fully realized mise-en-scène. In Appelfeld's later fictions the temporal specificity of history recedes before a mythic replay of fateful patterns, while the spatial backdrop on which that replay is enacted becomes more explicit. In the novella *Layish*, the pathways of an eternal Jewish journey traverse, in motion so slow that it is all but arrested, the identifiable geography of Austro-Hungary, which narrows to the confines of Appelfeld's native Bukovina.

The encounter between Bukovina and Jerusalem in Dan Pagis's poetry creates a series of satirical representations of the Jewish journey— through temporal and spatial detours and interrupted conversations. As scholar of medieval Hebrew poetry and master craftsman of modern Hebrew poetry, Dan Pagis viewed the regenerating Hebrew culture through the quizzical lens of a profound personal dislocation. His stereoscopic vision could also reveal the occluded species of flora, fauna, and humanity native to Palestine but not to the triumphal story of Jewish return; the landscape and language of the Holy Land are represented in his poems as containing their own alienated counterforms. His poems, like Appelfeld's stories, reflect not only the claustrophobia and confinement of the universe of concentration camps or the scorched landscapes of childhood, but also the claustrophobia and the oppressive force of a collective homecoming.

Such forces find their material expression in the commemorative culture, in the performative and ritual spaces designated for public memory with which Pagis's poems are in continuous dialogue. As symbolic burial grounds, the museums and monuments erected in Israel to commemorate the murdered Jews of Europe reflect a communal attempt to grant the wandering souls a proper resting place and to protect the living from their haunting, unmastered presence. They create new, fixed, iconographic references to combat a more dynamic interaction with the past. Between the monumental or ritual strategies that would codify, canonize, and fix memory and the language of poets like Pagis who dynamically engage memory is a paradigmatic tension between what I call the prosaics and poetics of memory. What can be distilled from the more static testimonial and literary as well as architectural sites is an insistence on "truth-telling," on a kind of historical positivism; it stands against the license for a more elastic collaboration between the ancient Aristotelian categories of what is "known" as historical fact and what can still be "imagined" as poetic possibility. When Dan Pagis turns at the end of his life from poetry to prose, he himself moves toward a form of reconciliation with the world of his childhood that is closer to plain truth-telling, to the onetime truth and stasis of experience, than are his oblique, embattled, elusive, and dis(re)membered verses. Like Appelfeld, Pagis only in his later writing uses the place of origin as the canvas for a more explicit and obligatory encounter with the past. I will argue further that the prose, coming so urgently at the end of this poet's life, constitutes the monument that, his task done, allows him finally to die.

The culture in the postwar Jewish world that licenses the most dynamic encounter with the Eastern European past is not in Israel or even Western Europe, but in America—the place that never became either a Jewish graveyard or an echo chamber for Jewish dybbuks. Having once embraced the vast spaces of the American imagination as supplanting the repressive diasporas of Eastern Europe, Jewish writers in late-twentieth-century America have begun to reengage those discarded realms—both offering an elegiac tribute and reflecting a genuine sense of patrimony. With Kafka enshrined as the remote father of the tragic muse, and Sholem Aleichem as the proximate father of the comic, writers as disparate as Isaac Bashevis Singer and Philip Roth have constructed a self-consciously artificial, literary surrogate for the ruins of Eastern Europe in post-Holocaust America. Their fictions of Jewish counterlives are the focus of my final chapters. Through an act of enchantment, the flora in Bashevis Singer's "Polish" stories, unlike the geraniums in Appelfeld's, are freed from the petrifying element of hindsight. A mischievous anachronism in Bashevis Singer's narratives challenges the boundary between defunct and imagined worlds, making more room for fiction than can be found in the work of any of his compatriots.

When Philip Roth's zany doppelgänger in *Operation Shylock* launches a scheme to "repatriate" the Israeli Ashkenazi Jews to their European lands of origin, he is both appropriating and caricaturing the pattern by which the devastated homeland becomes a shrine, a place of pilgrimage and of deferred return. In this audacious novel, Roth reinvokes the diasporic imagination as free from the "constraints" of Jewish reality (i.e., Israel).

With the extermination of Jewish life in Europe and the constitution of Jewish sovereignty in Israel, the relationship between negotiable and original places, between the map of Israel's wandering, its object of desire, and its burial sites, shifted radically. Over the last fifty years, what was destroyed has become an authentic original that can be *represented* but not recovered. In its poetic and empirical forms, it reminds us of the process of disengagement and separation from the holy sites, and then of substitution, reinvention, and mimesis, that evolved in the centuries following the destruction of ancient Jerusalem. Although the streets of Lodz are not sanctified in collective memory as were the hills of Zion, they become accessible to pilgrimages real and imagined, ritual and literary, as an unredeemable *and indestructible ruin*. Retrospectively, the dismantling of the European exile territorializes those lands as an (already lost) home. Eventually and inevitably, Yiddish, the language in which Bashevis Singer writes, begins to take on the status of a holy tongue: it becomes, in Naomi Seidman's words, "'*loshn koydesh*,' because it is '*lashon ha-kedoshim*,' the language of the holy ones, the martyrs."[4] As the eternal language of *golus*, it also maintains its position as mouthpiece of the itinerant Jewish story.

To dream fictional worlds will remain an act of *recovery* for the survivors, but it will also become an act of defiance of utopian vistas for Israeli writers and a reinvention of diasporic privilege for Jewish writers in America. The following chapters explore the new articulations, playful and defiant as well as mournful and respectful, of the ancient exchange between desire and fulfillment, between eros and death, between homelands lost and gained, between Jewish story and territory.

CHAPTER FIVE

Writing Poetry after Auschwitz

Paul Celan as the Last Barbarian

Paul Antschel, born in 1920 in Czernowitz, Romania, studied medicine and literature in France, returning home on holiday in 1939.

Viewed from our posttraumatic vantage point, that was the final act in a "normal" biography; from here on it becomes a life interpreted through the cataclysms of modern Jewish history. Czernowitz was occupied by Russian troops in 1940 and by the Nazis in 1941. Antschel's parents were deported in 1942 to an internment camp in Transnistria where they both died; he himself spent many grueling months in Romanian labor camps, but managed to survive and to return to Czernowitz before the end of the war.

Paul Antschel emerged in his postwar guise as Paul Celan to become the last of the great German Jewish poets.[1] German was his mother tongue: but more important, it was his *mother's* tongue. In the circumstances in which his poetic identity was forged, rewriting the language became a lifelong act of retrieval of what was at once the most precious and the most tainted of the lost voices of his childhood; the death by shooting of his mother, reported to him in 1943, became the most haunting echo in his poetry. And because Celan remained in exile in France—neither reclaiming, as did Primo Levi, his native land along with its language, nor participating, as did his compatriots Dan Pagis and Aharon Appelfeld, in the collective "repatriation" of the Jews in Palestine—his Czernowitz would recede more and more into the watery depths of a lost Atlantis, from which fragments persistently surface and wash up on the heart's shore.

After a few years in Bucharest and then in Vienna, the poet settled in
Paris, where he continued to live as writer, translator, and professor of
German literature until his death by suicide in 1970. In 1944 or early
1945, possibly while still in Czernowitz or in Bucharest, Celan wrote
"Todesfuge" [Deathfugue], the poem that was to establish his reputation and remain at the center of the debate over the nature and status of
writing in extremis that continues to this day.

> Schwarze Milch der Frühe wir trinken sie abends
> wir trinken sie mittags und morgens wir trinken sie nachts
> wir trinken und trinken
> wir schaufeln ein Grab in den Lüften da liegt man nicht eng . . .
>
> Black milk of daybreak we drink it at evening
> we drink it at midday and morning we drink it at night
> we drink and we drink
> we shovel a grave in the air there you won't lie too cramped . . . [2]

Both Celan's person and his poem have taken on the status of artifacts in
Germany, where, as poetic shards of a former universe, they constitute an
endless reprimand. In tracing the itinerary of that poem, we may find the
most compelling evidence both of dismantled Jewish geographies and
aborted Jewish journeys, and of the persistence of a diasporic poetics.

SYMBOLIC GEOGRAPHIES

Celan's language and the solitude of his journey have generated some of
critics' most powerful and contradictory statements on the authenticity
of poetic language, its mimetic function, and its effects on Western imagination. The controversy traces back to Theodor Adorno's dictum that
"to write poetry after Auschwitz is barbaric."[3] While generally invoked
in discussions of writers or texts that seem to violate implicit aesthetic
or moral norms, Adorno's statement, said to have been occasioned by a
reading of "Todesfuge," has become explicitly linked with it; the public
has thus seen the poem as the ultimate postwar challenge to the exercise
of the artistic imagination.

Since Adorno's death, his dictum has been appropriated without reflection or context by the very culture industry he so vigorously attacked in
his lifetime. But precisely because both his statement and Celan's poem
have been so fixed in discussions of the limits of language and of the imagination, they are candidates for a new diasporic discourse based on a kind
of phantom geography. Adorno himself "returned" to Auschwitz again
and again, refining and restating and qualifying his original statement in

subsequent essays, probing but never quite resolving the paradox at the heart of his argument that "the abundance of real suffering tolerates no forgetting . . . [:] this suffering . . . demands the continued existence of art [even as] . . . it prohibits it. *It is now virtually in art alone that suffering can still find its own voice, consolation, without immediately being betrayed by it.* The most important artists of the age have realized this" (emphasis mine).[4] But even if Adorno distanced himself from the categorical judgment implied by his initial statement, the image he generated— that the poem enacted vis-à-vis Auschwitz dangles in some barbaric space—has become part of a landscape littered with such icons. Within the terms both of Adorno's critical theory and of a theory of diasporic burdens and privileges, I will tease out the implications of such an image by drawing a distinction between "barbarity," as that which is by definition *outside* "civilized" discourse, and "liminality," as that which is not. The liminal spaces to which seekers go briefly before rejoining the community is the boundary of tolerated deviation; the barbarians at the gates are cast forever into the wasteland beyond the communal bounds. The stranger's babblings whose sound was for the ancient Greeks the paradigm of the speechless other, or the Wandering Jew's mutterings indecipherable to Western ears, become the poet's post-Auschwitz speech and an ongoing reproach to silence.[5]

When examined more closely, the critical norms that have their origins in (mis)readings of Adorno betray a widespread if unarticulated sense of the *propriety* of a symbolic geography that incorporates Auschwitz. Since the scorched earth that is the locus of this language cannot generate a natural audience for it, the issue of naturalization becomes crucial. Where, in this symbolic geography, do we locate Auschwitz—or, for that matter, the Warsaw Ghetto: in Poland? in Nazi-occupied Europe? in the vast resonant spaces of Jewish memory? as the metonymic limit of Western civilization? in some barbaric space outside? The disruption between this place and its signs is greater than the common disjunctions between referents and their signifiers—and the ongoing controversy over nominative and metaphoric language settles in that great divide. Is Celan's "Grab in den Lüften" an open space with no boundaries? "In der Luft, da bleibt deine Wurzel, da, / in der Luft" (In the air, there your root remains, there, / in the air), he writes in a poem composed nearly twenty years after "Todesfuge."[6] How far can such tendrils reach? Do certain images belong to specific symbolic worlds from which they are detached at considerable peril to both writer and reader? Are there Holocaust symbols or topoi so *over*determined that they cannot enter other existential

universes without being either disruptive or presumptuous—violating
an unspoken principle of incommensurability? Or is that which takes
"Auschwitz" as its sign in fact so *under*determined, in Jean-François Lyotard's terms so "dissipated" by the premise of extermination, that it disappears into a kind of phraseless space?[7]

Such questions highlight the artifactual status of certain metaphors
that come to mediate the past in the absence of their material references.
Like the survivors themselves, displaced poetic languages appear to move
randomly from one cultural realm to another, seeking a home. They are
the most radical expression of the footloose condition of the diasporic
Jew. But something fundamental has changed those cultural constructs
beyond recognition. We can perceive the dimensions of the change if we
consider that even the critical discourse has become suffused with geographical metaphors that are meant to somehow compensate for, but are
in fact the most important signifiers of, the loss of a material Jewish geography. Unconventional Holocaust texts are indicted for having transgressed some unspoken "limit." Clearly, in adopting a similar strategy
with regard to the poetry of Celan, in spatializing the critical vocabulary, I am deliberately (and sorrowfully) colluding in the preservation of
the physical geography of the prewar European Jew as the postwar Jew's
metaphorical geography—hoping thereby to call attention to the tragic
ironies of the post-Holocaust Jew as *luftmensch*, as the one who, having
long ago lost the ancestral home and sacred center, now experiences the
loss of its simulacrum, the diasporic fatherland. The effects of that loss
on the poetic imagination are far-reaching.

Even—or especially—in the wake of catastrophe, a "redemptive aesthetic" often emerges in the affected communities alongside public acts
of commemoration to create regenerative spaces. Referring to the idealizing function of art, Leo Bersani describes "a crucial assumption in the
culture of redemption": "a certain type of repetition of experience in art
repairs inherently damaged or valueless experience. . . . The catastrophes
of history matter much less if they are somehow compensated for in art,
and art itself gets reduced to a kind of superior patching function, is en-
slaved to those very materials to which it presumably imparts value; the
redemptive aesthetic asks us to consider art as a correction of life."[8]

Israel and Germany have each created regenerative and redemptive
spaces to overcome the trauma of the recent past. Celan's presence is subversive in both those realms in that it represents another paradigm altogether and another form of consolation, with its antecedents in the Hebrew Bible. The Jewish poetics of catastrophe and exile begins in the Book

of Lamentations with a radical premise regarding the power of metaphor. "To what shall I compare thee . . . *that I may comfort thee?*" asks the poet-prophet facing Jerusalem in her ruin (Lam. 2:13). This question not only seeks consolation through commiseration, offering the felicitous metaphor as the vessel of a most profound consolation, but actually launches the culture of an exiled people. Such tropes are the poetic expressions of a diasporic sensibility whose response to catastrophe is to build mimetic sites out of the ruins of original space. But after the Holocaust, it is very difficult to maintain the constitutive power of metaphor. Because human flesh has been metamorphosed into smoke, the temptation of the post-Holocaust imagination is to reground and literalize that which had become abstracted out of existence. Celan is one of those who, having struggled with that temptation, maintains the supreme value of metaphor over metamorphosis. His images can be seen in themselves as a plea for the poetic, mimetic imagination; the mandate to speak overcomes the petrified stance of the dumbstruck, and speech creates the mobility that makes memory and mimesis possible.

I am arguing that despite attempts in both Germany and Israel to domesticate or to limit the polysemous potential of certain symbolic vocabularies, some of the most decontextualized images remain disruptive in the ways that Jews have always been in their host cultures: ungrounded and migrant, they disrupt without either constituting alternative worlds or being absorbed into the regenerating culture. The attempts to appropriate the dislocated languages of exiles like Celan never quite succeed in domesticating the fragments of their broken worlds or in defending against the acidity of their irredeemably barbaric vision—a vision that not only resists corrective idealizing but also, through a series of defamiliarizing procedures, positively exemplifies as irretrievable and irreparable what has been lost. Celan's poetry constitutes a counteraesthetics of loss and catastrophe—and of consolation through verbal commensuration.

THE POEM AS ARTIFACT

The "black milk" that opens "Todesfuge" and provides its incantatory refrain is one of the most striking examples of a "displaced," defamiliarized, or "estranged" image in post-Holocaust poetry. As the trope of ultimate contradiction, this oxymoron seems to cancel itself and relinquish the compensatory function of both mimetic and metaphoric language. But because it is logically but not rhetorically impossible, because black is the color that incorporates while annihilating all color, the image reveals the power of metaphor to represent the most improbable reality. What proves to be so disruptive in such imagery is not its aesthetic properties or possibilities but its defiance of a redemptive aesthetic.

If we agree there is nothing redemptive in this or any of Celan's images, then how curious it must seem that "schwarze Milch" has become as much an icon of the Holocaust for Germans as is the photograph of the little boy with his hands raised in the Warsaw Ghetto for Israelis.[9] During Celan's lifetime the poem became a fixed item in the secondary school curriculum. It was recited in the West German Bundestag in 1988 to commemorate the fiftieth anniversary of Kristallnacht. The phrase has been frequently quoted in film, in art, in dance, in music—suggesting that it has actually become central to the official ritual of remembrance in Germany. The black milk and the ghetto child are constitutive texts in the regenerative semantic of their respective cultures.

The contradiction between the poem's defiant imagery and its position as object of public adulation, leaching out its subversive potential, forms the central paradox of this text and of Celan's poetic presence in the land of his people's murderers. The poem, which I am proposing as a kind of litmus test of the public attempt to come to terms with or to "master" the past—the *Vergangenheitsbewältigung*—remains subtly both central and extraneous to the cultural conversations taking place in Germany. In one of the most curious symptoms of its status, the "black milk," having achieved such a central place in German postwar discourse, nevertheless drew charges of plagiarism.[10] There is, I believe, an implicit connection between the disruptive potential of the text and both its legitimating function and its own provisional legitimacy within German society.

We have already noted that Adorno is invoked in those debates in which certain Holocaust texts are indicted for having transgressed some unspoken limit. The loss of Jewish geography in Eastern Europe has impelled both writers and readers to invent a metaphoric geography while interrogating metaphor itself as both a surrogate and instrument of consolation. At the same time, the material reference tends to shift from *place* to *person*: in the absence of Jewish places, survivors like Celan are seen as authenticating presences in the culture, carrying their authority within their own persons. The weight of the written historical record, of recorded facts and claims of propriety, decorum, protocol, and rules of evidence that would be admissible in some hypothetical court of law, often turn even the most abstract poetry into testimony—a reflection of the attempt to make even the most recalcitrant lexical fragments into some sort of "sentence." Rather than simply dismissing as irrelevant the accusations of plagiarism that were directed at "Todesfuge," critics like John Felstiner reinforce the artifactual, *ontological* status of the poem by suggesting that "'black milk' may have been no metaphor at all but the very term camp inmates used to describe a liquid they were given"—citing Celan's own declaration that "what counts for me is truth, not euphony."[11] On this account, Celan appears to be working to literalize the language, thereby undermining the power and privilege of metaphor.

By insisting on the veracity of the image or of the poem as a whole, Celan thus does more than take a defensive posture vis-à-vis perceived misreadings of his work, just as by showing interest in Celan's responses to them critics are concerned with more than questions of intentionality. It is the survivor's unmediated access to experience, *the survivor as ultimate reference* in light of the nearly total effacement of the material universe of his youth, that is being affirmed in the struggle over the text's cultural status; far more is at stake than the "correct interpretation" of the poem. Celan's authenticating role as survivor and his poem's authenticating role as testament are threatened *on their own terms* by public charges of plagiarism. It is hardly surprising, given what is at issue in this ongoing debate, to discover that as recently as 1988 (that is, forty-four years after its composition), a *New York Times* article described "Todesfuge" as having been composed in a concentration camp.[12] Such an error actually *elevates* the poem to the status of a "document" from the camps; locating its origin in the "black hole" of Auschwitz maintains Celan and his subject, the poet and his language, as authentic originals, separate from and incommensurable with every known place and mode of expression.[13]

Here, then, is one possible answer to the charge of plagiarism. Those texts, no matter how highly crafted, which appear to be *found* claim a valence that is essentially historical and documentary; like the survivors, they provide or constitute in themselves the citation or quotation that establishes authenticity. Salient and indigestible, separate and lonely, they remain appropriated by but never fully naturalized into the conversation of the cultures in which they appear. There is an implicit assumption here that accords the "reified text" an existence somehow beyond the artistic or aesthetic domain, yet not fully outside it—linked to some experience that, through art, can reproduce itself as document.

At some subliminal level, the generations growing up in postwar West Germany came to *know* the poem "Todesfuge" the way a people knows its anthems and its liturgies, learning the words at such an early age and during such solemn ceremonies that they become part of an incantation rather than an attended text. The "performative" function of "Todesfuge"—what it does as distinguished from what it signifies—reflects the specific nature of the dialogue between this exiled writer and the culture(s) he is addressing. It relates in large part to the differential status that a poem assumes within different interpretive communities and within the consensual spaces of ritual performance.

READING CELAN

Celan's encoded, private, opaque poetry has given rise to competing schools of criticism, which roughly divide into two: that which reads it as a buried text that can be deciphered and materialized by a laborious unearthing of every shard of biographical, empirical, and intertextual material; and that for which the obscurity of the writing is a barrier to be confronted—and respected—within the confines of the poem itself, understood as a texture woven of patterns of internal references and metaphoric ambiguities. Although these competing strategies are hardly unique in twentieth-century criticism, they do provide us with a kind of hermeneutic equivalent of the relation between sacred and diasporic space: they reflect presumptions not unlike the differential access of initiated or uninitiated persons to sacred space, defining levels of intimacy through degrees of devotion, attention, and proximity.[14] "Engführung" [Stretto] provides a paradigmatic example:

> *
> Verbracht ins
> Gelände
> mit der untrüglichen Spur:
>
> Gras, auseinandergeschrieben. Die Steine, weiß
> mit den Schatten der Halme . . .
> *
> Taken off to the
> terrain
> with the unerring track:
>
> Grass, written asunder. The stones, white,
> with shadows of the blades . . . [15]

The terrain, the track, the grass written asunder alternately invite and repel interpretive presumption. The poet who clung to his German, living and writing in the severed connections between language, primary audience, and ground of reference, spending a lifetime seeking his readers, seems to be desperately in need of acts of readerly collaboration: "A poem, being an instance of language, hence essentially dialogue," he said in one of his few public appearances, "may be a letter in a bottle thrown out to sea with the—surely not always strong—hope that it may somehow wash up somewhere, perhaps on a shoreline of the heart."[16] That is, perhaps, what makes his biography such a commanding element for most interpreters of his poetry. Like other survivor-writers whose native ground has been utterly obliterated not through the normal erosion of time but through expulsion and cataclysm, Paul Celan writes poetry that seems to tolerate or even demand more critical intervention through elaborate detective work than that of the writer whose home is remote, denied, outgrown, but still extant. The reader who takes the trouble to reconstitute Celan's world would, as an act of mercy, give back to the poetry both the materiality and the closure that it has lost.[17] But ultimately, if this reading attempts to return to the poet what was lost to him, it must be the *poem*, that desperate and life-giving surrogate, that is ceded.

An alternative hermeneutic strategy conspires with the poet in maintaining the obscurity of the referential world, in relinquishing, even in the act of reading, what was destroyed. By this logic, the poet's native ground has indeed become a grave; only set loose, ungrounded in its poetic representations—only as a "grave in the air"—can it become truly portable, hovering over the earth, freeing (or *compelling*) the survivor to become a wanderer. This is the reading of Celan that is most consistent with a diasporic poetics and, I believe, with a respectful acknowledgment of loss. One of Celan's earliest poems, probably composed during the war, was first called "Chanson Juive" and then retitled "An den Wassern Babels" [By the Waters of Babylon]:[18]

Wieder an dunkelnden Teichen
murmelst du, Weide, gram.
Weh oder wundersam
keinem zu gleichen?

Again at darkening pools
You murmur, willow, grieving.
Wounded or wondrous
Equal to none?

Beginning with "Wieder," *again*, and concluding with commensurability (the possibility of metaphor) as an open question, this verse constitutes a desperate acceptance of the inexorable Jewish burden and representation of exile—its waters, its willows, its wounds.

If Celan's self-selected decoders—those who insist on entering his poems as an act of piety and with a presumption of access—demand of themselves and each other a particular kind of "attention," it is the extension of that attitude—the automatic or even numbed response to an overexposed text or religious site—that makes the poem transparent to the larger public and connects it to the invisible spaces of monuments and liturgies: "There is nothing in this world as invisible as a monument," writes Robert Musil; "they are no doubt erected to be seen—indeed, to attract attention. But at the same time they are impregnated with something that repels attention."[19]

THE "BARBARIC" PLACE OF POETRY

The compulsive critical concern with the insularity or incommunicability of Celan's mature verses could be a symptom not only of their inherent obscurity and sanctity but also of their continued restless presence in the culture. The presumed impenetrability of his neologisms and of what has been called the "hermeticism" of his verses may instead be providing a kind of protective armor for texts that are footloose, uncontained.[20] It is in this sense that Celan's poetry becomes truly "barbaric," that the poet himself, as the last Jewish poet in German literature, remains the "barbarian" as foreigner or outlander—the one outside the community of selves, the one who in Germany most embodies an effaced, wandering otherness or nonidentity.[21]

Although Celan himself insisted that he was "'ganz und gar nicht hermetisch,' absolutely not hermetic,"[22] we can find in this accusation and its defense a key to both the autonomy and the corrosive potential of much of his poetry: uncontained because it is *self*-contained, at times it even encloses within itself the conversation that usually takes place between text and reader. In Celan's poem "In Eins," four languages—German, Hebrew, French, and Spanish—populate the first four lines:

> Dreizehnter Feber. Im Herzmund
> erwachtes Schibboleth. Mit dir,
> Peuple
> de Paris. No pasarán.[23]

Jacques Derrida finds in this and related poems a "multiplicity and migration of languages . . . within the uniqueness of the poetic inscription."[24] The languages that crowd such poems provide, in a sense, both the speakers and their audience.[25]

Not only do the languages constitute multiple interlocutors within a Celan poem but also the addressed others render it autonomous as a speech act incorporating its own recipient. What is the status of the "you" (*du*) so often summoned in Celan's verses? While a number of the poems, especially the later ones, appear to be firmly located in the conventional lyrical address to a specific beloved, the less-focused dialogical quest is thwarted in some of those texts in which it is most explicitly invoked. "The poem becomes conversation—often desperate conversation," Celan declares; "only the space of this conversation can establish what is addressed, can gather it into a 'you' around the naming and speaking I."[26] This *ars poetica* can inform a reading not only of his poetry but also of his much-interpreted prose parable "Gespräch im Gebirg" [Conversation in the Mountain]. The journey, which is both a parody and a recuperation of the romantic quest, begins, according to Stéphane Mosès, as a search for a true dialogue. But as the voice in the mountain echoes back upon itself, it becomes a kind of interior dialogue "of a single voice divided," and the search for otherness issues in a nostalgic gesture—an "encounter with an other who has not come."[27] This failed dialogic, this desperate search for the other that turns into a form of endless self-proliferation, seems to mimic the exile's yearning to return to native ground. Resembling at first the Zionist intoxication with a return to the primordial self, to the recovered archaeology and the remembered ecology of Palestine—indeed, incorporating the native "other" as primordial "self"—this search for a place of origin in Celan's poetry nevertheless comes to affirm the diasporic quest. The primordial mountainous landscape is represented as so generic, so nonspecific and elemental, that the writing offers less a recovery of lost vistas than a reversion to the legendary geography of the aimless and endlessly proliferating Jewish journey.

Whatever refuge is still provided by these generic landscapes, whatever romance and comfort still abide in the grandeur of the natural world, is mutilated, in poem after poem, by traces of the most private signpost of the poet's journey: his mother's death in the snows of the Ukraine. Celan writes in 1945:

> Aspen tree, your leaves glance white into the dark.
> My mother's hair never turned white.
> Dandelion, so green is the Ukraine
> My fair-haired mother did not come home.[28]

The death of the mother at a young, fair-haired age both consigns her to the perennially greening world of nature and is mocked by nature's indifference. Her violent death renders the world of nature as defaced as the language she spoke. Like the generic landscapes of collective memory, the utopian landscapes of childhood memory become the backdrop on which the hand of fate writes its own desperate story.

HEBREW MELODIES

For most of Celan's German audience, only one of his languages and landscapes would remain truly inscrutable—the Hebrew words scattered throughout the poems, especially those written in the last years of the poet's life, and the Jewish places they signify. Like the imperceptible mountains and valleys of the Jewish itinerary and the invisible horizons of a Hassidic tale,[29] like the small empty niches on the doorposts of formerly Jewish homes all over Eastern and Central Europe, Celan's Hebrew is a marker not only of the absent (and therefore indecipherable) Jewish culture but also of the absent reader. Recovering its status in his late poems as the language of origins, the primordial language, it remains uncorrupted, untried.[30] Translators and theorists have grappled with the untranslatability of many of the foreign phrases in Celan's verse; unique even within this polyphonic poetry, the Hebrew letters and words from a scriptural or liturgical vocabulary—"Ziv," "Hachnissini," "Kumi ori," "Kaddish," "Ashrei," "Yizkor," "Tekiah"—remain as salient, as resonant, and as unassimilated in his poetry as his poems are in German culture. The Hebrew words persist unexamined, maintaining the status of a document, a relic, a ritual—or an irretrievable memory.

The poet comes to Hebrew as a pilgrim. It is in the totemic images—incantatory fragments of a liturgical, scriptural lexicon—that his "nomad of the word" very tentatively enters redemptive, sacred space:

> The eye, dark:
> as tabernacle window. It gathers,
> what was world, remains world: the migrant
> East, the
> hovering ones, the
> human beings-and-Jews,
> the people of clouds[.]

The journey in the poem is to Vitebsk, Chagall's hometown and the canvas for all the lost hometowns, and then to "Ghetto" and to "Eden," as the eye moves, searches, gathers. Then it

musters the letters and the mortal-
immortal soul of letters,
goes to Aleph and Yod and goes farther,

arriving finally at:

Beth,—that is
the house, where the table stands with
the light and the Light.[31]

The scattered particles that inhabit Celan's grave in the air, like Chagall's visual and verbal vocabulary of floating parts, are momentarily ingathered by the centripetal force of the Hebrew language.[32] But the fragments collected through the "Aleph" and "Yod" ("Eretz Yisrael" . . .), which come together to constitute the "beth" that is *bayit* (the language that "houses"), wash up only briefly on that shoreline. Celan's "aleph" is always closer to the Kabbalists' aleph, to Borges's aleph—"one of the points in space that contains all other points."[33] The letters are *sacred in themselves*; positing the Aleph as the letter that is all letters, as the place that is all places—like Jerusalem, placed by medieval cartographers at the center of every map—takes measure of the land and the language that remain sacred, elusively utopian space for those who do not live within and need not be confined by its geopolitical borders.

In 1969, in what was to be one of his last major ventures before committing suicide, Paul Celan did visit Israel and even addressed the Hebrew Writers' Association. He spoke about the greening of the land and of the language: "Here," he said, "in your outer and inner landscape, I find much of the compulsion toward truth, much of the self-evidence, much of the world-open uniqueness of great poetry."[34]

The world-embracing possibility that emanates from a reclaimed landscape, the self-evidence that allows public surfaces to speak, and the privileging of "truth" over its simulacra are remarkable concessions, by this poet of private depths and unhinged languages, to the idea of repatriation. In that address, in that visit, and in the Hebrew words scattered throughout the poetry of his last years, Celan entered tentatively into a cultural space in which what he referred to as "Jewish loneliness"[35] was seeking, perhaps, a different resolution. But in the end Celan and the Hebrew writers he was addressing remained embedded in two distinct universes of discourse. For Celan, truly, the universe is bounded by discourse itself; the place is instantiated in the poetry. And even when he began to incorporate Hebrew words into his last poems, they were not elements in the lexicon of homecoming, not language with a territorial correlative, just as his German would not prove solid enough to support the weight of an adult return to the haunts of childhood. Paul Celan lived as fully in poetry as did any artist in our century.[36]

U-TOPIA

In defining a survivor's language, Celan may be seen as Primo Levi's foil. Levi struggled to overcome his own "Jewish loneliness" by regrounding himself not only in his native tongue and native soil, but also in the positivism of viewing language as transparent or as correlative to experience. Such language is clear insofar as it can "objectify" experience as a property of culture, rescuing it from the irredeemably unique, from the irremediably effaced and therefore utterly incommunicable. In Levi's view, at least as he stated it toward the end of his life, the urge to communicate, the mandate of lucidity, and the subordination of language to the writer's "message" are betrayed in Celan's more obscure verses: "If [Celan's writing] is a message, it gets lost in the background noise. . . . As long as we live we have a responsibility. We must answer for what we write, word by word, and make sure that every word reaches its target."[37] By these lights, Celan is attempting to integrate life with the inherent *irresponsibility* of a poetry surviving in a world whose symbolic geography has been convulsed, constituting a place "where," as he himself stated, "all tropes and metaphors want to be led *ad absurdum*."[38]

The landscape of Celan's native Bukovina exists wholly in its pastness, in its inaccessibility as the place of origin. It is the point of departure ever sought but retrievable only in the precincts of the imagination; "I am searching for my own place of origin . . . on a child's map," he said in a speech in 1960. "None of these places can be found. They do not exist. But I know where they ought to exist . . . and I find something else . . . something . . . which, via both poles, rejoins itself and on the way serenely crosses even the tropics: I find a meridian." The confessional presentation of the poem as a "sort of homecoming" defines home as a *process*, not a place—a yearning for a "meridian" or "u-topia" that is the "no-place" of the displaced soul. The "poem is lonely. It is lonely and *en route*," Celan added in what became known as the "Meridian" speech.[39] Poetry as a form of homecoming in the absence of the material universe, the very essence of the diasporic act, is here thematized quite explicitly; in other poems, *heimkehr* and *heimatlich* (homecoming; homeland-like) appear as adverbial or verbal constructions struggling, noun-*like*, for substantiation.[40]

Celan's u-topia, the irretrievable point of departure projected onto an endlessly deferred future, authorizes a version of the Jewish past and the Jewish place very different from and in many ways more familiar than the redemptive aesthetics of the Zionist utopia that connects an ancient memory with a real place on the map of the present, that connects origins with destiny and *destination* in a narrative of catastrophe and redemption.

THE LONELINESS OF THE LONG-DISTANCE RUNNER

George Steiner, who has always argued for the Jewish text as homeland and the Jew as housed in many languages, overstates the purgative force in Celan's writing. In *After Babel*, he claims that Celan wrote German as if it were a foreign language: "All of Celan's own poetry is translated *into* German. . . . It becomes a 'meta-German' cleansed of historical—political dirt and thus, alone, usable by a profoundly Jewish voice after the holocaust."[41] I am arguing, as many critics have before me, that the "historical-political dirt" is never fully eradicated, that through their trace elements the poet "intends to make readers aware" of just those absences within his language.[42]

But once again, who *are* these readers? The survivors form an inclusive and safe category of readers across all cultures and languages. Yet, notwithstanding their mediating presence, the exiled German writer has no more "chosen" them than the Hebrew audience he addressed in 1969. While his fellow survivors and friends such as Peter Szondi, who became self-selected readers and explicators of his work (joined by a host of contemporary critics), form a kind of cult of the initiated and constitute a protective, "attentive" buffer around him, the size of Celan's general reading community may correspond inversely to the degree of insularity in his language. In the mountain, the Jew remains a wanderer and a stranger; the conversation in the mountain is a conversation in an echo chamber. Whether we read Celan's last verses as "hermetic" in the sense of self-contained and autonomous, as incorporating text *and* audience— protected by a thick shield from the slings and arrows of outrageous readings—or as a gradual withdrawal into a private, impenetrable, and indecipherable universe, followed logically by death, his suicide becomes the ultimate inscription of the fate of the survivor-writer with a phantom audience.

What one reader has called his "host of invulnerable signs"[43] could thus signify a withdrawal into private space providing a unique form of inviolability. The more personal or idiosyncratic the inscription, the more immune it is to either the debasement of metaphor or its excessive reification in a specific empirical reference. Celan's writing becomes the most radical and insular postwar articulation of a diasporic poetics. Finally, the grave in the air is the locus of a poetry that hovers over the earth, still seeking readers while refusing all forms of containment and closure.

CHAPTER SIX

Reclaiming a Plot in Radautz

Dan Pagis and the Prosaics of Memory

In the voyage of recovery undertaken by every survivor who seeks a safe haven for untainted memories of childhood, Dan Pagis remained, like Paul Celan, an absent mariner. For most of Pagis's career, the world of his childhood in Radautz, near Czernowitz, and the war years in Transnistria remain the missing or nearly effaced texts that haunt his writing. The speakers in his poems are not volitional agents who travel between two points on the compass and two ends of the narrative, between departure and arrival, uprooting and resettlement. Scattered and distracted, they manifest a form of displacement unique in the modern Jewish poetics of exile and return:

> Hidden in the study at dusk,
> I wait, not yet lonely.
> A heavy walnut bureau opens up the night.
> The clock is a tired sentry,
> its steps growing faint.
>
> From where? In Grandfather's typewriter,
> an Underwood from ancient times,
> thousands of alphabets are ready.
> What tidings?
>
> I think that not everything is in doubt.
> I follow the moment, not to let it slip away.
> My arms are rather thin.
> I am nine years old.

> Beyond the door begins
> the interstellar space which I'm ready for.
> Gravity drains from me like colors at dusk.
> I fly so fast that I'm motionless
> and leave behind me
> the transparent wake of the past.[1]

The "transparent wake of the past" is produced by an act of effacement. Stubbornly resisting any narrative sequence, human fragments float like dead stars in "interstellar space." It is not the aborted or incomplete remembrance of things past but a *willed oblivion* that vitiates the restoration, in memory or in art, of native vistas and blocks the construction of any surrogate city of refuge.

A sequential narrative would go something like this: Born in 1930 into a German-speaking Jewish home in Radautz, Dan Pagis had, by the age of four, lost his mother to disease and his father through emigration to Palestine. He was raised by his grandparents until the age of nine when, with his "thin arms," he was forced to navigate the hostile spaces beyond the sanctuary and the promise of the library's unread books and the Underwood's unformed words. He survived the war in Transnistria's labor camps and in 1946 arrived in Palestine, where he was reunited with his father. Over the next four decades, until his death in 1986, Pagis came to be recognized as one of Israel's foremost scholars of medieval Hebrew poetry; his stature as author of some of the most powerful poems in modern Hebrew was, unfortunately, only fully acknowledged posthumously, after his collected works were published.

But the publication of his last writings also reveals a startling shift in direction: as the book of his life was about to be closed, Pagis moved from an amnesiac poetry to a remembering prose. As if mindful of the economy of unharvested words that would remain stranded at his demise, he began to build sentences of the discarded predicates and conjunctions, the continuities and chronologies, the properties and proprieties he had abandoned along the way. What appears at first as a series of prose poems solidifies as a map to the abandoned sites of childhood. This, I submit, is a prosaics of memory, the charter of a return as profound as only long-deferred, repeatedly circumvented homecomings can be.

POINTS OF DEPARTURE

Bukovina, the "point of departure," was pulverized into a cloud of dust in the postwar poetry of its native sons. In poems that began to appear in the early 1960s, Pagis generated a poetic stance that dissolved the frontier between the living and the dead, between presence and absence—the impenetrable boundary that every survivor-writer, from Orpheus to Rilke, struggles to cross: "Ready for parting, as if my back were turned, / I see my dead come toward me, transparent and breathing."[2] The poet appears here in direct, unmediated contact with his departed; his unfettered ego travels freely through space, incorporating the quick and the dead. But he achieves his triumph only by replacing poetic license with an act of cosmic recycling. For every one of Celan's nearly impenetrable metaphoric surrogates, Pagis projects a meta*morph*ic or metonymic remnant of the lost order. What had been human speech now emanates from discrete parts of the body, from prehistoric or posthistoric forms of evolution, and even from inert matter. The language of science fiction serves as a twentieth-century metaphysics.

In the poem "Honi" (1964), an act of ventriloquism refracts and disperses the speaking voice, both obliterating it as human discourse and conserving it as a law of nature; memory is set loose as a *property* of the universe, infusing interplanetary spaces with snippets of speech. Allusions to Scriptures and folklore, to Jewish gestures and geographies, are projected onto clouds and rain in what becomes a cosmic echo chamber:

> When [he] returned and opened his eyes and stood, uninvited,
> by the side of the roads, wrinkled in his old jacket
> he remembered and recognized the night and was not a stranger:
> as always the trespassing clouds rushed by
> and a blind rain went begging and rattled
> a can for charity,
> and a city of passersby turned
> With glass lights as if in another darkness[.][3]

There is no lyrical possibility when the ego has become so diffused and dehumanized. The self-effacement in this poetry is not the partial recovery of memory so common to survivor writing, when the main protagonist is the story itself, struggling—against amnesia, against repression—to be told.[4] Rather, by relinquishing the mimetic project in his poetry, by renouncing the available strategies for structuring experience—the myths or chronologies by which a community remembers, the mnemonics by which individuals remember—Pagis, more radically than any other post-Holocaust poet except Celan, surrenders the privileged status of the survivor. His survival seems to grant him instead the immunity of a "posthumous" voice, its liberation from rather than indebtedness to history and mortality. Like Celan's, Pagis's poetry resists the logic and compensations of narrative presumption, the comfort of *human* time ("time becomes human time to the extent that it is organized after the manner of a narrative," says Paul Ricoeur)[5] in either its personal, autobiographical or its collective, epic form:

> Well then, as the Lord has brought him back, he is still dreaming
> the year is not insistent, he is not late.
> He can yet ascend to the circle that opens above him
> and go back to sleep
> forgotten within the milky way.[6]

In this parody of Psalm 126 and the Talmudic legends of Honi, the Jewish Rip Van Winkle, sleep (*lishon*) replaces Zion (*tsiyon*) as the site of pilgrimage, and the vision of redemption is dismantled and reduced to a set of free-floating component parts. Like the smile of the Cheshire cat, disembodied gestures and mannerisms remain visible on the landscape long after the Jews who owned them have disappeared. In the poetry of Pagis's contemporaries, Honi had become a kind of modernist reinvention of the Wandering Jew. Time travel had largely replaced space travel in the version of the midrash embraced by a generation of poets who came of age with the State of Israel, as Honi's belated awakening was conflated with Odysseus's final homecoming.[7] Pagis's Honi, however, has returned to (outer) space; the centripetal force, the gravitational pull, is neutralized, releasing the Wandering Jew as a traveler not only across the earth and human history but also through the cosmos and intergalactic time.

Pagis's resistance to history as an intelligible narrative and to the logic and physics of repatriation is manifest in what can be read as a counter-epic. His survivors refuse to stay put. If contained, they and their memories could be compartmentalized and domesticated; by scattering their eyes and their voices over the entire plain of nature, the poet leaves no territory safe. Although, like Celan, Pagis has unleashed poetic fragments on a postwar world trying to ground—and bury—memory in ritual sites and practices, he is, unlike his compatriot, a public performer, brazenly juggling the intertexts of communal memory while camouflaging his own. While the reader of Celan's poetry constructs a profile out of the irreducible sounds that never quite enter public speech, the reader of Pagis's poetry tears off the public masks one by one, until the hollow contours of the skull appear where the self might have been.

Individual and collective destiny are supplanted by the impersonal fate of the species. The grammar of every humanly constructed universe comes unraveled, and the laws of evolution or planetary motion replace social systems by co-opting their signs. The familiar terms of Jewish reference, specifically those denoting displacement and exile, are recontextualized in startling images that deprive them of any historical resonance. Inside the skull, the Brain is carrying on a monologue: "Ever since his exile, he reasons: / there must have been a place to rest." In the jungle, an ape, who finds himself evolving into a humanoid, states: "This is it, I'm emigrating. Good-bye."[8] Locating the idea of exile in its anatomical nexus, recasting migration from a shared historical experience to an evolutionary phenomenon, undermines the primary terms of the Jewish code and substitutes Darwinian process for historical progress. On the beach

> the remains of a tank-tread
> are turning into a dinosaur's spine.
> An F-15 takes off, becomes obsolete,
> is gone.[9]

THE POEM AS ARTIFACT

Consider "Written in Pencil in a Sealed Railway Car," Pagis's best-known poem:

> here in this carload
> i am eve
> with abel my son
> if you see my other son
> cain son of man
> tell him that i[10]

On the face of it, this six-line poem emanates from a discrete human voice and historical occasion. It has, in fact, only two circumstantial markers—"sealed boxcar" and "carload" or transport (*karon hatum, mishloah*)—and even these are not unambiguous historical references. They are minimalist lines drawn on a canvas thick with public knowledge. The poet becomes a kind of prosecutor of the complacencies of consensual history. For most of his life, Pagis's Holocaust poems were conspicuously absent from both the school curriculum and the scripts for memorial occasions. It was only in 1995 that this poem achieved canonical status when it was inscribed on a railway car as part of an installation at Yad Vashem. If it has finally become as embalmed in official Israeli memory as Celan's "Todesfuge" is in German memory, the reasons are similar: as a defense against its toxic potential. Death is not *represented* in this truncated poem but *enacted*. "Here in this carload" there is, simply and suddenly, no time left. The shrieking silence that follows the introduction of quoted speech ("tell him that i") is barely contained in the ritual space to which it has been assigned after many years in limbo. There is no reflexivity in the voice that declares itself not as art but as *artifact*; the suspended present tense is not the eternity of figures preserved in the formaldehyde of fiction *sub specie aeternitatis* but interrupted speech, frozen time. Not the Grecian urn but the lava-covered bodies at Pompeii. Lack of closure here is the absolute refusal of art as triumph over mortality.

This is not to deny that "Written in Pencil" is one of the most highly crafted exercises in Hebrew literature. Or that the readers who are the direct recipients and addressees of the (enigmatic yet consequential) message to be relayed are more necessary for the completion of the poetic act than they would be vis-à-vis any text that is merely *overheard*; summoned to perform a speech act, the "you" addressed here in second-person plural ("*tell* him that i"; *tagidu lo she-ani*), grammatically encompassing the potential of both male *and* female witnesses, is absolutely integral to this most nonhermetic of poems. Pagis's poetic universe is a product of infinite self-division; there are no lyrical subjects or objects, no significant internal addressees,[11] no real search for the dialogic moment. In their place is the implied audience as recipient of an urgent message.

The appeal to an extratextual reader presupposes organic intralinguistic acts practiced by a living community. The subtle and changing relations between this poem and the public to which it is addressed illustrate Pagis's provocative presence in Hebrew culture. Although it poses as a "found" text, naming its place of composition, suspended as an interrupted inscription in its lack of closure, "Written in Pencil" does not perform either an authenticating or a delegitimating role in Israeli culture analogous to the "found" or "stolen" texts we have examined in considering Celan in Germany. Rather, this work invokes the transmission of an unspoken but intuited message ("tell him . . . ") as primary communal act. Celan's "Todesfuge" as a "performed poem" finds its counterecho in Pagis's poem-*as*-performance, which retains the full shock of its theatricality—its dynamic, unresolved presence—in the ritual community to which it is addressed. That it remained disruptive, unassimilable, even after being "safely" embedded in commemorative public space reflects the poem's resistance to the sanctities and proprieties of ritualized speech.[12]

To an extent hardly recognized during his lifetime, Pagis subtly forced a moral discourse out of the received vocabulary of martyrdom. In "Writ-

ten in Pencil" as elsewhere in his poetry, the archetypal Jewish sacrificial
victim, Isaac, is replaced by a composite figure—a fraternity of murder,
Cain *and* Abel. The universal moral imperative in these poems is addressed to a covenantal community with its own internal theodicy. In
Israeli civil as well as religious calendars, commemorative rituals protect the unchanging identity of victims and victimizers, facilitate the one-
way movement that holds the dead in their place and the living in theirs,
and confirm a linear and redemptive reading of modern Jewish history.[13]
Cain and Abel pose a challenge to such constructs when they appear as
moral *alternatives*. By intimating a possible exchange of identities between brothers, the poet captures an ongoing moral struggle. In "Brothers," Cain "dreams that he is Abel"; conceivably, his brother is dream-
ing a parallel dream. The poem "Autobiography" begins at the end of
an untellable story: "I died with the first blow."[14] So long as he was pre-
vented from being an acting subject in history, Abel's autobiography
could not be told. As victim, he remained without voice or accountability; but the moment he is recognized as potential subject, he too is eligi-
ble for the mark of Cain.

READING PAGIS

Since the language of social, profane discourse is Hebrew, and since that
young man who arrived on the shores of Palestine was hardly a pilgrim,
there is no area in Pagis's linguistic universe comparable to the sacred
space inhabited by the Hebrew words in Paul Celan's—no unexamined,
opaque, or totemic images. The riddle structure at the heart of much of
Pagis's later poetry presupposes encoded meaning, but it is potentially
accessible and public. Unlike Celan's, Pagis's personal exile is embedded
within the noisy semantic of a collective homecoming. The conversation
is entirely a social one between reader and text within a *community* of
readers. At home in the language and its literary genealogy, Pagis buries
his own displacement deep in the cultural matrix, in the collective resonances of the language of martyrdom. Within the public discourse that
presumes access to hidden sources, the poet camouflages and struggles
for the privacy of memory and the memory of privacy.

Pagis's most faithful readers have responded to the absence of confessional referents in his poetry with a widespread strategy of compensation, manifesting a kind of natural privilege that corresponds to the
rites of reading performed by Paul Celan's initiated or most "attentive"
decoders. There have been attempts, based on the consensual history of

that time and place, to reveal the repressed texts, to fill in the empty spaces, to attach specific autobiographical significance to elliptical or oblique references in the poems.[15] But critics have more often invoked, periphrastically, that remote place whose unmentioned status qualifies it as the (as-yet-undeciphered) source of a singular semiotic code; it is "another planet," a "genizah," the "world that was consumed," "that which haunts the poet."[16] Pagis's poems, according to one reader, are as lucid as crystals, but "beneath the transparent façade of the crystal there lurks an opaque riddle"—the riddle of the survivor.[17] They are thus understood as the traces or footprints of an inaccessible reality. But the unnamed reality behind the riddle, the opaque side of the crystal, is not unname*able* or unsay*able*; because the events have been officially incorporated into a teleological construct based on dialectical moves, they *must* have a name.

I submit that the imperfect correspondence between the *un*named and the name*able* leaves a small but significant space that contains Pagis's poetic struggle. The dramatic attribution of names to the hitherto unnamed will take place only in prose and only at the end of his life. Eve, universal mother, will yield to Yuli, the particular and irreplaceable mother; Abel, universal victim, will become "Dan," enabling the rebirth of the self.

A PHOTOGRAPHIC MEMORY

With the posthumous publication of Pagis's complete works, including previously unpublished material, it became possible to trace definite patterns in what had seemed unconnected episodes in his poetic career. We can now conclude that toward the end of his life he was moving rather steadily through a series of prose forms that signaled new possibilities for engaging the past, as the "public" struggles were giving way to a reconstruction of the private domain that had been shattered in early childhood.

The poetry of four decades attests to a process whereby the private domain, the "point of departure," had been all but erased. Rather than any coherent *picture* of reality, there remained the "thingness" or discrete "factuality" of reality, punctuating the poems like fallout from an extinguished star. Other Hebrew poets of European extraction, such as Avot Yeshurun, constructed a material world out of the *shmattes* of their former lives and the "found objects" of present-day Israel; their eclecticism is the political aesthetics of contemporary Israeli postmodernism.[18] For Pagis, the kind of animism that invests each object with vitality also precludes any larger system of meaning or rhetoric of representation, and thus his writing is marginal to both the modernist and the postmodernist projects.[19] The prose poem "Art of Contraction" [Omanut ha-tsimtsum] traces—over a lifetime, as it were—a perverse Platonic aesthetics of one who was "given" an entire meadow; out of a need for some order, he chose to limit his vision to a small plot of grass, then to but three blades of grass, and at last down to not one blade but a drawing of it. "Finally, after he hangs it on the wall, he understands: this painted blade of grass which implies the entire meadow, also denies the entire meadow."[20] But a new relation between the object world and its representation will, eventually, restore the meadow as ground zero of the poetic imagination. A rereading of the prose poem "Souvenir," which first appeared in Hebrew in 1982 as part of the last book of poetry published during Pagis's lifetime, suggests that memory was not only prodded by a relic of the past but was also reincorporated into it—even, in a sense, *replaced* by it.

> The town where I was born, Radautz, in the county of Bukovina, threw me out when I was ten. On that day she forgot me, as if I had died, and I forgot her too. We were both satisfied with that.
>
> Forty years later, all at once, she sent me a souvenir. Like an unpleasant aunt whom you're supposed to love just because she is a blood relative. It was a new photograph, her latest winter portrait. A canopied wagon is waiting in the courtyard. The horse, turning its head, gazes affectionately at an elderly man who is busy closing some kind of gate. Ah, it's a funeral. There are just two members left in the Burial Society: the gravedigger and the horse.
>
> But it's a splendid funeral; all around, in the strong wind, thousands of snowflakes are crowding, each one a crystal star with its own particular design. So there is still the same impulse to be special, still the same illusions. Since all snow-stars have just one pattern: six points, a Star of David in fact. In a minute they will all start melting and turn into a mass of plain snow. In their midst my elderly town has prepared a grave for me too.[21]

The belated reemergence, in the form of a photograph, of the material presence of the past registers a claim not unlike that felt by Italian artists in the sixteenth century when the ancient Greek statue of the Laocoön was discovered—or that felt by Jewish archaeologists and architects of national renewal in the twentieth when the Dead Sea Scrolls were found. Relics are both the metonymies and the authenticating evidence of our foothold in buried worlds—especially when, as in the case of the Laocoön, a person *chances* on them while planting a vineyard or plowing a field (or meadow). Legend has it that the unearthing of this sculpture and other ancient members of Rome's "silent population" took place in the presence of Michelangelo and other artists of the Italian Renaissance, reinforcing their sense of continuity with the material past of their city.[22] In the text before us, the physical place evoked by the photograph of Radautz becomes the repository of memories that, for so many years, had nowhere to land. But the memento takes on the aspect of a memento *mori*; the place of origin, the town that "threw him out" when he was ten, becomes the matrix for the poet's final return, the only possible grave for a life that has been haunted by—as the poetry has been enabled by—weightlessness.

In Nabokov's *Speak, Memory*, as in other autobiographies of exiles in the twentieth century, including those of many Holocaust survivors, photographs place the self in the primary context of family and native landscape, reconstructing and rescuing the past.[23] "Souvenir," however, is a verbal rendering of a visual image or artifact that contains a generic memory of the *place without the self*: a hollow place to which this survivor can return only by surrendering—at last—his mortality. The contrast becomes even more striking if one juxtaposes Pagis's image of the empty grave with the opening paragraph in Nabokov's autobiography, which invokes the photograph of a cradle awaiting the birth of the subject and his consciousness. Against the terror of the empty cradle that prefigures the coffin, Nabokov insinuates himself boldly into the foretime and the aftertime, searching for sparks of consciousness, the "faintest glimmers in the impersonal darkness on both sides of my life."[24] Well cradled in the world, even after he leaves it, Nabokov will never experience the total deracination suffered by the Jew from Bukovina under the sign of the swastika. "Life [and, one could add, imagination] begins well," writes Gaston Bachelard; "it begins enclosed, protected, all warm in the bosom of the house."[25]

In "Souvenir," the "bosom of the house" extends, with the help of genderized nouns in Hebrew, to the city itself; expelling its native son like a cruel aunt or unrequited lover, it becomes utterly inaccessible to him. The death warrant issued in 1939 against him and all his kin prevents a postwar return to the sites of childhood through memory's restorative vision and renders the poet's personal survival a kind of computational error ("I was a mistake, . . . forgotten in the sealed boxcar," is a phrase that recurs in poem after poem like a litany).[26] Having lived vis-à-vis his past "as if [he] had died," that is, having yielded his life unto the fictive, having died *into fiction*, he can now—once the encounter between town and self has been reestablished in the present—die for real or *into* reality. Once all the other deaths have been folded within the all-inclusive embrace of the poetic masque, the death of the *speaker* will designate the death of poetic speech itself. In the late writing of Dan Pagis we can explore a tentative but suggestive shift from the fictive to the "real," from the poetic mask to the autobiographical persona, from poetry to prose.

FOOTPRINTS

In a 1983 interview, Pagis referred to his earlier poem "'Akevot" [Footprints] as the first "crack in the wall of forgetfulness."[27] He suggested that "Footprints," like many of the poems in the volume *Gilgul* (1970), had been precipitated by an encounter with a physical emblem of his childhood; visiting distant relatives in New York, he entered a room in their apartment that struck him as a replica of the house in Bukovina in which he had been raised. A museumlike reconstruction of that lost world, this room becomes for the poet a "lieu de mémoire," in Pierre Nora's felicitous phrase, illustrating how "memory takes root in the concrete, in spaces, gestures, images, and objects."[28] In the poems written subsequently, that room (or its prototype in Bukovina) is refracted into its component parts, which, as we have seen, float about untouched by any gravitational force—with only a taut line of verse holding the particles in suspended sequence. The ancient chime clock, the Underwood typewriter, and the walnut bureau are destabilized sites of memory that must always give way to "the interstellar space" just beyond the door to the library.

It was the production of memories without conjunctions, without the privilege of the metaphoric imagination, without even the unities presumed in synecdochic procedures that fueled Pagis's poetry. Though the long poem "Footprints" comes closer than any of his other poems to a sustained memory, it too remained a narrative manqué, marking the incomplete synapses until some more compelling relic of the past could surface to force a reemplotment. Disembodied voices jostle each other in the heavenly spheres and their stories become a patchwork of interrupted conversations, uncompleted journeys. In the end the primary speaker, who "against my will . . . / was continued by this cloud," returns to the earthly stratosphere and hovers above his former home somewhere on "this ball of the earth, / scarred, covered with footprints."[29]

Footprints, like the mother's speech in "Written in Pencil," are the negative, empty traces of lives snuffed out in midmotion:

Maybe there's a window here—if you don't mind,
look near that body, maybe you can open up

a bit. That reminds me
(pardon me) of the joke about the two Jews
in the train, they were traveling to

Say something more; talk.
Can I pass from my body and onwards—

This is the view from the end of the line. Like the train itself, the truncated joke, an autobiographical sign of the father's sense of humor, is also a metonymic vehicle for Jewish storytelling. As locus classicus of the Jewish joke, the train becomes, after the war, a terrifyingly familiar juncture for frames of reference that cancel each other out; jokes and tales begun in the railroad stories of Sholem Aleichem and S. Y. Abramovitsh will echo faintly on ghost trains that trail "long convoys of smoke . . . from heaven to the heaven of heavens to the heaven of night."[30]

The physical properties that prodded memory in the poems in *Gilgul* begin to coalesce in the prose poems that appear twelve years later. In the 1983 interview (the interview itself is a sign of a new degree of self-regard), Pagis dwells on the autobiographical reference embedded in "Souvenir." Having heard that there was a photographic exhibition titled *The Last Jews of Radautz* at the Diaspora Museum in Tel Aviv, the poet asserts that he went out of his way to avoid seeing it: "I, of course, did not want to know anything about Radautz, my hometown, and I denied it [the reflexive term *hitkahashti* can connote self-denial or a kind of reciprocal denial], as if I were continuing to forget the place that had forgotten me."[31]

Yet one photograph seems to have pursued him with the force of destiny—the town in effect seeking out its native son insistently. On two other occasions, he tells the interviewer, and in entirely unrelated contexts, he found himself in front of that picture of Radautz. These would-be and actual encounters precipitated a crisis in what he defines as his "relation to place and time, to reality, to 'realia' that can be given a name, to palpable things in an actual situation." His "mythical," "distanced," highly "stylized" writing began to give way to an attempt to "take a stand" in the world through an exploration of the "biographical, the real product of place and time." He sees the change as transferring the weight of the creative from "form" to "content," and the result is a "linguistic liberation from certain stylized forms," from the "poetics of the 'well made poem' [in English in the original]" to a more open-ended attempt to enter real time. "The strong sense that history (my own, personal, collective) haunts me has only surfaced in my most recent writing." What

he describes as a liberation from closed forms prompts the writing to become "biographical, real, of time and place."[32]

The photograph from Radautz elicits an acknowledgment of the
presence—or insistence—of *the real* no less dramatic than Roland Barthes's
recognition of photography as the place in which "I can never deny that
the thing has been there."[33] Barthes and Susan Sontag affirm the authenticity and ontology of the photograph not only as a mimesis of the
experienced world, like writing or painting, but as an artifactual trace
of it: "A photograph is not only an image (as a painting is an image), an
interpretation of the real; it is also . . . something directly stenciled off
the real, like a footprint or a death mask."[34] Disallowing the alienation
of the thing from its representation, photography is presented here as the
medium to which "the referent adheres."[35]

Barthes's extraordinary meditation on photography, *Camera Lucida*,
was triggered by the death of his mother and the discovery of a picture
of her as a child (the "Winter Garden Photograph"), which provided a
reference for his own life that was fast unraveling. It has been argued
that *Camera Lucida* is the most referential and conventionally autobiographical of Barthes's writings, coming at the end of his life and reclaiming something approximating an essential self.[36] Perhaps for Pagis,
as for Barthes, a single photograph touched off an autobiographical quest
and a return to a kind of mimetic imperative at the end of a creative life
spent circumventing it. In any event, in "Souvenir" and other prose passages, an encounter with a physical trace of the past seems to relieve the
written word of its artifactual status.

Pagis seems in the short prose texts to begin to fit the pieces into a
more conventional tale told by a remembering self. First comes gravity.[37]
Next come the words: words "out of line," no longer contained in sparse,
unyielding poetic strophes;[38] words from that silenced Underwood;
words that behave like hungry locusts, covering the books, the face, the
mouth of one who used to choose among them so sparingly;[39] words
that reduce poetic ambiguity to simple equations: "since all snow-stars
have just one pattern: six points, *a Star of David in fact*."

The almost total absence of confessional referents in Pagis's poetry
finds compensation in the prose through a wry counterstrategy of inti-
mation, leading the reader to believe that the mystery in the poetry was
in fact an encoded message searching for a prosaic resolution:

> You ask me how I write. I'll tell you, but let this be confidential. I take a ripe
> onion, squeeze it, dip the pen into the juice, and write. It makes excellent in-
> visible ink: the onion juice is colorless (like the tears the onion causes), and

after it dries it doesn't leave any mark. The page again appears as pure as it was. Only if it's brought close to the fire *and ignited* will the writing be revealed, at first hesitantly, a letter here, a letter there, and finally, as it should be, each and every sentence. There's just one problem. No one knows the secret power of the fire, and who would suspect that the pure page has anything written on it?[40]

References to the "pure page," appearing in earlier poems as the "empty" page ("forty years now have gone by. / Still leaning above that empty page, / I do not have the strength / to close the book")[41] quite literally invite a decoding in this late prose poem, titled "For a Literary Survey." The empty page represented as an invisible text—like the empty space created by the footprint, or the empty grave in the photograph—now appears as a trace of places or lives abandoned. As a repressed memory, this invisible map to a specific site, a map that awaits deciphering, replaces the metamorphic imagination as a means of referring to the lost world.

"ABBA"

Pagis's most sustained autobiographical statement, a prose sequence posthumously titled "Abba" [Father], is a dramatic departure from the taut, enigmatic poetic line that had become the hallmark of his writing. Left unfinished at the poet's death,[42] "Abba" is in a way the text made visible, the blank page whose writing has materialized through the secret of the fire—even as it is nearly lost to the annihilating power of the fire. The manuscript, discovered in Pagis's estate, appeared on first reading to be a series of discrete prose poems, a number of which were published in the posthumous collection *Shirim ahronim*; further exploration revealed them to be sections of a larger prose composition. "Abba" features much of what had previously been omitted or denied in the poetry; but more important than the missing "information" it supplies is the striking shift in subject matter, tone, structure, and imagery that suggests new points of departure—and return.

The mise-en-scène of "Abba" is a cemetery; the temporal frame, the narrator's three annual visits to his father's grave on the anniversary of his death. When Paul Celan invokes the possibility of encounter and dialogue in prose, his "Conversation in the Mountain" actually becomes an exercise in monologic doubling, a self-proliferating voice.[43] Pagis's "conversation in the cemetery" is a truly dialogic encounter between two definable interlocutors—between a father and a son whose thirty-five years of estrangement had, it turns out, been caused by a radical misunderstanding. Although such an encounter would be consistent with Pagis's diaphanous poetic persona, relying on liminal places and times to facilitate rather than impede conversations that would be otherwise impossible between the living and the dead, this text is in all other respects prosaic and meticulous in its historical accuracy.[44] So immersed is the speaker in a *conversation* inimical to the overdetermined nature of poetic language that the reader is tempted to conclude that Pagis is slyly parodying or deconstructing the poetic gaze of a lifetime.

The autobiography or memoir of the survivor generally precedes the emergence of a fictive self and establishes a baseline of reference and authenticity; examples would include the Italian writer Primo Levi and the Yiddish writer Leib Rochman, among many others. Here, however, autobiography appears at the *end* of a life of the most elaborate evasions— and would seem to signify a major conversion rather than the need to establish credibility. While the autobiographical convention usually succeeds in creating a separation between the "self as author" and the "self as character,"[45] Pagis seems to be engaged in an even more radical act: establishing a "self" to supersede the selflessness of the poetic voice that had long ago been hurled into "interstellar space." It is not a separation but a *reintegration* of character and author that takes place in this text, preparing the ground for a profound, even sentimental, homecoming. "'You didn't understand your father [says the deceased father's card partner]. . . . You resemble him but only externally, if you'll forgive me for saying so.' I become nervous: 'So what then? Does he have to return to life so that I can understand him?' 'No, no,' says the card player. 'It's you who have to return to life. But if you'll forgive me for saying so, you don't stand much chance of doing that.'"[46] The son may not stand much chance but he is, at last, willing to try.

Having for some twenty-five years invoked and then refused the self-indulgence or self-confirmation that autobiography entails, Pagis now achieves dialogue by constructing a persona ("Dan") whose close resemblance to the author enables him to reenter and reappropriate the historical moment. Giving realia a name becomes a major task in the prose writing, a task nearly as consequential as crafting the circumlocutions that characterized the poetry. His native town now materializes as *Radautz*; his mother as *Yuli*.[47] But the most challenging of all is the act of self-naming: "Like the absent-minded professor who called home and asked, 'It's me here, where should I be?'—so I called and asked, 'I'm Dan, who should I be?' and in my absent-mindedness I didn't notice that the

line was busy" ("A Funny Question").[48] Only thinly disguised by the wit
is the existential shift from *where* to *who*—from tenuous location at the
very boundaries of existence to an attempt at self-definition. In expli-
cating Julia Kristeva's theory of the "borders of language," Shuli Barzilai represents topographically the collapse of "self-limits" in the psychotic
or borderline patient: "Instead of '*Who* am I?' [the borderline] patient
asks, '*Where* am I?' . . . The 'borderlander' is always an exile; "'I" is expelled,' or ceases to be, for, 'How can I be without border?' This absence
of identity—a psychic wandering or loss of place—is congruent with a
discourse produced on the borders of language"; and Kristeva locates
poetic language, which "'by its very economy borders on psychosis,'" as
a kind of borderline discourse.[49]

Pagis's move away from an altered set of voices echoing at the fragile borders of language, and toward the recovery of a particular voice
with recognizable limits, remains a gesture uncompleted in his life. "Dan"
the persona, like Dan the writer, is only a marker or signifier of an "original," unrevealed identity:

> "Your name? [asks the father.] Which of them, if you don't mind? The name
> I gave you (okay, it wasn't really me, Aunt Tzili suggested it), that resonant
> Latin name you erased when you came to Israel. You chose the most com-
> mon one: Dan. I never said anything. I understood that you wanted to dis-
> appear in the country, simply to be absorbed into it like water into sand. How
> does it go? If you change your name you change your luck, right? But I am
> grateful that you never changed our family name. Do you understand me?"
>   "No, Abba."[50]

The play on a Hebrew idiom—"he who changes his place changes his
luck"—substitutes *self* for *place* as the primary existential thrust and interrupted journey of the last years of the poet's life. It could come only
after he had initiated reconciliation with the place of origin.

While the son struggles on the brink of mortality and at the edge of
his own still-precarious identity, "Dan's" interlocutor, the father, appears
no less vigorous for being dead. The transparent film between the living and the dead had never been an impediment to communication in
Pagis's poetry—indeed, as we have seen, it actually facilitated dialogue;
but in "Abba" the centrifugal forces that make such "communication"
possible yield to a centripetal thrust that is a genuine homecoming. The
grave provides again (as in the photograph of Radautz) a compelling
center of gravity. As the biblical patriarch is "gathered unto his people"
in death, so the poet's father is ingathered by an act of poetic and filial
grace. He is reclaimed as an integral, sentient person; his humor, which

had floated in the outer space of disembodied spirits in "Footprints," is reincorporated here into a specific, focused center of consciousness. The poetics of self-transcendence yields to the prosaics of memory: the father's dematerialization through death suspends, for once, the imperative of surrealist *poetic* dematerialization and creates its own counter-imperative.

In imagining the father, the author gives him not only a sustained voice but also a defense, which in many ways compromises the son: "You think that you spared me by not speaking to me about the important things. You had to wait till I died?"[51] The "important things" revolve around the son's presumption that his father's immigration to Palestine, in 1934, amounted to an abandonment—an assumption reinforced by a failure to send for the boy after his mother's death a few months later, or, for that matter, at any time thereafter. Years of polite estrangement had followed the reunion between father and son in Tel Aviv after the war. The belated, posthumous reconciliation with the father is buttressed by written evidence of an alternative narrative: faded letters from the mother and grandmother in Bukovina, containing expressions of family devotion and confirming the father's intention to bring his wife and son to Palestine. It emerges that after the mother's death the family in Bukovina—convinced that a widower barely able to eke out a living for himself would hardly be able to care for a young child in Palestine—prevailed, and the child remained with his grandparents.

SELF-PORTRAIT

Marginalia on the pages of the manuscript indicate that in addition to the letters, the author had intended to incorporate his father's will and a number of photographs into the text of "Abba." We can speculate that such photographs might have included one of the mother taken a short time before her death, a picture to which the late poem "Ein Leben" refers: "In the month of her death, she is standing by the window frame, / a young woman with a stylish permanent wave."[52] But, by the same token, that very photograph might have remained, like Barthes's Winter Garden photograph, unreproduced—precisely because through it the mother has reengendered the writer to perform his last, autobiographical act: "(I cannot reproduce the Winter Garden Photograph. It exists only for me. For you, it would be nothing but an indifferent picture, one of the thousand manifestations of the 'ordinary'; . . . in it, for you, no wound.)."[53] Photography, Barthes insists, carries the ontological weight of a primary habitation; he describes looking at a nineteenth-century photograph of the "Alhambra" and being deeply touched by it:

> It is quite simply *there* that I should like to live . . . This longing to inhabit . . . is fantasmatic, deriving from a kind of second sight which seems to bear me forward to a utopian time, or to carry me back to somewhere in myself. . . . Looking at these landscapes of predilection, it is as if *I were certain* of having been there or of going there. Now Freud says of the maternal body that "there is no other place of which one can say with so much certainty that one has already been there." Such then would be the essence of the landscape (chosen by desire): *heimlich*, awakening in me the Mother.[54]

Such a photograph, *like* the mother, domesticates the wayward soul. And for that very reason, perhaps, the photograph *of the mother* is irreproducible. In the case of Pagis, the combination of a recently inaugurated narrative quest and the privileging of photographic material does invite speculation on what might have become new occasions for autobiography and self-portrait. The poem "Ein Leben" concluded:

> On the inside
> I'm the one looking at her, four years old almost,
> holding back my ball, quietly
> going out of the photo and growing old,
> growing old carefully, quietly,
> so as not to frighten her.[55]

There the artist, unable to capture himself in any fixed temporal or spatial frame, unable to invoke the normal license of poetic control to inhibit the march of time, was deprived of his own object (the discrete self in arrested moments) as a protected, frozen target of scrutiny. Now recontextualized as part of the documentary apparatus, fixed in time and place in the dialogue with the father, the same photograph *might* have furnished a more static autobiographical occasion from which the son would not have had to steal away.

Returning to the mother means abandoning the uncanny, the self-exile, the *unheimlich*, which has guided the poetry, for a "truer" place and a more congruent, even positivist, language.[56] In the poems of the late period, home almost achieves substance as a place frozen, and therefore preserved, in memory. Mental photographs of the poet's childhood begin to appear in a few of the late poems, marked by such conventions of memory and autobiography as the arrested past and images of circumference and containment—and by a respectful distance between the narrating and the experiencing self. In "Central Park, Twilight" (1982), the speaker imagines his grandfather among the bystanders at a skating rink and his own boyhood image reflected in the rink itself. This more conventional form of recall, which preserves the integrity of the remembering subject and the mirror reflection that fixes the self in a past moment, is also couched in the more traditional terms of a dream, maintaining the boundaries between the quick and the dead that had been trespassed by Pagis's diaphanous souls as they slipped so easily between worlds:

> Now, on the mirror of ice, in one daring loop,
> the boy glides toward me.
> That cap of mine. The woolen scarf with the stripes.
>
> Face to face, glowing with embarrassment
> and already turning away, I or I
> say very quickly: Please don't wake up.[57]

RECLAIMING A PLOT IN RADAUTZ

The narrative move in Pagis's late writing is a radical shift toward self-emplotment, and the addition of documentary material in the "Abba" text takes this process one step further. Whatever the intended final shape of this manuscript, the autobiographical text with its documentary "evidence" constitutes an unearthing of objects of the past that promise—or threaten—to replace the imaginative compositions of memory. And the draft found among the author's papers tells a tale as revealing as the story contained within it: many of the marginalia annotating the unfinished Hebrew text are written in Pagis's mother tongue, *German*.

The turn to prose manifest in the unpublished material signals the appropriation of a narrative of repatriation that could have accommodated the obliterated past in more conventional ways, providing room for that which was systematically omitted in the poetry.[58] Repatriation is achieved here in a double sense: both *within* narrative and as return to native grounds *through* narrative. After "forty years" of leaning over the "empty page," the poet receives a "souvenir" from his hometown of Radautz, "her latest winter portrait." The town, for so long a generic "city of passers-by,"[59] has won back its name. A quiet but persistent homecoming begins to unfold between these lines, as the poet enunciates his mother's name and admits to, even if he never actually enunciates, his own former name; as the father is rehabilitated through the dialogues and the letters; and, finally, as an interlinguistic dialogue emerges between the Hebrew text and the marginalia written in the poet's native tongue.

I therefore see Pagis's last composition not only as an act of reconciliation with his father and his fatherland, his mother, and his mother tongue but also as a generic reconciliation with story- (and history-) telling. And it prepares the way for his belated induction as a major figure in contemporary Hebrew letters. The Zionist elevation of history itself as an epic story grants a certain privilege to the "emplotment" of each of its subjects. Hebrew literature, so saturated with memory and countermemory, so invested in narratives of survival that follow a *chronology* of submersion in and emergence from the abyss, could barely contain Pagis's dismembering poetry, which was a radical dis-remembering. But his prosaic "I," newly situated in time and space, relocates the moral center from an imaginary universal space to a particularized territory.[60] Although the prose material does not constitute a sustained fiction, this new entry into the prosaic with a restored human voice clearly located in the present and reconciled with the past, now fully named, privileges the everyday, the ordinary, the historically real[61]—and, by projection, privileges a vision of a future of personal and social order.

Even in its incomplete, raw state, the material under discussion has the spell-binding quality of both a story and a confession. As hermeneutic map, Pagis's late prose is valuable for fixing interpretive strategies: the poetry becomes the encoded text and the prose, with its access to the "truth," its code. Pagis appears to have moved out of an absurd world of inscrutable riddles into an answerable, disenchanted universe.

But the recentering of the poetic self involves a subtle displacement of the reader. It was, we saw, the absence not only of a subject in the present but also of any specifically addressed and definable *other* in Pagis's poetry that had made the community of his readers the primary audience and the act of reading so consequential for the dynamics of moral discourse. In "Abba," however, the address to a specific other *within the text* relegates the reader to the more conventional status of voyeur/observer. Any sense of impoverishment in the prose may therefore be a function of such subtle reorientations, which leave readers deprived of their role as subjects in the poetry. As full of *presence* as these prose texts are, what is missing is precisely the absences—all the circumlocutions and open-ended mysteries—that had characterized a Pagis text. A poetry of unfathomable depths poised at the borders of language, of enigmatic signals sent directly to the reader, yields to a sane set of surfaces that beckon the reader merely to eavesdrop.

Nevertheless, we find that after the death of the author, the reader has an even more consequential task to perform—or avoid. As with Paul Celan, Primo Levi, and other writers whose formative years were spent in the world of labor and death camps, it is only too seductive to read the author's death and his last words back into the life as a terribly appropriate—or appropriately terrible—form of closure and hermeneutic tool. One can overstate the finality of Pagis's last work by placing so much weight on the scanty lines of prose that crisscross his last years, though between his father's death in 1983 and his own in 1986, his writing is indisputably filled with a sense of the urgency that prompts one to set one's house in order. We are, by "backshadowing,"[62] in even greater danger of providing closure to relieve our own anxiety at the ongoing reproach of the open-ended scream of the mother, Eve, and at the same time foreclosing what may have been an even more daring departure into other literary realms.

My own reading of the scant and unfinished manuscript that was to become Pagis's last work is inevitably skewed; had the writer lived, "Abba" would have assumed additional dimensions and would, no doubt, have been succeeded by other work. The text before us remains no more than a signpost of one direction Pagis's writing was taking into the precincts of a history that seemed to deny or defy imagination, that seemed to claim that the unworked, prosaic matter of life is its "truest" form. I thus end my discussion by following another direction, pointing out that while his death grants the prose passages the status of a last will and testament, a longer life might have made them just that: *passages*. They might well have yielded to another poetic space: a space free from the burden of testimony. Once having reconstructed his lost Atlantis on the physical foundations of photographs and documents, having buried his dead and concluded his own journey of the self in the graveyard of his hometown, Pagis might have been at liberty at last to engage in what I have described as the most profound act of the diasporic imagination: the mimetic license that presupposes both distance from and completed mourning for the homeland. That is, this new archaeological process that locates memory in the shards of physical evidence—the letters, the photographs, the graveyard in Radautz—could ultimately have relieved the poetic trope of its testimonial, iconic status. If the imagination need no longer "bear witness" through preserving meta*morphic*ally the fragments of an obliterated civilization, if the imagination has been liberated from its status as *evidence* through the appearance of other material traces of that world, then it can recover its mimetic *and* its meta*phoric* function as surrogate and consolation ("to what shall I compare thee *that I may comfort thee*?"). This hypothesis is, of course, as much a projection into an unrealized future as backshadowing is an insistence on the iron grip of the past. But it is the next *logical* step toward reinventing a diasporic poetics in the wake of the destruction of the Jewish Diaspora that first invented it.

Whether we read Pagis's prose as an alternative construct of memory, as final words that provide an ultimate deciphering, as hermeneutic code for that poetry of spare lines and empty spaces, or as a stage in the liberation of the poetic imagination, and whether our uneasiness concerning this shift to a prosaics of memory simply reveals us as petulant readers deprived of fictive unlikeliness, of a more obvious type of lyric enchantment, one thing seems certain. Four decades in the wilderness of a self-enforced oblivion culminated in an arrival of sorts: a narrative exploration of native grounds that enabled this poet, finally, to reclaim a plot in Radautz.

Between Bukovina and Jerusalem

Aharon Appelfeld and Pilgrimage
to the Ruined Shrine

For the bereaved, a lost continent, like a lost beloved, is a construct of the imagination that must be large enough to contain the objects that memory produces. Whether recovered objects are seen as metonyms for the submerged wholeness of the past or as the fragmented, ever-surfacing but utterly elusive changelings of history, they are above all a test of the survival of remembered worlds as the legitimate domain of the imagination. Three writers from Bukovina record, in three different registers, the resonant sounds of objects as they resurface. We have seen how Dan Pagis succeeds in his late prose in penetrating the surface itself—which, in turn, serves as the matrix and the burial ground for his own story—and how Paul Celan keeps the objects sealed in an internally referential poetry like the floating hope chest of an unconsummated marriage. For Aharon Appelfeld, the object world remains suspended in eternal anticipation of the demise of the beings that animated it. What begins in his early fiction as an aborted return to the sounds and sites of memory becomes, over time, a return to discarded cultural paradigms and languages of representation—most saliently, the representation of the Jewish journey. Whether such a dramatic reconnection with the past proves enabling or disabling in the context of modern Hebrew fiction is one of the questions I want to explore. We will also examine whether, between geographies lost and gained, there is another place that can never be recovered but covers itself and its surroundings with utter blankness.

Although we take it as axiomatic that the Holocaust survivor is lost among the shattered worlds of his or her own survival, it is remarkable, if little remarked, that in the artistic reconstruction there are as many points of entry into a *post*-Holocaust universe as there are of *reentry into the past*—and that these points are often reflections of each other. Paul Celan's dialectical engagement with German, his language of origin, and Dan Pagis's with Hebrew, his adopted language—each with its persistent, ghostly echoes of the *other* language and landscape—furnish very different referential and poetic sites.

Generic moves also reflect and influence this process. I argued in the previous chapter that the shift to prose from a poetry riddled with the evasive signs of the past provided the narrative space in which Pagis could realign his language with his biography. But for Aharon Appelfeld, who also refuses to represent history in explicit terms, prose not only does not facilitate the recovery of memory: it actively undermines the very discourse in which it is logically embedded. What might have become Appelfeld's "prosaics of memory" is filtered inexorably through Nazism's "final act," stubbornly eschewing the comforts of narrative, the temporality of telling that can construct a future not only after but *out of* the past. Whatever memories of childhood are recycled in Appelfeld's fictions are suffused with the pathos of what is to come. Writing emerges as an obsessive and always incomplete compensatory act.

Appelfeld's travel narratives seem to exhaust the genre by fully realizing its potential. Some of the later and longer fictions move between Europe and Israel as the two points on the Jewish compass that both mirror and undermine each other. *Mikhvat ha-or* [Searing Light] (1980) promises to be a novel of "repatriation" of Jewish refugees in Palestine after liberation; instead, it records their peregrinations along the shores of Italy, their "transport" to and arrival in Palestine, and their failure to be absorbed into the Jewish community of the Yishuv. *Tor hapla'ot* [The Age of Wonders] (1978) is a two-part "return" to the European home before and after its destruction. The first book relates the twilight hours of bourgeois Jewish culture in Austria on the eve of World War II from the perspective of a child voiced over by a brooding sentience of what is to come. The second part, narrated in the third person, takes place many years later when the protagonist leaves Jerusalem in order to revisit his hometown and try to piece together the physical traces of his past.[1]

Many of Appelfeld's early narratives trace random wartime movements of Jews through the vast spaces of the Austro-Hungarian empire,[2] and many of the later ones chart the homing patterns of those who dare to return to postwar Europe; but only with the publication of the novella

Layish (1994) does this author provide a powerful *literary* resolution to the struggle to reclaim the past through forms of representation belonging to the geosocial space in which it unfolded. *Layish* is the story of an ostensible journey to Jerusalem by a group of ragtag Jews; their identity and itinerary are more generic than specific, creating an ambiance in which, eventually, Jerusalem reclaims its traditional status as unattainable goal, as destiny rather than destination.

"Return" in an Appelfeld story is a gesture not so much of "going back" as of "repeating." The earlier fictions present less a narration of return than a deformation of both the idea of the journey and the narrative as its vehicle; that stance reaches a kind of formal perfection and even affirmation in *Layish*. This novella, approximating in some places a reconstruction of the past and in others a mimesis of repressed memory, evolves along patterns whose undecidability can be read in Freudian terms as either "acting out" *or* "working through." It can be approached, that is, either as a compulsive attempt to *repeat* or to *repair* past traumas by relating the cognitive-epistemological flaws of those who were its agents and its victims. *Layish* may represent the first true literary homecoming in Appelfeld's fiction; it is written in a language that constitutes a rendezvous with Eastern European Jewish culture on its own grounds, archaic and, therefore, more resonant than his earlier narratives had been with the literary tradition we traced in the first half of this book as stretching from Yehuda Halevi to S. Y. Agnon.

A TIME OF INNOCENCE

For most survivor writers, the imagined postwar return to their birthplace is strewn with the rubble of a childhood not simply lost through the normal course of time and distance, but ruined. The compositional strategies of recall reveal both aesthetic and ideological positions. Abba Kovner, leader of the Vilna ghetto partisans and a major poetic voice in Israel's first decades, presents a complex exchange between geographies lost and gained. The towns in his long poem cycle *A Canopy in the Desert* are a pastiche of ancient Hebrew settlements, European Jewish villages, modern Israeli development towns, and decimated Arab villages. In the desert, wasteland of dreams and heroic visions, at an unspecified but belated hour, the quiet act of rebuilding a city unfolds; the composite, compensatory landscape of desert and sea is sketched from acacia, roads and their signs, a policeman's dog, and the "little sister" carried on the poet's back like Jacob's bones from another place and another poem.[3] In the unending search for a "better story," this storyteller's wanderings through the desert culminate in the construction of a home on "naked soil" out of the recovered layers of memory. Kovner's city, unlike Pagis's, is as transparent as a highly crafted pane of glass, the poetic act rendering the past somehow visible.[4]

But the composite picture drawn by Abba Kovner is rare in Israeli literature, in which round-trip journeys to native grounds are generally informed by a rigid dialectic of exile and return—studies in contrasting climate and geography, gravitational pull, patterns of light and darkness. The narrator of Shulamith Hareven's story "Be-dimdumim" [Twilight] (1980) dreams herself back into the European city in which she was born, now a murky, lightless wasteland. At the end of a nocturnal year among the dead souls of her native town, she awakens in Jerusalem, "in my other house. It was morning. A great sun shone straight into my eyes."[5] Itamar Yaoz-Kest's story "Ha-kav ha-zarhani" [The Phosphorus Line] (1978) concludes a dreamlike revisit to a concentration camp with a return to the land of "the sun."[6]

The Israeli sun that rehabilitates the survivors in these Hebrew poems and narratives exudes a "searing light" in the fiction of Aharon Appelfeld, burning away the vestiges of private memories in the process of welding the parts into a solid mass of undifferentiated collective memory. By resisting the lure of the sun, Appelfeld challenges and engages, at its most elemental level, the ethos of ingathering. Perhaps the sun provides no balm because the abandoned world of childhood presents no wasteland. The horror of the survivor's discovery that his or her world has been utterly *effaced* can only be surpassed by the discovery that it has been completely *preserved*. Sparse attention to the phenomenological world characterized Appelfeld's earlier fiction, which has been described as shrouded in an impressionistic mist that obscured any real engagement with reality.[7] But out of these misty landscapes evolves, in the stories of return, a kind of *hyper*realism, a close focus on the physical properties that remain somehow untouched by the earthquake that shook the town and emptied it only of its Jews. Returning to his hometown of Knospen "many years later, when everything was over," Bruno, the adult protagonist of the second part of *The Age of Wonders*, rivets his attention to the minutest details of his physical environment; his fixation with geometrical patterns and designs, with the positioning of objects in an unchanged world, betrays the cool dispassion of a perfectly displaced despair:

> A week already gone in this familiar exile and nothing done. Most of the day he spends sitting on a bench measuring the shadows of the church spires; re-

alizing again that nothing has changed here, only him—he is already his father's age.

And when he tires of measuring the shadows, he strolls along Hapsburg
Avenue, and here too nothing has changed. As if the scenes of his childhood
have been embalmed in all their subtlest nuances of light and shade, from the
awnings above to the paving stones below. . . . Even the Jewish shops have
preserved their outward appearance, like the Lauffers' drapery shop. None
of them have survived but their shop is still standing at exactly the same angle as before, perfectly preserved, even the geraniums in their pots.[8]

Such operations, which at one level seem to recapitulate the child's-eye
view of the world, are in a more basic sense what Frederick Hoffman
would call "calculations of existence": "they attempt to answer the question, not why do I exist but do I exist at all; that is, is there a recognizable set of spatial and temporal coordinates which, by means of certain
calculations, I can use to arrive at the fact of my existing?"[9] A new spatial calculus emboldened Pagis to establish a foothold among the fading
footprints of his childhood. In the case of Appelfeld's lone survivor who
returns to his former home, the spatial coordinates are the measure not
so much of his present existence as of all the *absences* by which his present existence is calculated. On the platform of the train station, "paving
stones lay side by side in the familiar pattern, but they seemed more
worn."[10]

These exertions both establish the locus of authentic space and challenge the entire mimetic enterprise, recalling the way that, in Walter Benjamin's analysis, the original work of art relates to its reproductions. Like
Benjamin's irreproducible masterpiece, the authority of the object world
encountered by Appelfeld's survivor inheres in "its unique existence at
the place where it happens to be."[11] The work is original here in the sense
of delineating the material world of one's origins. It is even more immediate, more urgent and inflexible, than the photographic reproductions that trigger the remembering prose of Dan Pagis. The hyperrealistic representation of this landscape thus follows from assuming the
irreplaceable nature of original space whose contours, revisited, can only
be a measure of absence.

What characterizes Bruno is that as he can no longer find a foothold
for himself between the worn paving stones of the train station and the
immutable shadows of the church spires, so he can never quite touch
down in Jerusalem, either; like the other survivors in Appelfeld's stories
and Pagis's poems, those who cannot repatriate their memories in some
innocent landscape of their childhood can hardly be repatriated in postwar Israel. "Bertha," an early story (1962), is set in Jerusalem but in-

habits another geography altogether, one that is as primordial as it is irretrievable—the interior space of effaced memory. Bertha is the girl/
woman whose mental development was literally retarded by her wartime
experience and her transplantation to Jerusalem: "From the day that they
had reached this country, oblivion had overcome her. Her memory froze
at a certain point."[12] The street semiotics of modern Jerusalem, that peculiar palimpsest of Hebrew territory and text, serves to locate Bertha's
abode somewhere beyond "Ibn Gabirol Street and Ramban Boulevard,"
inviting resonances that the rest of the narrative will repeatedly silence.
The male protagonist, Max, is portrayed as a traveling soft-drink sales-
man who disappears on the job for months at a time, returning with the
change in seasons to the small room he shares with Bertha: "In winter,
he would return. Perspiring, a knapsack on his back, he would bring with
him the fresh scent of worlds unknown here."[13] Even were his journeys
to stretch the entire length and breadth of (pre-1967) Israel, from
Metulla in the north to Eilat in the south, from Tel Aviv to Jerusalem,
Max could cover the whole country in a day or two. Both Max's peregrinations and Bertha's confinement take place in prototypical landscapes: he is doomed to repeat the wandering of a Jew lost in the limit-
less vistas of the Austro-Hungarian Empire, she to replay the broken
chords of an unfinished childhood refrain.[14]

Even when the surface would indicate otherwise, the narrative space
requires the physical expanse of the cities and forests of Europe. In *The
Immortal Bartfuss*, the characters orient themselves toward Vienna as if
it were a neighboring city and only at the end of the narrative is it established that the events have been taking place in Jerusalem.[15] On the
dust jacket of the English translation of Appelfeld's novel *Katerina*, the
author is described as having been born in Bukovina and as "currently
living in Jerusalem."[16] Using this paratext as a code for deciphering Appelfeld's work, one could argue that all of his stories are located in some
nomadic space *between* Bukovina and Jerusalem. It is in the novel *Layish* that this nomadic space reacquires its appropriate geographic and narrative topography.

A "safe trip" back to Europe can be constructed from one of two
points of reference: from Israel as place of refuge, as demonstrated in the
stories mentioned above by Hareven and Yaoz-Kest, or from the prewar
reserve of uncontaminated memories. The existential quest is structurally
related to, though not necessarily nourished by, the Zionist romance that
seeks to recover a lost paradise. "That," says Yehuda Amichai, "is the
way memory works in this country, where childhood is as distant from

the people as the time before the destruction of the Temple."[17] One of the most sustaining principles in fictions, poetry, and memoirs of survival is the positing of an untainted area of reference, the soul's temple, generally located in the childhood of the narrator or the central protagonist. This area serves as a kind of nature preserve—and nature itself is invariably a part of the childhood idyll; in the case of the Hebrew narrative, it provides a shady European counterpart to the Mediterranean sun that illuminates and scorches the postwar years. By admitting time and the unidirectional linearity of memory as pretraumatic reference, such writers summon a protected past that can furnish a foundation for constructing possible futures.[18] We saw how in his late poem "Ein Leben," Dan Pagis may have located such a point in the framed photograph of mother and child taken in his fourth year, which was also the year that his mother died. Appelfeld's post-Holocaust Jerusalem, empty of resonance, is a projection of the absence of innocent points of origin in the world of childhood. But the war itself, experienced "in nature" by a child on the run, is configured in the fictions as both refuge and menace, the sphere in which the primordial struggle for survival is enacted.[19]

The endlessly repeated efforts to write and rewrite an elusive story structure Appelfeld's fiction and reveal its central themes. The characters' endemic homelessness—their failure to retrieve the past or connect to the future, to be domesticated within their acquired languages and landscapes—is represented in a kind of hyperrealistic suspended present tense, a formal hedge against the inescapable discontinuities of an interrupted narrative. Though the construction of a viable identity in the postwar period depends largely on the preservation of a protected prewar reference, Appelfeld posits no such point d'appui; the missing set of concentric circles with the self in the center, safe even for a moment in the bosom of family and nature, is here replaced by concentric circles with a "black hole" as its nucleus.

THE BLACK HOLE, THE WHITE PAGE

Effaced memory recurs emblematically in Appelfeld's short stories, novellas, and novels. In *The Age of Wonders*, the blank page separating the long novella that relates life on the eve of the war from the short story that traces a return to that world decades after its destruction signifies the great silence or the "black hole"—the place or event that cannot be articulated or the trauma from which one cannot recover that disrupts the normal continuity of biography and subverts the conventional course of the bildungsroman. Where the young narrator would normally have gone out into the world to shape his destiny, he falls instead into the abyss of the white page. Those events that appear as a blank page (*Age of Wonders*) or a blank memory ("Bertha") are in other wartime narratives rendered as a series of reflexive responses to unspecified terror, persecution, and flight.

Few readers have failed to note the emblems of oblivion in Appelfeld's writing that correspond to the war years. It is possible to adduce many, albeit conflicting, sources of this phenomenon, all relating to the writer's childhood as a fugitive. He was born in 1932 into a German-speaking assimilated Jewish family in Czernowitz in the Bukovina region of Romania, not far from the birthplaces of Paul Celan and Dan Pagis. When he was nine years old, the Germans entered the town; he was separated from his family and sent to a work camp in Transnistria. He managed to escape and to survive the remaining war years hiding in the forests and villages of the Ukraine. The months between liberation and the journey to Palestine were spent among Russian troops and groups of displaced persons in Yugoslavia and Italy.

The limbo in time and space that corresponded to Appelfeld's coming of age found its fictional expression in a dismantling of the mystery of the open-ended narrative, in a denial of the novelistic premise of life as ongoing negotiation between will and fate. Appelfeld's representation of childhood is consistently overwritten by a knowledge of what is to come. When the war catches up with the characters, it has been fully anticipated at the level of the metanarrative. Michael André Bernstein argues that Appelfeld's double vision—the reconstruction of events from the heights of historical hindsight, or "backshadowing"—is flawed both aesthetically and ethically: Appelfeld treats "his characters as marionettes whose futile gestures on an absurd stage we watch, half in horror, half in anxiously bemused melancholy at their foolishness. We know they are doomed; they stubbornly refuse to know it, and in the interaction between our knowledge and their ignorance a fable of willed self-delusion unfolds."[20] "What was I to do?" asks Appelfeld in an essay, as if anticipating Bernstein's critique. "Every time I tried to reconstruct those forgotten resorts [where 'we, like all the other petit-bourgeois families,' would spend the summers], I had visions of the trains and the camps, and my most hidden childhood memories were spotted with the soot from the trains."[21]

Underlying (and facilitating) such determinism is the rigid adherence to a mythical structure of memory that does not admit any life beyond.

The settings in fortresses or monasteries in war-torn Europe are not entirely unrealized; but they remain unconnected to larger contexts or social systems, to any historical or chronological continuum, or to the surprise that accompanies a sense of the contingent. Life before and during the war is, in a fundamental sense, nonmimetic; as it does not acquire historical status, it cannot constitute a resource for memory or the narrative impulse.

The suspended narrative belongs to that third place, neither the Holy Land nor the European home, but the "concentrationary" universe with a black hole as its center and *absence* as its aesthetic foundation. Art functions as the measure of distance: proximity to the black hole is often signified by an object world frozen in a suspended present tense, in the "black milk" of morning, of midday, of evening that "we drink and drink" in Celan's "Todesfuge" and will never finish drinking, and in the barren movements of errant characters who will never arrive.

In the decades after the war and in the shadow of Adorno's pronouncement about poetry "nach Auschwitz," two major strategies of representation have evolved: the static or absolutist approach, which locates a nonnegotiable self in the unyielding experience or site of persecution and extermination (or, as in the case of Appelfeld, in its signifier, the blank page), and the dynamic or relativist position, which approaches the reconstruction of that place as an ongoing process of *re*negotiation. For the latter, the immobility of the past is mitigated by the very conventions mobilized to represent it. For the former, an invented language grounded in a sense of suspension or unmastered trauma prevents convention and commensurability, the pillars of mimetic and poetic structure, from relativizing the absolute, frozen reality of the place. In each case, of course, the work of history or art is being performed in the aftermath, at a "safe" distance—but it is distance itself that is at stake.[22]

When one is inside an Appelfeld story, there is no reality beyond or without, no distance from what is not yet or no longer visible. The absolute, mythic suspension of time and of outside reference is the prism that collapses chronological and geographical distance. Singular events are supplanted in this fiction by an inexorable *condition*, a state of *being*; historical sensibility gives way to static consciousness. Even stages of accommodation or change that can be discerned in Appelfeld's world cannot, strictly speaking, be located on a historical plane. "Years and Hours" (the name of another two-part novel: *Shanim ve-sha'ot*, 1975) are not normal measures of human time but rather compressed eons in which individuals in a given group acquire the habits and the parts necessary to survive in new circumstances. In short narratives like "Hish-tanut" [Transformation] (1968), which traces the adaptive mannerisms and appearance of a Jewish couple in the forest to which they have escaped, evolution is substituted as a scientific measure for both biographical time and suprapersonal Jewish time.[23]

The operation of time in many of these stories thus seems to be more "phylogenic" than historical or metaphysical; the survivors who populate Appelfeld's universe are a new breed. Even the volume of autobiographical essays, which appears to have a confessional tone and in its original Hebrew version was titled *Masot be-guf rishon* [Essays in the First Person], is in fact cast almost entirely in the first-person *plural*—as is the novel *Mikhvat ha-or* [Searing Light]. When a story is narrated in the singular—whether first- or third-person—the character rarely appears significantly differentiated from his or her comrades. In the stories that chart the course of Jewish refugees in Palestine, the dramatic struggle takes place not between the individual and the group, but between two species: the native-born and the refugees. The protagonists in these stories are not bound by a social contract but by a kind of biological homogeneity—and the plight of the lone individual is not alleviated by flocking instincts.

LANGUAGES LOST AND GAINED

In Appelfeld's fictional reconstruction of a world on the verge of extinction, the first and most fundamental property of which the hapless German-speaking Jews are dispossessed is their language, their mode of intercourse with the world at large. The fog that occludes events and places not only is a form of amnesia (a response to trauma) but also reflects the muteness of those who have, quite simply, *lost their tongue*. The stories repeatedly dramatize how, in the earliest stages of exile, in the crush of deportation to ghettos and train stations, "the words got lost."[24] The language of home was not simply forgotten, having fallen into disuse—it was *denied*. None of the lessons that had been learned could be applied to the present struggle—neither algebra, nor Latin, nor the pride of belonging to German culture. German was now the language of National Socialism, of a territory that had no room for Jews.

In the fictions that trace the wanderings of groups of refugees during the war and of survivors following liberation, the characters begin to appropriate fragments of speech from one another. And the more their original speech becomes obsolete, the more it takes on a material, palpable presence. Each acquisition seems to consign to oblivion another article from their own past: "The bit of warmth that resided in the few words we had brought from home, evaporated."[25] The younger one was at the time of deportation, the more far-reaching the ultimate effects of linguistic displacement. The child who had barely mastered the rudiments of language could hardly have acquired the verbal formulas that protect the integrity of the past. Memories, associations, one's own native tongue— all remain trapped forever in that prearticulate stage of young childhood and are never regained in the adult's search for compensatory literary forms.

Still words, or phonemes, mediate between body and spirit; they persist as the primary associative mechanisms, struggling to survive the ultimate ruin of the physical world and to reproduce it acoustically as an echo chamber. Memory is thus triggered primarily through verbal rather than nonverbal sensory association.[26] In *Mikhvat ha-or*, the narrator is confronted on the ship to Palestine by the man who claims to have been his father's literary adversary, who tells the boy: "'I wrote about 12 long articles and not a few critical essays (*retzenziot*) against your father, mostly in German, but some in French.' The word *retzenzia* evokes in me, like magic, the smells of home. Books, galleys, my father sitting bent over his table, writing. He is engulfed in a screen of cigarette smoke and the aroma of coffee: 'What does the *retzenzia* say?' I hear mother's voice."[27] The old words are independent entities. They are of the essence of time past; they *are* the past, as palpable as any artifact salvaged from one's childhood—a picture or a scarf—could be. But they are lighter than the past, because they are reported undeciphered, freed even from their semantic weight. It is not the content or the effect of the critical review of the father's work but the pure sound of the word *retzenzia* that releases memory. Retrieval of childhood will, inevitably, remain partial, incomplete, obsessive, because the process of remembering is involuntary[28] and because when an Appelfeld character succeeds in retrieving one detail, he loses the others. "How many years has it been since I saw father's study," muses the narrator; "Even my mother tongue, German, comes out of my mouth corrupted irreparably. I lost it somewhere along those endless roads. Now I speak Yiddish in all the jumbled accents of the refugees."[29]

In an essay written in memory of Leib Rochman, Appelfeld acknowledged that this Yiddish writer, whom he first met in Israel in the early 1950s, awakened within him his "mother tongue"—that Rochman took him, through his writing and his oral tales, on long journeys through Jewish Poland.[30] The reference is clearly to Yiddish as *mame-loshn*, the matron presiding over the linguistic realm of Eastern Europe's Jews. As is the case for Primo Levi and other survivors of Western or Central Europe, Yiddish functions for Appelfeld as the generic Jewish language that he reveres (and despises) *by maintaining his own distance from it*. He grew up, as did most of his characters, in an assimilated family ("assimilation was passed on as our inheritance") that had totally embraced German culture.[31] The word *retzenzia* appearing in a Hebrew text has in fact escaped from the repressed domains of both German *and* Yiddish.

On the shores of Italy and after the survivors' arrival in Palestine, a few words of Hebrew are learned—and they succeed in forming a thin cover, camouflaging the negated past. The new culture facilitates the escape from and denial of one's former identity. Whatever remained of the languages of *galut* to which the "smell of death"[32] still clung was baggage that the refugee had to cast off in order to qualify for the Procrustean bed provided by the Jewish Agency. The image of the helpless, ignominious Jew was to be exchanged, along with one's name and mannerisms, for the proud, swarthy appearance of the self-reliant Israeli. It is, presumably, relatively easy to pour language into a mind that has been vacated.

Rather than providing a vocabulary to rescue private as well as public memory, the language of the Sabra spoken in Appelfeld's house of fiction appears as an effective shield *against* any claims the past might still assert. Cliché is the language of enforced consensus that intrudes on and usurps the remnants of memory that still guard the private domain. Soon after his arrival in Palestine, the narrator of *Mikhvat ha-or* dozes in the company of a group of refugees who spend their time playing cards and declaring their political and religious allegiances:

> And I close my eyes for a moment and see clearly the small village where my mother and I spent our last vacation. It was a sparse village bisected by a stream. And when it was time to leave, mother packed the suitcases and wept. I, fool that I was, tried to comfort her. But she refused to be comforted and continued to cry. As if her whole world had been destroyed. I can now see her teary face clearly, as if under a magnifying glass.
>
> "Now we are all in one boat." This sentence penetrated my daydream and awakened me. One of the card players, who was losing, had said it.
>
> "You are asleep. Who will build the country? We need *halutzim* here and not dreamers."
>
> "What do you want from the boy?"
>
> "I want him to be a *halutz*. A fighter."

There is no meaning to the words. They issue forth by themselves and do not harm anybody, but they roused me from my sweet daydream. How long has it been since I last saw my mother. Now that she has appeared to me, they have snatched her from me.[33]

The mother's words, like the dreamscapes that preserve them, are usurped by the masculine and dream-defying discourse of the Palmach generation. It is only later that the narrator learns the pragmatic value of those Hebrew idioms and clichés that he is mastering so reluctantly. "We spoke a broken babel of tongues, and now to this mix were added a few Hebrew words. He [Dormant, the refugee who has made the quickest adjustment] absorbed the clichés first and made effective use of them. At that time we did not yet realize that they were his fins and that it was with their help that he navigated."[34] In the Darwinian drama of acculturation, acquired words are like new appendages enabling this transplanted species to adapt to a new environment. But unlike the porous language of Sholem Aleichem's Motl, who celebrates his Americanisms as paving stones on the road to cultural and economic enfranchisement, every Hebrew cliché in the narrator's lexicon is mourned as a nail in the coffin of the past.

It is not only in the represented speech of the newcomers that languages of the past and present collide. The Hebrew novel itself, a testament to the writer's triumph over his stuttering beginnings, also bears the evidence of his struggle; there is an ungrounded, oblique quality to Appelfeld's prose, like the aimless tendrils of an air plant. Permeable boundaries and an unparticularized realism are the signposts of a literature of displaced persons. The writer moving into Hebrew could acquire a discourse on Jewish suffering—a set of paradigms of protest and consolation, of piety and irony. For Dan Pagis, deeply immersed in classical Hebrew, medieval poetry came to serve both as muse and as formal refuge from the shattered syntax through which the world of childhood had to be refracted in his own postwar poetry.[35] But Appelfeld's language still bears the chisel marks of a writer who encountered modern Hebrew unencumbered—and unenriched—by layers of intertextual allusion. Neither his native German, lost "somewhere among those endless roads" and delegitimated as the language of the murderers, nor the submerged Yiddish of his ancestors, nor his adopted Hebrew would facilitate access to the collective *or* the personal past. Like the holy place, the holy language has no resonances for Appelfeld's characters; in such narratives as *An Age of Wonders* or "Bertha," Jerusalem remains a city without shadows and Hebrew a language without echoes.

Nevertheless, the old words from home do continue to erupt, unbidden and autonomous, into the business of constructing one's present life out of Jerusalem stone and Hebrew cliché. There is a clear dialectical antagonism in *Mikhvat ha-or* between the languages of past and present, between the diminishing store of warm words salvaged from home—like the vestiges of speech organs from an earlier phylogenic phase—and the foreign words grafted on but never fully assimilated, between the privacy of a would-be biography and the tyranny of the collective saga.

Unsafe journeys to the sites of childhood are narrated as physical catalysts to memory, and the sojourn on native ground invokes and sustains, for just a moment, images of the past. The second part of *Age of Wonders* is the narrative of Bruno's return to his hometown of Knospen; here, rather than being antagonistic, the linguistic environment is organic with the memories themselves, and the suppressed words are allowed to surface freely. The speech Bruno hears in the familiar dialect is exhilarating and liberating: "Words he had not used for years rose to the tip of his tongue and he was glad to have them back again. [Later, Bruno heard two old women speaking and it was] as if the words had filtered toward him through a heavy curtain of water."[36]

Inevitably, though, the past that was so unnaturally aborted and that is so discontinuous with the present cannot yield a coherent narrative, and the seeker is condemned to begin again and again. Staring at the "dark green geranium pot, looking as out of place and artificial as ever" after several days in his old hometown, Bruno suddenly says, "in any case what difference does it make." Then "words deserted him, as did the fevered excitement. Only weariness remained. *It was as if a scaly armor had sprouted on his back*" (emphasis mine).[37] When the survivor who had adapted to his new environment by acquiring the requisite appendages dares to return home, he becomes, by the logic of natural selection, an anachronism, a scaly creature who no longer fits his time and place.

At the end of *The Age of Wonders*, Bruno is at the train station waiting to leave Knospen and return to Jerusalem. In a rather obvious denial of the Proustian model of the protected realm of childhood, retrieved through sensory association and infused with meaning through art, Bruno orders a cake and dips it into his coffee, realizing that "not a memory remained with him. It was as if they had been devoured and left not a trace behind."[38] The writer whose protagonists are "posthumous" or anachronistic figures who have forfeited their emplotment in the world cannot take (or provide) the simple pleasures of character and plot development that the novelistic form affords.

The search for home nonetheless remains a perpetual and lonely one that each survivor undertakes simultaneously with but in isolation from his or her fellows. Different narrative strategies provide different avenues of return. What is constant is what cannot, what *must not*, be remembered and the consistent refusal of an epic or even biographical structure that would incorporate childhood's paradise and its loss.

Within the broad exigencies of a Zionist literature of "return," the *helekh* or restless wanderer, animated by personal memory, continued to act as control and reproach. The land envisioned as a haven by prophets, poets, philosophers, and politicians had to make room, if only at the margins, for the yearnings and the murmurings of dislocated souls. Tel Aviv became their city. The pioneers, the pilgrims, and the expatriates have always known that the closer one is to the sea, the more accessible are the great metropolises and small towns of Europe, America, Asia, North Africa. Even during the early years of this century, the tallest of Y. H. Brenner's transplanted trees could see a long way, perhaps even catch a glimpse, if they craned their top branches, of the great cities across the sea.[39] "And—so it seemed—if / you but turn your head, there's your town's church floating in the sea," writes Leah Goldberg in her poem "Tel Aviv, 1935."[40] For Avot Yeshurun, Tel Aviv became "the Holy City" by virtue of its affinity to the profane spaces of childhood: "I walked in you in the town I left. / In your city, in my town. / My city that's behind your back." A short time before his death in the spring of 1992, he confessed that he had written "a poem of gratitude to Tel Aviv—for having allowed us to be immigrants [*mehagrim*, as opposed to *'olim*]."[41] Nostalgia and neck craning were, it seems, built into the project almost from the beginning.

But Appelfeld's characters were anarchic selves who lived outside historical time and personal memory and who undermined society and culture simply by their inability to connect to the present or to remember the past, by the inexorability of their fate as refugees. They remained exiled even inside the adaptive behaviors and gestures of their own survival—until the *language of exile* itself resurfaced as authentic mode of representation. Only when the figure of the displaced Jew reconnected with the language of the Jewish journey and its ultimate destination as infinitely deferrable would he recover something "authentic" and canonic in what was otherwise a series of nonresonant fictions. What then emerges as the most allusive element in Appelfeld's stories is not linguistic or cultural memory but the unresolved, recurrent patterns of Jewish *destiny*. Though in nearly all of Appelfeld's stories, beginning with the earliest

ones collected in *'Ashan* [Smoke] (1962), Israel remains a wanderer
among the nations—even in Jerusalem itself—in *Layish* there is finally
a confluence between Jewish geography and the Jewish journey.

I am arguing that the search for the "lost continent" in Appelfeld's
later fiction may be characterized less by backshadowing, in Bernstein's
terms, than by the practice of return as a form of déja vu. Appelfeld's
characters are not free—not only because they are judged by the finality of history but also because they are trapped in a world of recurrence,
in patterns that have been repeated for thousands of years. His essays,
like his narratives, address absences in the world of the parents—the pe-
tite bourgeoisie who, having tried to disengage from the "anachronistic" collective, were doomed like everyone else to live (and to die) as part
of the Jewish corpus. "Fate was already hidden within those people like
a mortal illness"[42]—yet it was only *they*, he insists, embedded as they
were in a delusive physical and spiritual state, who had lost the code by
which they might have deciphered the circumstances of their lives. The
absence created when collective consciousness goes underground becomes, during and after the Holocaust, a kind of tabula rasa on which
the code may someday be reinscribed: "The Jewish experience in the Second World War was not 'historical' . . . ; we came into contact with archaic mythical forces, a kind of dark subconscious the meaning of which
we did not know, nor do we know it to this day."[43]

Appelfeld's voice entered the Jewish story at a point of access that I
would define as prearticulate—both on account of the young, *prearticulate*, age of the child who is banished from his own childhood and on account of the parents' relegation of Jewish consciousness to mute or *sub-
articulate* precincts. The process of decoding Jewish fate culminates in the
novel *Layish*, which describes the most basic, primordial exilic pattern—
the topos of the journey to the Holy Land as a tale of the endlessly deferred end.

LAYISH: PILGRIMAGE TO THE PAST

> Kayn kotsk fort men nisht,
> Kayn kotsk geyt men;
> Vayl kotsk iz dokh bimkoym-hamikdesh,
> Kayn kotsk darf men oyle-regl zayn.
>
> 'Regl' iz dokh der taytsh a fus—
> Kayn kotsk darf men geyn tsu fus,
> Zingendik un tantsndik,

Un az khsidim geyen kayn kotsk,
Geyt men mit gezang.

'Regl' is dokh der taytsh a gevoynshaft—
Men darf zikh gevoynen tsu geyn kayn kotsk,
Zingendik un tantsndik.
Un az khsidim geyen kayn kotsk,
Geyt men mit a tants.

'Regl' iz dokh der taytsh a yontev—
Gut-yontev, gut-yontev gut-yontev!
Un az khsidim geyen kayn kotsk,
Is dokh a groyser yontev.

One doesn't ride to Kotsk. One walks to Kotsk, for Kotsk is in place of the
Temple. To Kotsk you have to make the pilgrimage on foot.
Regl means "foot," to Kotsk you have to go on foot, singing and dancing.
And when Hassidim go to Kotsk, they go with a song.
Regl also means "habit." One must get in the habit of going to Kotsk,
singing and dancing. And when Hassidim go to Kotsk, they go with a
dance.
Regl also means "holiday." A happy holiday! And when Hassidim go to
Kotsk, it's a great holiday.[44]

A convoy of wagons carrying a motley group of Jews who are mainly
social outcasts—petty thieves, thugs, and murderers—along with a sprin-
kling of old folks, musicians, rabbis, and visionaries who disappear and
reappear by turns, is making its way over what seem to be great geographical distances and many years. Their ostensible destination is
Jerusalem (the "Land of Israel" is hardly mentioned). Although there are
no clear historical indices, a few markers limit this story to an undefined
period in the early part of this century. As the youngest, Layish, the eponymous narrator, plays the role of both *ingénu* and scribe.

One can read *Layish* as a teleological narrative whose final station is
Jerusalem and whose final chapter—which takes place at the port of Galati, Romania, on the shores of the Danube, just "before" embarkation—
is a sign that the destination is within reach. This reading provides the
anticipated redemptive closure to a two-thousand-year-long voyage.[45] It
is, however, far more plausible to read the text as an *anti*teleological narrative; after all, the actual sea voyage and arrival are extratextual and
dependent on a readerly act. But a recontextualization of the entire discussion can yield an alternative strategy—one that could reach beyond
this dialectic altogether to a *reincorporation* of discarded modes of Jewish consciousness into the dominant structure.

The aborted conclusion, the *'aliyah* to Jerusalem that is not enacted

in the text, may be a sign of the thwarted teleology of the voyage; but if
we retrace our steps (as some of the travelers themselves attempt to do),
we will discover that the linear structure is undermined throughout the
journey. The appearance of progress is really a series of digressions: "The
distance from Sadigora to Czernowitz is a one-hour journey, but the heavy
rains and the squabbles impeded us and we arrived in Czernowitz two
weeks later"; "afterward the convoy proceeded slowly and apparently
aimlessly. . . . [W]e meandered along the Prut as if we had lost our way."
And, toward the end, after the death of two of the elderly passengers,
"our progress was halted."[46]

What appeared to be a major movement in space is now revealed as
a sluggish journey within the confines of the Bukovina region, particularly along the shores of the Prut River. As I have been arguing, this picaresque chronotope of the road, in which random encounters, digressions,
diversions, and chance stations—and not the final destination—are what
determine the essence of the journey and the structure of the narrative,
is a parody of the great Jewish epic and tells the story of the "losers." To
repeat David Quint's observation, "to the victors belongs epic, with its
linear teleology; to the losers belongs romance, with its random or circular wandering."[47] But after the realization or depletion of the epic impulse at the end of the twentieth century, such wandering could also reveal the scaffolding of the Jewish myth: that is, what remains without the
superstructure of Zionism or Enlightenment, messianic or Marxist faith.

The "official" pilgrimage to Jerusalem, it turns out, is composed of
mini-pilgrimages to the local saints (*tzaddikim*) of Vizhnitsa and Sadigora. In some stark way it both recapitulates the localization of sacred
space in Hassidic communities before the war and anticipates the evolving ritual of *geyn af keyver oves* (visiting ancestral graves) in postwar
Europe. Even more striking, it is the quintessential enactment of the cultural representations and suspended teleology of *golus*; the mimetic activity of *oyle regl*, of pilgrimage, is based on the premise that Kotsk, or
Vizhnitsa—like the Yiddish translation of the Hebrew Bible—is *bimkoym-
hamikdesh*, a movable simulacrum of the Temple.

But *Layish* is a disenchanted world; it is Agnon without miracle,
Mendele without satire. It is devoid of the cosmic miracles that facilitate
Hananiah's voyage, the magical thinking that impedes Benjamin's, and
the exuberance that animates Motl's.[48] When Agnon directs "our comrades" to the Holy Land through the actual topography of the Prut River,
the port at Galati, and the voyage over a stormy sea, and when Hananiah travels on a magic carpet the size of a handkerchief, the characters

move by an authorial fiat that incorporates historical/mimetic and mythological journeys into one tapestry, an act of grace that holds in suspended tension the Jewish folkloric and material universes. Layish and his companions go through more or less the same places—with Czernowitz replacing Buczacz as the autobiographical point of reference—and they are even joined by someone named Shmuel Yosef, by another named Yosef Hayyim, and, if not by Chaim Nahman himself, then by a few of his verses.[49] Paradoxically, however, such aggregations actually impede the journey; the sacred center these pilgrims are trying to reach *recedes* from the material world into the sphere of legend the closer they come to their destination.

As the narrative proceeds, it approximates more and more a journey as a retrograde textual enterprise. The Prut River comes to resemble those Babylonian waters by which the song of exile was first chanted. The rhetoric becomes increasingly biblical and formulaic: "'What will be?' Menahem the Blind purses the orbs of his eyes (*arubot eynav*)." Only twenty-five pages from the end of the narrative that is meant to be the end of the journey itself ("for the end of the journey is the true test," says Srul), one of the teamsters requests to return to his hometown; when he has finally been convinced that Piotrkow has been burned to the ground, "he is driven crazy with longing" and jumps into the Prut River and drowns. At that moment the river, which until then has provided nourishment for the convoy traveling its length, becomes "as turbulent as the Sambatyon."[50] As he leaps into the aggadic river that for centuries had protected the borders of the known world and the inviolability of the unknown, that had been the sign of deferred access to the lost tribes of Israel and to Jerusalem as the site of a ruined past and a messianic future, the mythological map usurps both geography and history.

Perhaps it would be more accurate to say that at this point in the narrative, Europe is represented more or less in its real topography and Jerusalem returns to its status quo ante: the focus of eternal Jewish desire, the place beyond the Sambatyon where "everything will be repaired."[51] Reverting to that archaic space out of which Agnon's characters and their *pesukim* emerged to be reincarnated in sacred soil, these characters seem to find not refuge or redemption but the solace of a familiar tale of suspended animation. Jerusalem reacquires its dimensions as the site of Jewish longing and the journey is revealed as a traditional pilgrimage with a two-way thrust, a round-trip.

When Appelfeld's minimalist, amnesiac language becomes textured and allusive, granting access to collective memory, the change is in the

service of reinventing the primordial topos of the (unending) Jewish journey. Another novella published around the same time as *Layish*, *The Iron
Tracks*, is structured not by intertextuality but by the journey itself. "Since
the end of the war I have been on this line," begins this first-person narrative of a man whose only postwar activity is to ride the rails of Europe. Admitting to a loss of emplotment and emplacement, he is also reclaiming Jewish wandering and space as its element: "Others may possess
spacious houses, shops, even warehouses. I have an entire continent. . . .
In this repetition lies a strange hopefulness. As if our end were not extinction but a sort of constant renewal."[52]

What is the resonance of this paradigm of "renewal" or repetition in
Israeli literature of the late twentieth century? That is, how can such a
deferment of the telos unfold within the telos itself? Can we say that in
some crucial sense, Appelfeld's story, like his convoy of refugees, like
Bertha incarcerated in her room, never really arrived in Jerusalem?

On the one hand, of course, "return" to the fatherland in any true
sense is no longer possible.[53] When, in *Benjamin the Third*, the Quixote
figure and his sidekick declare that they are "bewived" and ask to be
released from the czar's army so that they may return home, they are
voicing a kind of skepticism regarding all schemes of redemption—but
above all they are delivering a proleptic rejection of Zionist utopianism.
Yet, as we have seen in chapter 2, it turns out that the journey of Benjamin and Sender did not end in their home in Batalon; after having served
for years in Israeli schools as exempla of the degradation of *galut* culture, they managed via a circuitous route to "reenter" the culture to serve
as indictments of the teleological-monumental structure itself, of politics
and militarism that dwarf the human being. If the speech delivered by
these shlemiels resonates as loudly at the end of our century as it did at
the end of theirs, then the miserable, lost characters in Appelfeld's universe may also constitute, in their circular, reflexive movement, a gesture
of some weight.

However, Appelfeld's characters can be said less to supply a critical
or skeptical gesture than to reiterate a pattern of collective self-representation. This reading depends on a set of hermeneutic adjustments in
the relative status not only of Czernowitz and Jerusalem but of desire
and arrival, of narrative and closure, of the "real" and the mimetic. As
the journey proceeds, the number of travelers shrinks. Some die, some
run away. But for those deserters who leave the convoy and look for a
way home, there is no hope in the (no)place that exists always in the
reader's mind under the (back)shadow of Nazism. And since Jerusalem

becomes more and more occluded as the journey approaches its end, the narrative makes clear how radical their displacement is. Given what we are invited to know from hindsight to be the absence of any *historical* option of return to their homelands in that infinitely deferred moment before embarkation, the travelers remain frozen in their posts on the shore in a state of pure, eternal longing for the city on the "other side." *We* know how lethal is the fate that awaits them, that both pursues and impedes them in all the spaces of Europe—but their fear of arrival in Jerusalem is no less great, for it is also the fear of death. The traveler who never arrives is guaranteed eternal life, like Yehuda Halevi, whose longing for Zion echoes in the ears of all the pilgrims of all the generations, a longing trapped and embalmed in the artistic act itself.

(Re)Imagining Europe

The Anachronistic Tales of I. B. Singer

In 1914, Sholem Aleichem's nine-year-old narrator, Motl, transplanted his shtetl to America, which he embraced as the country of endless self-invention. After two world wars, a child*like* naïveté, sustained against all odds, will prove the next best thing to the naïveté *of* a child as passport to American culture. In 1945, Isaac Bashevis Singer's man of faith, Gimpl, came to America by never leaving the world of the shtetl; his naïveté or gullibility protected him from the historical events that had just destroyed that world. Bashevis Singer manages to suspend him and some of his compatriots in an airtight bubble of innocence that preserves their world from the ravages of the times—betraying the degree of artifice enlisted in such a massive act of denial. It is one of the earliest and most enduring of cultural strategies for securing for the Jewish imagination the vanishing continent of Eastern Europe.

I. B. Singer himself arrived in New York from Warsaw as an already-acclaimed Yiddish writer in 1935, but he remained avowedly an exile, never an immigrant, in America. Yet in some ways he became an exile in his own community as well—one of those rare examples of a writer widely read and venerated in every language but his own. America would free I. B. Singer to perform radical acts of fantasy to replace what could not be remembered, but over time it would also provide the stage for mourning what could not, ultimately, be forgotten. His early, "Polish" stories are as strangely self-contained and immutable as his later "American" narratives are catalogues of displaced, nomadic words, refugees from *some other* sentence; the Jewish streets in Poland remain a protected ground of reference, while the streets of New York, Buenos Aires, and other cities of the New World cannot provide semantic space for the stray fragments of the Jewish story.

Throughout the second half of the twentieth century, Bashevis Singer maintained his position as the most authentic and authenticating Jewish reference, his shtetl the most genuine, *albeit nonmimetic*, Jewish geography. I am deliberately limiting my discussion here to his short fiction, for there is a significant generic difference between his short stories and novellas and his novels. Many of the longer, dynastic novels have a kind of mimetic quality and act as weathervanes of the winds that propel Jewish history. But in the carefully reauthored, defamiliarized world of the short story, the *hurbn* remains the endlessly deferred scenario. The suspension of apocalyptic endings, like the deferral of messianic closure, is a peculiarly diasporic gesture, defiant and humane as well as repressive and delusional. Its expression in Bashevis Singer's fiction is the verbal-textual re-creation of a lost center. Over the years, the hometown of Frampol or Bilgoray or Warsaw, reinvented in the early stories, takes on a kind of ontological status of its own. Ultimately, it will rescue this singer, his characters, and his readers from the fate of the utterly dispossessed.

GIMPL IN A BAPTIST CHURCH: TRANSLATING BASHEVIS SINGER

Saul Bellow's translation of Isaac Bashevis Singer's Yiddish story "Gimpel the Fool" appeared in the American journal *Partisan Review* in May 1953, eight years after its Yiddish appearance; it launched the English career of I. B. Singer and a new phase in the representation of Jewish culture in America. The narrative condenses the life of a long-suffering *ingénu* into a series of acts of faith, which in turn constitute a license for storytelling.[1]

There is a curious nuptial scene early in the English version in which Gimpel and his bride, the "virgin" Elka, stand under the canopy while the "master of revels makes a 'God 'a mercy' in memory of the bride's parents" (E 12; Y17). The traditional dirge "El maleh rahamim" [God full of mercy], chanted for the deceased relatives of a bride or groom, is a conventional folkloristic expression of the Jewish ritual incorporation of the memory of loss into celebratory occasions.[2] But delivered tongue-in-cheek by a *badkhn* or jester in a story written just as the camps were being liberated, it is metonymic of what will become Bashevis Singer's complex representation of the past for the American reader. The most obvious accommodation is to the idioms of the host culture. The distance between "God 'a mercy" and "El maleh rahamim" represents, presumably, the cultural terrain that Gimpl had to cross in order to enter the pages of *Partisan Review* and become naturalized as an American fool. The deterritorialized "God 'a mercy"—Gimpl in a Baptist church, as it were— serves as a dissonant marker, flagging this absence until compensatory readings can reinvest it with some of its original sounds. Such lacunae both mark a discarded culture and leave room for its recovery. The passage of time and the acts of compensation that followed the radical displacement and eventual destruction of the language and the culture of Jewish immigrants from Europe would invite American readers, later in the century, to strain to hear "El maleh rahamim" under the *huppa*.[3]

We begin to see that there was as much cover-up as exposure in Bellow's "Gimpel." But in some ways the English translation mimics the contested authority of the Yiddish original. Gimpel responds to the taunts of his fellow townspeople with the gullibility of either a true believer or a true fabulist: "'Gimpel, a cow flew over the roof and laid brass eggs.' . . . 'You, Gimpel, while you stand there scraping with your baker's shovel the Messiah has come. The dead have arisen. . . . Gimpel, your father and mother have stood up from the grave. They're looking for you.' I like a golem believed everyone," Gimpel the narrator admits, invoking the authorizing power of Scriptures: "In the first place, everything is possible, as it is written in the Wisdom of the Fathers, *I've forgotten just how*" (E 10; Y 17; emphasis mine).

Is it *faith* or *memory* that is being tested here? or perhaps faith and memory as competing modes of imagination? Forgetting, like remembering, is a collaborative process that requires an implicit social contract over the generations. And the suspension of disbelief that is a profound state of forgetfulness is as necessary a condition for entering the realm of fiction as for entering the realm of faith. The widely acclaimed translation that inaugurated Bashevis Singer's American career made the text available without making it transparent; this story in its English reincarnation both enacts and very partially redresses the widespread cultural amnesia that had followed the mass migration of Jews from Eastern Europe and the displaced access to Jewish territories, languages, and texts.

Images of the American Adam were so empowering that immigrants writing in Yiddish, who had disengaged from traditional Jewish practice, believed at least for a moment that they might succeed in inscribing their lives on the American landscape. Their faith that the cultural pluralism embedded in the American ethos would provide a more tolerant center for a new Jewish culture fueled an energetic modernism in the Yiddish poetry of the early decades of the century. The poet H. Leyvik envisioned the words "do voynt dos yidishe folk" (here lives the Jewish people) emblazoned on the New York skyline.[4] That the acculturation of these poets—and of their children—would be so successful that their writing would, within one generation, become all but invisible is one of the profound ironies of this enterprise;[5] it is, nevertheless, consistent with the larger cultural patterns of repression, substitution, and selective recovery that constitute the history of ethnicity—most dramatically, perhaps, of Jewish ethnicity—in America.

It is through allusion as well as translation that this process manifests itself. There develops in the *English* writing of both Jewish immigrants and their American-born sons and daughters a strange dialectic of simultaneous reference to and effacement of the Jewish literary and linguistic canons—marking the place of the discarded culture through reference, through *partial* translation, and through transmutation of an inherited vocabulary into indigenous terms. The most powerful site or mise-en-scène of this process is Henry Roth's *Call It Sleep*, first published in 1934. In this remarkable text, mediated like *Motl the Cantor's Son* through the consciousness of a child, the Jewish languages and texts are in fact made salient by their *absence*. Yiddish is the normative language, yet the warm dyadic speech that flows between Genya Shearl and her son David is a "Yiddish" translated for purposes of the narrative into a lyrical English. That is, the Yiddish is presumed but not really enacted as a linguistic layer, except for occasional aphorisms or inflected phrases. The culture or language of origin is thus marked off and engaged through the most radical act of translation, of carrying over, into the highest register of the host language.[6] Hebrew, by contrast, as repository of the language of revelation, is present as an untranslated, indecipherable medium: Hebrew is a "strange and secret tongue. . . . If you knew it, then you could talk to God. (Furtively [in *heder*], while the rabbi still spoke David leaned over and stole a glance at the number of the page.) On sixty-eight. After, maybe, can ask. On page sixty-eight. That blue book—Gee! it's God."[7] Here place, in its sense of *makom* and *HA-makom*, human and divine, is not only marked or embedded in the text: it *is* the text. But it is the text seen through a glass darkly, the text as eclipse, absence, substitution. For the moment, for these writers and their readers, both the Hebrew and the Yiddish canonic languages and texts are as present as those dark squares in the family photo album where the pictures of the patriarchs are missing.

But after the war this process of selective amnesia and absent reference is manifest more in the proximity of the writer to the original, lost culture than in lacunae in the English texts. And Bashevis Singer, in translation, will embody that proximity.

ONE MORE STRANGER IN A STRANGE LAND?

"What exactly is American about Singer's American fiction?" Leslie Fiedler asks in a whimsical book of essays, *Fiedler on the Roof.* Surveying terrain generally inhabited by males who share a yearning for the "wilderness, [the] unlimited space, the untamed ocean," he finds at Bashevis Singer's hand a far less promising landscape: "Outside of Singer's half mythological city, we are permitted to imagine only squalid bungalows huddled on the slopes of alien hills; and if the sea laps the shores of his Coney Island, it remains always a sea seen from apartment house windows, into whose waves his protagonists are never moved to plunge."

But Fiedler does find what he is looking for in the quality of "lostness" that pervades all of Bashevis Singer's American stories; "It is this theme which, paradoxically, makes him seem finally one of us, one more Stranger in a Strange Land."[8] To convey it, Bashevis Singer does not need wilderness or vast spaces. Without a doubt the characters in his American fiction have nearly all lost something, and are nearly all lost themselves. But even if Fiedler is riding on the coattails of a fashionable confusion between the refugee as alien and the critical posture of the American intellectual as alien*ated*—a posture common to the generation of writers who came of age in the 1940s—it is through an inclusive strategy of the excluded that he welcomes Bashevis Singer as an "American" writer. This honorary citizenship in the republic of letters to which so many Yiddish writers aspired takes on a bittersweet cast if one recalls that Bashevis Singer gained his American audience at the very moment his primary audience in Eastern Europe was being wiped off the face of the earth. What Fiedler is not taking into account here is that the appeal of this Yiddish writer came not from his refugee stories but from his reinvention of the shtetl. And what is transpiring in this shtetl of the mind, at its most fundamental level, is a creative resolution of the struggle between *remembering* and *forgetting,* a shadow play of what is being enacted in the postwar world as it embraces Bashevis Singer.

There are, then, two levels of effacement or estrangement operative in stories like "Gimpel the Fool." That the connection between Gimpl's own "amnesia" and the "forgetful" English text goes deeper than the changing decorums of translation can be seen in how knowledge internal to the text functions. When Gimpl forgets the prooftext from Pirkei Avot ("everything is possible, as it is written in the Wisdom of the Fathers, *I've forgotten just how . . .* "), the implication is that his primary, *intra*textual, audience—his silent interlocutors whose presumed presence constitutes an internal and intimate dialogic space—will "remember." The correctives for individual lapses of memory are embedded in the knowledge shared by a storytelling circle, which provides the locus for much of the humor in Yiddish fiction; the malapropisms and misquotes of Sholem Aleichem's semiliterate characters, as we have seen, are a function of group memory and can help us delineate the boundary between collective knowing and collective forgetting. But Isaac Bashevis Singer, writing the original Yiddish story in America in 1945, is signaling a more fundamental loss.

Although America may have offered its immigrants a kind of milk of amnesia as antidote to the heartburn of ethnic memory, after 1945 the mandate to remember takes on deadly earnestness for Jewish writers; every act of recollection becomes a gesture of *re*-collection, of rescue, measured not within the normal parameters of intralinguistic discourse or within the fanciful frameworks of supreme fictions but by its function as one more defense against oblivion. The attention to fragments, which began as a "kaleidoscopic" embrace of the modern world,[9] a celebratory shoring-up of its disparate voices, of its signs and sights and sounds, becomes after the war a conservational strategy for salvaging the past. Because those who could really remember have died, those who have almost forgotten feel compelled to create new repositories of memory. With the appearance of Bellow's Gimpel and Irving Howe and Eliezer Greenberg's "treasury" of Yiddish stories, 1953 becomes the year that inaugurates the enlistment of Yiddish writers in the American attempt to reclaim a lost Jewish place and an interrupted Jewish story.

GULLIBLE'S TRAVELS: GENEALOGY OF THE SHLEMIEL

In his translation Bellow provided not only cultural mediation but also the subtext for his own writing: "I am Gimpel the fool. I don't think myself a fool," the American Gimpel announces (E 9; Y 17). Eleven years later, in 1964, Gimpl's translator published a novel that begins, "If I am out of my mind, it's all right with me, thought Moses Herzog."[10]

The privileged reader approaches the text with the expectation that Herzog is no more out of his mind than Gimpl is a fool. There is, nonetheless, a great distance between Gimpl as *tam*—a spiritual category that, as critics have shown, connotes integrity and fullness as well as gullibility and receptivity[11]—and Herzog's psychic imbalance, which represents alternative moral postures in a disenchanted world. The transmigration of the fool, with his clearly defined social role in the European as well as the specifically Jewish imagination, into the neurotic academic in his American isolation suggests something about the cultural contexts and their respective definitions of the outsider who expresses critical distance.

Yet we can recognize in this little intertextual transaction between Bashevis Singer and Bellow an archetype who managed to survive the war and the rocky voyage between Jewish spaces and languages. In her study of the shlemiel as modern hero, Ruth Wisse identifies him as the most representative diaspora figure and, in the writings of S. Y. Abramovitsh and Sholem Aleichem, as a remarkably viable moral and cultural response to the condition of the disempowered Jew:

> Almost without warning, [a character like Mendele's Benjamin the Third becomes a] serious moral alternative to the organized evil that would destroy him. . . . In an insane world, the fool may be the only morally sane man. . . . The schlemiel becomes a hero when real action is impossible and reaction remains the only way a man can define himself. . . . [Sholem Aleichem] conceived of his writing as a solace for people whose situation was so ineluctably unpleasant that they might as well laugh. . . . [Through language, the schlemiel] reinterprets events to conform to his own vision, and thereby controls them.[12]

Following the thinking of Dov Sadan, Wisse then suggests an affinity between the Wandering Jew and the shlemiel in popular novels of the nineteenth century, beginning in 1813 in German with Adalbert von Chamisso's *Peter Schlemihl*. We should take note of the unacknowledged overlap between the prototypes of the fool, the insane man, and the wanderer in Wisse's profile of the shlemiel, caused by their resonance in non-Jewish as well as Jewish cultures; implicitly, that is, the shlemiel becomes acculturated by "borrowing" the characteristics of the liminal figures in Western literature and drama. A talking culture whose self-understanding and self-narration are grounded in acts of interpretation can then focus on the centrality of the shlemiel as its cultural ambassador and on homelessness as his endemic condition. In his kinship with Ahasuerus, with the social outcast as changeling, and with the "golus Jew," Peter Schlemihl's lack of a shadow is perceived as "the closest metaphorical equivalent for the lack of a homeland."[13]

Bashevis Singer plays this rather anachronistic role to the hilt. Standing in Stockholm in 1978, he began his Nobel Prize acceptance speech by accentuating, in Yiddish and with no small amount of hyperbole and distortion, the peripatetic and peaceful nature of his native tongue and the discourse it produced: "The high honor bestowed upon me by the Swedish Academy is also a recognition of the Yiddish language—a language of exile, without a land, without frontiers, not supported by any government, a language which possesses no words for weapons, ammunition, military exercises, war tactics. . . . In a figurative way, Yiddish is the wise and humble language of us all, the idiom of frightened and hopeful humanity."[14]

Acknowledging in that august forum the values of a deterritorialized language as a medium of tales whose global itinerary qualifies them as "universal," Bashevis Singer is also claiming a place for the Jewish imagination that is, patently and proudly, *in*consequential. As prototype of the diaspora Jew, the shlemiel thrives in the wordy gap between inner and outer reality or between ideal and real worlds, in the space where fiction is generated. Bred of a fatalism and resignation that resist all prevailing utopian schemes to "enter history" as a plotting character, Gimpl becomes a positive reincarnation of I. L. Peretz's Bontshe Shvayg, the scorned figure who doesn't know how to petition heaven for more than a buttered roll. Like Sholem Aleichem before him, Bashevis Singer elevates the logocentrism of his characters to an article of faith, turning their monologues into an affirmation of the unparalleled empowerment of speech. Dan Miron writes that for Bashevis Singer passivity was not a function of a ruined order but rather a normative posture vis-à-vis the order (or disorder) of things. Miron compares him to S. Y. Agnon, for whom a character's passivity was a tragic response to an unfulfilled Zionist-religious vision of redemption through social (or divine) agency, a desperate resignation to the shattering or deterioration of the ideal order.[15]

Compulsive speech and the self-conscious flights of imagination built around it, symptomatic of a passive and obligation-free relation to the affairs of the world, have been presented as the very essence of Jewish humor. But the implications of such representations bear tracing. The humor in Sholem Aleichem, like the playfulness in Bashevis Singer, yields to irony and then to despair in Agnon, as the discrepancy between the ideal and the real produces different cultural responses to universes conceived in different modes: the credulous and self-mocking or the utopian

and self-aggrandizing. Utopia as a *program* mandates a claim to ownership of the territory of this world and therefore of the gaps as well; angst
and anomie come to replace laughter in those gaps and, it seems to me,
partly account for a certain humorlessness in much of Israeli fiction. There
is considerable irony and satire, which is utopia unmasked, but little of
what we have come to identify as "Jewish" humor—the compensatory
humor of the disempowered.

Gimpl takes charge only of his inner reality; he is, ultimately, the
shlemiel as spinner of tales, as wandering bard, his gullibility a kind of
negative capability that can generate an infinity of possible worlds: "The
longer I lived the more I understood that there were really no lies," he
declares as he exits the stage. "Whatever doesn't really happen is dreamed
at night. It happens to one if it doesn't happen to another, tomorrow if
not today, or a century hence if not next year" (E 22–23; Y 20).

Speech acts would become the ticket into cultural forums of the late
twentieth century; positivist concepts of reality would yield to literary
and linguistic inquiries into reality as a rhetorical or discursive construct;
narrativity would become the ascendant order of the imagination. It is
no wonder that at this moment, the Jews of the American Diaspora are
performing a profoundly American and profoundly modern as well as
profoundly Jewish act in canonizing the fictions of I. B. Singer. It is one
of the signs that, not unlike the remaking of its civilization two thousand years ago, Jewish culture survives the devastation of its material
universe by creating ersatz, fanciful forms that tell the tale, mark the place,
and set it free.

REFUSAL TO MOURN

The process of creating a culture of substitution and replica took some
time. The war was followed by twenty years or so of intense mourning,
which appeared to be the only task left for Yiddish writers surviving in
the Diaspora. Yet it was a process in which Isaac Bashevis Singer seemed
to take little or no part. One wonders, in fact, whether the scorn heaped
on him by the Yiddish critical establishment was spurred by this perceived
delinquency no less than by the sexual license and the presence of the supernatural in his stories and by the uneven quality of his Yiddish prose.
The Yiddish American poet Jacob Glatshteyn wrote the most scathing
of the attacks: "The author seemingly takes pleasure in the desecration
of the dead, which shames the living. Again and again he describes the
partially decomposed bodies garbed in the Devil's clothing. . . . I'd wa-

ger that this sort of jest would never have occurred to the Devil if Singer had not prompted him to engage in this weird act of grave desecration."[16] That is, the problem for Glatshteyn, here defined in terms of a decorum of historical accountability, lies not so much in the intimidating presence of the Devil as in the desecration of graves, the necrophilic carnival, the playful and irreverent clothing of "decomposed bodies" in the Devil's garb. The post-Holocaust writer should rather—by these lights—be the ultimate gravedigger for those bodies that had no proper burial.

Before the commemorative gesture had been exhausted, the documentary impulse sated, and memories embedded in mimetic texts with referential (and reverential) status fully explored, certain forms of countermemory would have appeared suspect to one's fellow writers. For over two decades after the war, Bashevis Singer continued writing about Polish Jewry, often using the shtetl as his setting, as if it still existed. In an interview with Irving Howe in 1966, he admitted that at the heart of his writing there is an "illusion which is consciously sustained."[17] Bashevis Singer thus quite deliberately undertook to exempt the characters in many of his short fictions from their awful historicity. Are the monologues in these narratives delivered before a group of interlocutors—that same internal audience—now silently entombed, as in a great wax museum? Spared the fate of their fellows, separated out and placed in a hermetically sealed chamber, they replay indefinitely the final polyphonic moments of their civilization—unburdened by the terrible knowledge of the end. Here may lie an act of commemoration more dramatic and powerful than all the monuments and eulogies to a destroyed civilization. "In literature, death does not exist," Bashevis Singer is quoted as saying; "we never say: 'the *late* Anna Karenina.'"[18] One might problematize the argument by adding that the *late* Anna Karenina—Anna dead at the end of the novel—carries no more ontological weight than the *early* Anna Karenina, whom we retrieve by simply flipping back to the front of the volume. And how much more true is this of Gimpl, whose immortality is secured not only by his kinship to the Wandering Jew but also by the lack of closure in his story, narrated in the first-person continuous present.

That the characters in fiction live generally *sub specie aeternitatis* takes on particular resonance in the literature before us—where the bravest defiance of the death of the Jews is the eternal life granted their fictional counterparts. But we have seen that eulogy, not suspended animation, was the order of the day. In some cases, final rites of poetic tribute also served hidden ideological agendas. Setting sail as an illegal immigrant, braving the rough seas and the transport into colloquial Hebrew, the shlemiel could hardly get past the port authorities in Palestine—even as the crematory chimneys were still smoldering in Europe. The Hebrew poet Natan Alterman wrote his epitaph in the wartime poem "Mikhtav shel Menakhem-Mendl" [Letter from Menakhem-Mendl]. Published in Alterman's column, "Ha-tur ha-shvi'i" [The Seventh Column], in *Davar* on March 9, 1945, Menakhem-Mendl's "letter" to his wife Sheyne Shendl contains a graphic report of the deaths of the characters in Sholem Aleichem's house of fiction. But these lines are more than a memorial to the Yiddish spirit; they also serve as a compassionate barrier of exclusion of certain nonviable figures from Eretz Yisrael:

> . . . 'ad nitzavnu be-tokh ha-gola,
> abirei he-halom,
> geonei ha-'oni,
> giborei ha-sifrut ha-yehudit ha-gdola
> ha-nofelet ba-sheleg kamoni.[19]

Tevye, Motl, Pini, Stempenyu, and Menakhem-Mendl himself—the quixotic "knights of the dream," "geniuses of penury," "heroes of the great Jewish literature / that falls in the snow" in the very midst of (*be-tokh*) a place called *gola*—are by definition unsuited for the topography and climate of Palestine. Some forty-five years later, Sholem Aleichem's characters will again prove nonviable in the harsh climate of Israel; as we have seen, Motl, Sholem Aleichem's eternal child, becomes an imaginary companion to Momik, the nine-year-old protagonist of David Grossman's Hebrew novel, *See Under: Love*, licensing Momik's most daring attempts to rewrite history (see chapter 4). In the end, however, Motl is delivered over to his hapless fate and "killed off" in Momik's dream, as his friend looks on in terror.

The afterlife of the shlemiel in America and his extinction in Israel become a barometer of the selective cultural authority of the past; the act of burying the characters along with their real-life models, rather than granting them eternal life in a suspended present tense, can be seen as a form of distancing as well as of historical representation. By reenacting or reinventing the destroyed shtetl as fictive possibility, and the shlemiel as its primary citizen, Bashevis Singer also enabled American Jews to *continue* the acts of simultaneous reference and effacement that were directed formerly at the living culture of European Jews. He thus helps to preserve, at some level, the dialectic of American Jewish identity premised on a voluntary editing of the past undisrupted by the burden of the survivors' moral responsibility for total recall. Here, then, is a curious if subtle denial of the essential distinction between communities lost by voluntary immigration and communities destroyed by external force.

Eventually even Bashevis Singer could not sustain the illusion at the heart of his writing; but in the short fiction, at least, it is the stories located elsewhere—mainly in America, and mainly in New York—that come to reflect the destruction of the primary referent. There is a crucial difference, that is, between those stories published *in* America and those whose mise-en-scène *is* America. Most of the stories published in English since *The Seance* (1968) take place in the United States; they mark a clear shift toward an exploration of the effects of cataclysmic history on the lives of refugees. The cosmology and mythopoiesis of the "Polish" stories are here replaced by a kind of metaphysics of human potential and vision; for Bashevis Singer, acknowledging the Holocaust means revealing the vast empty spaces in the universe that only *human* compassion can fill.

In I. B. Singer's fiction, the link between the death of the Jews and the collapse of their cultural universe is measured most dramatically in the utter transfiguration of the supernatural world; eventually, even the ghosts and demons come to share the fate of the community that believed in them: "I, a demon, bear witness that there are no demons left. . . . I've seen it all, the destruction of Tishevitz, the destruction of Poland. There are no more Jews, no more demons. . . . No more sins, no more temptations. . . . I am the last, a refugee."[20] Most of the characters in these stories are refugees living in anomie in the no-places of Jewish migration; human kindness has largely replaced eros and simple affection has replaced cosmic forces as the prime movers in this pathetic drama of remaindered lives.

ANACHRONISM AS POETIC LICENSE

The Jews in Bashevis Singer's "American" narratives may be survivors and mourners at the largest funeral procession in recent memory, but the "Polish" stories were what secured his place in the pantheon of modern fiction. The force of Bashevis Singer's success as a writer in America lies precisely in that temporal remove which rendered him anachronistic in the eyes of his contemporaries: those who were committed, in the first half of the century, to inscribing a brave new world in Yiddish and, in the second half, to keening for the dead from the old world.[21] *Anachronism* itself—not nostalgia—becomes the article of faith and the temporal logic that governs Bashevis Singer's writing. Far from being a radical departure, anachronism has been a principle of the Jewish imagination since Talmudic times and finds its most forceful expression in Yiddish retellings of biblical tales.[22] Yet Bashevis Singer invoked it, implicitly, as a substitute for grieving. He began by insisting, as early as 1943, while the war was still raging and its ravages yet uncounted, that Yiddish had already become an artificial language capable of rendering only the Eastern European Jewish past. As a medium for representing the present (life in America or even in the big cities of Europe) there is, he argued, no "hope" for Yiddish, which is a "caricature of a language, if you wish to use it for contemporary secular purposes, but full of unexploited resources if you use it for describing our past and for creating works of art linked with yesterday": "Our mother's tongue (*mame-loshn*) has become old. The mother is by now a grandmother and a great-grandmother. . . . She makes funny mistakes and mixes things up. But only when she wants to be modern, to stride with the times in order to show how worldly she is. When she starts talking about times gone by, . . . precious stones fall from her lips."[23]

This is a rather disingenuous denial of the forms of Yiddish modernism—including that of his own brother, I. J. Singer—that fed his own. But however self-servingly, Bashevis Singer is representing the (Yiddish) word that has outlived its world as a reinstatement of the text as memory and metonymy: the thing itself and its signifier. Now, as in the wake of former catastrophes, patterns of exodus, of recuperation and return through acts of pilgrimage to the place or to its surviving texts, represent for the Jewish generations "in exile" the narrative of their origins in a destroyed civilization. Whether they are constructed as narratives of origins or of endings, however, determines the nature of the sites and of the pilgrimage itself.

Jacob Glatshteyn, whose scathing criticism of Bashevis Singer's work we have already noted, provides the counterexample in his own poetry. In some ways he traveled a far greater distance than did his compatriot. His poetry of the 1920s and early '30s is counted among the most daring of modernist experiments in Yiddish in America; happily deterritorialized from the burden of the Jewish past, Glatshteyn and his fellow "Introspectivists" reclaimed the language for its American chapter and a new universalist cultural embrace. Described by Benjamin Harshav as "immersed in listening to the secrets of the Yiddish language," the young poet (who had arrived in the United States from Lublin at the age of eighteen and studied law at New York University before devoting himself to poetry) invoked the sounds of places real and imaginary. "Gradually but persistently, the rhyme *erter-verter* . . . emerges in Glatshteyn's poetry. . . . There are no words ('*verter*') without places ('*erter*')." Yet while the latter are contained in the former, they also, by their very existence, safeguard the language that names them and set it free to roam in spaces both nostalgic and exotic. In the names of the Polish towns of his childhood the poet can evoke a geography resonant, warm, and at the same time unobligated by memory, time, or distance. "But after the Holocaust," argues Harshav, "the relation is inverted . . . : in Glatshteyn's early poetics, places carried words; now the words are the carriers of a lost world."[24]

Harshav's gloss on Glatshteyn provides a foil for Bashevis Singer and a very different model for rescuing Jewish places. Acts of the imagination that had once disburdened themselves of historical accountability are now utterly shaped by it; the realm of the fantastic, proudly claimed as the province of the unfettered Yiddish word, yields to the Jewish town whose ghostly presence has become as exotic as were the shores of the Ganges River or the Shinto shrines in Japan just a few decades before. Glatshteyn's poem "I Shall Transport Myself," which appeared in Yiddish in the very year of Gimpl's English debut, is an exercise in realities invented not out of magnificent marble and precious stones from the Far East or from the Xanadus of the mind—"kaleidoscopic" pictures of an infinitely accessible world—but out of the shards and rubble of the scarcely buried past:

> I shall transport myself inside the mote of wonder
> that blots the view
> As far back as my dark gaze
> Can dream, can see . . .
>
> I shall stubborn myself,
> Plant myself
> In a private, intimate night
> That I totally invented
> And wondered-in on all sides.
> I shall find a spot in space
> As big as a fly,
> And there I shall impose,
> For all time,
> A cradle, a child,
> I shall sing into it a voice
> Of a dozing father,
> With a face in the voice,
> With love in the voice,

With misty looks
That float in the child's sleepy eyes
Like warm moons.
And around the cradle I shall build a Jewish town
With a *shul*, with a vigilant God,
Watching over the poor shops,
Over the Jewish fear,
Over the graveyard
Alive all night
With its worrying dead.[25]

"These were words that carried in themselves the memory of places; you could conjure up whole Jewish worlds from them," Harshav comments on this poem. "(Did these worlds ever exist? Is he inventing them now?)" he adds,[26] not daring to reclaim the compensatory value of invention as equal to that of the lost referent. It is in fact clear that these later poems are not an architectural but an archaeological enterprise, a world admittedly reconstructed from "half of / a saved star . . . a piece of a gutted planet"[27]—underscoring the impossible task of the demiurge whose materials are recycled relics of a former creation.

A solitary figure among Jewish poets and storytellers, I. B. Singer succeeds for over two decades after the war in mobilizing narrative strategies to paint a universe in which the balance between places and words is maintained *in the illusion of their synchronicity*. Whereas virtually all the Yiddish writers and many of the Hebrew writers are engaged in rescuing fragments of the destroyed culture, Bashevis Singer's mythopoiesis encompasses a world in its totality, with its cultural dichotomies intact and with the legitimacy of humor and the arena of fictive possibility defended against history itself. While it may resemble in form what Hebrew writers were engaged in *proleptically* at the end of last century, theirs was built on an act of faith in worlds yet uncreated; in contrast, Bashevis Singer's re-creation of a world that no longer exists is a lonely act of willful amnesia.[28] Glatshteyn concludes his poem by consigning his reinvented Yiddish town to its cataclysmic fate:

I shall cling to it with my last days.
Spitefully, I shall count them in you, frozen past,
You, who mocked me,
You, who invented
My living, talking
Jewish world.
Then stilled it,
And in Maidenek-woods,

With a few shots
Killed it.[29]

Bashevis Singer suspends the awful finality of endings fictive or true. At the close of his narrative, Gimpl takes up his staff and goes out into the world, invoking in his wandering the consciousness, the theodicy, and the narrativity of exile—of a story with an endlessly deferred end.

VIRTUAL JEWISH GEOGRAPHIES

The endemic American quest for a lost—and irrecoverable—community will dovetail eventually with a nostalgia for Jewish spaces in the poetry and prose of the two or three generations of writers spanned by Bashevis Singer's lifetime. Whether through acts of translation or imaginative appropriation, both the shtetl and the Lower East Side will become mythic Jewish fields of reference in the postwar imagination.[30] The distance between the shtetl and the American Jewish ghetto as "mythic space" should not be minimized, of course; while their affinities can be judged as symptoms of a pervasive romantic sensibility, the distance should be measured in terms of access. Kazin can walk the streets of Brownsville where "Alfred" grew up, however remote and transfigured they may have become in the natural order of things;[31] but Bashevis Singer cannot revisit the landmarks of Itzik's boyhood without hearing (or *refusing* to hear) the echoes of the unnatural death of his townspeople, rendering the streets of Bilgoray or Frampol or even Warsaw a memory place of a different order.

That the shtetl had become mythic space for its own writers even *before* the war only highlights this process. The writers—Sholem Aleichem, I. L. Peretz, S. Y. Abramovitsh—who "invented" the shtetl as fictive geography in the late nineteenth and early twentieth century lived and wrote in the large urban centers of Eastern Europe.[32] Fiction fulfilling its promise as alternative reality is predicated here on the *presence of the referent* for both the writer and his public. The disappearance of the referent threatens to turn the fiction into a relic or an icon, undermining the critical tension between art and life. Distance as well as nostalgia is built into all subsequent acts of homage. Yiddish poet Y. Y. (Judd) Teller writes that because "the bearded generations . . . decimated by German genocide . . . are remote and unreal, like the weightless, levitating figures of Chagall's canvases, one may vaguely relate to them, without the risk of being mistaken for them."[33] Taking this further, we can see Gimpl's radical gullibility ("Gimpel, a cow flew over the roof and laid brass eggs . . .") as a way of

iconicizing the lost culture—a verbal counterpart to Chagall's aerody-
namic cattle; literalizing the folk idiom, it also confesses its own coun-
terfactuality as the most daring act of commemoration.[34]

On artists and writers more remote from the life and death of Eastern Europe than were Chagall and Bashevis Singer, such icons have an
effect like that of an embalmed ancestor. Cows (and fiddlers) on roofs
vie with caftaned grandfathers both as points of origin and authenticity
and as measures of distance. The image of his grandfather in Hassidic
garb serves as a touchstone of authenticity for Bellow's Herzog as he
stares at himself in the mirror of a men's clothing shop. The walking
anachronism of a survivor in a musty black suit becomes the point of
reference for Philip Roth's Eli in "Eli the Fanatic" (1959). Yet both the
middle-aged intellectual appraising his reflection in downtown Chicago
and the young lawyer parading down the streets of Woodenton, New
York, are engaged in a masquerade that is more like a Halloween prank
than a true conversion; neither would dream of claiming this moment of
sartorial authenticity as more than a symbolic point of departure.

Because Bellow's Moses Herzog and Roth's Eli Peck are more removed
in time, in place, and in language from the shtetl "original" than Bashevis
Singer's Gimpl, the latter's status is heightened as an authentic representation based on self-conscious anachronism rather than on nostalgia.
The surviving Roman imitations of the extinct Greek sculptures have been
viewed by later generations as authoritative visual representations of classical sculpture; by a similar logic, the progressively more removed American references to the European Jewish experience contribute to the canonization of Bashevis Singer's fictions as truer and more authentic
representations. In both cases, an original does not authenticate the
"best" representation; instead, the more removed and partial reproductions or referents authenticate the more proximate and less partial ones.
Canonization is effected here in the absence of opportunity to foreground
the literature against the life to which it refers. Bashevis Singer's characters, unlike Appelfeld's, are generally not overdetermined by the historical catastrophe that, as every reader knows, annihilated their living
correlatives—and in this paradoxical situation, that only reinforces their
credibility as "authentic" (if not mimetic) representations of pre-Holocaust Jewish lives, as delegates from a past that is eternally present.[35]

Anachronism based on willful amnesia is becoming a strategy in some
of the more experimental Jewish fictions of the late twentieth century.
See, for example, Melvin Jules Bukiet's Stories of an Imaginary Childhood, Arieh Eckstein's Doda Ester [Auntie Esther], and Allen Hoffman's

Small Worlds.[36] The first is by an American Jewish writer, the second by an Israeli, and the third by an American writer living in Jerusalem. The question worth considering is whether the opposite of what Michael André Bernstein calls "backshadowing," or reading history backward from its cataclysmic end, is something like "back*whitewashing*"—and we should also consider what the comparative aesthetic and ethical implications might be.

THE LITTLE SHOEMAKERS: A SHTETL IN NEW JERSEY

Given the authority invested in him, I. B. Singer's shlemiel becomes increasingly consequential for certain readers as he is filtered through his pale reflections in the American fiction of Bellow or Roth, Bukiet or Hoffman. Having just barely caught the last ship leaving Europe and escaped both the annihilation that awaited him there and the gentle but firm acts of exclusion that greeted him in Israel, he reclaims his "other fate" as the Wandering Jew endowed with eternal life. The shlemiel-storyteller becomes, once again, a competing cultural hero; his verbal acts are a challenging substitute for action and his wandering a countertrope both to the demise of the diasporic imagination and to the teleology of homecoming.[37]

One of the most dramatic enactments of this pattern is Bashevis Singer's "Di kleyne shusterlekh" [The Little Shoemakers], published in Yiddish in 1945, the same year as "Gimpl tam." It traces a voyage from Frampol to America propelled by hermeneutic strategies that cast a spell over land and sea—not to expedite the journey, as in the case of Agnon's Hananiah, nor to expose the deluded gullibility of the religious imagination, as in the case of Abramovitsh's Benjamin the Third, but to preserve the entire territory safely within the confines of the imagination. The central figure, Abba, is the last patriarch in the line of shoemakers who are as firmly rooted in Frampol as is their ancestral house, which is sinking into the ground under the weight of its own antiquity. Even Abba's vision of redemption maintains Frampol as the center of the universe and brings him to the Holy Land only on Sabbaths and Holy Days: "It seemed to him that his little town was the navel of the universe and that his own house stood at the very center. He often thought that when the Messiah came to lead the Jews to the Land of Israel, he, Abba, would stay behind in Frampol, in his own house, on his own hill. Only on the Sabbath and on Holy Days would he step into a cloud and let himself be flown to Jerusalem."[38] By these lights, Eretz Yisrael, even in messianic times, will be a place to visit, a place of *pilgrimage* but not of settlement.

Abba's oldest son, Gimpl, whose namesake began the diasporic saga in the other story, may be enacting its next, American, chapter: as he and his six brothers move to America, they shift the center of gravity to the New World. Abba, like Sholem Aleichem's Tevye, remains in Europe, minding the shop as his progeny scatter and the world seems to spare him its atrocities. But the time comes when even he must flee, as did Tevye before him. Hitler's hordes enforce historical consciousness just long enough to induce Abba to leave Frampol and head for America (to Elizabeth, New Jersey, to be exact). And if Bashevis Singer must finally concede his character to the force of history, he does so by providing him with the same supplies that served Benjamin and Hananiah and Tevye: cognitive blinders that convert every unknown event and site into a familiar landmark in a decipherable and divinely countenanced universe. The voyage itself is coded as a redemptive journey—and since Abba is so locked into biblical landscapes and seascapes, his departure only reinforces his status as composite, generic Jew:

> He had abandoned the house of his forefathers and the place of his birth and, staff in hand, gone wandering into the world like the patriarch Abraham. The havoc in Frampol and the surrounding villages brought Sodom and Gomorrah to mind, burning like a fiery furnace. . . .
>
> He was put on board the last ship for the United States. . . . The ship would leap up as if mounting the sky, and the torn sky would fall as though the world were returning to original chaos. Then the ship would plunge back into the ocean, and once again the firmament would be divided from the waters, as in the Book of Genesis. . . .
>
> Just as he was unable to remember when he began his voyage, so he was unaware when it came to an end. The ship had already been made fast to the dock in New York harbor, but Abba hadn't the vaguest notion of this. He saw huge buildings and towers, but mistook them for the pyramids of Egypt. . . . Suddenly he thought of Jacob arriving in Egypt, where he was met by Pharaoh's chariots.[39]

After such a trip, one would expect an afterlife of epic proportions. But the epic is quickly swallowed up in the accommodation that life in *galut* exemplifies at its most viable: American words and phrases punctuate the Yiddish narrative, but the original venue remains fundamentally unaltered. Like another Bontshe Shvayg, who will ask for a buttered roll when he reaches heaven (but unlike Motl, who asks for watermelon when he reaches New York), all that Abba requires when he arrives in Elizabeth, a "shtetl in New Jersey," are his old cobbler's

"last, hammer and nails, . . . file and awl, even a broken-down shoe" he
brought from Frampol.[40]

The Holy Land maintains its place in the "authentic" Jewish imagination as the site of redemption, and by retaining its mythical dimensions, it also remains necessarily embedded in a messianic vision. Like
Jonah's being lost and found in the whale, like Hananiah's trip to
Jerusalem, Abba's trip to America is coded in the language of miracle;
but its psychological geography resembles that of Benjamin's return to
his backwater shtetl or of Tevye's open-ended journey. Going to America is going to another familiar diaspora—transporting Frampol to Elizabeth and keeping the Holy Land safe as the always-deferred referent.

THE RUINED SHRINE

In the critical discourse in which the voice of the nomad is perceived as
articulating a new urgency, Isaac Bashevis Singer becomes a player with
an authority that could hardly have been anticipated by the Yiddish writers who came to the United States in the early decades of the century
looking for cultural as well as physical asylum. Instead of focusing on
choosing burial rites for characters whose life models had none, writers
following I. B. Singer's lead are concerned with the survivability and viability of likenesses of those characters in the postwar world.

For all the centuries of the Diaspora, Jerusalem was entombed as the
ruined shrine in the mind, in the poetry, and in the ritual behavior of
Jews. After Jerusalem had been reclaimed, *Judea capta* dusted off and
rebuilt, and even the remains of the temple incorporated into the iconography of political space, the Jewish imagination that needed *ruins* began
to turn back to Poland.[41] The small towns and cities, the cemeteries and
concentration camps of Eastern Europe have come in the last decades of
the twentieth century to replace Jerusalem as a site of pilgrimage to a
lost civilization.

Europe's function as the source of an authentic as well as a discarded
or denied American self is nearly as old as America itself. In his study of
Europe as "the great museum," Donald Horne argues that tourists "trying to imagine the past . . . [have] turned parts of Europe into a museum
of authenticated remnants of past cultures." He describes the "restored
hull of a seventeenth-century Swedish warship, the Wasa," which lies on
display in Stockholm "like a patient in an intensive-care ward. Put together from the 14,000 bits and pieces that were lifted out of the har-
bour where it sank in 1628," the Wasa is "propped up by steel pipes and

220   Jewish Geographies

sustained by rubber tubes, its temperature and humidity being tested several times during the day as if it were still near death."[42] Many kilometers from Stockholm, the Jewish cemeteries that survived the carnage in Poland crumble before the eyes of today's pilgrims, as if there were still some dying to be done.

American readers go to the stories of Isaac Bashevis Singer as Americans have gone to European, especially Russian, literature for over a century: to encounter the passions, the whiff of evil, the Gothic structures and sensibilities, the social stratifications and stratagems that they do not find in the American landscape. They go to Europe in the late twentieth century as Americans have gone to Europe for nearly as long as their severance from it: in search of the picturesque, in search of authenticity and points of departure.[43] To one specific interpretive community in quest of its lost civilization, Bashevis Singer's narratives have come to seem like an exquisite replica of the Wasa. Whether these stories are regarded as reproductions or as free interpretations of the European Jewish past is a function of the weight assigned to authentication; not unrelated to the widespread American fascination with replicable culture, the preoccupation with possessing the authentic through forms of duplication characterizes not only ethnographic museums but rites of recovery as well. In America, unlike Europe, the authentic is replaced by the didactic and accessible. The contract purchasing Manhattan, sold at historical monuments along with copies of the Declaration of Independence as an authentic replica of the original, is presented in English in "pseudo-antique characters," Umberto Eco reminds us, "whereas the original was in Dutch"; in fact, "it isn't a facsimile, but—excuse the neologism—a fac-different."[44] The English Bashevis Singer is often visited by tourists to the site as if it were a facsimile, whereas it is a fac-different of the Yiddish Bashevis Singer—which is in turn a fac-different of the lives buried under the reconstructed cities and small towns of Eastern Europe.

The next phase in the quest for the authentic takes these travelers to those very cities and towns in Poland and Czechoslovakia and Hungary—much as Jews have gone to *Jerusalem* for centuries: on pilgrimage to the ruined shrine.

The Grapes of Roth

Diasporism from Portnoy to Shylock

When the European Jewish civilization that had accommodated *galut* or exile as a "provisional" but viable Jewish condition, suspended between ancient memories of destruction and visions of redemption, was itself destroyed in the middle of this century, it appeared that *galut*, beyond insular religious forms and a few nostalgic shudders, could no longer furnish a normative model for the rehabilitation of Jewish life. A majority of Jews continued to live outside of the Holy Land even after the founding of the State of Israel, but the philosophical, ideological, and cultural apparatus for validating life in exile had been shattered. The establishment of Israel as the ultimate resting place of the Jewish people invited a process of ingathering not only of the scattered people but of the fragmented relics of their material world and the diffuse elements of their imagination.

Isaac Bashevis Singer, over decades of postwar Yiddish writing, reimagined an Eastern European Jewish geography largely uncontaminated by foreshadowings of catastrophe; but his remained for some time a unique, idiosyncratic presence in Jewish letters. Paul Celan's "grave in the air" is a self-contained force field that floats forever above but never resettles on fertile ground. The obstinacy of particles that refuse to be reabsorbed anywhere pervades the Hebrew poetry of Dan Pagis and the prose of Aharon Appelfeld, contributing eventually to the rise of postmodernist or post-Zionist discourse.

The last decades of this century have witnessed a subtle reshifting of centers of gravity. Post-Zionism has reintroduced shards of the repressed past into Israeli culture. In France and America, the existential virtues of life in exile and the essence of Judaism as a culture in exile have reconverged as a new philosophical-political platform. When "nomadism" competes with "nativism" among Jews who are increasingly ambivalent and puzzled over the uses and abuses of Israeli power, and when the storyteller competes with the soldier for cultural privilege, "Diasporism" takes on the dimensions of a new cultural agenda. In the literary realm, what was formerly encapsulated in a handful of anachronistic stories that preserved the shtetl as a reference untainted by its historical fate, or in the poetic relics and icons of a destroyed universe, reemerge as the foundation of a new Jewish aesthetics.

In *Operation Shylock* (1993) Philip Roth has added another voice to the growing chorus of "diasporists" in the academy and the arts. This narrative contains a kind of manifesto that not only finds value in recuperating discarded or defunct models, like crinolines crumbling in old attic trunks; it reflects in its very ambiguities and contradictions a postmodern search for value in the interstices, in the outskirts and on the peripheries of sacred centers, and in the imagination of alternative worlds.

Jewish letters had already been radically reshuffled to accommodate the changing status of *fictitious* and *real* worlds by the time Philip Roth appeared; what makes him different from the writers we have considered up to now is that he navigates between these worlds with the audacity, the naïveté, and the adventuresomeness of an American native son. Cynthia Ozick argued in 1970 that "America shall, for awhile, become Yavneh" and that "the Aggadists, the makers of literature[, were] just now gathering strength in America," writing an English permeated with Jewish "liturgical" sensibility that she called the "New Yiddish."[1] Her claim was based on a tiny sampling of contemporary fiction whose dominance proved quite short-lived, as she herself admitted a decade later.[2] In the intervening period, the debate over whether a handful of American Jewish writers, roughly covering the fifty years between Roth (Henry) and Roth (Philip), constitute a renaissance in Jewish letters or provide just one more shelf of good Jewish books has nearly exhausted itself.[3] What Philip Roth's late fiction suggests is less a cultural revolution than a reconfiguration, from within the American purview, of the dichotomy between "original" and "imitative" space—between place designated as real, and therefore nonnegotiable, and places designated as spots on blueprints that are infinitely negotiable. It is Diaspora as polemic option and aesthetic process rather than as a cultural canon or a "way of life" that I want to consider here.

OPERATION SHYLOCK:
"MORE DRASTIC THAN A MERE BOOK"?

Operation Shylock: A Confession is rather surprising in its grimness. Readers had gotten accustomed to that series of acrobatic feats by which Roth had helped to rescue Jewish humor from the dustbin of Jewish history. It didn't really matter all that much whether Alex Portnoy masturbated into a piece of liver or his sister's underclothes. What mattered in 1969 was that he did it on the pages of Jewish fiction, succeeded in delighting many Jews and enraging many others—and their rabbis ("defenders of the faith")—and, eventually, changed the norms and the proprieties of American Jewish literature.[4] Twenty-four years later, however, Roth raised the stakes so that nothing short of a global reshuffling of Jewish populations and a total redefinition of Jewish civilization hung in the balance.

Operation Shylock is a narrative that, by its own admission, aspires to be "something more drastic than a mere book."[5] At times it appears to be drastic *as* a book, that is, as an act of fiction whose conventional mandate and popular appeal lie in its ability to entertain or edify. It is long and diffuse and quite tedious, in places. But its main achievement makes it a fitting subject to conclude a study of Jewish journeys and Jewish geographies: it enacts some of the more ludic—and ludicrous—dimensions of the larger diasporic enterprise. In the process, the novel lurches recklessly between the worlds we invent and the world we inhabit.

The "real" world is the Jerusalem of the Demjanjuk trial and the Intifada. Bridging the various narratological and political realms is the figure of a man who claims to be Philip Roth and who espouses the theory that in the late twentieth century, as for so many centuries before Hitler, the Diaspora remains the only viable place for Jews. The Jews of Israel, or at least the Ashkenazim among them, face imminent destruction at the hands of the Arabs, and should therefore be dispatched back to Warsaw, Prague, Berlin, and Kiev—after the remaining anti-Semites in those places have undergone a process of reeducation to rid them of their lingering prejudices. "For the European Jews, Israel has been a . . . temporary interlude in the European saga that it is time to resume," says "Roth" (pp. 42–43). His encounters with the narrator (Philip Roth) and the latter's encounters with Hebrew writer Aharon Appelfeld, with a number of Palestinians, and with members of the Israeli Mossad highlight a roster of characters who claim varying degrees of extratextual status and credibility.

There are, as readers have observed, at least three Philip Roths in *Shylock*: Philip Roth the author of the novel, Philip Roth the author-narrator *in* the novel, and Philip Roth the impostor—who comes to be referred to alternatively as "Moishe Pipik."[6] "I've been putting myself in difficulties like this all my life," admits the narrator; "but, up till now, by and large in fiction. How exactly do I get out of this?" (p. 142). Precisely what he is trying to "get out of" may be the clue to something quite extraordinary hidden beneath the refracted surface of interlocking mirrors.

This struggle can be construed on one level as the attempt of an author who as a young man seemed intent on writing the naughtiest page of the Jewish Story to enter his seventh decade with less animosity and maybe even some plaudits from the other elders of the tribe. On another level, given the endless diatribes in the novel delivered by different characters representing interested parties, the struggle appears to be a contest between Zionism and Diasporism. Both of these readings boil down to a choice at the heart of this novel and of nearly everything Roth has written in the last twenty-five years—the choice that is, I submit, at the heart of Jewish culture at the end of the second millennium as it was at the beginning of the first: between life as "fiction" and life as "fact"; between fiction that is diasporic privilege, unmoored and fanciful, and fact as the ingathering of the material, obligatory world.

DIASPORA AS POSTMODERN PRIVILEGE

The two-way traffic across the great divide between life and fiction is a postmodern version of the parade through the looking glass and back again. In the "Zuckerman" trilogy (*The Ghost Writer*, 1979; *Zuckerman Unbound*, 1981; *The Anatomy Lesson*, 1983) and *The Counterlife*, Roth had already begun a vertiginous process of endless self-invention. *The Counterlife* (1986) and *Facts* (1988) were particularly dense experiments in trying on alternative destinies and rescuing one's dear ones from their mistakes and their coronaries through the power of the pen. The former is built on the idea of constructed lives and the divine power of the writer to imagine, simultaneously, the road taken and the roads not taken. What Nathan Zuckerman defines as his fabricated identity may capture the protean profile of the Jew in the twentieth century: "Being Zuckerman is one long performance and the very opposite of what is thought of as being *oneself*. In fact, those who most seem to be themselves appear to me people impersonating what they think they might like to be, believe they ought to be, or wish to be taken to be by whoever is setting standards. So in earnest are they that being in earnest is *the act*. For certain self-aware people, however, this is not possible: to imagine themselves being themselves, living their own real, authentic, or genuine life, has for them all the aspects of a hallucination."[7]

Such an affirmation of fragmented or masked selves is also an assault on the modernist creation of a new Jewish subjectivity. The Zionist dream of transforming the Jewish self into something utterly *other* may have been the greatest act of impersonation in modern Jewish history; nonetheless, it is predicated on the return of *ontology* as Jewish reference, on the ultimate valorization of a place and time that signals the end of exile and alienation. That is why *Operation Shylock* might represent a watershed in popular Jewish self-representation: here, the game of fact and fiction has found its objective correlative in the renewed struggle between Israel and Diaspora for a place of privilege in the economy of the post-Holocaust Jewish imagination. In this narrative the struggle manifests itself as an act of poetic license—but never in Roth's fiction has authorial intervention been so *consequential*. The fate of whole peoples seems to depend on it.

If *Operation Shylock* is something of a departure, it is not because it signifies the author's return to the fold, or, as Hillel Halkin puts it, a move from "me" to "us," acknowledging an "authorial debt" to fathers, mothers, and the Jewish fraternity at large after his transgressive act in *Portnoy's Complaint*.[8] Roth, it seems to me, has been playing the role of public penitent for two and a half decades, going so far in his novel *The Ghost Writer* as to resurrect Anne Frank so that he could bring her as a prospective fiancée to every Jewish mother who personally identified with the long-suffering Sophie Portnoy ("Nathan, is she Jewish?" "Yes . . . [she's] Anne Frank").[9] But Roth may indeed be doing something different here, facing the ultimate "authorial debt" for audacious acts of poetic license in the form of a temptation to relinquish authorship altogether by capitulating to a Hebrew space where *dvarim* (words) are also *things*, an object world that reifies our fictions. And even if he never fully capitulates, that pull has the weight of gravity itself.

DIASPORA AS POETIC LICENSE

The struggle between the diasporic lure of the imagination and the Zionist pull of "the *real*" unfolds in stages over three decades. In Israel in

1967, Portnoy found his sexual nemesis in the person of Naomi, the emas-
culating Sabra: "Where other Jews find refuge, sanctuary and peace, Portnoy now perishes," wailed this latter-day Hamlet, impaled, as it were,
on his own limp member. *Portnoy's Complaint* ends with the protagonist singing desperately, "Im-po-tent in Is-rael, da da daaah," to the tune
of "Lullaby in Birdland." Admitting to Naomi that he is the "epitome
of what was most shameful in 'the culture of the Diaspora,'" this character, who has worked so hard to "put the *id* back in 'Yid,'" is sent skulk-
ing back home, "back into the exile" of the psychiatrist's couch.[10] It was
from that supine position, a few months later, that Alex Portnoy would
have watched the Israeli soldiers on television as they enacted in the Six-
Day War the spectacular military equivalent of the sexual victory of the
reembodied Jew in Israel over the disempowered diaspora Jew. It is the
very moment when the shlemiel as cultural hero is superseded by what
critics of Zionism call the "tough Jew," when "images of Jewish wimps
and nerds are being supplanted by those of the hardy, bronzed kibbutznik,
the Israeli paratrooper, and the Mossad agent."[11]

In spite of Roth's deliberate disengagement from the pieties of self-
representation found in other Jewish writing of the 1950s and 1960s, his
impotent characters call to mind the fantasies of violence that characters
like Bernard Malamud's "Fixer" and Saul Bellow's Herzog prove incapable of carrying out. They contrast markedly and dialectically with the
violent fantasies that *are* realized, often but not exclusively in the context
of the Arab-Israeli conflict, in Hebrew literature of those same years.[12]
"When I was younger my Jewish betters used to accuse me of writing short
stories that endangered Jewish lives—would that I could! A narrative as
deadly as a gun!" confesses the narrator of *Operation Shylock* (p. 186).

And yet when Roth "himself" returns to Israel in *Operation Shylock*,
he encounters the self-identified, latter-day diasporist: "a Jew for whom
authenticity as a Jew means living in the Diaspora, for whom the Diaspora is the normal condition and Zionism is the abnormality—a Diasporist is a Jew who believes that the only Jews who matter are the Jews
of the Diaspora, that the only Jews who will survive are the Jews of the
Diaspora, that the only Jews who *are* Jews are the Jews of the Diaspora"
(pp. 170–71). What has happened to turn powerlessness into a competing
cultural claim and Diaspora into the most authentic and secure form of
Jewish existence? Once again Roth's hero is defeated in Israel, but this
time in a different kind of battle, fought with weapons—the pen and the
sword—no less phallic but more consequential. Israel has become the
place where Reality writ large has the same effect on the psyche as Naomi

did on the libido. First the phallus and then the "fictus" of the diaspora Jew are blunted by the reality of Israel. "Exile," now redefined as "Diaspora," is no longer limited to the realm of therapy but extends to the much larger realm of fiction.

There is in fact an immanent connection between the two. Israel, after all, was founded on the premise of a Jewish emergence from the state of dreaminess. The dream is necessary as blueprint but is superseded by the will, by the fulfillment of desire: "if you will it, it is not a dream"; *its realization abolishes desire.* With the ingathering of the exiles, with the territorialization of the dreamscape, there is, officially, no more room for dreaminess. It is the dreamers, then, who continue to cause trouble by imagining alternative worlds and undermining the ontology of the created world. The writers of fictions—those, at least, who are not socialist realists painting the perfect fit between map and territory—remain dreamers.

When the century was young, another utopian enterprise being launched in America was also founded on the unabashed principle of impersonation and dream enactment: the Jewish empire in Hollywood and the images that came to be associated with its reproduction in the mass media. The difference between the two undertakings sheds light on what would later become the diasporist agenda: Hollywood's mandate is to continue to spin dreamscapes, while Israel as Utopia Realized is the place where dreams must be fulfilled—*or abandoned.* In the words of the commercial poster based on a common orthographic error: ISREAL is REAL. Indeed, the utopian imagination of the Jews of America continues to look more like Hollywood than like Israel; Barbra Streisand's *Yentl* and Haim Topol's *Fiddler on the Roof* are not just reproductions or trivializations but are fantastic reinventions of the shtetl sanctioned by the fictions of I. B. Singer and of younger writers who are exploring Eastern Europe as a newly available site of Jewish fantasy.

So it is the authenticity of self-invention, the privilege to dream and to create counterlives, that all the "Philip Roths" are defending in *Operation Shylock*, and the Diaspora is presented as the only place where that is still possible, legitimate, and maybe even necessary. Even if Diasporism is espoused by a madman and an impostor, he is allowed to bear the name of the author and the limited and retractable but nonetheless significant claim to authorship.

In an illustration accompanying its front-page review of *Operation Shylock*, the *New York Times Book Review* portrayed Roth as a composite figure, Moses and Ahasuerus, holding tablets and a staff against an urban backdrop.[13] As we have seen, the Wandering Jew in his modern incarnation is nearly always a storyteller. When Eastern Europe is the reference, antiquity and loquacity appear to be his primary attributes. In "The Prague Orgy," which constitutes the epilogue to Roth's Zuckerman trilogy, the narrator describes Prague as the very place he had imagined the Jewish homeland to be when as a child he collected money for the Jewish National Fund:

> What I privately pictured the Jews able to afford with the nickels and dimes I collected was a used city, a broken city, a city so worn and grim that nobody else would even put in a bid. . . . In this used city, one would hear endless stories being told—on benches in the park, in kitchens at night, while waiting your turn at the grocery or over the clothesline in the yard, anxious tales of harassment and flight, stories of fantastic endurance and pitiful collapse. What was to betoken a Jewish homeland to an impressionable, emotional nine-year-old child . . . was, first, the overpowering oldness of the homes . . . ; second were the stories . . . the construction of narrative out of the exertions of survival.

This process, so long the burden and privilege of Jews, became the common lot under communist and other repressive regimes: "Where the literary culture is held hostage, . . . stories aren't simply stories; it's what they have instead of life."[14] So it is natural that Roth, for whom Eastern Europe is the place of an alternative diasporic identity, would design a program to actually ship his people back there, after the end of communism, with the license to tell stories. This may be the ultimate expression of the nostalgic mode that both Hana Wirth-Nesher and Norman Finkelstein have identified as driving Roth's obsessive orientation toward Eastern Europe. The culture of nostalgia is manifest in American Jewish writing ranging from the more sentimental to the more ironic, eclectic efforts at recovery and projection. It informs Roth's editorial activities as initiator of the Penguin series Writers from the Other Europe and his fictional attempts to "retrieve" a lost writer who resembles Bruno Schulz or to reimagine the life of Franz Kafka or Anne Frank in America.[15] Based on anachronism and on the impossibility of actual return, such stories unfold neither in "time" nor in "place" but in some acoustical space.

Shylock is, in fact, a very noisy novel. Words are flung like stones, done and undone like refugee bundles on an endless highway. Exile is always the beginning of narrative—and Diaspora is the place where people talk. It is also the place where people eat—just another form of orality, after all. Even the whitefish salad has a genealogy: in a "Jewish food store on Amsterdam Avenue . . . the bitter fragrance of vinegar, of onions, of whitefish and red herring, of everything pickled, peppered, salted, smoked, soaked, stewed, marinated, and dried, smells with a lineage that . . . more than likely led straight back through the shtetl to the medieval ghetto" (pp. 378–79). These are passages we can sink our teeth into, words with the promise of a story.

ISRAEL: EVERY WORD A SWORD

In the Middle East, however, where exile comes to an end, so too, it seems, do the stories and the compulsions of orality. Talk becomes consequential. Words can kill. The narrator says of the Israeli Mossad agent, Louis B. Smilesburger: "He's swimming in the abrasive tragedies of life and I am only swimming in art" (p. 378). Each of these swimmers, each of the pale speakers in this series of endless monologues, presumably conceals a knife or an Uzi (although a few of the non-Mediterranean types use weapons from Roth's more conventional erotic arsenal). While the names of some of the characters have been "changed" to protect their "identity," the American-educated Palestinian, who might still have been talking about Raskolnikov had he remained at the University of Chicago, is "actually" gunned down in the streets of Ramallah. The Mossad's secret weapon, "loshon hora" [sic] (slander), has the power to silence any potential defector (p. 397).[16] The American Jewish writer—or his double—is recruited by the PLO and the Mossad, invited to speak with Lech Walesa, the pope, and Arafat. His only shield is the thought that when all this becomes too threatening, he at least can find some way out of the plot and return to New Jersey, to fiction that doesn't really count so much, to textuality that doesn't kill. For that is what Diasporism amounts to here: the privilege to "swim in art," to try out any role, any character, without paying the consequences of fixed identity: "This is the plot up to the moment when the writer leaves the woman still dolefully enmeshed in it, and, suitcase in hand, tiptoeing so as not to disturb her postcoital rest, he himself slips silently out of the plot on the grounds of its general implausibility. . . . The story so far is frivolously plotted, overplotted, for his taste altogether too freakishly plotted, with outlandish events so wildly careening around every corner that there is nowhere for intelligence to establish a foothold" (245).

We can of course argue that just as he writes himself out of the plot, leaving the woman and slipping quietly back to Newark, so could Roth the author have saved the Palestinian by writing him out of his fateful connection with Ramallah and injecting him with some flu virus or the idea for some academic conference that would have kept him in Chicago. After all, Roth is perpetrating the *illusion* of a loss of fictionality here: even the "real people" have ink running through their veins. Once again, Thomas Pavel's disarming query about the relative suspensions of disbelief has particular resonance: "In *War and Peace* is Natasha less actual than Napoleon?"[17] In *Operation Shylock* the author is invoking precisely that distinction as a quality that bifurcates Jewish existence.

Determined, as it were, not to become a latter-day Quixote (or Benjamin the Third) unable to distinguish between actual and fictional worlds, Roth places them in different *geographical* locations. "A universe is composed of a base—an actual world—surrounded by a constellation of alternative worlds," argues Pavel; "taking the division of the ontological space into central and peripheral models as a very general formal organization of the beliefs of a community, we may localize fiction as a peripheral region used for ludic and instructional purposes."[18] If we accept this geographical imaginary, we can then explore the idea of Diaspora as the "ludic" region, the region where experiments and games are still possible. In the Aristotelian scheme that Roth inherited, the poet's representation of "the kind of things that would happen" is superior to the historian's presentation of "what happened" (*Poetics*, chap. 9); the diasporic, poetic option is thus the privileged one.

The identification of exile with *textuality* has, as we have seen, been forcefully advocated by Edmond Jabès and George Steiner and by an increasing number of students of contemporary Jewish culture.[19] I am proposing, in a somewhat different vein, that the fictive word and the mimetic mode that have replaced sacred scriptures and sacred space are the essence of diasporic privilege; at this late date in Jewish history, they represent the freedom of invention in the face of or *in place of* territorial sovereignty and "historical" imperative.

The power of alternative fictions is most successfully challenged by the two events, one catastrophic and the other epic, that form the very center—as black hole and as magnet—of the Jewish twentieth century. Prague (and Eastern Europe in general) may be the marketplace of the Jewish story; but, as the ambivalent reception of I. B. Singer indicates, its disappearance as Jewish geography leaves as little tolerance for fiction as does the creation of the Jewish state. In Roth's novel, Aharon Appelfeld represents both events, in his person and in his writing. "Aharon and I each embody the *reverse* of the other's experience; . . . each recognizes in the other the Jewish man he is *not*. . . . [W]e are heirs jointly of a drastically *bifurcated* legacy," says the narrator of *Operation Shylock* (p. 201). As survivor and

Israeli, in whom "fiction" as a ludic exercise is defeated by the two forms
of inexorable reality, Appelfeld's "authorizing" presence helps to ground
the imaginative flights of the other characters. Appelfeld's own publication in English, *Beyond Despair*, is subtitled "Three Lectures and a Conversation with Philip Roth"; parts of that "conversation" appear more
or less verbatim in Roth's own novel, functioning as an authenticating intertext that insists on the documentary status of its subject even as it parodies the very dichotomy between fiction and fact.

What at first appears to be an unlikely connection between the writer
of the Jewish catastrophe and the author of the Jewish farce thus reveals
itself to be an affinity of another order. They are both investigating quintessential elements of the diasporic experience: its inexorable tragedy,
on the one hand, and its tentative, fictive qualities, its masquerade and
rich counterlives, on the other. That is, amid all the proliferations of identity represented by the various Philip Roths, and amid the unstable geography of Appelfeld's own fictions, Appelfeld remains for Roth the
writer as static point of reference, much as Israel remains the nonnegotiable reality, the center of gravity for the drifting, ex-centric, diasporic
imagination.

DIASPORA AS THEATER

Once again, it is distance from the center and the trajectory of the journey that constitute the coordinates of a global reconfiguration of (post-
Holocaust) Jewish civilization. A diasporic aesthetic based on the principle of dispersion and diffusion is explicitly endorsed by the British
American painter R. B. Kitaj, Roth's friend and fellow (part-time) expatriate.[20] The presence in his writings (and as subjects in his paintings)
of writers such as Franz Kafka and Walter Benjamin renders Kitaj's
theories fairly predictable, but his particular "obsession with the Jews"
qua exiles is relevant here in its self-representation as an "art-obsession,
an *aesthetic*."[21] While the diasporist aesthetic he identifies is bleaker by
far than Roth's—restless, uneasy, "depressive," and broken, based on
eclectic definitions of art and of the Jewish condition as "being elsewhere
combined with the desperate wish to 'be at home'"[22]—it is also an artistic license perceived as "magical" in its generative powers:

> [Diasporists are people who] have not taken Pascal's advice, which is some-
> thing like: all the trouble in the world is caused by people who do not know
> how to stay in their own room. I'm glad they didn't because their dispersed
> lives have broken mediocre patterns and searched out cosmopolitan treas-

ure. . . . Nietzsche defined art the way I really like it: "the desire to be different, the desire to be elsewhere." . . . So, I set sail, as Gauguin had done for Samoa, into the storm of Jewish dispensation, which felt like forbidden excitement feels—that's how I knew it was true for my art, or at least akin to Kafka's "rumour of true things."[23]

The image of diaspora as a journey yields to that of a theater, underscoring the affinity between the transient and the make-believe: as against the "primordial . . . human instincts for kin and home, . . . the Diasporic condition presents itself as yet another theater in which human, artistic instinct comes into play, maybe not primordial . . . but a condition, a theater to be treasured." It is a traveling theater, embodying the "mystery of dispersion," the "illusion of truth," and the destabilization of meaning.[24]

Even if the ultimate reference for the authentic Jew in Roth's nostalgic geography is Eastern and Central Europe, the theatrical logic of his imagination mirrors an American version of the Purim sensibility, of what has been called the "rite to be reckless."[25] Roth's predecessors in this enterprise include I. B. Singer, who in his "Polish" stories reinvented the shtetl, and Sholem Aleichem, who in *Motl* extended the Purim license to America as the site of diasporic transformations.

In the ongoing differentiation between exilic and "autochthonous" forms, between Judaism as a mimetic culture or masked ball in *galut* and as a "genuine" or "real" culture in the sacred center, Philip Roth's novel, like Sholem Aleichem's novel or Kitaj's paintings, becomes one of the popular enactments of the gaps and the bridges between them. Avoiding resolution, the author Roth (like his clones) evinces deference for and even submission to the "actual" world of generals and guns and bombs—to such an extent that he even "deletes" the "final chapter" of this narrative, in which certain secrets of the Israeli Intelligence Operation might have been "revealed." In persuading the narrator to delete chapter 11 of *Shylock*, Smilesburger invokes "fiction" and "fact" as two opposed and inviolable spheres. The narrator protests:

"Calling fiction fact would undermine everything."
    "Then call it fiction instead. Append a note: 'I made this up.' Then you will be guilty of betraying no one—not yourself, your readers, or those whom, so far, you have served faultlessly."
    "Not possible. Not possible in any way."
    "Here's a better suggestion, then. Instead of replacing it with something imaginary, do yourself the biggest favor of your life and just lop off the chapter entirely."

(p. 387)

The final "Note to the Reader" asserts that "this book is a work of fiction" and concludes, "this confession is false" (p. 399). In the novel, unlike the polemical literature, the tension between Israel and Diaspora, between real and imagined geographies, between the "true" and the "false" need never be resolved.

SHLILAT SHLILAT HA-GALUT

In the Israeli context, the attempt to redefine an Israeli "place" as detachable from Sacred Space[26] finds its philosophical justification in the argument of Amnon Raz-Karkotzkin on the value of exile or *galut* as the repressed function of the dialectic of homecoming: "How can we once again feel *galut* here in Israel[;] . . . that is, [recognize that] the yearning for redemption is itself [a form of] redemption. . . . *Galut* signifies absence, the acknowledgment of the present as an imperfect time, of the world as a defective place."[27] What Raz calls negating the negation— "shlilat shlilat ha-galut"—is the recognition of *galut* as the repressed other. By reintroducing it into the realm of the self, the Israeli can be liberated from the very act of repression. This signifies a postmodern sociocultural hermeneutics freed from the dialectical thinking that has plagued the Zionist enterprise *and* its detractors from the beginning.

Such gestures provide not so much a historical option or a social contract as a valuable critical sensibility, reintroducing the suppressed and generative potential of *galut*. Its practice in the Homeland is an exilic enactment of fiction not only as alternative to but as critique of "the real," creating a very different epistemology and aesthetics from those that prevail in the exile defined as the place-that-is-not-real. Whether or not it proves to be an enduring response to the realignment of Israel's geopolitical and psychosocial borders, this sensibility has appeared as the most recent stage in the ongoing dialectic between the spaces that form Jewish collective consciousness.

There are border crossings that are possible, as Thomas Pavel argues, between myth, fiction, and actuality. Those who work toward reconstituting Israel as a state with open borders are amenable to a renegotiation of these realms, a relinquishing of guardianship over the boundaries of the real, and a new exploration of the no-man's-land of fiction at the margins, of alternative worlds, of counterlives.

Conclusion

The Imagination of Return and the Return of Imagination

. . . I didn't kiss the ground
when they brought me as a little boy
to this land. But now that I've grown up on her,
she kisses me,
she holds me,
she clings to me with love,
with grass and thorns, with sand and stone,
with wars and with this springtime
until the final kiss.

> Yehuda Amichai, "Travels of
> the Last Benjamin of Tudela,"
> tr. Chana Bloch and Stephen Mitchell

The literary gestures of the "homeward bound" describe a peculiar trajectory between symbol and history. Because life in exile never carried ultimate ontological weight, all the countries of the Diaspora could be "non-historical" experimental sites, containing an infinite number of detours and generating an infinite number of stories. Having managed to preserve for nearly two millennia a community of rememberers with deferred claims to sovereign and sacred space within the praxis of nonsovereign boundaries, Jews who have attempted in the twentieth century to fit such a richly imagined community into specific geopolitical boundaries may have won a Pyrrhic victory. The opportunity for self-enshrinement, the lure of consecrated stones and burial sites, encounters an inbred and persistent Jewish resistance to stasis. Scattered across the landscape and frozen in granite and marble, the monuments to Israeli tragedies and triumphs, like the political rhetoric and the public ceremonies of commemoration and consecration, may temporarily arrest but cannot resolve the restless dybbuk's claims on the Jewish body.

The Zionist alternatives to Diaspora offered utopian or messianic closure to the narrative of exile: even the chapter telling the extermination of the Jews of Europe could be incorporated into a redemptive vision of resurrection in real time. The implications of this exchange are as considerable for the Jewish imagination as for Jewish politics. How do closure and containment compete with open-endedness to provide narrative possibilities in a culture newly obsessed with boundaries, magnetized by the soil and by the sheer pull of gravity? How does the appropriation of geographies of the mind, of sacred spaces, as sites of civic negotiations affect the long, rich life of the Jewish imagination in fictional landscapes? What are the minimal conditions for fiction in paradise reclaimed, so to speak, where all stories, *aggadot, märchen, bobe-mayses,* are meant to end?

JERUSALEM GAVE YOU THE MARVELOUS JOURNEY . . .

And if when you arrive you find her poor . . .
remember . . .
Jerusalem gave you the marvelous journey.
Without her you wouldn't have set out.
She has nothing left to give you now[.]

After C. P. Cavafy, "Ithaka"

The Jewish representations of exile that offer Auschwitz as touchstone of the ultimate fate of the silenced and the disenfranchised must also acknowledge the postwar status of Hebrew as a reterritorialized culture enlarged—and tainted—by national identity. Something of a paradox begins to emerge between the increasingly problematic status of the Jew who comes belatedly to history—the sovereign Jew, the land-intoxicated Jew, the colonizing Jew of the late twentieth century—and the enduring privileged status of the *symbolic Jew*, whose ur-language is Hebrew, whose point of departure (and deferred return) is always east of Eden, who persists in the imagination as the prototypical wanderer, exile, and nomad, as the marginal figure who defines the center, who expands, in his ubiquity and his immortality, the parameters of every narrative.[1] This paradox in contemporary political and cultural theory corresponds to a persistent anxiety in Jewish self-definition, as Zion and Exile resurface as alternative organizing principles of the Jewish imagination.

At this late moment in a century that radically disfigured and transformed Jewish civilization, we face the possibility of a more synoptic vision that could read the mutually subversive perils and seductions of *both* the reterritorialized and the deterritorialized Jewish selves as elements in a larger critique.

AND IF WHEN YOU ARRIVE YOU FIND HER POOR . . .

The city plays hide-and-
seek among her names:
Yerushalayim, El-Quds, Shalem, Jeru, Yeru, all
the while
whispering her first, Jebusite name: Y'vus,
Y'vus, Y'vus, in the dark. She weeps
with longing: Ilia Capitolinia, Ilia, Ilia.
She comes to any man who calls her
at night, alone. But we know
who comes to whom.

        Yehuda Amichai, "Jerusalem 1967"

The poet in Jerusalem who manages to write a poem of longing has outwitted death. As long as there is desire, the stones glitter with enchantment; arrival necessarily brings disenchantment. The secret of the Jews in the years of their exile was in having and not having: in having the memory and the promise of home *and* the freedom of the road, in cherishing a home without having to defend it or even keep its roads free of potholes. Turning toward Jerusalem in prayer from whatever spot one inhabited, the Jew was reminded that the sacred center was somewhere *else*; it was *the not-here*. On the level of the theodicy of exile and the ever-deferred return, the places outside of the Land of Israel were provisional, never invested with the ultimate status of real, original space.

Jerusalem, for her part, is preserved in the imagination over the centuries of Israel's wandering as a *hurva* awaiting redemption, a shrine suspended in its ruin.[2] Nothing significant can happen elsewhere, but nothing significant will happen *there* until the Jews return to complete the redemption. Even if it tarries a bit, the real drama will unfold only in Jerusalem. And the only official municipal designation for the city until that drama begins is as a vast graveyard and a dusty shrine. The only death that really counts will take place in—or be translated to—Jerusalem. For centuries the Jews of Samarkand, Uzbekistan, in preparing to meet their Maker, would buy one grave site in the local cemetery and another plot in Jerusalem. It was, by all reports, a valid legal transaction, with a bill of purchase placed in the hands of the deceased and buried with him or her; thus on the day of redemption, when there will no doubt be a grand traffic jam in the subterranean passages to Jerusalem as all the bodies are rolling toward the site of the resurrection, the dearly departed Samarkandians will already have reserved places.[3] In terms of narrative as diasporic privilege and Zion as its deferred end, it is the best way to preserve *both plots*.

Where death and resurrection are the ultimate ratifiers of place, distance becomes insignificant. As long as the vision remains unrealized, it creates an infinitely elastic umbilical cord to link the dispersed tribe of the faithful to the matrix of their faith. Reconnection with the material world, reacquisition of the territorial dimension, reduces the elasticity and releases toxins into the erotic forces. The poet who heads back to Jerusalem, to her vineyards and gardens, to her alleyways and gates, recovers the real, material world from under the allegorical weight of her imagery. But here, in the *ultimate* resting place from which there can be no more departures, and in its most sensuous poetry, lurks the danger of death and (that is) literalization: the landscape that becomes so palpable in Yehuda Halevi's last poems seems about to lose its symbolic, poetic status. Images of death are as abundant in this poetry as images of consummated love: *thanatos* as significant other and devourer of *eros*. Jerusalem as a ruin welcomes the poet into her rubble and lures him to his death. For all the travelers we have followed, beginning with Yehuda Halevi, the final port of disembarkation is the place of death. Distance is diminished to the point where it is nearly eradicated by an ecstatic, mystic vision of arrival. So the danger of arrival is also the challenge to the symbolic universe, the materialization of desire, the move from symbol to sacrament.

The tension between "Eretz" as the idea of sacred, redemptive territory and native soil as the natural human realm, between "large" and "small" space, has escalated into tribal warfare in our own time. In the poetic imagination the boundaries of the city expand easily to include all of Zion and then just as easily contract to the dimensions of the Old City: "May the day come when Jerusalem extends as far as Damascus, and in every direction," says the 104-year-old Tehila to the narrator in S. Y. Agnon's story by that name. "But the eye that has seen all Jerusalem enclosed within her walls cannot accustom itself to viewing what is built beyond the walls as the City itself. It is true that all the Land of Israel is holy and, I need hardly say, the surroundings of Jerusalem: yet the holiness that is within the walls of the City surpasses all else."[4] When this poetic image *denies its status as poetry*, it makes such claims on the political imagination that the "final status" of Jerusalem becomes nonnegotiable. The Jerusalem of the mind can extend as far as Damascus. The most landlocked city in the world, Jerusalem-of-the-mind can abut rivers and even oceans, the Jordan as well as the Sambatyon. Earthly Jerusalem must be divided into distinct boroughs and many intersections. It is only when the symbolic and the material dimensions are *severed* that dreamscapes can be preserved alongside well-groomed landscapes.

The psalm that inaugurates the poetics of exile concludes with a pledge to vengeance, demonstrating that the other side of the apocalyptic death wish is the apocalyptic vision of revenge. The links between the remembering community's amazing capacity for total recall and its undying vow to even the score are the consequence of the obliteration of distance, as the act of return entails picking up the old stories and finishing them, leaving no forgotten enmities, no loose ends. Words that were hypothetical in exile become consequential when they are repatriated. Put just one letter back into the canon and you have a ballistic device.[5]

The insistence that endings must reconnect with beginnings—that what has traveled through space as a symbol, when finally (re)grounded in sacred soil, stakes an incontrovertible, inalienable, and *total* claim—reveals the seduction of an *aesthetics of the whole*. The whole holy land. Undivided Jerusalem. The aesthetics and politics of wholeness are built on sacrifice and exclusivity, on a messianic perfection of the form that can be fully realized only in death. The eternity of Jerusalem is privileged over the ephemeral lives of its inhabitants, fulfillment over deferral, original and indivisible space over all forms of partiality, imitation, fragmentation, or duplication. Death celebrated as glorious, as sacrificial or heroic, preserves the image of the integrity of the body, unsullied by the ravages of the battlefield. It is the postromantic imagination that has come to the recognition that death is rarely beautiful.[6]

. . . EXPAND THE FRONTIERS OF FICTION

Thomas Pavel's *Fictional Worlds* explores the "frontiers of fiction" that "separate it on one side from myth, on another from actuality."[7] In contemporary Israel, a reconnection with sacred space and the powerful myths of death and rebirth, of the already-arrived, of the perfection of form, have made significant inroads into the frontiers of fiction on the one side, claiming more and more space for the *mythic* imagination; at the same time, the grounding of previously fictional constructs in the material, public space of the actual world erodes the frontier of fiction on the other side—leaving a significantly diminished arena for anyone of fictive mind.

One can appreciate this process by examining the language of biblical exegesis that suffers from literalization and reification, undermining the legitimacy of all "metaphoric travelers." A people used to living in narrative suddenly begins to use its texts as highway maps. The Bible becomes a code of memory, a deed, a travel guide, and a farmer's almanac. In fundamentalist interpretations of any sacred text, the map of desire is not an imitation or a microcosm but a perfect fit over the territory it describes. This insistence on the exact correspondence between map and territory, or between the Jerusalem of prayer and dream and desire and the Jerusalem of its citizens and its traffic jams, demonstrates the struggle between utopian and pragmatic negotiations with place in modern Israel.

Regarding the relative hermeticism of fictional territories, Kendall Walton observes that "we never intrude into a play to save a damsel from the clutches of the villain."[8] Yet to live in Israel, to read its texts, and to be present at its performances is to sit rather precariously at the edge of one's seat, waiting to be called onstage. This phenomenon exceeds the usual explanations— the mobilizing power of political theater or engaged literature in a postrevolutionary society; it relates also to the obsession with what I have called "return" and "recovery" as tropes of conquest and self-confirmation. Only with the return from the drama of exile do the opportunities and the dangers of reterritorialization, literalization, and reification emerge—when memory, empowered, becomes so consequential.

Travel and trespass, and fiction as their vehicle, may therefore retain in modern Israel the significance they have enjoyed in Western culture from the Renaissance to the present.[9] Alongside the persistence of stories of that beast slouching ever more single-mindedly toward Bethlehem to be born, there are growing signs of dislocation, shifts in the center of gravity corresponding to the increasingly mobile boundaries of the Hebrew self. "Exile" as the repressed other becomes the critique of a culture of the static and the whole. The stagnant waters and mirrors that reflected an ossified relationship to sacred space are beginning to show ripples and cracks.[10]

Granted, the search for cracks or fissures in the so-called bedrock of a culture, for signs of infiltration in the fences at its borders, for the dissonant voices in the chorus or the "desolate silences of the wandering people,"[11] can be a very seductive process. In the desire to redress the suffocating power of totalizing national visions and signifying processes that efface signifying others, the forgotten and the marginalized, the disinherited and the disenfranchised, can be embraced with a kind of indiscriminate enthusiasm. But consider the attention given to Palestinian Israelis such as Anton Shammas and their representations of exile in their homeland,[12] or the belated recognition of the poetry of Avot Yeshurun, who changed his name from Yehiel Perlmutter when he came to Palestine but maintained a large space for the chattel that included his own discarded name and home as well as the names and homes of evicted others;[13] we can see the beginnings of an internal Israeli deconstruction of the exclusive Jewish discourse of exile and homecoming—a process that, when expanded, grants privileges to all the writers and artists, citizens and sojourners, who touch down lightly but are never quite grounded.

In such a context this book becomes part of the project tracing radical changes in the relations between the fictional (or symbolic) and the historical as shifts in the relations between two paradigms of the Jewish imagination. What appeared at first as mutually exclusive may actually be much more complex: an exchange between Jewish culture as a *minority* culture, whose paradigmatic experience is exile, and as a *majority* culture struggling with new definitions of time and space and the imagination—with telling time and telling stories in utopia. The sanctuary for fiction is created here on the slopes of a volcano; it is threatened either with being overrun by the molten lava of the myths, with their mobilizing and homogenizing force, or with being raked into the soil by the literalizers who turn ancient fires into fertilizers for today's crops.

What for decades after the wars that had destroyed one Jewish culture and created another was a claim for the cultural supremacy of the return to Zion and a negation of the remnants of *galut* can now be reconfigured in a more global context that contains Jewish minority *and* majority cultures. Elements from the periphery or minority voices move to the center, are reprocessed, while centrist elements are continually marginalized. There is, then, an ongoing dynamic of selection and transformation, a reciprocal recycling of the energies that constitute contemporary Jewish imagination.

Pavel calls attention to the difference between self-interpreting or parabolic texts, "which strongly influence us" even if they "subsist outside the limits of actuality," and those by such writers as Kafka and Borges, which in their playfulness "expand our perception of fictional possibilities." He insists, "fictional colonies established as bases for traveling back and forth to the actual world must therefore be distinguished from fictional settlements founded for the sake of adventure and investigation, after burning the ships."[14] When settlements beyond the constituted borders of Israel were moved from their temporal space at the End of Days and incorporated into the "actual" world, "fictional settlements founded for the sake of adventure and investigation" all but disappeared. A genuine peace treaty between Israel and its neighbors, and a withdrawal to morally as well as militarily defensible borders, could have the effect of restoring some of our "fictional territory."

Epilogue

At Nisibis there [are] . . . two synagogues built by Ezra the
Scribe. In one of them is a red stone, fixed in the wall, which
Ezra had brought with him and which had been one of the
stones of the Temple.

"Petahia of Regensburg [Ratisbon]," late twelfth century

But, if you do not wish it, all this that I have related to
you is and will remain a fable.

I had meant to compose an instructive poem. Some will
say, it contains more poetry than instruction. That it has
more instruction than poetry will be the verdict of others.

Now, dear Book, after three years of labor, we must part.
And your sufferings will begin. You will have to make your
way through necessity and misrepresentation as through a
dark forest.

When, however, you come among friendly folk, give them
greetings from your father. Tell them that he believes Dreams
also are a fulfillment of the days of our sojourn on Earth.
Dreams are not so different from Deeds as some may think.
All the Deeds of men are only Dreams at first. And in the
end, their Deeds dissolve into Dreams.

Theodore Herzl, epilogue to Altneuland

A prayer for Jerusalem: Each pilgrim who comes to Jerusalem will take
one stone from the Wailing Wall, and use it as a cornerstone to construct
a little shrine, a *mikdash m'at,* in true diasporic fashion, so that there
will be thousands, tens of thousands, of little temples constructed from
tens of thousands of ancient rocks, and each of them will contain a sliver
of the divine aura, enough to illuminate the whole of Nisibis or Naples,
of Princeton or Paris, of Butte or Buenos Aires, of Kansas or Kiev. . . .
Jerusalem will then be bereft of its Wall, so the Jerusalemites will, natu-

rally, have to build another wall (we all know that good walls make good neighbors), and everyone will pitch in. Its primary dimensions, marking and invoking the Temple of Solomon and its Christian and Moslem offshoots, can be extended to divide the city into its natural municipal sectors, capitals of two sovereign states. And when it will be finished, it will be a lovely work of construction but it will be worth nothing, because after all it will not be the REAL THING, just a facsimile. It won't be worth fighting for and killing over. It will, that is, be worthless and therefore it will be priceless. It will have the value of imitation diamonds that sparkle like the real ones but are not in danger of theft, of dreams and desires that need never arrive, and of tolerance for everyone else's fake diamonds and glittering dreams.

Notes

INTRODUCTION

1. Theodor Herzl, *Altneuland, Roman* (Leipzig: Hermann Seemann Nach-folger, 1902); *Tel Aviv, Sipur* [Hebrew], tr. Nahum Sokolov (Warsaw: Hatzefirah, 1902); *Altneuland* [Yiddish], tr. Isidor Elyshev (Warsaw: Hatzefirah, 1902); *Old-Newland ("Altneuland"),* tr. with revised notes by Lotta Levensohn (New York: Bloch Publishing Company and Herzl Press, 1960) (first published in English as "OldNewLand," in *The Maccabean* 3, no. 4 [October 1902]). We should not miss the irony in the specific genre of storytelling that Herzl invokes—the *märchen*—as reflection of the German folk imagination. Naturally, the resonances of this dictum will vary with the place reserved in each culture for the folktale.

2. For a critique of the "Eastern European model" of Zionism represented as having emerged victorious over the Central or Western European models, see Uri Eisenzweig, *Territoires occupés de l'imaginaire juif: Essai sur l'espace sion-iste* (Paris: Christian Bourgois, 1980).

3. Leonard Barkan, "Rome's Other Population," *Raritan* 11, no. 2 (fall 1991): 40.

4. Ibid., pp. 41–42.

5. Yadin is quoted in Amos Elon, *The Israelis* (London: Weidenfeld and Nicolson, 1971), pp. 247–49. "Through archaeology [Israelis] . . . learn that their forefathers were in this country three thousand years ago," Yadin continues. "This is a value" (ibid.). The symbolism of the scrolls for him is "heightened by the fact that the first three scrolls were bought by my father for Israel on 29 Nov., 1947, the very day on which the United Nations voted for the recreation of the Jewish state in Israel after two thousand years." Yigal Yadin, *The Message of The Scrolls,* ed. James H. Charlesworth (New York: Christian Origins Library, 1992), p. 14.

The ongoing fascination with the scrolls focuses on their as-yet-undeciphered substance—on what Robert Alter calls the "ultimate secret of origins" the scrolls are expected to reveal, the "material substance of the past" that could help us "understand . . . how we came to be what we are." Alter argues that "our" true origins lie with another narrative—the early rabbinic and early Christian systems of belief and religious practice—rather than with the Qumran sectarians who lived in the arid, apocalyptic atmosphere of "hypnotic words that insulated them from the changing winds of history," and whose writings and message "seem narrow and rigid and shrill." Alter, "How Important Are the Dead Sea Scrolls?" *Commentary*, February 1992, p. 41. For a more recent and illuminating discussion of the ideological import of archaeology generally and its import in validating the place of Massada in the recovery of ancient sites, see Yael Zerubavel, *Recovered Roots: Collective Memory and the Making of Israeli National Tradition* (Chicago: University of Chicago Press, 1995).

6. "The significance of the emergence of Zionism and the birth of Israel is that the former marks the reimagining of an ancient religious community as a nation, down there among the other nations—while the latter charts an alchemic change from wandering devotee to local patriot," writes Benedict Anderson in *Imagined Communities: Reflections on the Origin and Spread of Nationalism*, rev. ed. (London: Verso, 1991), p. 149. In his study of the psychosocial dynamics by which communities imagine themselves as nations—especially where he focuses on the territorialization of religious communities—Anderson might have expanded or challenged his own categories by examining such a well-imagined community as the collectivity of Jews in the Diaspora and their reconfiguration as a nation-state in the twentieth century. His passing reference marks a missed opportunity.

7. Pierre Vidal-Naquet, "Atlantis and the Nations," *Critical Inquiry* 18, no. 2 (winter 1992): 300–326.

8. Jacques Derrida, *Of Grammatology*, tr. Gayatri Chakravorty Spivak (Baltimore: Johns Hopkins University Press, 1976), p. 115.

9. Maurice Halbwachs, "The Legendary Topography of the Gospels," in *On Collective Memory*, ed. and trans. Lewis A. Coser (Chicago: University of Chicago Press, 1992), p. 219.

10. See, for example, Shimshon Bloch Halevi, *Shvilei Olam* [Pathways through the World; Hebrew] (Warsaw: n.p., 1855).

11. See Peter Berger, Brigitte Berger, and Hansfried Kellner, *The Homeless Mind: Modernization and Consciousness* (New York: Random House, 1973).

12. On the creation of a Talmudic culture as response to catastrophe and exile, see Jacob Neusner, *Judaism: The Evidence of the Mishnah* (Chicago: University of Chicago Press, 1981), and the debates that his work has generated. See also Arnold Eisen's discussion of tractate Avodah Zarah and the subsequent sociological and philosophical permutations of the Jewish discourse on exile in *Galut: Modern Jewish Reflection on Homelessness and Homecoming* (Bloomington: Indiana University Press, 1986); Eisen's study, which is an invaluable companion to my own work, proceeds by a close reading of constitutive texts spanning some three thousand years. For philosophical and theological discus-

sions of the Jewish theodicy of exile and homecoming, see also Yehezkel Kaufmann, *Golah ve-nekhar* [Exile and Foreignness], 2 vols. (Tel Aviv: Dvir, 1962);
Yitzhak Baer, *Galut*, [trans. Robert Warshow] (New York: Schocken Books,
1947); Eliezer Don-Yehiya, "'Galut' in Zionist Ideology and in Israeli Society,"
in *Israel and Diaspora Jewry: Ideological and Political Perspectives*, ed. Eliezer
Don-Yehiya (Tel Aviv: Bar Ilan University Press, 1991), pp. 219–57; Eliezer
Schweid, *The Land of Israel: A Homeland or Land of Destiny?* tr. Deborah Greniman (New York: Herzl Press/Associated Universities Press, 1985). The more recent discourse on the subject in the writings of Zali Gurevitch, Gideon Aran,
Amnon Raz-Karkotzkin, and Daniel Boyarin and Jonathan Boyarin will be considered later in this volume.

13. Mark Taylor, *Erring: A Postmodern A/theology* (Chicago: University of
Chicago Press, 1984), p. 153; the second ellipsis is mine.

14. Maurice Blanchot, *The Space of Literature*, tr. Ann Smock (Lincoln: University of Nebraska Press, 1982) pp. 70–71. Michael Seidel argues that "exilic
imagining . . . is both the mirror and the 'other' of narrative process; mimesis
becomes an alien (or allegorical) phenomenon that establishes fictional sovereignty on fictional ground." *Exile and the Narrative Imagination* (New Haven:
Yale University Press, 1986), p. 198.

15. Franz Rosenzweig, *The Star of Redemption* (Notre Dame, Ind.: University of Notre Dame Press, 1985), part 3, book 1, p. 300.

16. Edmond Jabès, "This Is the Desert: Nothing Strikes Root Here," interview by Bracha Ettinger Lichtenberg, in *Routes of Wandering: Nomadism, Voyages, and Transitions in Contemporary Israeli Art*, ed. Sarit Shapira, exhibition
catalogue, bilingual edition (Jerusalem: Israel Museum, 1991), pp. 247, 248, 250.

17. George Steiner, "Our Homeland, the Text," *Salmagundi*, no. 66 (winter–
spring 1985): 5, 24–25. References to modern Judaism as a text culture can be
seen in Yiddish literary circles much earlier in this century. See, for example, Ba'al-
Makhshoves [Israel Isidor Elyshev], who wrote in 1918 that "the literature of
oppressed peoples has always been their own territory, where they feel entirely
at home. . . . We Jews have been able to survive history because of this exterri-
toriality. . . . The term 'People of the Book,' with which history has crowned us,
clearly contains the notion that our earth, our very home, has always been literature." Ba'al-Makhshoves, "Tsvey shprakhen: Eyn eyntsiker literature," tr. as
"One Literature in Two Languages," in *What Is Jewish Literature?* ed. Hana
Wirth-Nesher (Philadelphia: Jewish Publication Society, 1994), p. 75. In France,
the growing influence of Emmanuel Levinas and, through Levinas, of Franz Rosenzweig, adds to the impact of Jabès and Steiner in redefining a late-twentieth-
century "text-centered" polemic with Jewish statehood. See Harold Bloom, *Agon:
Towards Theory of Revisionism* (New York: Oxford University Press, 1982); see
also Robert Gibbs, *Correlations in Rosenzweig and Levinas* (Princeton: Princeton
University Press, 1992), p. 137; and Jill Robbins, *Prodigal Son—Elder Brother:
Interpretations of Alterity in Augustine, Petrarch, Kafka, and Levinas* (Chicago:
University of Chicago Press, 1991).

18. Steiner, "Our Homeland, the Text," p. 19. For a discussion of Jewish intellectuals and postmodernism, see Norman Finkelstein, *The Ritual of New Cre-*

ation: Jewish Tradition and Contemporary Literature (Albany: State University of New York Press, 1992); relying heavily on Harold Bloom and Gershom Sholem, Finkelstein defines the "modern ritual of new creation" as comprising "the matter of 'wandering meaning' . . . [and] the matter of loss and exile" (p. 3). See also his discussion of the utopian/messianic element in George Steiner's thought and of the role of art as the arena of the struggle between the real and the ideal (pp. 97–116).

19. Paracelsus is quoted in E. R. Curtius, *European Literature and the Latin Middle Ages*, tr. Willard R. Trask (New York: Pantheon Books, 1953), p. 322. For a general discussion of "the book of nature" and "the book as symbol" generally, see chap. 16.

20. Vladimir Nabokov, *The Real Life of Sebastian Knight* (London: Weidenfeld and Nicolson, 1960), p. 150.

21. "Because he travels there by way of Venice, Athens or Constantinople, Chateaubriand approaches the 'term' Jerusalem (signifying 'term' as a sign and 'terminus') in a certain way," writes Michel Butor. "One stopping-place produces the effect of a parenthesis or a digression, while another is, on the contrary, an essential stage of an argument." The correlative of travel as writing is "writing as travel": "The terms Rome, Athens, Jerusalem are arranged in a particular order by the sentence which is my journey, and they can be varied at the instruction of my travelling-writing." Butor, "Travel and Writing," *Mosaic* 8, nos. 1–2 (fall 1974): 15.

22. Jesse Gellrich finds the poetic language of such medieval writers as Dante and Chaucer to be a kind of "fictional signifying" that both endorses and expands the boundaries and destabilizes the fixity of meaning inscribed in both the "Book of God's Work (nature)" and its "speculum," the "book of His Word (the Bible)." *The Idea of the Book in the Middle Ages* (Ithaca: Cornell University Press, 1985), p. 18.

23. Maurice Samuel, *The World of Sholem Aleichem* (1943; reprint, New York: Schocken Books, 1965), pp. 194–95. See, among others, the Hebrew writing of Y. H. Brenner and H. N. Bialik; and see in chapter 2 my discussion of Abramovitsh's *Travels of Benjamin the Third* for a satiric, maskilic representation of the effect of "text-centeredness" on the Jewish powers of observation. See also Jonathan Z. Smith, *Map Is Not Territory: Studies in the History of Religions* (Leiden: E. J. Brill, 1978), pp. 104–28.

24. Genesis Rabbah 49:4. In commenting on this passage, Israeli anthropologists Zali Gurevitch and Gideon Aran note the astounding correlation or identification between the Land of Israel and the text. "'Al ha-makom" [On Place], *Alpayim* 4 (1991): 16. For the abridged English version of this essay, see note 37 below.

25. Bland cites a fifteenth-century Hebrew grammarian who wrote that "because this sacred Book is equal in its properties to the Temple, it was originally divided into three sections just as was the arrangement of the Temple." Kalman Bland, "Medieval Jewish Aesthetics: Maimonides, Body, and Scripture in Profiat Duran," *Journal of the History of Ideas* 54, no. 4 (October 1993): 549. See also Bland, *The Artless Jew: Medieval and Modern Affirmations and Denials of the Visual* (Princeton: Princeton University Press, forthcoming).

26. The vision of confluence of the temporal and the divine Sabbath was homologized to the return to Zion and an end to exile. Elliot K. Ginsburg, *The Sabbath in the Classical Kabbalah* (Albany: State University of New York Press, 1989), pp. 85–92; see also Schweid, *Land of Israel,* pp. 79–90.

27. For intrabiblical prooftexts of the changing relations of territory, blood, and faith, see I Samuel 26:19; I Kings 20:28; Ruth 1:16; Ezra 9; Esther 3:8. For a succinct but thorough discussion of the classical biblical and postbiblical sources on territoriality, see W. D. Davies, *The Territorial Dimension of Judaism* (Berkeley: University of California Press, 1982). For a discussion of the violence entailed in group identity formation, see Regina M. Schwartz, *The Curse of Cain: The Violent Legacy of Monotheism* (Chicago: University of Chicago Press, 1997).

28. See, for instance, Jonathan Z. Smith's claim that the Temple in Jerusalem was itself a "self-referential system" that in an arbitrary way signified, quite simply, *difference,* and that, like the "phonemes in Roman Jakobson's linguistic theories[,] . . . [formed] . . . a system 'composed of elements which are signifiers and yet, at the same time, signify nothing.'" The priestly documents recorded in the Bible "already reduced the rituals of the Temple from performances to systems— primarily by mapping modes of emplacement . . . [and] these maps allow a prescission from place. They could be thought about in abstract topographies; they could be transported to another place; they could be extended to other sorts of social space." Smith's reading of the temple described in Ezekiel 40–48, a temple envisioned from the perspective of the Babylonian exile, together with the very different renderings in the Mishnah, is of a "systemic" rather than a primarily "historical" phenomenon; therefore it can be replicated. *To Take Place: Toward Theory in Ritual* (Chicago: University of Chicago Press, 1987), pp. 108–9, 73.

29. "Simulation is no longer that of a territory, a referential being or a substance," writes Jean Baudrillard. "It is the generation by models of a real without origin or reality: a hyperreal. The territory no longer precedes the map, nor survives it. Henceforth, it is the map that precedes the territory[;] . . . it is the map that engenders the territory." *Simulations,* tr. Paul Foss, Paul Patton, and Philip Beitchman (New York: Semiotext(e), 1983), p. 2.

30. "'Al 'aravim be-tokha talu ha-kabtzielim tarmilehem u-smartutehem vayishtatakhu lahem shatoah 'al pnei ha-adamah." S. Y. Abramovitsh, "Hanisrafim," in *Kol kitvei Mendele mokher sfarim* [The Complete Works of Mendele Mokher Sfarim] (Tel Aviv: Dvir, 1958), pp. 444–45.

31. Paul Celan, "Todesfuge," tr. John Felstiner, in Felstiner, *Paul Celan: Jew* (New Haven: Yale University Press, 1995), p. 31; Dan Pagis, "'Akevot" [Footprints], from *Gilgul,* in *Points of Departure,* tr. Stephen Mitchell (Philadelphia: Jewish Publication Society, 1981), p. 29.

32. Parallels with the literary and then the literal pilgrimages of Jews from Arab countries to their countries of origin, especially to North Africa, as the walls of enmity between Israel and its Arab neighbors crumble and these Jews challenge the Ashkenazi hegemony over Israeli culture and reconstruction of the past, are drawn by Amiel Alcalay, *After Jews and Arabs: Remaking Levantine Culture* (Minneapolis: University of Minnesota Press, 1993).

33. Primo Levi, who "remembered" Auschwitz and narrated his own salvaged humanity through his native Italian, claims in later stories that the "lager jar-

gon" was in fact Yiddish, which should be granted a "privileged position in the reconstruction of memory." This claim is only surprising, argues Sander L. Gilman, because Levi didn't really know Yiddish. Gilman, "To Quote Primo Levi: 'Redest Keyn Jiddisch, bist nit kejn jid' [If you don't speak Yiddish, you're not a Jew]," *Prooftexts* 9, no. 2 (May 1989): 143. See especially Levi's 1982 novel, *If Not Now, When?*

34. See Gershom Scholem, *The Messianic Idea in Judaism* (New York: Schocken Books, 1971) and later discussions by Jacob Talmon, Moshe Idel, and others who further advanced the debate on the continuities and discontinuities between messianism and Zionism. See also *Jews and Messianism in the Modern Era: Metaphor and Meaning*, ed. Jonathan Frankel, Studies in Contemporary Jewry 7 (New York: Oxford University Press, 1991); and Rahel Elboim-Dror, *Ha-mahar shel ha-etmol* [Yesterday's Tomorrow] (2 vols. [Jerusalem: Yad Ben-Zvi, 1993]) for a study of the major texts and influences of Zionist utopianism.

35. Frank Kermode and Michael Hamburger, among others, have identified the apocalyptic undercurrents in modernist forms and sensibility that are the legacy of romanticism; writers such as D. H. Lawrence, W. B. Yeats, T. S. Eliot, R. M. Rilke, and even Wallace Stevens share what Kermode defines as "the conviction that [they] exist at the end of an epoch, in a time of transition, on a ridge of history from which the contours of the whole are visible. That vision [encompasses] . . . the design of history . . . the outcome of the great narrative plot." Kermode, "Apocalypse and the Modern," in *Visions of Apocalypse: End or Rebirth?* ed. Saul Friedländer, Gerald Holton, Leo Marx, and Eugene Skolnikoff (New York: Holmes and Meier, 1985), p. 94. This position is more fully explored in Kermode, *The Sense of an Ending: Studies in the Theory of Fiction* (New York: Oxford University Press, 1967). See also Michael Hamburger, "Absolute Poetry and Absolute Politics," in *The Truth of Poetry: Tensions in Modern Poetry from Baudelaire to the 1960s* (London: Methuen, 1982), pp. 81–109.

36. Ernst Bloch remains one of the most powerful exponents of the utopian function of art as a theory of desire and "anticipatory illumination" that does not detach landscapes from "wish-landscapes." *The Utopian Function of Art and Literature: Selected Essays*, tr. Jack Zipes and Frank Mecklenburg (Cambridge, Mass.: MIT Press, 1988), p. 155. See also Theodor Adorno, *Minima Moralia: Reflections from Damaged Life*, tr. E. F. N. Jephcott (London: New Left Books, 1974), pp. 247 ff. The binary structures that evolve in response to an absence of utopian fulfillment can yield to the more organic, postmodern thrust of the not-yet-realized, generating an infinitude of fictive possibilities.

37. Zali Gurevitch and Gideon Aran, "The Land of Israel: Myth and Phenomenon," in *Reshaping the Past: Jewish History and the Historians*, ed. Jonathan Frankel, Studies in Contemporary Jewry 10 (New York: Oxford University Press, 1994), pp. 195–96. This is an abridged version of their essay "Al ha-makom." For an elaboration of this idea, with special attention to the sense of place gleaned by modern Zionist pioneers from the ancient biblical story of Israel, see Zali Gurevitch, "The Double Site of Israel," in *Grasping Land: Space*

and Place in Contemporary Israeli Discourse and Experience, ed. Eyal Ben-Ari and Yoram Bilu (Albany: State University of New York Press, 1997), pp. 203–16.

38. Conversely, the sacralization of territory can result in attempts to expand sacred space so that place and Place will correspond; religious Jewish settlers' ongoing staking of claims to the West Bank can be understood in this light.

39. A. B. Yehoshua, *Mr. Mani*, tr. Hillel Halkin (San Diego: Harcourt Brace, 1992), pp. 265–56.

40. In one of the earliest analyses of responses to claustrophobia in Israeli literature, Robert Alter argues that there was an essential difference between the "imaginative horizons" in fiction and in poetry, especially among those Hebrew writers who came of age in the 1950s and 1960s; the poets more naturally manage to overcome the "geographical limits that define the imagined world of the literary work" while the fiction becomes more often than not a representation of "claustrophobic collective existence, . . . a nervous shuttling between home and horizon." Alter, "A Problem of Horizons," in *Contemporary Israeli Literature*, ed. Elliott Anderson (Philadelphia: Jewish Publication Society, 1977), pp. 329, 332.

41. "Jerusalem is a port city on the shore of eternity. / The Temple Mount is a huge ship, a magnificent / luxury liner." Yehuda Amichai, "Yerushalayim 'ir namal 'al sfat ha-netzah" [Jerusalem Is a Port City on the Shore of Eternity], in *Songs of Jerusalem*, bilingual edition (Jerusalem: Schocken, 1987), p. 79.

42. Yehuda Amichai, "If I Forget Thee, Jerusalem," in ibid., p. 13.

43. See Ernst Renan's often-quoted lecture, "Qu'est-ce qu'une nation?" (delivered at the Sorbonne on March 11, 1882), in which he argued that "forgetting . . . is a crucial factor in the creation of a nation." He referred to different forms of forgetting: the effacement of individual origins in the forging of a nation as well as the effacement of "deeds of violence which took place at the origin of all political formations." Renan, "What Is a Nation?" tr. Martin Thom, in *Nation and Narration*, ed. Homi K. Bhabha (London: Routledge, 1990), p. 11.

44. Uri Zvi Greenberg, "Bizkhut em u-vena viyirushalayim" [For the Sake of a Mother and Her Son and Jerusalem], in *Kol Ketavav* [Collected Work] (Jerusalem: Mossad Bialik, 1994), vol. 7, pp. 57–59.

45. Eisen, *Galut*, p. 10.

46. See, for example, Y. H. Brenner in " 'Atzabim" [Nerves], in which the "hof" which is the shore of the Land of Israel is also the *final* shore (see note 48 below); Ya'acov Fichman, "Tzlalim 'al sadot" [Shadows over the Fields]—and Dan Miron on Fichman in his *Bodedim be-mo'adam: le-diyukana shel ha-republika ha-sifrutit ha-'ivrit be-tehilat ha-mea ha-'esrim* [When Loners Come Together: A Portrait of Hebrew Literature at the Turn of the Twentieth Century] (Tel Aviv: Am Oved, 1987), pp. 545–48. On the "Charon complex" as a theme in modern Israeli art, see Sarit Shapira, "Vehicles," in Shapira, *Routes of Wandering*, p. 197. One could argue, though, that it is the figure on that other shore, Jacob at the Jabbok ford (Gen. 32), that mimics Charon and his ferry; see Silvie-Anne Goldberg, *Crossing the Jabbok: Illness and Death in Ashkenazi Judaism in Sixteenth- through Nineteenth-Century Prague*, tr. Carol Cosman (Berkeley: University of California Press, 1996), esp. pp. 87–88. The biblical equivalent of

the modern site of return, the pioneer's landing in Jaffa Port, would be the crossing of the Jordan River.

47. "The necrophore is a coleopter beetle that buries carrion, cadavers of moles and mice, on which it lays its eggs." *Le Petit Robert*, quoted in Henri Raczymow, *Writing the Book of Esther*, tr. Dori Katz (London: Holmes and Meier, 1995), p. 93.

"Modern psychoanalytic theory teaches us that fictions of closure are linked to the death drive," writes Regina M. Schwartz; "that, as the end of desire, fulfillment is tantamount to death. Desire itself, however, perpetual desire, ensures textuality—in our parlance, scripturality. The Bible complicates this picture for it gives us at once desire (the promised land is, after all, promised) and nostalgia. . . . [In the Hebrew Bible] there are many dyings and risings rather than a single resurrection." Schwartz, "Joseph's Bones and the Resurrection of the Text: Remembering in the Bible," *PMLA* 103, no. 2 (March 1988): 122.

Freud's connections between psychoanalysis and archaeology, between the mother's body/mother earth/motherland as original home and transcendental homelessness as the state of civilized humanity, developed in *Totem and Taboo* and *Civilization and Its Discontents*, as well as the connections he draws between the fulfillment of desire and death, have not yet been fully explored in the context of Zionist images of return and the fulfillment (= denial) of desire. On Freud's sense of "homelessness" and fascination with archaeology and the "primitive," see Marianna Torgovnik, *Gone Primitive: Savage Intellects, Modern Lives* (Chicago: University of Chicago Press, 1990), pp. 194–209.

48. I may have been living all that time with the hope . . . of finding a foothold . . . in our picturesque ancestral corner of Asia, in which Bedouin, the great-grandchildren of Abraham the Hebrew, pitch their tents to this day and bring to the well real camels as once did his bondsman Eliezer . . . and in which . . . third- and fourth-generation children of Polish Jewish money-lenders are learning to follow the plow. . . . So that I thought . . . "Let me cross over and see that goodly land, its fair mountains and the Lebanon." . . .
"Well, what do you think now? Did you find your foothold?"

Y. H. Brenner, "Nerves" ['Atzabim], tr. Hillel Halkin, in *Eight Great Hebrew Short Novels*, ed. Alan Lelchuk and Gershon Shaked (New York: New American Library, 1983), p. 36.

49. shiru lanu mi-shirei tzion!
eikh nashir shir tzion 'al admat tzion
ve-'od lo hithalnu lishmo'a?

Leah Goldberg, "Mi-shirei Tzion,"
in *Shirim* [Poems] (Tel Aviv: Sifriat
po'alim, 1986), vol. 2, p. 219.

50. "Rearticulating the bones" by assigning absolute and redemptive value, the value of total recall, would thus be a defiance of Jewish hermeneutics understood as a lack of completion. See Schwartz, "Joseph's Bones and the Resurrection of the Text."

The unburied dead of the Holocaust, like the unmarked grave of Moses, maintain the tension and critique of the well-articulated narrative in modern Israel. See Don Handelman and Lea Shamgar-Handelman's fascinating comparison between the memorials to the dead in Israel's wars and to the dead of the Shoah:

they argue that because the dead of Europe *and their world* are so absent in the landscape of Israel, the memorials to them must be elaborately realized, unlike the simple and uniform cemeteries and memorials to the dead of Israel's wars. "Each type visualizes some relationship of the dead to the land, such that their absence on its surface signifies their presence within its earth . . . [contributing differentially] to the molding of landscapes of collective memory." On the one hand, in a kind of "synthetic holism," the bodies of the soldiers are perceived as "belonging" to the land, while the "land is felt to acquire contours that resonate with the bodies buried within it." On the other hand, the absence of both the "authentic body of sacrifice and of the place of sacrifice, that typifies Holocaust memorialism in Israel," depends on "metaphorization"—figuration or "copies," in the Baudrillardian sense—of that life above ground, stressing their "discontinuous relationship to the surrounding landscapes." Handelman and Shamgar-Handelman, "The Presence of Absence: The Memorialism of National Death in Israel," in Ben-Ari and Bilu, *Grasping Land*, pp. 89, 90, 101, 114–15.

51. Yehuda Amichai, from "Songs of Zion the Beautiful," in *Songs of Jerusalem*, p. 109.

PART ONE.   JEWISH JOURNEYS

1. David Quint, *Epic and Empire: Politics and Generic Form from Virgil to Milton* (Princeton: Princeton University Press, 1993), p. 9.

2. Leopold Zunz, "On the Geographical Literature of the Jews from the Remotest Times to the Year 1841," in vol. 2 of Benjamin of Tudela, *The Itinerary of Rabbi Benjamin of Tudela*, tr. and ed. by A. Asher (New York: Hakeshet Publishing, 1841), p. 304.

3. Smith calls the "two basic structures of human symbolization and experience . . . the 'centripetal' and the 'centrifugal.'" Jonathan Z. Smith, *Map Is Not Territory: Studies in the History of Religions* (Leiden: E. J. Brill, 1978), pp. 137, 131, 157.

4. A study complementary to the present volume, with its admittedly Eastern European bias, would consider the literature of such figures as Albert Memmi, Albert Cohen, and André Aciman (*Out of Egypt*) as well as Edmond Jabès—with Yehuda Halevi as the same poetic point of departure. See Ammiel Alcalay's representation of the culture of the Arab world and the Levant as mediating not only between former enemies but also between Zionist and diasporist orientations that were largely determined by an Ashkenazi bias; *After Jews and Arabs: Remaking Levantine Culture* (Minneapolis: University of Minnesota Press, 1993).

5. David Frishman's remark is cited in Benjamin Harshav, *Language in Time of Revolution* (Berkeley: University of California Press, 1993), pp. 4–5. Highly unconventional in his perception of "the place of place" in modern Jewish literature, Frishman remains a subversive figure in the canon of literary critics.

6. Dan Miron, "The Literary Image of the Shtetl," *Jewish Social Studies* 1, no. 3 (1995): 1–43. Originally published in Hebrew as a five-part article, "Hadimui ha-sifruti ha-klasi shel ha-'ayara," *Ha-do'ar* (55 [1976], 56 [1977]), and in Yiddish as *Der Imazh fun Shtetl: dray literatishe shtudiyes* (Tel Aviv: I. L. Peretz, 1981).

1. THE POETICS OF PILGRIMAGE: YEHUDA HALEVI
    AND THE UNCOMPLETED JOURNEY

1. Philo, *Contra Flaccum* 45–46; quoted in Jackie Feldman, "The Pull of the Center and the Experience of Communitas in Pilgrimage to the Second Temple" (M.A. thesis, Hebrew University of Jerusalem, 1988), part 6, p. 1.

2. For a discussion of the protean topography of the Holy Land even before the fourth century, and the relation between testimony and dogma in shaping sacred places, see Maurice Halbwachs, "The Legendary Topography of the Gospels in the Holy Land," in *On Collective Memory*, ed. and tr. Lewis A. Coser (Chicago: University of Chicago Press, 1992), pp. 191–235; on the elasticity of Jerusalem and its environs in accommodating the spiritual needs of many religious sects and its importance relative to other holy sites, see John Eade and Michael J. Sallnow, eds., *Contesting the Sacred: The Anthropology of Christian Pilgrimage* (London: Routledge, 1991), especially Eade and Sallnow's introduction (pp. 1–29) and Glenn Bowman, "Christian Ideology and the Image of a Holy Land" (pp. 98–121).

3. The Karaites appear in Babylonia in the eighth century with possible antecedents in earlier forms of resistance to the oral tradition and rabbinical Judaism. The most valuable repository of documents on these groups and their activities is the Cairo Geniza. See *Karaite Anthology: Excerpts from the Early Literature*, tr. and ed. Leon Nemoy (New Haven: Yale University Press, 1952). For a discussion of pilgrimage to the Holy Land during the period of the "First Moslem Conquest" (634–1099), and particularly of the movement of the Karaites after 825, as well as the polemic between the Karaites and the rabbis, see Moshe Gil, "'Aliya ve-'aliya la-regel bi-tekufat ha-kibbush ha-muslemi harishon (634–1099)" [Pilgrimage and Settlement in the Time of the First Moslem Conquest], *Katedra* 8 (1978): 124–33, and the responses by Shmuel Safrai, Avraham Grossman, and Hai ben Shamai (pp. 134–46). This discussion should be viewed in light both of modern attempts to establish evidence for the continuous presence of Jews in the land of Israel after the destruction of the Second Temple and of the connections between various messianic movements and the phenomena of pilgrimage to and settlement in Palestine.

4. "The Pseudo-Qumisian Sermon to the Karaites," tr. Leon Nemoy, bilingual text in *Proceedings of the American Academy for Jewish Research* 43 (1976): 64, 74 (English) and 93, 98 (Hebrew). See also Haim Hillel Ben-Sasson, ed., *A History of the Jewish People* (London: Weidenfeld and Nicolson, 1977), pp. 448–52; Barry Walfish, "The Mourners of Zion (Avelei Siyyon): Karaite Aliyah Movement of the Early Arab Period," in *Eretz Israel, Israel, and the Jewish Diaspora: Mutual Relations*, ed. Menachem Mor, Studies in Jewish Civilization 1 (Lanham, Md.: University Press of America, 1991), pp. 42–52.

5. "Ye mourners for Zion, remember your Mother from afar" wrote Japeth ben 'Ali in a late-ninth- or early-tenth-century hymn (Nemoy, *Karaite Anthology*, p. 107). Israel in the Diaspora is referred to as both "virgin of Israel" and as a wayward and rebellious daughter or wife ("The Pseudo-Qumisian Sermon to the Karaites," pp. 74–75). Worth noting in this context is not only the

image of women but also the role of women. Women mourners who recited lamentations were prominent in the activities of the Karaites who settled in Jerusalem.

6. Among the more illustrious travelers of this period who have left traces of their voyages—and, in some instances, whole itineraries—were Rabbi Ahima'az the Elder of Venosa, Italy (ninth century), Nasir Khosraw of Persia (eleventh century), Phinhas ha-Kohen from Babylonia (eleventh century), Petahia of Regensburg ([Ratisbon] twelfth century), and Judah al-Harizi (thirteenth century). After the Spanish expulsion, the number of pilgrims increased dramatically, especially among the Jews who had resettled in Turkish territories.

7. Shelomo Dov Goitein, "'Meeting in Jerusalem': Messianic Expectations in the Letters of the Cairo Geniza," *AJS Review* 4 (1979): 45. See also Ammiel Alcalay, *After Jews and Arabs: Remaking Levantine Culture* (Minneapolis: University of Minnesota Press, 1993), pp. 128–43, for an elaboration of the natural social, cultural, and economic intercourse between Jews and Arabs represented in the "*geniza* world."

8. Compare the Hyperboreans in Herodotus's geography, who were literally the "people beyond the north wind." The lands that lie beyond the ken of the Greek historian of the Persian Wars, who provides personal testimony based on extensive travel, contained such marvels as Indian tribes who extract gold from sand heaps, islands where gold dust covers the bottom of the lake, horned donkeys, and dog-headed men. The *History of the Persian Wars* is discussed in Lionel Casson, *Travel in the Ancient World* (Toronto: Hakkert, 1974), pp. 108, 110–11. Percy Adams cites passages from what might be called the "discovery" narratives of North America that could furnish interesting parallels and contrasts to the descriptions of the mythical river and the Red Jews: references to real places alongside imaginary ones—the nonexistent "rivière Longue" and the strange people living along it—and the encounters with either savage or highly developed "Red Men" punctuated the accounts of travelers as recent as the *Nouveaux Voyages . . . Dans l'Amerique* by French baron Lahontan in the early eighteenth century. Percy G. Adams, *Travel Literature and the Evolution of the Novel* (Lexington: University Press of Kentucky, 1983), pp. 74, 78.

For a discussion of imaginary Jewish geography, see A. Z. Eshkoli, "Yehudei habash ba-sifrut ha-'ivrit" [Jews of Ethiopia in Hebrew Literature], *Zion* 1 (1936): 316–36. For a relatively recent endorsement of the location in Africa of the tribe of Dan—and three of the other Lost Tribes, Naftali, Gad, and Asher—see the introduction by the editor, Avraham Epstein, to the 1891 edition of Eldad the Danite with a separate article on the Falashas: *Eldad Ha-dani: sipurav ve-hilkhotav be-mahadurot shonot 'al pi kitvei-yad ve-defusim 'atikim 'im mevo ve-he'arot* [Eldad the Danite: Editions of His Story and Precepts, Based on Ancient Manuscripts, with Introduction and Annotations] (Pressburg: Druck von Adolf Alkalay, 1891), p. vii. See also Rahel Elboim-Dror, *Ha-mahar shel ha-etmol* [Yesterday's Tomorrow], vol. 1, *Ha-utopia ha-tzionit* [The Zionist Utopia] (Jerusalem: Ben-Zvi and Mossad Bialik, 1993), p. 224 n. 36.

For a discussion of the clash between the known world and the world beyond knowledge in the age of exploration, and the ensuing change in epistemological strategy from texts to empirical observation, see Anthony Grafton, *New Worlds, Ancient Texts: The Power of Tradition and the Shock of Discovery* (Cambridge, Mass.: Harvard University Press, 1992).

9. As late as the mid–nineteenth century, the American Jewish playwright Mordekhai Immanuel Noah advocates conducting a search for the Ten Lost Tribes among the Native Americans. "Only Mordekhai Noah of New York, still upholds the opinion of Menasse B. Israel, that the ten tribes must be looked for in America," writes Leopold Zunz in 1841. "On the Geographical Literature of the Jews from the Remotest Times to the Year 1841," in vol. 2 of Benjamin of Tudela, *The Itinerary of Rabbi Benjamin of Tudela,* tr. and ed. A. Asher (New York: Hakeshet Publishing, 1841), p. 313. One of the symptoms of a new claim to territorialism and the "demystification" involved in returning to original space is the renewed attempt in present-day Israel, using the most sophisticated technology, to ingather the remnants of the tribes from their alleged abodes in India or Ethiopia, thereby rearticulating the lost parts of the primordial self. Similarly, the reluctance of Israeli authorities to dig the ruins of the Khazar Jewish kingdom that flourished over a thousand years ago in what is now southern Russia is symptomatic of the resistance to competing claims to "original" space.

10. Ibid., p. 241.

11. In the section chronicling Benjamin's journey through Babylon, for example, the paragraph that describes a passage of "five parasangs to Hillah, where there are 10,000 Israelites and four Synagogues," is followed by "Thence it is four miles to the Tower of Babel, which the generation whose language was confounded built of the bricks called Agur. The length of its foundation is about two miles. . . . One can see from there a view twenty miles in extent, as the land is level. There fell fire from heaven into the midst of the tower which split it to its very depths." Benjamin reports, with all the authority of a modern geographer, that the Jewish community in Tiberias numbers "about fifty," a rather meager flock shepherded by no fewer than three rabbis. Benjamin of Tudela, *Itinerary of Rabbi Benjamin of Tudela,* vol. 1, pp. 106–7, 81.

12. For a full discussion of the relationship between travel and pilgrimage literature and the birth of the novel, see Adams, *Travel Literature and the Evolution of the Novel,* and this volume, chapter 2.

13. Stephen Greenblatt, *Marvelous Possessions: The Wonder of the New World* (Chicago: University of Chicago Press, 1991). Greenblatt explores the representational strategies used by the explorers to describe what they encountered in the New World to their fellow countrymen and the implications of the transition from the "language of the marvelous" to the "ritual of appropriation." "Wonder," he concludes, with a gesture toward modern norms of tourism and travel, still "remains available for decency as well as domination"(pp. 24–25). See especially his discussion of Herodotus, Mandeville, and the discursive principles that they instituted regarding travel and attitudes toward the unfamiliar and the alien.

14. Yehoshua Ben-Arieh, *The Rediscovery of the Holy Land in the Nineteenth Century* (Jerusalem: Magnes Press, Hebrew University; Detroit: Wayne State University Press, 1979), pp. 5, 12; emphasis mine.

15. "One mode by which nineteenth-century male poets could sustain the

intensity of their profound yearning for a return to a site free of strife was to link this threatened female space with death," writes U. C. Knoepflmacher in a study of ruins in romantic poetry. "Ruins, rather than living buildings, predominate in works in which a woman's abode, rather than a man's, becomes directly or indirectly associated with what Bachelard sees as a 'dream-memory' of an original maternal envelope. . . . Romantic poetry all too often depicts a ruthless razing of the structures it persistently identifies with a feminine enclosure." Knoepflmacher, "Hardy Ruins: Female Spaces and Male Designs," *PMLA* 105, no. 5 (October 1990): 1056. See also John Michael, "History and Romance, Sympathy and Uncertainty: The Moral of the Stones in Hawthorne's *Marble Faun*," *PMLA* 103, no. 2 (March 1988): 150–61.

16. Mark Twain, *Traveling with the Innocents Abroad*, and Herman Melville, *Journal of a Visit to Europe and the Levant, Oct. 11, 1856–May 6, 1857*, are quoted in Walker Franklin, *Irreverent Pilgrims: Melville, Browne, and Mark Twain in the Holy Land* (Seattle: University of Washington Press, 1974), pp. 179, 125–26; Albert Heusser, *The Land of the Prophets*, is quoted in S. Friedman, *Land of Dust: Palestine at the Turn of the Century* (Lanham, Md.: University Press of America, 1982), p. 15.

On the death wish associated with arrival in Palestine, see also Alfred Kazin's discussion of Melville's anticipated trip to Palestine. As Melville and Nathaniel Hawthorne walked along the shore of the Irish Sea at Southport at Lancashire (according to Hawthorne's journal entry of November 12, 1856), Melville spoke of his desire both "to be annihilated" and to make a trip to the east, ending in the Holy Land. Kazin, *God and the American Writer* (New York: Knopf, 1997), p. 90.

17. Such images, of course, are not limited to the Jewish imagination. See, for example, Rembrandt's *Jeremiah Lamenting the Destruction of Jerusalem* (1630), with its representation of the prophet sitting on the moss-covered steps of the ruined Temple of Solomon. On this painting and its construction and deconstruction of home, see Sanford Budick, "Rembrandt's and Freud's 'Gerusalemme Liberata,'" in *Home: A Place in the World*, special issue of *Social Research* 58, no. 1 (spring 1991): 189–207.

18. Yehoshua Ben-Arieh notes that as late as the middle of the nineteenth century, no major scientific study of Palestine had been undertaken; there were not even any "maps with accurate measurements. . . . Numerous historical sites could not be identified, and the flora and fauna were 'terra incognita.'" Ben-Arieh, "Perceptions and Images of the Holy Land," in *The Land That Became Israel: Studies in Historical Geography*, ed. Ruth Kark (New Haven: Yale University Press, 1989), p. 45. Without here considering the ideological and spiritual value of maintaining the Holy Land as a ruined shrine, he goes on to document the scientific activity that took place in the second half of the nineteenth century—which of course can be seen as parallel to a political appropriation of the territory.

Zunz claims, typically, that it was only a matter of the denial of civil liberties that had impeded a more scientific Jewish approach to the Holy Land; the "bare accounts of Jews are converted into history and statistics, the reports of the holy land are converted into archaeology and biblical Geography" ("On the Geographical Literature of the Jews," p. 304).

19. "In wisdom poems and other genres [of medieval Hebrew poetry], Time and the World, both implicitly capitalized, [are] ruthless characters who devour their own children," writes Dan Pagis. *Hebrew Poetry of the Middle Ages and the Renaissance* (Berkeley: University of California Press, 1991), p. 8.

20. Yehuda Halevi, "Ode to Zion" [Tzion, ha-lo tishali] in *The Penguin Book of Hebrew Verse*, ed. T. Carmi (Harmondsworth: Penguin, 1981), pp. 347–49. In his gloss on the words from the Song of Songs, "I sleep, but my heart waketh," the "Haver" in the *Kuzari* says that Solomon "designates the exile by *sleep*," the ultimate state of suspension. Yehuda Halevi, *Book of Kuzari*, tr. fr. the Arabic by Hartwig Hirschfeld (London: George Routledge and Sons, 1969), book II, para. 24.

21. Yehuda Halevi, "Admonition to the Soul" [Yeshena vehek yaldut, le-matai tishkevi], tr. Gabriel Levin, *Jerusalem Post*, November 21, 1986, p. 18. I gratefully acknowledge my conversations with Gabriel Levin and with Kalman Bland, which contributed much to my understanding of Yehuda Halevi's poetics and philosophy.

22. The *Kuzari* becomes a constitutive reference for the territorial nationalism and political messianism that emerge some seven centuries later. See, for example, Yitzhak Baer, who argued in an influential essay first published in 1936 in Berlin that "Judah ha-Levi is the first thinker after the political decline of the Jewish nation to give a full theoretical consideration to the problem of the Galut. . . . He undertakes his memorable journey to Palestine in order by his own example to teach his contemporaries and all who come after him that redemption may be won only by a real and active longing for reunion with God in Palestine— that man himself must create the conditions that will lead to redemption." *Galut*, [tr. Robert Warshow] (New York: Schocken Books, 1947), pp. 31–33. See also Eliezer Don-Yehiya, "'Galut' in Zionist Ideology and in Israeli Society," in *Israel and Diaspora Jewry: Ideological and Political Perspectives*, ed. Eliezer Don-Yehiya (Tel Aviv: Bar Ilan University Press, 1991), p. 219.

Alcalay emphasizes the poet's embeddedness in the Arabic culture of his time rather than the argument that his entire life was a journey to the Land of Israel. "It is the journey of Yehuda Halevi . . . that has assumed the status of nationalist myth and model in the Zionist phase of the 'new modern' period. . . . At its most vulgar, the [use to which these poems are put] makes Halevi into some kind of proto-Zionist, [even though most of his poetry,] like that of his Andalusian counterparts, was steeped in the material and spiritual culture of Islam" (*After Jews and Arabs*, pp. 173–75). See also Marc Saperstein, "Halevi's West Wind," *Prooftexts* 1, no. 3 (September 1981): 306–11; and Yisrael Levine, "Masa'o shel Rabi Yehuda Halevi le-eretz yisrael—siyumo shel tahalikh ruhani" [R. Yehuda Halevi's Voyage to the Land of Israel—the Conclusion of a Spiritual Process], *Apiryon*, nos. 26–27 (1993): pp. 7–13.

23. Yehuda Halevi, "Hard-Pressed for the Living God" [Hetzikatni teshukati], from *On the Sea* [Shirei yam], part 5, tr. Gabriel Levin (Jerusalem: Ibis Editions, 1997), pp. 26–27.

24. See also Yehuda Halevi, "My Soul Trusts in You" [Lekha nafshi betuhah], in *Shirei ha-kodesh le-rebbe Yehuda Halevi* [The Liturgical Poetry of R. Yehuda Halevi], ed. D. Yarden (Jerusalem: Kiryat no'ar, 1978–1985), vol. 4, pp. 937–40.

On the sumptuous life of such courtier poets as Yehuda Halevi, see Gerson Cohen, "Abraham Ibn Daud's Universe of Discourse," introduction to Abraham Ibn Daud, *The Book of Tradition* [Sefer Ha-Kabbalah] (Philadelphia: Jewish Publication Society of America, 1967), pp. xvi–xxv.

25. Ross Brann, "Judah Halevi: The Compunctious Poet," *Prooftexts* 7, no. 2 (May 1987): 124–25. Brann expanded this argument in *The Compunctious Poet: Cultural Ambiguity and Hebrew Poetry in Muslim Spain* (Baltimore: Johns Hopkins University Press, 1991). And see, for example, Yehuda Halevi's poem "Ha-fashat ha-zman bigdei haradot ve-lavash et begadav ha-hamudot" [In Alexandria], part of a qasida written in Alexandria in response to a letter from a friend in Cairo (discussed later in this chapter).

26. Yehuda Halevi, "The Poet Imagines His Voyage" [Ha-tirdof na'arut ahar hamishim], in Carmi, *Penguin Book of Hebrew Verse*, p. 350.

27. Yehuda Halevi, "Has a Flood Washed the World to Waste?" [Hava mabul], no. 2, in *On the Sea*, p. 22.

28. Yehuda Halevi, "Greetings Ladies, Kith and Kin" [Kiru 'alei vanot], in ibid., pp. 36–37.

29. Don Pagis, "Individuality and the Poetic Tradition," in *Hebrew Poetry of the Middle Ages and the Renaissance* (Berkeley: University of California Press, 1991), p. 28. The existential aspects of the poetry have come into prominence only recently; Pagis stresses the highly individual aspects of theme and form against those who read the poetry of the Hebrew-Spanish school as generally conventional and formulaic.

30. For example, the *muwashshah* or "girdle poem" is an Arabic strophic form used by Yehuda Halevi even in his long poem cycle *Shirei yam* [On the Sea].

31. See Ross Brann's discussion in *The Compunctious Poet* (pp. 23–58) of the plethora of biblical references and allusions that characterize the Hebrew poetry of Spain in the Golden Age and the Andalusian poets' astounding proficiency in imitating biblical Hebrew—along with their abiding ambivalence about the entire bicultural enterprise.

On the larger issue of the place of Hebrew as language and literature for an exiled people, see Moses Ibn Ezra's essay (in Arabic!) on Hebrew poetics, which includes an indictment of the Jewish forefathers for neglecting their "Hebraism"; *Kitab al-Muhadara wal-Mudhakara: Liber Discussionis et Commemorationis (Poetica Hebraica)*, ed. A. S. Halkin, bilingual edition (Jerusalem: Mikitzei nirdamin, 1975), pp. 50–51. In "The Medieval Jewish Attitude toward Hebrew," Halkin analyzes the struggle that medieval Jewish writers in the Islamic world underwent, unlike their counterparts in Christian cultures who were not tempted by the vernacular. He cites the positions of both Judah ibn Tibbon and of Yehuda Halevi who link the plight of the Jews to the plight of their language (as for example, in the *Kuzari*, book II, para. 68). In *Biblical and Other Studies*, ed. Alexander Altmann (Cambridge, Mass.: Harvard University Press, 1963), pp. 233–48. For a summary of the development of medieval Hebrew poetry and the influence of Spanish-Arabic forms on Hebrew poetics, see Benjamin Harshav, "Note on the Systems of Hebrew Versification," in Carmi, *Penguin Book of Hebrew Verse*, pp. 57–72.

The bilingual edition of Yehuda Halevi's poems based on the critical text edited by Heinrich Brody includes scriptural sources as part of the scholarly apparatus. See *Selected Poems of Jehudah Halevi*, tr. Nina Salaman (Philadelphia: Jewish Publication Society, 1928).

32. See my discussion of Abramovitsh's *Mas'ot binyamin ha-shlishi* and Agnon's *Bilvav yamim* in chapters 2 and 3.

33. Yehuda Halevi, "Past Fifty, Still Hot on the Heels of Juvenile Pastimes" [Ha-tirdof na'arut ahar hamishim], tr. Gabriel Levin, unpublished MS, p. 51.

34. Halevi, "The Poet Imagines His Voyage," in Carmi, *Penguin Book of Hebrew Verse*, p. 350. This is the last section of the poem that I cited in Levin's translation in the previous quote. I have used Carmi's translation here as it is more literal and accentuates the image of "the heart of the seas."

35. Hamori claims that what is specific to this poem, which was most likely written in Alexandria while the poet was awaiting the ship to Palestine, is "its insertion of personal time into the time of divine and Jewish history." Andras Hamori, "Lights in the Heart of the Sea. Some Images of Judah Halevi's," *Journal of Semitic Studies* 30, no. 1 (spring 1985): pp. 82–83.

36. Yehuda Halevi, "Ode to Zion" [Tzion ha-lo tishali], in Carmi, *Penguin Book of Hebrew Verse*, p. 347; "My heart is in the East and I am at the / edge of the West" is the opening line of Yehuda Halevi's best-known poem, "Libi ba-mizrah" (ibid.).

37. Levin translates "east wind" (*mizrah*) as "levant" (Halevi, *On the Sea*, p. 36). Goitein has established that this poem was written in Alexandria while the poet was waiting to leave for the Holy Land. Goitein, "Ha-im higia' rav Yehuda Halevi el hof eretz-yisrael?" [Did R. Yehuda Halevi Ever Reach the Land of Israel?], *Tarbiz* 46, nos. 3–4 (autumn 1977): 245–50. Another poem written in the same circumstances, "Ze ruhakha, tzad ma'arav" [To the Western Wind], designates the east wind as *kadim*; translated in Carmi, *Penguin Book of Hebrew Verse*, pp. 350–51.

38. Halevi, *Book of Kuzari*, book II, para. 20.

39. Tikva Frymer-Kensky traces the image of Jerusalem as woman—mother, wife, lover—through the biblical prophets; it is Micah who first "transmutes the Judean attachment to Jerusalem to a love for the 'spirit' of the city, a movable indwelling presence." At the time of the destruction, Jeremiah envisions Jerusalem as both female persona and intercessor on behalf of its inhabitants; and later, "when the exile finally came, Deutero-Isaiah imagines Bat-Zion as a solitary figure, alone among the ruins of the city of Jerusalem, waiting for the people to come back, [while] Zachariah [sees her] as the portable city, the spirit of Jerusalem who has accompanied the people into their exile and awaits their return." *In the Wake of the Goddesses: Women, Culture, and the Biblical Transformation of Pagan Myth* (New York: Fawcett Columbine, 1992), p. 175.

40. Johan Huizinga, *The Waning of the Middle Ages: A Study of the Forms of Life, Thought, and Art in France and the Netherlands in the XIVth and XVth Centuries* (New York: Doubleday, 1954), p. 201.

41. Yehuda Halevi, "Lovely Slopes, Earth's Delights" [Yefeh nof m'sos tevel], tr. Gabriel Levin, unpublished MS, p. 47.

42. Yehuda Halevi, "Ode to Zion" [Tzion ha-lo tishali], tr. Gabriel Levin, unpublished MS, pp. 43–46.

43. Ibid.

44. The "filthiness" in her skirts in Lamentations has been otherwise interpreted as referring to Zion as menstruating. See Frymer-Kensky, *In the Wake of the Goddesses*, p. 269 n. 3. This would reinforce the palpable and coherent structure of the biblical metaphor of Jerusalem as woman.

45. Heinrich Heine, "Romanzero," *Hebraische Melodien*, in *Heinrich Heine Werke* (Frankfurt am Main: Insel Verlag, 1968), vol. 1, section 3, p. 207.

46. Moshe Idel, "The Land of Israel in Medieval Kabbalah," in *The Land of Israel: Jewish Perspectives*, ed. Lawrence Hoffman (Notre Dame, Ind.: University of Notre Dame Press, 1986), pp. 176, 178–81.

47. Yehuda Halevi, "In Alexandria" [Ha-fashat ha-zman bigdei haradot velavash et begadav ha-hamudot], tr. Gabriel Levin, unpublished MS, p. 69.

48. Halevi, *Book of Kuzari*, book II, para. 22.

49. Ja, das ist das Zionslied,
Das Jehuda ben Halevy
Sterbend auf den heilgen Trümmern
Von Jerusalem gesungen—

Barfuß und im Büßerkittel
Saß er dorten auf dem Bruchstück
Einer umgestürzten Säule;—
Bis zur Brust herunter fiel

. . . Also saß er und er sang,
Wie ein Seher aus der Vorzeit
Anzuschaun—dem Grab enstiegen
Schien Jeremias, der Alte—

. . . Doch ein frecher Sarazene
Kam desselben Wegs geritten,
Hoch zu Ross, im Bug sich wiegend
Und die blanke Lanze schwingend—

In die Brust des armens Sängers . . .
Ruhig floss das Blut des Rabbi,
Ruhig seinen Sang zu Ende
Sang er, und sein sterbeletzter
Seufzer war Jerusalem!—

            Heine, "Romanzero,"
            pp. 210, 216–217.

A Hebrew poem on the same subject, "R. Yehudah ha-Levi," was written at around the same time by Micah Joseph Lebensohn (1828–52). The earliest expression of the legend can be found in *Shalshelet ha-Kabbalah*, written by Gedaliah Ben Joseph Ibn Yahya (Venice, 1587). Not the least of the mysteries surrounding such accounts of Halevi's death is the contradiction between the image of the Arab assassin and the fact of Christian hegemony in this Crusader-dominated moment in the history of Jerusalem.

Over the years, S. D. Goitein refashioned his own reading of the poetry and the biography as new documents from the Cairo Geniza came to light and were deciphered; he was finally able to reconstruct Yehuda Halevi's life until his last days in the Alexandrian port, citing poems and letters written aboard ship and entrusted to a friend. In projecting into the murky time between the poet's departure for the Holy Land and his end, which came sometime in the summer of 1141, Goitein remains cautious about confirming the legends; however, he finds it likely that the poet made it to Palestine and probably met an "unnatural end" there. See "Ha-im higia' rav yehuda halevi el hof eretz-yisrael?" See also Goitein, "The Biography of Rabbi Yehudah Ha Levi in the Light of the Cairo Geniza Documents," *Proceedings of the American Academy for Jewish Research* 28 (1959): 41–56. And for a more recent overview of this subject as well as of the different modern interpretations of Yehuda Halevi's pilgrimage as indices of the interpreter's ideological stance, see Levine, "Masa'o shel Rabi Yehuda halevi le-eretz yisrael," pp. 7–13.

50. Yehuda Halevi, "Trusting, or Flustered, My Soul" [Lekha nafshi betukha], in *On the Sea*, p. 24.

51. Halevi, "Ode to Zion," unpublished MS, p. 43.

52. Michael Fishbane, *The Kiss of God: Spiritual and Mystical Death in Judaism* (Seattle: University of Washington Press, 1994), pp. 11, 20.

53. Yehuda Amichai, "Travels of the Last Benjamin of Tudela," in *Selected Poetry of Yehuda Amichai*, tr. and ed. Chana Bloch and Stephen Mitchell, with foreword by Chana Bloch (New York: Harper & Row, 1986), p. 71, bilingual ed. (New York: Sheep Meadow Press, 1996), p. 159.

2. LOST IN SPACE: S. Y. ABRAMOVITSH AND THE SKEPTICAL VOYAGE

1. On the whole issue of "Mendele" as pseudonym or as persona, see Dan Miron's definition of the "pseudonymic fallacy." Tracing the evolution of the Mendele-Abramovitsh conflation and the critical discussion surrounding it, he argues persuasively that Mendele is not Abramovitsh's pseudonym, comparable to "Sholem Aleichem" or "Mark Twain," but rather a masked character, an insider-outsider, one who dresses and behaves like the folk and mingles with them, telling and selling stories, peddling his wares (books of course, but also prayer-shawls, copperware, candles, amulets . . .); he is never fully the benighted shtetl Jew or the gentrified, urbanized maskilic Jew. Miron, *A Traveler Disguised: A Study in the Rise of Modern Yiddish Fiction in the Nineteenth Century* (New York: Schocken Books, 1973), chap. 5. Whereas Gershon Shaked claims that in Abramovitsh's fiction there are really only two characters, the narrator (Mendele) and "the people" of Israel (*Bein s'hok le-dema': 'iyunim bi-yetzirato shel Mendele Mokher Sefarim* [Between Laughter and Tears: Studies in the Work of Mendele Mokher-Sefarim] [Ramat Gan: Massada, 1965], p. 63), Miron comes closer to a Bakhtinian reading in claiming that "polyphony" characterizes the complex structure of *Benjamin the Third*—a "multiplicity and quick interchangeability of the authorial 'voices'" that include those not only of Mendele and Benjamin but also of people in conversation and the ancient sources quoted as authorizing texts (*A Traveler Disguised*, pp. 222–23).

2. Joachim Neugroschel's raunchy translation of the Yiddish original into idiomatic American English presents an interesting late-twentieth-century resolution to the challenge of an archaic satiric text. Except where otherwise specified, I am using the Yiddish, in Neugroschel's translation, as the "normative" text.

The English place-names, which translate those in the Yiddish text, will be followed in brackets by transliterations of both the original Yiddish and the Hebrew terms; page references will be given parenthetically in the text, first to the Yiddish, then to the English translation from the Yiddish, and then to the Hebrew (designated Y, E, and H). The use of place-names as semantic and satirical focal points is duplicated to varying degrees in the different translations. The editions used are *Masoes binyomin hashlishi*, vol. 10 of *Ale verk fun Mendele moykher sforim (S. Y. Abramovitsh)* (Cracow: Farlag Mendele, 1911); "The Travels of Benjamin the Third," in *The Shtetl*, tr. and ed. Joachim Neugroschel (New York: Richard Marek, 1979); and *Mas'ot Benyamin ha-shlishi* (Tel Aviv: Dvir, 1950). All translations from the Hebrew text are my own. Another English edition of *Benjamin the Third* has recently appeared, translated by Hillel Halkin; this translation is based on the Yiddish version but includes the epilogue found only in the Hebrew version. See *Tales of Mendele the Book Peddler: Fishke the Lame and Benjamin the Third*, ed. Dan Miron and Ken Frieden (New York: Schocken Books, 1996).

3. The self-styled "Benjamin the Second" was Israel Joseph Benjamin, who as late as the mid–nineteenth century regarded himself as successor to the medieval pilgrim/explorer and set off from his native Romania in search of traces of the Ten Lost Tribes; his *Cinq années de voyage en Orient* was published in French in 1856 and then translated (slightly modified) into German, Hebrew, and English. The English version was J. J. Benjamin II, *Eight Years in Asia and Africa from 1846 to 1855*, tr. and published by the author (Hanover, 1863).

4. See above, chapter 1. In his *Itinerary*, Benjamin of Tudela refers to his visit to the community of Jews in Amadiah, Kurdistan, who speak the language of the "Targum" (Aramaic) and, reportedly, descend from the "first [Babylonian] exile." One of the earliest if not the first to mention the tradition that connected the Ten Tribes and the Jews of Kurdistan, Benjamin of Tudela was followed by Benjamin the Second and, naturally, by . . . Benjamin the Third. Benjamin of Tudela, *The Itinerary of Benjamin of Tudela*, tr. and ed. A. Asher (New York: Hakeshet Publishing, 1841), vol. 1, pp. 76–77 (Hebrew) and 121–22 (English).

In the metastylistic analogy between Aramaic and Yiddish, Abramovitsh is establishing a translating convention for the vernacular; his Hebrew *nusah*, accommodating a multilayered linguistic culture, will designate Aramaic as place marker for colloquial Yiddish.

5. The folk etymology of Poland as "Po-lin," the place where God instructed the exiles from the Holy Land to make their dwelling in the *mean-time*, is the whimsical version of a (provisional) sanctification of diasporic time and place. In his essay on the literary image of the shtetl, Miron adds that even if Glupsk is mocked as "Jerusalem in exile," Abramovitsh's "shtetl image . . . needed to comply with [the myth] of the aboriginal Polish shtetl . . . founded by divine decree as the temporary home of the Jerusalem exiles." Dan Miron, "The Literary Image of the Shtetl," *Jewish Social Studies* 1, no. 3 (spring 1995): 36–37.

6. Being "led to the bathhouse" is idiomatic Yiddish for being duped, being sold a bill of goods. "Usually the bathhouse theme is used for a portrayal of Jewish society in its naked truth," note Dan Miron and Anita Norich in "The Politics of Benjamin III: Intellectual Significance and Its Formal Correlatives in Sh. Y.

Abramovitsh's *Masoes Benyomin hashlishi,*" in *The Field of Yiddish: Studies in
Language, Folklore, and Literature, Fourth Collection,* ed. Marvin I. Herzog et
al. (Philadelphia: Institute for the Study of Human Issues, 1980), p. 98. They
proceed to give a detailed analysis of the political and anatomical allegories in
each chapter, reading the bathhouse as parody of the British political system at
the time of the Crimean War and each of the towns as a specific "body politic."

7. The insidious participation of *khappers* in the conscription of Jewish boys
into the czar's army had already been discontinued by Abramovitsh's time, after the end of the reign of Nicholas I in 1855.

8. See, for example, Menakhem Perry, "Thematic and Structural Shifts in Autotranslations by Bilingual Hebrew-Yiddish Writers: The Case of Mendele
Mokher Sforim," *Poetics Today* 2, no. 4 (summer/autumn1981): 181–92.

9. In the popular genealogy of Yiddish letters, Abramovitsh was represented
as the paterfamilias and Sholem Aleichem and I. L. Peretz as his descendants.
The "grandfather's" life, which was considerably longer than that of his two
younger "progeny," spanned much of the nineteenth century and ended, like
theirs, during World War I.

10. Benjamin Harshav, *The Meaning of Yiddish* (Berkeley: University of
California Press, 1990), p. 151. For a comprehensive discussion of the relative
place of Yiddish and Hebrew in Abramovitsh's life and in the Jewish culture
of the nineteenth century, see Miron, *A Traveler Disguised,* chap. 1. For earlier
overviews of internal bi- and trilingualism in modern Jewish literature, see Ba'al-
Makhshoves, "Tsvey shprakhn—eyneyntsige literatur," in *Geklibene verk* (New
York: CYCO, 1953), pp. 112–23, tr. as "One Literature in Two Languages," in
What Is Jewish Literature? ed. Hana Wirth-Nesher (Philadelphia: Jewish Publication Society, 1994), pp. 69–77. See also Dov Sadan, "Masat mavo," in *Avnei
bedek* [Foundation Stones] (Tel Aviv: Ha-kibbutz ha-me'uhad, 1962), pp.
26–38; Max Weinreich, *History of the Yiddish Language* (Chicago: University
of Chicago Press, 1980). On the construction of modern Hebrew, see also Robert
Alter, *The Invention of Hebrew Prose: Modern Fiction and the Language of Realism* (Seattle: University of Washington Press, 1988), and "Inventing Hebrew
Prose," in *Hebrew and Modernity* (Bloomington: Indiana University Press,
1994), pp. 40–74.

11. Harshav, *The Meaning of Yiddish,* pp. 151–52. The reasons for a given
writer's movement between the two languages may be as much economic or sociological as ideological. For the argument that Abramovitsh left Hebrew and
began writing in Yiddish not out of a particular love of that language, and that
twenty-eight years later he returned to Hebrew not out of *hibat Zion*—love of
Zion or love of the lovers of Zion—but because in each case he was influenced
by an assessment of the size of his readership, see Dan Miron, *Bodedim be-
mo'adam: le-diyukana shel ha-republika ha-sifrutit ha-'ivrit be-tehilat ha-mea
ha-'esrim* [When Loners Come Together: A Portrait of Hebrew Literature at the
Turn of the Twentieth Century] (Tel Aviv: Am Oved, 1987), pp. 82–83. Nonetheless, having reentered the semantic universe of Hebrew letters, the text would
perforce be brought into the nationalist polemic that monopolized the agenda
in those years.

12. Miron, comparing Mendele's intertextuality with that of Sholem Alei-

chem's Tevye, calls the first a "'spoiled' theologian . . . a 'black' rabbi who enjoys the subtle desecration of the scriptures, who dexterously mingles the holy with the profane and then offers the explosive mixture to his readers, expecting it to blow up in their faces" (*A Traveler Disguised*, p. 177). I would add that Mendele is undermining or challenging the traditions he misquotes, while Tevye is *preserving* them through misreadings—anticipating the cultural process of partial amnesia that will take place in America just one generation later. See discussions of Sholem Aleichem and I. B. Singer in chapters 4 and 8.

13. Ruth Wisse, *The Schlemiel as Modern Hero* (Chicago: University of Chicago Press, 1971), p. 34. For a discussion of the satire created between the promise of heroic exploits contained in the language and the pathetic conditions of the protagonists, see also Shaked, *Bein s'hok le-dema'*; Menakhem Perry, "Ha-analogia u-mekomah be-mivne ha-roman shel Mendele mokher sfarim" [The Place of Analogy in the Structure of the Novels of Mendele Mokher Sefarim], *Ha-sifrut* 1, no. 1 (spring 1968): 94.

14. Of course it is only relatively true that Hebrew was a hermetic, nonporous language, as anyone who has studied the diglossia in the early rabbinic period (Hebrew-Aramaic) or in the High Middle Ages (Hebrew-Arabic) can see. See the interesting study by Rina Drori of the influence of the Karaites on rabbinic language: "'Al tafkida shel ha-sifrut ha-karait be-toldot ha-sifrut ha-yehudit ba-mea ha-'asirit" [On the Role of Karaite Literature in Jewish Literature of the Tenth Century], *Dapim le-mehkar be-sifrut* [Pages in Literary Research] 9 (1993–94): 101–10. On its long-range implications for the Yiddish-Hebrew diglossia of the modern period, see part 2 of this volume.

15. Perry demonstrates the enactment of the Yiddish idiom in both the linguistic and the mimetic dimensions of the Hebrew *Benjamin the Third*, arguing persuasively that the Hebrew text presumes a Yiddish reader and in places even actualizes (unarticulated) Yiddish expressions ("Autotranslations by Bilingual Hebrew-Yiddish Writers," pp. 181–92).

16. In *Bein s'hok le-dema'*, Shaked dwells at length on the Jewish noses (*be-hotem ha-hotem*) in Abramovitsh and on what he calls the "secularization" and the "materialization" of the language of Scriptures and liturgy, meant to produce the comic effect of maskilic irreverence toward the sacred.

17. Within only a few years of its appearance in Yiddish, the novel was translated into Polish (1885) and Czech under the title *The Jewish Don Quixote*—and so it continued to be known for decades in the Americas as well as in Europe.

Don Quixote's prominence in the Jewish imagination reflects his diffusion in the culture at large. Sholem Aleichem wrote a Hebrew fragment titled "Don-Kishot mi-mazepfke ve-simha-pinhas re'ehu" [Don Quixote of Mazepfke and His Friend Simha Pinhas], which appeared in the journal *Pardes: osef sifruti* 1, ed. Y. H. Ravnitzky (Odessa, 1892): 267–73. While it has been generally acknowledged, since Abramovitsh's own time, that *The Travels of Benjamin the Third* was patterned after *Don Quixote*, most of the critical discussions of the influence of Cervantes, and of the element of the picaresque in Abramovitsh's writing, have centered on the impact of European models on the emerging Jewish novel in general and on Abramovitsh as a derivative or "original" writer in particular.

18. The figure of the Wandering Jew, implicated in both the crucifixion and the projected Second Coming of Christ, first surfaced in the thirteenth century and became prominent in the *Volksbücher* of seventeenth-century Europe; he has a complex and still largely unexplored presence in the Jewish domain. For a very extensive history of the Wandering Jew and his place in Christian ritual and thought, see George K. Anderson, *The Legend of the Wandering Jew* (Providence, R.I.: Brown University Press, 1965). For discussions of the attraction and resistance of the Jewish imagination to the Wandering Jew, the affinities between the "*golus* Jew" and the Wandering Jew, see Galit Hassan-Rokem and Alan Dundes, eds., *The Wandering Jew: Essays in the Interpretation of a Christian Legend* (Bloomington: Indiana University Press, 1985). See also Richard Cohen, *Jewish Icons: Art and Society in Modern Europe* (Berkeley: University of California Press, 1998).

19. Percy Adams cites several arguments for according the contested title of "first modern novel" to *Don Quixote*, including that it became and remained, for at least two hundred years, the most influential work of prose fiction and that it supports those who, like Ortega y Gasset, have claimed that the "novel" was born of the conflict between romance and realism. Adams, *Travel Literature and the Evolution of the Novel* (Lexington: University Press of Kentucky, 1983), p. 23. On the Cervantean narrative as a quest for justice and an inquiry into the practice of practical jokes, see Alexander Welsh, *Reflections on the Hero as Quixote* (Princeton: Princeton University Press, 1981); as an allegory and a multilayered inquiry into life as a journey, see Steven Hutchinson, *Cervantine Journeys* (Madison: University of Wisconsin Press), 1992.

20. See the introduction for a discussion of poststructuralist readings by Jabès, Derrida, Steiner, Taylor, and others; in chapter 9 I consider postcolonial readings of Jewish nomadism as a privileged as well as an "indigenous" condition. On the romantic configurations of the Wandering Jew, see Anderson, *The Wandering Jew*.

21. Hyam Maccoby, "The Wandering Jew as Sacred Executioner," in Hassan-Rokem and Dundes, *The Wandering Jew*, p. 252. Maccoby explores the nineteenth-century construction of Jews as inherently "nomads who had invaded Palestine from the desert and remained at heart creatures of the desert, . . . [as] 'rootless cosmopolitan[s]'"—a view that would, he argues, later be "taken up with enthusiasm by the Nazis."

22. Michael Butor, "Travel and Writing," *Mosaic* 8, nos. 1–2 (1974–75): 4. See also Hutchinson, who quarrels in *Cervantine Journeys* with structuralist and poststructuralist readings that privilege the spatial over the temporal, structure over process; he instead explores the ramifications in Cervantes' writing of readings of journeys *in* and *as* discourse.

23. Thomas Mann, "Voyage with Don Quixote" (1934), in *Essays by Thomas Mann*, tr. H. T. Lowe-Porter (New York: Vintage Books, 1957), pp. 326, 330, 332.

24. M. M. Bakhtin, *The Dialogic Imagination: Four Essays*, ed. Michael Holquist, tr. Caryl Emerson and Michael Holquist (Austin: University of Texas Press, 1981), pp. 165, 412; Michel Foucault, *The Order of Things: An Archaeology of the Human Sciences* (New York: Vintage Books, 1973), p. 49.

25. *Map Is Not Territory* is, as we have seen, the title of a study by Jonathan Z. Smith (*Map Is Not Territory: Studies in the History of Religions* [Leiden: E. J. Brill, 1978]).

26. James D. Fernandez, "The Bonds of Patrimony: Cervantes and the New World," *PMLA* 109, no. 5 (October 1994): 972.

27. See ibid., p. 978 n. 2. Anthony Grafton argues that the voyages of discovery and exploration so changed the epistemology of the West that "between 1550 and 1650 Western thinkers ceased to believe that they could find all important truths in ancient books; [in effect,] knowledge had burst the bounds of the library." *New Worlds, Ancient Texts: The Power of Tradition and the Shock of Discovery* (Cambridge, Mass.: Harvard University Press, 1992), pp. 1, 3. The analogous process in Jewish life at the end of the nineteenth century is brilliantly captured in *Benjamin the Third* and, as we will see, takes on even more far-reaching implications in the afterlife of the text.

28. See Perry, "Ha-analogia u-mekomah," pp. 65–100.

29. The Hebrew differs in nuances from the Yiddish version.

30. Georges Van Den Abbeele, *Travel as Metaphor: From Montaigne to Rousseau* (Minneapolis: University of Minnesota Press, 1992), pp. xiv, xxiii, xxx. Many of the travelers whom he considers went to Italy, which was the "the early modern and secular equivalent of the medieval pilgrimage to Jerusalem" (pp. 6, xxix).

31. Ibid., p. xxiii.

32. On the function of this literature, see also Percy Adams, *Travel Literature and the Evolution of the Novel*, pp. 273, 274.

33. S. Y. Abramovitsh, "Ma anu?" [What Are We?], translated and quoted by Miron and Norich, "The Politics of Benjamin III," pp. 28–29.

34. Abbeele, *Travel as Metaphor*, p. 8. "*Oikos* (the Greek for 'home' from which is derived 'economy') [is the term] in relation to which any wandering can be *comprehended* (enclosed as well as understood)" (p. xviii). Gershon Shaked suggests that *Benjamin the Third* is a narrative of arrested movement that amounts to a "frozen picaresque novel" (*Bein s'hok le-dema'*, p. 117). My argument here is that the movement "back" is neither frozen nor retrograde but critical.

35. Adams, *Travel Literature and the Evolution of the Novel*, p. 51.

36. Claude Lévi-Strauss, *Tristes Tropiques*, tr. John and Doreen Weightman (New York: Atheneum, 1973), p. 102; quoted in Adams, *Travel Literature and the Evolution of the Novel*, p. 38.

37. Abbeele, *Travel as Metaphor*, pp. 9, 67, referring to Montaigne's *Journal de voyage en Italie* (written in the 1580s but published only two centuries later) and Montesquieu's *Persian Letters* (1721).

38. "What we have here is not a marriage plot as such, but a hovering pseudo-marriage plot (*kemo-'alilat-nisuin merahefet*), which appears as a comic device devoid of any pretense to reality." For Perry, this pseudo-plot appears within the framework of the parallel structure he discerns between the departure-from-home (*'alilat ha-yitziah*) and the military plots (*'alilat ha-tzavah*); see "Ha-analogia u-mekomah," p. 92.

39. Shaked's remark refers not to *Benjamin the Third* but to the passage in

Abramovitsh's *Sefer ha-kabtzanim* [The Book of Beggars] (1909) in which the father, so distracted by economic woes, does not realize that he has betrothed his son to another man (*Bein s'hok le-dema'*, p. 121). See also "Biyemai ha-ra'ash" (1894; referred to below, note 57), in which a similar coupling or pseudo-marriage takes place in the context of a journey to the Land of Israel.

40. Miron and Norich, "The Politics of Benjamin III," pp. 63–70. Perhaps the more common form of "cross-dressing" is women dressed as men; within the context of the yeshiva world, the male-populated world of Jewish learning and prayer, it forms a particularly interesting dimension of the homoerotic as represented in narratives stretching from Abramovitsh to I. B. Singer. For a contemporary example, see Bashevis Singer's "Yentl" and its Hollywood interpretation.

41. Jeffrey Fleck, "Mendele in Pieces," *Prooftexts* 3, no. 2 (May 1983): pp. 169–88.

42. Daniel Boyarin, "Epater L'embourgeoisement: Freud, Gender, and the (De)colonized Psyche," *Diacritics* 24, no. 1 (spring 1994): 33. He considers these issues more broadly in *Unheroic Conduct: The Rise of Heterosexuality and the Invention of the Jewish Man* (Berkeley: University of California Press, 1997), esp. pp. 221–70.

43. Naomi Seidman, *A Marriage Made in Heaven: The Sexual Politics of Hebrew and Yiddish* (Berkeley: University of California Press, 1997).

In his study of Abramovitsh, Miron analyzes the writer's representation of Yiddish as a "'strange woman' and Yiddish compositions as her illegitimate issue." The respectable writers who sometimes "'visited that cursed woman,'" including Abramovitsh himself, are engaging in illicit acts tinged with both the stigma and the allure of sexual transgression (*A Traveler Disguised*, p. 14).

David Aberbach catalogues the evidence of what he calls "latent homosexuality" in the fictions of Abramovitsh and Agnon, observing that Benjamin was "intent on belatedly proving himself a man by making the hard trek to the Land of Israel." Aberbach, "Homosexual Fantasies in Mendele and Agnon," in *Tradition and Trauma: Studies in the Fiction of S. Y. Agnon*, ed. David Patterson and Glenda Abramson (Boulder, Colo.: Westview Press, 1994), p. 175. See also his *Realism, Caricature, and Bias: The Fiction of Mendele Mocher Sefarim* (London: Littman Library of Jewish Civilization, 1993). He barely explores the implications of the trope as a significant border crossing in Yiddish and Hebrew fiction or as part of the larger cultural enterprise (inherent in Freudian and Zionist rhetoric) of masculinizing the Jewish self, as Seidman, Boyarin, David Biale, and others have done.

44. See S. Niger's 1912 essay on the female readers of Yiddish, "Di Yidishe literatur un di lezerin," reprinted in *Bleter geshikhte fun der yidisher literature* [The History of Yiddish Literature] (New York: World Yiddish Cultural Congress, 1959), pp. 35–108; tr. and abridged by Sheva Zucker as "Yiddish Literature and the Female Reader," in *Women of the Word: Jewish Women and Jewish Writing*, ed. Judith R. Baskin (Detroit: Wayne State University Press, 1994), pp. 70–90.

On Yiddish and Hebrew as "gendered," not because of some quality "intrinsic" to the respective language but because of the literary audience and sociolinguistic standards they address and constitute, see Seidman: "Abramovitsh's tracing of his course from Hebrew to Yiddish combines with his apparent fondness for sexual/linguistic metaphor to produce an astonishingly intricate inquiry into the psychosexual dynamics of language choice. . . . Whereas the Hebrew writers reject Yiddish as both sexually and ethnically alien, for Abramovitsh, Yiddish is the primary emblem of *Jewish* otherness; standing in for a people whose degradation is figured . . . as a kind of feminization" (*A Marriage Made in Heaven*, pp. 45–46).

On Yiddish as "mother tongue," and on postwar Yiddish as "domesticated in a different way as the sign of both mourning and memory," see Anita Norich, introduction to *Gender and Text in Modern Hebrew and Yiddish Literature*, ed. Naomi B. Sokoloff, Anne Lapidus Lerner, and Anita Norich (New York: Jewish Theological Seminary of America, 1992), p. 4.

45. For discussions of how Abramovitsh's interest in nature developed from viewing it as direct target of scientific inquiry to employing it as analogue of the human condition, see Shaked, *Bein s'hok le-dema'*, pp. 80–83, and Miron and Norich, "The Politics of Benjamin III," pp. 4–6.

46. Miron, *A Traveler Disguised*, p. 267. Miron goes further than Shaked, who invokes the "Eiron" as a Mendelean character whose primary function is to "reveal the nakedness . . . of prevailing social forces"—including the Haskalah, Zionism, and other ideological and cultural enterprises that have strong supporters in the public square and can therefore suffer his slings and arrows without being destroyed by them (*Bein s'hok le-dema'*, p. 150).

47. See especially the preface to Abramovitsh's fictional autobiography, *Shloyme Reb Chayim's*, partially translated as "Of Bygone Days" in *A Shtetl and Other Yiddish Novellas*, ed. Ruth Wisse (New York: Behrman House, 1973), pp. 249–358.

Shmuel Werses analyzes the evolution of folkoristic materials in Abramovitsh's prose and his oscillation between the maskilic agendas of uprooting the superstitious and irrational forces in Jewish culture and the ethnographic urge to preserve a record of communal behaviors and practices; complicating matters at the end of his life is his sentimental evocation of his childhood, especially his mother's populist practices. Abramovitsh, like so many others of his and succeeding generations, remains on a pendulum that swings incessantly between "apologetics and satire vis-à-vis Jewish reality." Werses, "Olam ha-folklor bi-yetzirat Mendele" [Folklore in the Works of Mendele], *Dapim le-mehkar be-sifrut* [Pages in Literary Research] 9 (1994): 23.

48. For a discussion of Ahad Ha-am and "cultural Zionism," as well as Herzl and "political Zionism," see Bernard Avishai, *The Tragedy of Zionism: Revolution and Democracy in the Land of Israel* (New York: Farrar, Straus, and Giroux, 1985), pp. 22–66; for a biography of Ahad Ha-am, see Steven Zipperstein, *Elusive Prophet: Ahad Ha-am and the Origins of Zionism* (Berkeley: University of California Press, 1993).

49. For the classical sources of *komemiut*, see Lev. 26:13 and "ahava raba" in the *shaharit* prayer; echoed in the rhetoric of Haim Nahman Bialik and Y. H. Brenner, the word is connected with the "uprising" that signals national self-determination and that will bring Zionists to refer to the War of Independence in 1948 as *milhemet ha-komemiut*.

50. See, for example, Perry, "Ha-analogia u-mekomah," p. 86. Miron and Norich call attention to the connection between Benjamin and both Herzl (in his Hebrew incarnation) and Benjamin *Disraeli*. In discussing the political satire embedded in the early chapters of the narrative, they argue that "if Tuneyadevke is a mock Brittania, Benjamin then is a mock Disraeli" ("The Politics of Benjamin III," p. 54).

51. One of the more interesting questions is whether the "practice of utopia" enlarges or constrains how utopias are imagined in this period. The first Jew accredited with writing a Zionist utopia was Edmund Eisler, whose book *Ein Zukunftsbild* was published anonymously in 1885; the second was Elchanan-Leeb Levinsky, who in 1892 published *A Voyage to the Land of Israel in 2040* (in Hebrew). Theodore Herzl published his *Altneuland* in 1902. Sholem Aleichem also began a utopian novel whose first installments were published in the Yiddish Zionist newspaper *Die Welt* in 1901. (On Sholem Aleichem, see chapter 4.) On the general subject of Zionist utopias, see Rahel Elboim-Dror, *Ha-mahar shel ha-etmol* [Yesterday's Tomorrow], vol. 1, *Ha-utopia ha-tzionit* [The Zionist Utopia] (Jerusalem: Ben-Zvi and Mossad Bialik, 1993), and, for a short version in English, "Gender in Utopianism: The Zionist Case," *History Workshop Journal*, no. 37 (1994): 99–116.

52. Perry, "Ha-analogia u-mekomah," p. 98.

53. Miron and Norich, "The Politics of Benjamin III," pp. 102–3. They present Abramovitsh's polemic with political Zionism in much sharper terms than does Wisse, who argues that "whatever anti-Zionist sentiment the book contains is directed at the early sentimentalists [hovevei tzion], not the political activists of the end of the century" (*The Schlemiel as Modern Hero*, p. 33). Shaked reads the end of the text as a "pathetic" demonstration of the vulnerable position of the weak and innocent in the face of the powerful, consistent with the rest of the narrative (*Bein s'hok le-dema'*, p. 120). Y. Carmel, in a much earlier evaluation of the novel, claimed that Benjamin and Sender were the two figures in Abramovitsh's workshop who most successfully exceeded the bounds of the local or provincial, achieving a level of both dignity and mobility. See "Shirat ha-historia shelanu" [The Poetry of Our History], *Gilyonot* 1 (1934): 42.

54. Miguel de Cervantes Saavedra, *Adventures of Don Quixote*, trans. J. M. Cohen (Harmondsworth: Penguin, 1950), part 2, chap. 74, p. 936.

55. While in Yiddish the self-mockery related to acknowledged weakness, in Hebrew it took on, originally, the Zionist connotions of satire on the Jews of exile. A very interesting and curiously timed survey was carried out in the Beit ha-kerem high school in Jerusalem in 1945: seventy-eight young teenagers who had been required to read *Kitzur Mas'ot Binyamin ha-shlishi* were polled as to their responses and attitudes toward the shtetl as it is portrayed there; the evaluation was presented in Yiddish in 1948 and appeared in English translation as Haim Ormian, "Israeli Students and Mendele," *YIVO Annual of Jewish Social Science* 5 (1950): 292–312.

56. David Quint, *Epic and Empire: Politics and Generic Form from Virgil to Milton.* (Princeton: Princeton University Press, 1993), pp. 9, 147, 168. Quint's

discussions of the "deformation of narrative" focus on the poems of the Roman poet Lucan and his imitators; he argues that in "dismantl[ing] teleological narrative structures in the name of a losing political opposition for whom nothing is settled and history remains an open book," the [sixteenth-century] *Araucana* of Ercilla, like the [first-century] *Pharsalia* of Lucan, "remain epics of empire . . . even as they contest Virgilian norms by telling the losers' other side of the story" (p. 137).

57. S. Y. Abramovitsh, "Biyemai ha-ra'ash" [In a Tumultuous Time], in *Kol kitvei Mendele mokher sfarim* [The Complete Works of Mendele Mokher Sfarim] (Tel Aviv: Dvir, 1956), pp. 406–19.

58. S. Y. Abramovitsh, "Ha-nisrafim" [Burned Out], in *Kol kitvei Mendele*, pp. 444–47.

59. S. Y. Abramovitsh, "Aggadot ha-admonim" [Legends of the Reds], in *Kol kitvei Mendele*, pp. 469–74.

60. Miron, *A Traveler Disguised*, pp. 171–202. Miron describes Mendele not only as performer in but as judge of the drama he is mediating, akin to a Greek chorus. And it is not only Tevye but also Menakhem-Mendel and others whose stories are delivered to us through the mediation of Sholem Aleichem. Motl, as we will see later, appeals directly to his (world-embracing) audience, but the response he solicits is one of universal affirmation or assent.

61. "Don Kishot hot far keynem keyn moyre nisht; . . . [er] shteyt kegn der velt azoy vi di tmimes kegen der falshkayt, azoy vi der ekstaz kegn der nichterkayt. . . . Benyomin shrekt zikh far a hunt; . . . [er] shteyt . . . antkegen der velt . . . vi a nar kegn kluge." Shmuel Niger, *Vegn Yidishe shrayber* [On Yiddish Writers] (Vilna: S. Shrabark, 1912), vol. 1, pp. 56–7.

62. See Wisse, *The Schlemiel as Modern Hero*. The radical change in Wisse's own evaluation of the shlemiel whom she so definitively established as cultural hero will be discussed in chapter 8; see esp. note 37.

More or less the same qualities inhere in what Shaked defines as the "pathos" of the Mendelean sensibility, the "tragi-comic" view of a "revolutionary satirist" who is paralyzed by his sense of impending catastrophe and who succumbs increasingly to excesses of the absurd and the grotesque on the one hand and the sentimental on the other. Twenty years after the end of the Holocaust and eighteen years after the War of Independence and the establishment of the State of Israel, Shaked pronounces compassionate judgment on a writer whose characters, "heroes of the *kapote* and *streimel*, are not about to don helmets or fortified breastplates and go off armed against the sea of troubles." Having learned, nonetheless, to swim in that sea, they emerge from it only to find themselves "cast into the lion's den to suffer their dolorous fate in a world without miracles" (*Bein s'hok le-dema'*, pp. 135, 191, and passim). Shaked's reading, expressive of contemporary Israeli attitudes, sees the world evoked by Abramovitsh as shaped by circumstances that were oppressive until they proved lethal. It provides a sensitive but limited analysis of the complexities of Mendelean humor and literary strategies from an existential distance safeguarded by helmets and breastplates.

63. Miron and Norich, "The Politics of Benjamin III," p. 104.

3. IN THE HEART OF THE SEAS:
    S. Y. AGNON AND THE EPIC OF RETURN

1. One of the earliest studies of Agnon in English, Arnold Band's *Nostalgia and Nightmare: A Study in the Fiction of S. Y. Agnon* (Berkeley: University of California Press, 1968), captured the spectrum of Agnon's imagination during the author's lifetime as a constant swing between the extremes of the innocent, nostalgic, or mythic and the absurd, grotesque, Kafkaesque—even before some of his darker, posthumous writings had come to light. Contemporary readings sensitive to the ironic possibilities latent even in "mythic" or innocent stories such as the one before us somewhat refine this sharp dichotomy.

2. S. Y. Agnon, *In the Heart of the Seas: A Story of a Journey to the Land of Israel*, tr. I. M. Lask (New York: Schocken Books, 1947), p. 7. All subsequent references in the text to page numbers, cited parenthetically as E, are from this English edition. *Bilvav yamim: sippur aggadah shel S. Y. Agnon*, from the cycle "Sippurim shel Eretz Yisrael" [Stories from the Land of Israel] is collected in the volume *Elu ve-elu* (Jerusalem: Schocken, 1971); all references to the Hebrew text, cited parenthetically as H, are to this edition unless otherwise specified. *Bilvav yamim* was first published in Hebrew in *Sefer Bialik* (Tel Aviv: Va'ad ha-Yovel, 1934) and separately by Schocken (Berlin, 1935).

3. Hananiah's kerchief, in which "all his worldly goods were tied up" (along with some of his other-worldly properties), is believed to have imparted its magical powers to the Emperor Napoleon, who "saw it and made a flag out of it and was victorious in his wars." But, the narrator hastens to add, "that is not the truth either, since, when Hananiah had passed away, they covered his eyes with his kerchief" (E 125; H 550). Whatever the "truth" may be, this allusion reinforces the dating of the represented events to the beginning of the eighteenth century, as Napoleon enters the story when Hananiah is already a centenarian.

4. The group leaves from Buczacz, Agnon's hometown. There is, however, little evidence of any pilgrimage of Hassidim from Buczacz at that time. A veiled allusion to R. Nahman of Bratzlav, who had come on pilgrimage and managed to flee Palestine on the eve of Napoleon's siege of Jaffa (1798–99), is reinforced by Hillel Zeitlin's claim that one of the subtexts of *Bilvav yamim* is the travelogue written by R. Nahman's faithful student and scribe, R. Natan from Nemirov. Cited in Shmuel Werses, *Sipur ve-shorsho: 'iyunim be-hitpathut ha-prosa ha-'ivrit* [Story and Source: Studies in the Development of Hebrew Prose] (Ramat Gan: Massada, 1971), p. 203. Werses, on the basis of other internal evidence, argues that the narrative spans the years from 1825 to 1835, but he calls attention to the anachronisms that interrupt the natural chronological flow of events (pp. 209–10). An English translation of Martin Buber's retelling of the story, "Rabbi Nachman's Journey to Palestine," concludes Buber's *Tales of Rabbi Nachman*, tr. Maurice Friedman and Stanley Goodman (Atlantic Highlands, N.J.: Humanities Press International, 1988), pp. 179–214.

On the subject of autobiographical elements in Agnon's writing, see my essay "Agnon Before and After," *Prooftexts* 2, no. 1 (January 1982): 78–94, and Anne Golomb Hoffman, *Between Exile and Return: S. Y. Agnon and the Drama of Writing* (Albany: State University of New York Press, 1991), chap. 4.

5. Gérard Genette finds heterodiegetic autobiography in Borges's writings, notably his "Epilogo." Genette, "Fictional Narrative, Factual Narrative," *Poetics Today* 11, no. 4 (winter 1990): 765–66.

6. What I identify as the homodiegetic mode appears in Agnon's writings from "Tehila" (1925) through *Ore'ah nata la-lun* [A Guest for the Night] (Jerusalem: Schocken, 1939) to posthumously published narratives like "Kisui ha-dam" [Covering the Blood] (1975), in *Lifnim min ha-homa* (Jerusalem: Schocken, 1975), pp. 51–104. See also "Tale of a Scribe" [Aggadat ha-sofer], in *Twenty-One Stories*, ed. Nahum Glatzer (New York: Schocken Books, 1970), pp. 7–25, and "'Im kenisat ha-yom" [At the Outset of the Day], in *'Ad hena* [This Far] (Jerusalem: Schocken, 1974), pp. 171–77.

7. Robert Alter, *Hebrew and Modernity* (Bloomington: Indiana University Press, 1994), p. 73. See also the work of Mikhail Bakhtin on novelistic thinking, especially *The Dialogic Imagination*.

8. Nancy Huston, "Novels and Navels," *Critical Inquiry* 21, no. 4 (summer 1995): 716. For a discussion of wife as the de-eroticized emblem of home and of "other women" as the detours, the seductresses that distract the man on his travels, see Georges Van Den Abbeele, *Travel as Metaphor: From Montaigne to Rousseau* (Minneapolis: University of Minnesota Press, 1992), pp. xxv–xxvi, 96–98.

9. The satiric subtext for Hananiah's act is the Yiddish spoof on Hassidic miracles; "Kum aher du Philosof" [Come Here, Mr. Philosopher] is a popular song describing a rebbe who spreads his kerchief and travels over the ocean. I am grateful to Chana Kronfeld for bringing this to my attention. Reading Agnon through his own bilingual context, which embraces the secular iconoclastic strand in both Yiddish folk literature and Yiddish modernism, reveals an implied ironic subculture against which the norms of this text are struggling.

10. For a Yiddish representation of the "Eternal Jew" early in this century, see David Pinsky, "Der Eybiker Yid: Tragedya in eyn akt" [The Eternal Jew: Tragedy in One Act], in *Meshihim* (Warsaw: Farlag Ch. Brzoza, 1906), pp. 4–36.

11. Hillel Barzel, introduction to *Shmuel Yosef Agnon: Mivhar ma'amarim 'al yetzirato*, ed. Hillel Barzel (Tel Aviv: Am Oved, 1982), p. 78. See also Gustav Krojanker, *Yetzirato shel Shai Agnon* [The Work of S. Y. Agnon], tr. Jacob Gotschalk (Jerusalem: Mosad Bialik, 1991), pp. 125–31.

12. Agnon's more conventional, or folkloric, representation of this theme can be found in the short story "Ma'agelei tzeddek," which narrates the last years of a poor vinegar maker who pursues his miserable trade in "one of the towns of Poland." He is transported in his moribund state by a Christ figure/band of angels directly to the Wailing Wall: "That night a knocking was heard upon the door of the Kotel in Jerusalem. Those who went outdoors saw a flight of angels which had come from the exile bearing a mortal form, which that very night they took and buried, in keeping with the custom in Jerusalem not to hold over the dead." Published in *Elu ve-elu*, pp. 283–87, it is translated by Amiel Gurt as "Paths of Righteousness, or the Vinegar Maker," in *A Book That Was Lost and Other Stories*, ed. Alan Mintz and Anne Golomb Hoffman (New York: Schocken Books, 1995), p. 197.

See again Buber's "Rabbi Nachman's Journey to Palestine," one of the possible subtexts of Agnon's narrative, especially the reference to the tomb that "achieves its perfect form" in the land of Israel; as the site of the "resurrection of the dead," it alone is "the place of perfect burial" (p. 208).

13. Sanhedrin, 98a. Critics including Dov Sadan, Hillel Barzel, and Arnold Band have noted the coincidence of the composition of *Bilvav yamim* and the short story "Ha-mitpahat" [The Kerchief] in the early 1930s, as well as other Agnon narratives in which the kerchief appears as a central metonymy. Dov Sadan, "Ma'aseh mitpahat" [On Kerchiefs], in *'Al Shai Agnon* (Tel Aviv: Ha kibbutz ha-me'uhad, 1959), pp. 65–73; Barzel, introduction to *Shmuel Yosef Agnon*, pp. 77–78; Arnold J. Band, *Nostalgia and Nightmare: A Study in the Fiction of S. Y. Agnon* (Berkeley: University of California Press, 1968), pp. 224, 227.

To reinforce our own intertextual journey, I could cite a report in the *Itinerary* of Benjamin of Tudela of a contender for the messianic title, David Alro'i, who lived in Kurdistan and actually endangered the entire Jewish community there with his defiance of the reigning authorities some dozen years before Benjamin's visit; he is said to have miraculously escaped several tight spots, once removing his mantle and spreading it "on the face of the water to cross thereon" (Benjamin of Tudela, *The Itinerary of Rabbi Benjamin of Tudela*, ed. and tr. A. Asher [New York: Hakeshet Publishing, 1841], vol. 1, pp. 79 [Hebrew] and 55 [English]).

14. From the rabbi in "'Agunot" through Menashe Haim in "Ve-haya he'akov le-mishor" [And the Crooked Shall Be Made Straight] and Yudel Hasid in *Hakhnasat kallah* [The Bridal Canopy], the *na' va-nad*, or wanderer who is not a pilgrim, describes a kind of penitential arc in space. This movement can be also traced in the Yiddish fiction of both Isaac Bashevis Singer and his elder brother, Israel Joshua Singer. See I. J. Singer's *Yoshe Kalb* (1932) and Anita Norich's commentary on it in *The Homeless Imagination in the Fiction of Israel Joshua Singer* (Bloomington: Indiana University Press, 1991), pp. 19–39. For a discussion of I. B. Singer, see chapter 8.

15. The opening passage of *Bilvav yamim*, for instance, can be seen as a revisionary performance of the opening of *Benjamin the Third*.

16. Abbeele, *Travel as Metaphor*, p. xx.

17. For a full discussion of Agnon's sources, see Werses, *Sipur ve-shorsho*, pp. 221–33. The geography of the voyage from Galicia to Jaffa through Moldavia and Turkey is as accurate as the geography in *The Travels of Benjamin the Third* is imaginary.

18. In a hostel in Istanbul, for example, the pilgrims meet a Sephardic emissary who unrolls before them the mystical geography of Jerusalem, Safed, Tiberias, and Meron (E 84–88; H 527–28).

19. For a discussion of the Hebrew "republic of letters," see Dan Miron, *Bodedim be-mo'adam: le-diyukana shel ha-republika ha-sifrutit ha-'ivrit be-tehilat ha-mea ha-'esrim* [When Loners Come Together: A Portrait of Hebrew Literature at the Turn of the Twentieth Century] (Tel Aviv: Am Oved, 1987), pp. 13–19.

20. Benjamin Harshav, *Language in Time of Revolution* (Berkeley: University of California Press, 1993), pp. 20–21.

21. Paraphrasing Dov Sadan here, Alter goes on to argue that to the extent that such an extreme statement holds, it is true primarily through hindsight, as it was mostly "on Central and Eastern European soil" that writers of the Hebrew Enlightenment such as Abramovitsh, Gnessin, and Berdichevski thought they were creating an "authentically *European* Hebrew fiction" (*Invention of Hebrew Prose*, p. 71; emphasis mine).

22. The term *kinus* is applied to the ingathering of people and of books. Bialik refers to the "heziyon ha-kinus ha-sifruti," and the centripetal dynamic is envisioned as literary as well as human. If, Bialik declared in a speech delivered before the Second World Congress for Hebrew Language and Culture (Vienna, 1913), we desire to revive the energy, vitality, and influence of literature, then we must generate a new national "*kinus*—not religious, of course—of the best Hebrew writing of all the ages." *Ha-sefer ha-'ivri* [On the Hebrew Book] (Jerusalem: Goldberg, 1913), n.p.

23. Ruth Wisse argues in *I. L. Peretz and the Making of Modern Jewish Culture* (Seattle: University of Washington Press, 1991) that Peretz in the 1890s is the counterpart to Herzl in advocating the renewal of a modern, secular Jewish culture that would acquire an autonomous minority status in Poland. On acts of literary rescue as forms of "creative betrayal" that account for the proliferation of Yiddish storytellers at the turn of the century, see David Roskies, *A Bridge of Longing: The Lost Art of Yiddish Storytelling* (Cambridge, Mass.: Harvard University Press, 1995).

24. Sh. Ansky is the pen-name of Solomon Zanwil Rapaport. His particular act of *kinus* in the early years of the Soviet Union has an even more interesting afterlife as a traveling exhibit, which provides a more contemporary dimension to the entire story of exile and homecoming. Ansky's "dybbuk," the restless spirit of the unburied dead, is reconfigured in the post-USSR world as an emblem of the indigenous homelessness of Ansky himself and of the Jews at large. One Israeli reviewer of the 1994 exhibit of Ansky's collection at the Israeli Museum, *Be-hazara la-'ayara* [Back to the Shtetl], writes that "the *golah* is here and the shtetl is here. . . . [T]he exhibit presents the shtetl to present-day Israel in a concave mirror—without either of the participants in the specular dialogue being capable of knowing who is the representative of the banished dybbuk (*ha-dybbuk ha-meshulah*) and who is the true expression of the root culture." Eli Shai, "Kemihah mistit le-negi'a ba-kame'a" [Mystical Yearnings to Touch the Sublime], *Ha-aretz*, Book Section, July 13, 1994, p. 8. This statement and the exhibit itself, like a previous installation at the Israel Museum titled *Wandering*, are symptoms of the restlessness, the nostalgia, and the postmodern or "post-Zionist" yearnings for a free and creative reconnection with the past complicated by a fear of the resurgence of constrictive religious forms in late-twentieth-century Israeli culture.

25. For a critical discussion of the parallel invention of national and modernist cultures in Greece and Ireland, and of the roles that literature plays in forming the modern nation-state and that the language wars play in "consolidating" national identity, see Gregory Jusdanis, *Belated Modernity and Aesthetic Culture: Inventing National Literature* (Minneapolis: University of Minnesota Press, 1991), and David Lloyd, *Nationalism and Minor Literature: James Clarence*

Mangan and the Emergence of Irish Cultural Nationalism (Berkeley: University of California Press, 1987).

26. On Bialik's work on *Sefer ha-'ivri* and *Sefer ha-aggadah*, see Dan Miron, *Bo'ah, laylah: ha-sifrut ha-'ivrit bein higayon le-i-higayon be-mifna ha-mea ha-'esrim* [Come, Night: Hebrew Literature between the Rational and the Irrational at the Turn of the Twentieth Century] (Tel Aviv: Dvir, 1987), pp. 183–89. Whereas the evaluations of Bialik and Ravnitzki's enterprise have been many and varied, Michael Fishbane finds such anthologies as *Sefer ha-aggadah* inherently valuable as acts of canon formation. He argues that even when considered in terms of the national cultural movement that it was meant to serve, and even with its flawed or controversial presentation of the aggadic texts, *Sefer ha-aggadah* can be "compared to the periodic collections of Hebrew literature that have occurred earlier in Jewish history such as the redactions of the Bible, the Mishnah, and the Talmuds over the course of a millennium. . . . Each act of ingathering produced an anthology (the quintessential Jewish genre) of certain favored traditions and it marginalized others." Fishbane, "The Aggadah: Fragments of Delight," *Prooftexts* 13, no. 2 (May 1993): 187.

27. In a more formal recuperation, Agnon collected source material on the High Holy Days, *Yamim nora'im*, and he viewed the project as equivalent or complementary to Bialik's *Sefer ha-aggadah*. On Agnon's responses to the challenge of *kinus*, on his rather complicated relationship to Bialik and *Sefer ha-aggadah*, and on the ill-fated enterprise that he began with Buber and that Buber was left to complete on his own, see Haim Be'er, *Gam ahavatam, gam sinatam: Bialik, Brenner, Agnon, ma'arekhet yahasim* [Their Love and Their Hate: H. N. Bialik, Y. H. Brenner, S. Y. Agnon] (Tel Aviv: Am Oved, 1992), pp. 207–9, 220–25, 286–87. Buber, Bialik, and even the paralyzed Franz Rosenzweig strongly petitioned Agnon not to abandon the Hassidic book after the catastrophic fire, but to no avail.

28. "The ship went on, the waters moved as usual, and a still small voice rose from the ship. It was the sound of song and praise rising from one firmament to another": the voices of boys and girls exiled by Titus after destroying the Temple, who jumped into the sea and were taken by God ("in his right hand," as it were) and brought to an island where they spend the ages speaking of the "glory of Jerusalem" (E 61–64; H 515–17). These children are Israel's memory, as encapsulated in its myths and its mythic geography. Here they facilitate the journey that finally reaches its destination.

29. See Ezrahi, "Agnon Before and After," pp. 90–93.

30. Thomas G. Pavel, *Fictional Worlds* (Cambridge: Harvard University Press, 1986), p. 16.

31. S. Y. Agnon, "Ha-nidah" [The Outcast], in *Elu ve-elu*, p. 56.

32. Once the signifier of the mobility of generations of Jews, the key is a metonymy of the Temple itself and the key that was relinquished when Israel went into exile. See Ezrahi, "Agnon Before and After," pp. 78–94.

33. S. Y. Agnon, *Tmol shilshom* [Just Yesterday] (Jerusalem: Schocken, 1971), p. 7. Hereafter references will be made parenthetically to this edition.

34. Yitzhak obviously is also the namesake of Isaac, the prototypical sur-

vivor; and he is great-grandson of Yudel Hasid, the picaresque hero of Agnon's earliest novel, *Hakhnasat kallah* (Jerusalem: Schocken, 1974) (*Bridal Canopy*, tr. I. M. Lask [N.Y.: Literary Guild of America, 1937]), whose progress is facilitated by a miraculous monetary endowment and semimiraculous climatic events. On that novel and its relevance to Agnon's portraits of wandering Jews, see Dan Miron, *Histaklut be-ravnekher: 'al Hakhnasat Kalah me-et Shai Agnon ve-sviva* [The Motley Canopy: A Study of S. Y. Agnon's Narrative Art in *The Bridal Canopy*] (Tel Aviv: Ha-kibbutz ha-me'uhad, 1996).

35. On *Tmol shilshom*, see Amos Oz, *Shtikat ha-shamayim: Agnon mish-tomem 'al elohim* [The Silence of Heaven: Agnon's Fear of God] (Jerusalem: Keter, 1993); Hoffman, *Between Exile and Return*, chap. 7; and Nitza Ben Dov, *Agnon's Art of Indirection: Uncovering Latent Content in the Fiction of S. Y. Agnon* (Leiden: E. J. Brill, 1993).

36. One of the earliest of the modern pilgrims to the Holy Land, Herman Melville's Clarel (*Clarel*, 1876), also traces a labyrinthine pattern through the city of Jerusalem—and through eighteen thousand lines of iambic tetrameter.

37. Like many of Agnon's narratives, parts of this long novel were published separately; the chapter on "Rav Geronam yakum purkan" appeared in *Moznayim* (May 14, 1931, pp. 5–7) some fifteen years before the novel was published, at the time Agnon was working on *Bilvav yamim*.

38. What Gustav Krojanker describes as an "old world epic," in which there is still an unmediated relation to the Divine, a confluence between outside and inside, is not the province of the modern novel. Krojanker identifies the fusion of the "real" and the legendary planes, the "historical-fictional journey," as a peculiar form of "aggadic epic" (*Yetzirato shel Shai Agnon*, pp. 78–79, 126–27).

Along complementary lines, Dan Miron argues that the modern novel was an alien form that Agnon explored nearly to its fullest degree, stopping just short of drawing the conclusions to which the novelistic inquiry inevitably leads, conclusions that are the equivalent of a form of exile from the "spiritual, personal source" located in Scriptures. In the later novels, especially in *Shira*, which he never finished, the demands of the hour and the demands of the genre as it was practiced by his contemporaries made closure, with its resolution of the tensions between the world of faith and the historical reality of the twentieth-century Jew, harder to achieve. See "Agnon's Transactions with the Novel," *Prooftexts* 7, no. 1 (January 1987): 26. See also Hoffman, *Between Exile and Return*.

39. Originally published in a limited edition of 300 copies, *Die Gabe* was reprinted by the Leo Baeck Institute with comments and short translations by Martin Goldner: *Die Gabe: For Franz Rosenzweig on His 40th Birthday, 12/25/26* (New York: Leo Baeck Institute, 1987).

40. Hoffman, *Between Exile and Return*, p. 177.

41. Ibid.

42. Ibid., p. 178 (quoting *Die Gabe*, p. 9).

43. Ibid., pp. 178, 57. "I use the term 'textuality' to suggest that issues of boundary and transgression, exile, and return are acted out within the domain of the writing itself," says Hoffman; "in a geography of language and text, [Agnon's] writing moves between exile and return" (pp. 2, 5).

44. Cited from the Agnon-Schocken letters in Be'er's *Gam ahavatam, gam sinatam*, p. 287. Whereas it now appears that Bialik did not fully endorse Agnon's own high opinion of his story, and may in fact have withheld the first "Bialik Prize" from Agnon in 1934 because of his ambivalence about *Bilvav yamim*, Agnon did receive the prize for the story the following year, a judgment taken after Bialik's death. This incident is discussed in the addendum to the 1993 third edition of Be'er's book, pp. 414–21.

45. Krojanker, *Yetzirato shel Shai Agnon*, p. 128; Hoffman, *Between Exile and Return*, p. 180. One could perhaps argue further that what gnaws at the heart of Agnon's fiction and comes out most powerfully in manuscripts such as "Kisui hadam" [Covering the Blood], which was published posthumously, is not only the threat to authority of the self-authorized modern text but also the despair over a world from which these carefully preserved schemes of meaning have been withdrawn.

46. *Bayit* is the Hebrew word for both a house and a stanza in a poem; in medieval poetry, the opening line of a verse is referred to as a *delet* (door) and the closing line as a *soger* (shutter). For a more explicit allusion to the language "housed" in the poetry of Paul Celan, see chapter 5.

47. S. Y. Agnon, "Tehila," in *'Ad hena*, p. 183; tr. as "Tehila" by Walter Lever in *Firstfruits: A Harvest of 25 Years of Israeli Writing*, ed. James A. Michener (Greenwich, Conn: Fawcett, 1973), p. 62. I have slightly emended Lever's translation, although the result is still far from satisfactory.

48. Mircea Eliade, *The Sacred and the Profane: The Nature of Religion*, tr. Willard Trask (New York: Harcourt Brace and World, 1959), p. 63.

49. Earlier in this homodiegetic fictional narrative, the first-person scribe-narrator effects another kind of passage from text to territory; sitting at the feet of one of Jerusalem's many "men of learning," he finds relief from the tedium of the man's scholarship by allowing his eyes to escape through the window and his language to escape through a rhetorical trompe d'oeil:

> I asked my questions, and he replied; or spoke of problems, which he resolved; or mentioned obscure matters which he made clear. How good it is, how satisfying, to sit at the feet of one of the scholars of Jerusalem, and to learn the Law from his lips! His home is simple, his furnishings austere, yet his wisdom ranges far, *like* the great hill ranges of Jerusalem which are seen from the windows. Bare are the hills of Jerusalem; no temples or palaces crown them. Since the time of our exile, nation after nation has come and laid them waste. But the hills spread their glory like banners to the sky.
> "Tehila," p. 40 (emphasis mine)

The transport from language to landscape, from tedious discourse to holy space, is effected by means of a simile ("like the great hill ranges . . . ") that conveys both the instrumental power of poetry and its ultimate subordination to sacred soil.

The theme of the book that is "lost" by being incorporated into the material of Jerusalem appears with a different twist in Agnon's story "A Book That Was Lost," which appeared posthumously in *Ir u-melo'ah* [An Entire City] ([Tel Aviv: Schocken, 1973], pp. 207–11) and is the title story of the collection of his stories edited by Alan Mintz and Anne Golomb Hoffman, *A Book That Was Lost and Other Stories* (New York: Schocken Books, 1995), pp. 128–35.

4. BY TRAIN, BY SHIP, BY SUBWAY: SHOLEM ALEICHEM AND THE AMERICAN VOYAGE OF SELF-INVENTION

1. From Mary Antin's *From Plonsk to Boston* (New York: M. Wiener, 1986), originally published in 1899, to Eva Hoffman's *Lost in Translation: A Life in a New Language* (London: Heinemann, 1989), Jewish journeys to America have been well documented over the last century. Writers from the Other Europe is a Penguin series launched by Philip Roth that features writers from Eastern Europe who were relatively unknown in the West.

2. Dov Sadan, "Three Foundations: Sholem Aleichem and the Yiddish Literary Tradition" (1959), tr. David G. Roskies, *Prooftexts* 6, no. 1 (January 1986): 57 (translated from *Avnei miftan: masot 'al sofrei yidish* [Corner Stones: Essays on Yiddish Writers] [Tel Aviv: Y. L. Peretz, 1961], vol. 1, pp. 45–54). Critical interest in Sholem Aleichem has increased dramatically since Sadan wrote those words, as witnessed by the very issue of *Prooftexts* that reproduced this essay.

3. See above, chapters 2 and 3. In the original version of the epistolary narrative, the shtetl to which Sheyne Shendl was attached was Mazepfke, not Kasrilevke.

We might note Natan Alterman's 1945 Hebrew "elegy" to the Jews of Eastern Europe, written in Palestine as the "last" letter from Menakhem Mendl to his wife, Sheyne Shendl; Menakhem Mendl remains in the Hebrew imagination as the quintessential Wandering Jew, as his wife remains "in the shtetl" even after it has been destroyed. (This poem is discussed later in this chapter and in chapter 8.)

For an interesting Marxist critique of *Menakhem-Mendl*, written in the mid-1930s, see Max Erik, who maintains that while Menakhem Mendl, the irrepressible traveler and petty businessman, is intoxicated with the metropolis (Odessa, Yehupetz [Kiev]), Sheyne Shendl remains "frozen and immobile, contentedly stuck in the Kasrilevke mire." Erik equates the "faith" she exhibits in the status quo and in divine providence with the "precapitalist [but also premodernist] fantasies" that characterized Benjamin's position in *The Travels of Benjamin the Third*. Erik, "*Menakhem-Mendl*" (1935), tr. David G. Roskies, *Prooftexts* 6, no. 1 (January 1986): 36–38.

4. Hillel Halkin calls Tevye a "God-arguer." Introduction to Sholem Aleichem, *Tevye the Dairyman and the Railroad Stories,* ed. and tr. Hillel Halkin (New York: Schocken Books, 1987), p. xxiv.

5. The cycle was originally called simply "Ksovim fun a komi-voyazher." A few of the stories that Sholem Aleichem adapted and appended to the text when he reworked it from 1910 to 1911 had been written between 1902 and 1903.

6. Sholem Aleichem, "Tevye Leaves for the Land of Israel," in *Tevye the Dairyman,* pp. 108, 110, 111; from the Yiddish original, *Gants Tevye der milkhiker,* in *Ale verk fun Sholem Aleykhem* (New York: Sholem-Aleykhem Folksfond oysgabe, 1927), vols. 1–2, pp. 183, 185, 187. All subsequent page references to these stories, made parenthetically in the text, are to these Yiddish and English editions (designated Y and E). Halkin added "go to die," which is a gloss on the more allusive Yiddish that translates literally as "all old Jews go to Eretz Yisroel."

7. When he reported on his wife Golde's death, Tevye had told Sholem Aleichem that "I only hope she puts in a good word for her daughters where she is,
because the Lord knows she went through enough for them" (E 98; Y 168). Here,
in a departure from the convention of woman as/at home, it is Tevye who stays
put while his women move: Golda to Heaven ("Zion") and the daughters to (and
beyond) the geographical and existential borders of the Pale of Settlement.

8. Y. D. Berkovitz, "Tuvya ha-holev nose'a le-eretz Yisrael," in *Ha-rishonim
ki-vnei adam: sipurei zikhronot 'al Shalom 'Aleichem u-vnei doro* [The Founders
as Human Beings: Memories of Sholem Aleichem and His Generation], vol. 8 of
Kitvei Y. D. Berkovitz [The Writing of Y. D. Berkovitz] (Tel Aviv: Dvir, 1954),
pp. 192–94.

9. I have emended Halkin's translation somewhat here.

10. Dov Sadan, Dan Miron, Benjamin Harshav, and Ruth Wisse, among other
contemporary scholars, have debated the nature and function of Tevye's malapropisms, misquotes, and misprisions. Michael Stern takes the discussion one
step further by closely examining some of the biblical and liturgical intertexts in
his essay "Tevye's Art of Quotation," *Prooftexts* 6, no. 1 (January 1986): 79–96.
The significant shift in meaning that takes place in this and other passages between the biblical phrase "el ha-aretz asher areka" (to the land that I will show
thee) and Tevye's "wherever your eyes will take you" (which Halkin changes in
the English translation to "wherever your legs will carry you") could, he says,
be a gloss on the difference between Abraham's mission, "assured of God's watchful protection," and Tevye's, enacted in its absence (p. 94). But it can also mark
the shift from directed to aimless movement, as discussed later in this chapter.

11. As with "I'm a real *al tashlikheynu le'eys ziknoh*" in the passage above,
Halkin's liberal translations always maintain the spirit of the original; here, the
translation also tends to accentuate the tension between the explicit textual references to a physical return to the Holy Land and Tevye's interpretive strategies
that reinforce exile as the normative condition of the Jew.

12. "Tevye fort kein eretz-yisroel" was the final story in the cycle as it appeared in the 1911 edition; because that story ended with the death of Golda,
and because the romantic theme had been exhausted with the marriages of Tevye's
daughters, it would be fitting, argues Chone Shmeruk, to take leave of Tevye as
he departs for the Holy Land. He further maintains that the impetus behind the
story "Lekh-lekho" relates to the author's own unrest at having facilitated,
through Chava's marriage to a non-Jew, the ultimate boundary crossing. So he
"returns" Tevye to his village, stages a little pogrom, and brings Chava back into
the fold. Written around the time of the Beiliss trial, "Lekh-lekho" also reflects,
in its subtheme of persecution and banishment, Sholem Aleichem's concern with
actual events. On the composition of the *Tevye* stories and the conflicts that are
revealed through revisions appearing in the various editions, see Shmeruk, "Tevye
der milkhiker—toldoteha shel yetzira" [The History of "Tevye the Dairyman"],
Ha-sifrut 7, no. 26, (April 1978): 26–38. Shmeruk is clearly dissatisfied with
the 1918 edition, which was edited by Berkovitz and appeared after the author's
death as *Gantz Tevye der milkhiker* [The Complete Tevye the Dairyman];
Shmeruk reveals his own ideological (and aesthetic) position by insisting that

"Tevye's departure for Eretz Yisrael would have been more convincing not in the context of Beylke but especially after the banishment from the village and the return of Chava. But with the text of *Gantz tevye der milkhiker* before us, we cannot but contemplate the unrealized potential for a great work (*yetzirat mofet*)" (pp. 37–38).

13. "Oh, God likes to play games with us, He does. He's got a favorite game He plays with Tevye called *Oylim Veyordim*, which means in plain language Upsy-Daisy—now you're up, and now you're pushing daisies" (E 119; Y 202–3). Hillel Halkin, who finds a wonderful equivalent in daisies for the double entendre of the language of Fortuna (*yordim* as those who are down-at-the-mouth), nevertheless is therefore forced to omit the allusion in this passage to the pioneering language of *'aliyah* (ascent) to and *yerida* (descent) from the Land of Israel.

14. There is some disagreement among critics about the status of the final chapter, "Vekhalaklakoys." In his translation of the last few *Tevye* stories, Hillel Halkin spliced the final passages from "Vekhalaklakoys" onto the penultimate chapter, "Lekh-Lekho," with the result that the return to the Land of Israel, reinforced by the biblical resonances from Genesis 12 in the title and in Tevye's supposed destination, is effectively subverted by the final paragraph. Halkin justifies his editorial practice by citing the inferior quality of this last story, published a short time before Sholem Aleichem's death and written two years previously; he does not, however, dwell on the ideological import of adding to the natural conclusion of the Tevye cycle (the reconciliation of Tevye and his beloved daughter Chava) a chapter whose primary purpose seems to be to affirm the nature of Jewish wandering and preclude other "resolutions" to the homeless condition of the Jews. It is hardly surprising that in his Hebrew translation of the text, Sholem Aleichem's son-in-law Y. D. Berkovitz left out this chapter altogether.

For discussions of closure in this and other of Sholem Aleichem's fictions, see Shmeruk, "'Tevye der milkhiker,'" pp. 34–37; David Neal Miller, "Don't Force Me to Tell You the Ending: Closure in the Short Fiction of Sh. Rabinovitsch (Sholem-Aleykhem)," *Neophilologus* 66 (1982): 102–10; David G. Roskies, *A Bridge of Longing: The Lost Art of Yiddish Storytelling* (Cambridge, Mass.: Harvard University Press, 1995), pp. 176–88.

15. While still an adolescent, Agnon published "City of the Dead" as a feuilleton in Buczacz; see Arnold Band, *Nostalgia and Nightmare: A Study in the Fiction of S. Y. Agnon* (Berkeley: University of California Press, 1968), pp. 37–38.

16. See chapter 7 for a discussion of Michael André Bernstein's notion in *Foregone Conclusions: Against Apocalyptic History* (Berkeley: University of California Press, 1994) of "backshadowing" and "sideshadowing" as compositional and critical strategies. An example of the inevitable backshadowing that prevails in post-Holocaust readings of the texts before us can be found in David Roskies's argument that because many of the pogromists of the 1880s were either train workers or transported to the *shtetlakh* by train, "the train was already being transformed in Sholem Aleichem's fiction from a vehicle of dislocation to a vehicle of death." Roskies, "Sholem Aleichem and Others: Laughing Off the Trauma of History," *Prooftexts* 2, no. 1 (January 1982): 63. (It is worth noting

that these stories contain as many tales of miraculous rescue as of danger on the train.)

The train had become so identified as a context for Jewish stories that it survived as one of the artifacts of the fragmented postwar poetic imagination. For one of the most radical expressions of this, see the long poem "Footprints" by Dan Pagis ("'Akevot," in *Kol ha-shirim; 'Abba' (pirkei proza)* [Collected Poems and "Father" (prose passages)], ed. Hanan Hever and T. Carmi [Jerusalem: Hakibbutz ha-me'uhad and Bialik Institute, 1991], pp. 141–46), and my discussion of it in chapter 6.

17. See Leo Marx, *The Machine in the Garden: Technology and the Pastoral Ideal in America* (London: Oxford University Press, 1964). Marx's path-breaking study of the forms of American cultural response to technology in general and to the railroad in particular generated many subsequent studies, and he himself reconsidered the subject in the mid-1980s. See Marx, "Pastoralism in America," in *Ideology and Classic American Literature*, ed. Sacvan Bercovitch and Myra Jehlen (Cambridge: Cambridge University Press, 1986), pp. 36–69.

18. To be sure, Jewish literature is not unique in recording the train from the inside; from Agatha Christie's *Murder on the Orient Express* to Italo Calvino's "Adventure of a Soldier," many dramas have been enacted on trains in fiction and in film. Yet peculiar to the Yiddish and Hebrew literature is both the report on life viewed from within the third-class coaches and the absence of the view from the outside. The "commercial traveler" who narrates Sholem Aleichem's train stories concludes his tales by admonishing the reader to "avoid going first or second class. . . . What can be the point, I ask you, of a Jew traveling in total solitude without a living soul to speak to?" (E 279; Yiddish original is from *Ayznban-Geshikhtes* in *Ale verk fun Sholem-Aleykhem*, vols. 25–26, p. 296). Halkin claims that "though the notion of trains running through Russia with almost no one in their third-class cars but Jews who tell each other stories may seem like an artificial literary convention, this is actually not the case"; because of the social structure of the society, Jews as petty merchants were far more mobile than the peasants who rarely traveled and were more garrulous than the aristocracy who never traveled third-class (introduction to *Tevye the Dairyman*, p. xxxiii). The class consciousness presented in these stories is, nonetheless, more proletarian than petit-bourgeois.

19. Michel de Certeau, *The Practice of Everyday Life*, tr. Steven F. Rendall (Berkeley: University of California Press, 1984), pp. 1, 112–13.

20. The famous lithograph by Fanny Palmer that became a Currier and Ives print in 1868, *Across the Continent: "Westward the Course of Empire Takes Its Way,"* incorporates all the icons of the Westward Movement: Native Americans and white settlers, covered wagons and the new schoolhouse, mountains and plains—bisected and foregrounded by the steam locomotive and cars headed west. For a new evaluation of these images, see Henry Nash Smith, "Symbol and Idea in *Virgin Land*," in Bercovitch and Jehlen, *Ideology and Classic American Literature*, pp. 21–35.

21. De Certeau, *The Practice of Everyday Life*, p. 112.

22. The commercial traveler who narrates Sholem Aleichem's railroad stories demonstrates the narratological principle governing this perspective in a

prefatory note "To the Reader," which in English translation reads as follows: "Since we travelers often spend whole days on end sitting and looking out the window until we want to bang our heads against the wall, one day I had an idea: I went and bought myself a pencil and notebook and began jotting down everything I saw and heard on my trips" (E 135; Y 7). But it is the translator who adds "looking out the window"—as if it were obvious that that is what a passenger on a train does; the original Yiddish is a *domestic* image connoting indolence, "having nothing to get one's hands wet for" (*nisht tsu tun keyn hant in kalt vaser*). "Everything that [he] saw and heard" as related in the subsequent stories is confined to the pageants inside the railway cars, an internal discourse with virtually no reference to what might have been seen had the narrator *really* been looking out the window. Rare references to life or to the weather outside are part of the minimal circumstantial framing of the stories.

23. Mendele, who narrates the story, admits regretfully to having relinquished the freedom of the open-air horse and buggy for the incarceration of the crowded railway coach: "All this business of a railway journey is new to me. . . . In the train there is no feeling of independence. One is like a prisoner, without a moment's respite." S. Y. Abramovitsh, "Shem and Japheth in the Train," in *Modern Hebrew Literature*, ed. Robert Alter (New York: Berman House, 1975), pp. 20–21 (for the Hebrew, see "Shem Ve-yefet ba-'agala," in *Kol Kitvei Mendele mokher sforim* [The Complete Works of Mendele Mokher Sfarim] [Tel Aviv: Dvir, 1957], pp. 399–405).

Traveling in the open air had allowed Mendele to be a free spirit, having an affinity with but a nonproprietary relationship to the world through which he passed. Along with his former mode of conveyance, Mendele has, by his own report, abdicated his position as semidetached Jew and now appears beside his characters in the guise of a fellow traveler; the irony that we identified in *Benjamin the Third* as inhering in the distance between Mendele and the subject of his narrative seems to be replaced here, willy-nilly, by acts of empathy and identification. But something has also been gained: the third-class compartment in a train is the perfectly enclosed environment for an exchange of stories, and each family or personal unit is a tale waiting to be told.

Mendele's traveling companions in "Shem and Japheth" are generic samples of the human race, such as it has become since the Flood; it is not so much their story but their companionship that piques Mendele's interest. In joining the ranks of the Jewish beggars, a Polish cobbler who is traveling third class is reported to have "converted"—not to Jewish faith but to Jewish destiny: "Stay a Christian as you have always been," he is told, "but . . . come to master the Jewish art of living, and cleave to that, if you are to preserve yourself and carry the yoke of exile"(pp. 35–36). "Shem" in his earlier incarnation had struggled to leave the confines of his tent and travel in the footsteps of the world's great adventurers and liberators; now he ends up by bringing "Japheth" into his own quarters. But along with the acts of empathy and incorporation is a deep satire on the death-in-life of the shtetl Jew and a kind of proto-socialist solidarity among the hungry of the earth.

24. Trunk refers specifically to the "slowpoke express" (*Der leydik-geyer*) as "Kasrilevke on wheels." Y. Y. Trunk, *Sholem Aleykhem: zein vezen un zeine*

verk [Sholem Aleichem: His Being and His Work] (Warsaw: Kulturlige, 1937), p. 218.

25. Dan Miron, afterword to Sholem Aleichem, *Sipurei rakevet* [The Railroad Stories], ed. and tr. Dan Miron (Tel Aviv: Zmora Bitan, 1989), pp. 246, 243, 236, 247, 244, 263, 298. This long essay traces the publishing history of the stories and, in addition to arguing for their unique status collectively as a cultural watershed, analyzes many of them in detail.

Each of the critical positions Miron alludes to reflects, naturally, the ideological agenda to which the respective critics were responding. That Y. D. Berkovitz, Sholem Aleichem's son-in-law, literary confidant, and official Hebrew translator and mediator for generations of Israeli readers, did not translate more than a few of these stories into Hebrew may well be related to his decisions not to translate the last chapter of *Tevye* and to eliminate, as we will see later, many of the "American" chapters from *Motl*. All of these sections are affirmations of the phenomenon we have been probing in the fiction of Abramovitsh and Sholem Aleichem: the connection of wandering and mobility in a nonepic, nonteleological scheme. The translations by Aryeh Aharoni (1986) and Dan Miron (1989) of these stories into Hebrew and by Hillel Halkin (1987) into English make them available in those languages for the first time as a whole. Halkin's interpretation of these stories, as reflected in his translations, is not as sombre as Miron's.

26. Compare this to the instant sexual intimacy created between two complete strangers, a soldier and a "widow," who never exchange one word as they engage in their erotic encounter in Italo Calvino's "Adventure of a Soldier," in *Difficult Loves*, tr. William Weaver, Archibald Colquhoun, Peggy Wright (London: Picador, 1983), pp. 185–96.

27. From Sholem Aleichem's letter to Noach Zablodovski, reproduced in the *Sholem Aleykhem-Bukh* [Sholem Aleichem Book], ed. Y. D. Berkovitz (New York: n.p., 1926), p. 295.

28. Quoted by Halkin in his introduction to *Tevye the Dairyman*, p. xxxiv, and by Miron in his afterword to *Sipurei Rakevet*, pp. 231–32.

29. Berkovitz quotes Sholem Aleichem as saying to the yeshiva student (in his own Hebrew translation): "Likhtov—zohi melakhti. Ata tzarikh lidaber. Ve-lo dimyonot—uvdot tisaper!" (Writing is my craft. You have only to speak. And nothing imaginary—only relate the facts!) (in *Kitvei Y. D. Berkovitz*, vol. 8, p. 257).

30. Roskies, *A Bridge of Longing*, p. 173.

31. Such is the intention of "the man from Buenos Aires" who, in the story of that title, returns from white slave trading in South America to his hometown of Soshmakin to marry a "hometown girl" (E 175; Y 86).

32. De Certeau, *The Practice of Everyday Life*, p. 114.

33. See, for example, the distinction Ruth Wisse draws between the two: "Kafka's heroes are themselves a part of the universal horror confronting them. Sholem Aleichem's heroes are confronted by horror, but within a universe of meaning." *The Schlemiel as Modern Hero* (Chicago: University of Chicago Press, 1971), p. 53.

34. Kafka's dreams of escape or refuge did project, as we know, as far as Palestine—imagined as an ideal pastoral or cultural construct by his sister Ot-

tla and by such friends as Max Brod, Martin Buber, Gershom Sholem, and, finally, Dora Dymant.

35. *Amerika*, Kafka's first full-length novel, was begun in 1912. The first chapter, "The Stoker—A Fragment," published separately by Kurt Wolff in 1913 (*Der Jungste Tag*), remained the only section to be published during Kafka's lifetime; *Amerika, roman*, as reconstructed and edited by Max Brod, was published posthumously (Munich: K. Wolff, [1927]).

36. Perhaps the most salient sign of this is the dog image that recurs in Kafka's fiction and that will resonate throughout the narratives of subjugation in the twentieth century, from Agnon to Günter Grass. Joseph K. dies like a dog; the condemned man in *The Penal Colony* submits like a dog. However, when Karl's unsavory traveling companion, Robinson, explains that "if you're always treated like a dog, you begin to think you actually are one," and invokes the same paradigm, Karl *resists*, neutralizing the threat. *America* in *The Penguin Complete Novels of Franz Kafka*, tr. Willa and Edwin Muir (Harmondsworth: Penguin, 1983), p. 592.

37. The phrase comes from a diary entry where Kafka records that he has started a novel in which two brothers (based evidently on two cousins) quarreled—the one went to America, while the other remained behind in a "European prison." Quoted in Ernst Pawel, *Nightmare of Reason: A Life of Franz Kafka* (New York: Farrar, Straus, and Giroux, 1984), p. 254.

38. Amerika is *not* Combray. When Karl loses the photograph of his parents, he seems to lose the parents themselves—and the past itself—as a reference (*America*, pp. 507, 530). We receive one or two more glimpses of them later, but memory is not an organizing or enabling principle in the narrative or in the character's existential development.

39. In some ways, the machine that functions—or malfunctions—in so much of Kafka's fiction reaches a level of ultimate, Chaplinesque, American (not Prussian) efficiency in *Amerika*. In the first chapter, "The Stoker," the boiler room is a piece of machinery; the desk in the uncle's home is an invention of great intricacy. The social machine is configured with the individuals appearing as cogs and gears—in the hotel, in Uncle Jacob's office, in the political demonstrations that run with "machine-like regularity" (*America*, p. 606; see also pp. 570, 573, 471). In the final chapter, Karl declares his desire to be an engineer—though he is subsequently lowered to the status of "technician" in the Nature Theatre (pp. 628–29). Gilles Deleuze and Félix Guattari maintain that every enumeration is a manifestation of a machine and follows sets of rules and procedures; each statement "constitutes the real instructions for the machine." *Kafka: Toward a Minor Literature*, tr. Dana Polan (Minneapolis: University of Minnesota Press, 1986), p. 82.

On America as the context for "technological optimism," see Yaron Ezrahi, *The Descent of Icarus: Science and the Transformation of Contemporary Democracy* (Cambridge, Mass.: Harvard University Press, 1990).

40. It is true that Karl gets himself evicted from every safe refuge—his uncle's house, the hotel where he lands a job—and that he is taken in and mistreated by his traveling companions. But, just as inevitably, in the following chapter he finds himself by some miraculous narrative means—or by the sheer corruption of the text—out of danger.

41. Hannah Arendt is generally credited with having introduced Kafka to America. Although there were some earlier translations of Kafka into English, Arendt, as the first director of the newly established American branch of Schocken Press, bought the rights to all of his works and oversaw the translations. "Arendt had the unfortunate intuition that America needed Kafka, and people who lived quite comfortably in the world he had scorned, assured each other gleefully that they were living in a Kafkaesque world," writes Henry Pachter; "perhaps it was meant to épatez les bourgeois, but it only tickled them." Pachter, "On Being an Exile," in *The Legacy of the German Refugee Intellectuals*, ed. Robert Boyers (New York: Schocken Books, 1969), pp. 27, 43. For a less cynical view, see Walter Kaufmann, "The Reception of Existentialism in the United States," in ibid., p. 85.

Kafka remains, of course, the brooding presence in this study, as in nearly every cultural enterprise in the twentieth century. It is Kafka who is credited with inventing the modern language of exile and Kafka who is hailed as the prototype of the nomadic imagination; see above, chapter 1.

42. See Pawel, *Nightmare of Reason*, pp. 254–57; Michael Löwy, *Redemption and Utopia: Jewish Libertarian Thought in Central Europe, a Study in Elective Affinity*, tr. Hope Heaney (London: Athlone Press, 1992), pp. 71–94; Gershon Shaked, *The Shadows Within: Essays on Modern Jewish Writers* (Philadelphia: Jewish Publication Society, 1987), pp. 9–10.

43. Marx, *The Machine in the Garden*, p. 228. The American myth, Marx adds, is a "variant of the primal myth described by Joseph Campbell: 'a separation from the world, a penetration to some source of power, and a life-enhancing return.'"

44. The first story of the second section, "Vasershtub" [The Floating House], was revised and renamed "Mazl tov! mir zenen shoyn in amerike!" [Hurrah, We're in America!] before appearing in the book. Three of the stories were still unpublished at the time of Sholem Aleichem's death; one of them, "Mir mufn" [We Move] was unfinished. For the publishing history of *Motl* as well as a critical evaluation of its fate at the hands of Sholem Aleichem's official literary executor and Hebrew translator, Y. D. Berkovitz, see Chone Shmeruk, "Sipurei Motl ben he-hazan le-Shalom Aleichem: ha-situatzia ha-epit ve-toldotav shel ha-sefer" [The Tales of Motl the Cantor's Son by Sholem Aleichem: The Epic Situation and the History of the Text], *Siman Kri'a*, nos. 12/13 (February 1981): 310–26. See also Chone Shmeruk, "Nokhvort" [Afterword], in Sholem-Aleykhem, *Motl Peyse dem Khazns* (Jerusalem: Magnes Press, 1996), pp. vii–viii.

45. There is good reason to assume that when Sholem Aleichem published the first of the *Motl* stories, called "Haynt is yomtev—me tor nisht veynen" [Today Is a Holiday: It Is Forbidden to Cry] and "related" by Sholem Aleichem "in honor of Shavuoth," he had at best a vague conception of the shape of the narrative as a story of immigration to and settlement in America. Each of the stories had autonomy even as each was governed by the voice of the first-person child narrator and by a loose geographical and chronological structure. "Ein mukdam u-me'uhar" (there is no chronological order), writes the author in a letter to Yiddish critic S. Niger, adopting the Talmudic code for sacred narrative as justification of whatever anachronisms appear in the text (quoted in Shmeruk,

"Sipurei Motl," pp. 312, 315–16). A Russian version of the first part of *Motl* presented as a consecutive narrative appeared a year before the first Yiddish version of 1911.

Dan Miron discusses the author's concern with the problem of serialization that brought him to accommodate an "undefined mass of readers." On this and other issues related to the publication history of the text, see "Bouncing Back: Destruction and Recovery in Sholem Aleykhem's *Motl Peyse dem khazns*," *YIVO Annual of Jewish Social Science* 17 (1978): 136–37.

46. Werner Sollors, "Immigrants and Other Americans," in *Columbia Literary History of the United States*, general ed. Emory Elliott (New York: Columbia University Press, 1988), p. 588.

47. For a description of the funeral of Sholem Aleichem, attended by a crowd estimated at somewhere between 100,000 and 250,000 people, see Ellen D. Kellman, "Sholem Aleichem's Funeral (New York, 1916): The Making of a National Pageant," *YIVO Annual* 20 (1991): 277–304. Examining it as a public performance and rite of social cohesion and as the largest funeral New York had seen up to that time, Kellman notes that the path traced by the funeral cortege, which covered the city from the Bronx to Brooklyn, was orchestrated in such a way that the "hundred thousand or more mourners were laying claim to New York as their turf in a physical as well as a political sense" (p. 289).

The funeral itself, Jeffrey Shandler points out, takes on symbolic power not unlike the ritual of reading Sholem Aleichem as a form of "'geyn af keyver-oves' (visiting the graves of one's parents or ancestors), a substitute for visiting the inaccessible and later effaced graveyards of one's actual relatives." Shandler, "Reading Sholem Aleichem from Left to Right," *YIVO Annual* 20 (1991): 327.

48. Sholem Aleichem, *Adventures of Mottel the Cantor's Son*, tr. Tamara Kahana (New York: Henry Schuman, 1953), pp. 25, 293; *Motl Peyse dem Khazns*, vol. 1, p. 35; vol. 2, p. 129. Subsequent references to these editions, E and Y, will be made parenthetically in the text.

49. Motl's age ranges from five to nine in the different (not necessarily chronological) stories and versions. What is important, as we will consider at greater length in a moment, is that he does not grow.

50. The different translations of this sentence—which literally means "it is well with me—I am an orphan"—will largely reveal the interpretive strategies for translating all the inversions to come.

51. Miron, "Sholem Aleykhem's *Motl Peyse dem khazns*," p. 180.

52. The work of Mikhail Bakhtin on the carnivalesque, the comic, and the grotesque informs much of the discussion below. The cultural implications of the Jewish celebration of Purim and its modern transformations provide fertile material for his theories.

53. "Haynt, az ikh derher dos vort pogrom, antloyf ikh. Ikh hob beser lib freylekhe mayses" (E 190; Y 1:269). In the earlier passage, I have incorporated Naomi Sokoloff's translation, which is more accurate than Kahana's. Sokoloff develops the idea of the denial of threatening reality in Sholem Aleichem's fictions that was defined by David Roskies as "laughing off the trauma of history." The "grim humor" in this passage, she writes, "also defuses pathos and even makes for a conundrum or riddle game that mocks referentiality." Sokoloff, *Imagining*

the Child in Modern Jewish Fiction (Baltimore: Johns Hopkins University Press, 1992), pp. 51–52. The referents are, however, encoded in the Yiddish idioms themselves; Sholem Aleichem's "autobiography" was ambiguously titled *Funem Yarid* [From the Fair] (New York: Warheit, 1917).

In some versions of this story, explicitly intended for children, Sholem Aleichem himself deleted the first pogrom passage. On this see Shmeruk, "Sipurei Motl," pp. 316–17, and Sokoloff, *Imagining the Child*, p. 50.

54. Isaac Babel, "The Dovecot," in *Collected Stories*, ed. and tr. Walter Morison (New York: Meridian Books, 1955), p. 165.

55. See Chone Shmeruk, "Sholem-Aleykhem un Amerike" [Sholem Aleichem and America], *Di Goldene Keyt*, no. 121 (1987): 58–59.

56. Miecke Bal, "Lots of Writing," *Poetics Today* 15, no. 1 (spring 1994): 101 and passim.

In the passage from *Motl* just cited, Pini invokes Purim just before his reference to America; his comment ("Purim nokhn kaltn kugl") is translated into English as "sheer idiocy!" (E 252; Y 2:64).

57. In tracing the evolution of Motl from a promising musician into a cartoonist, Miron evokes the real-life model, a painter-cartoonist whom Sholem Aleichem met on his way back to Europe after his first failed visit to America ("Sholem Aleykhem's *Motl Peyse dem khazns*, pp. 120–21, 169).

58. The textual nature of the holiday and the cultural sensibilities it promotes are explored in two very different directions by Harold Fisch and Miecke Bal in the special volume of *Poetics Today*, "Purim and the Cultural Poetics of Judaism," edited by Daniel Boyarin. Fisch's study of the "semiotics of Purim" is a fascinating inquiry into the process by which the "sign" mediates between history and theology. "Reading and Carnival: On the Semiotics of Purim," *Poetics Today* 15, no. 1 (spring 1994): 55–74. Bal emphasizes the destabilizing effects of *writing itself*, which she sees as central to the Esther narrative; the writing which begins as official kingly edict moves to the word of Esther as a "fully realized agent, or subject" ("Lots of Writing," pp. 89–114).

59. Some studies in the 1990s have traced the sinister implications of the holiday not only in its "tropic" or performative but also in its behavioral dimensions— and have examined the dilemmas they posed for the more apologetically minded Jewish historians in the nineteenth century and their intimidated counterparts in Hitler's Germany. See Elliott Horowitz, "The Rite to be Reckless: On the Perpetration and Interpretation of Purim Violence," *Poetics Today* 15, no. 1 (spring 1994): 9–54. It is commendable that such an essay is included in the issue, given the editor's declared commitment to a diasporic sensibility and to Purim as the quintessential diasporic holiday; the evidence of Purim-related acts of anti-Christian violence beginning in the early medieval period and renewed in the early modern era complicates a reading of Diaspora as a disempowered and inherently nonviolent cultural form.

60. Mikhail Bakhtin has shown that the world of the comic and the grotesque incorporates death "in close relationship with the birth of new life and—simultaneously—with laughter." Death is "something that occurs 'just in passing,' without ever overemphasizing its importance"; it is, then, "an unavoidable aspect of life itself," part of the "temporal series of life that always marches for-

ward." *The Dialogic Imagination: Four Essays*, ed. Michael Holquist, tr. Caryl Emerson and Michael Holquist (Austin: University of Texas Press, 1981), pp. 198, 194, 193.

61. Natalie Zemon Davis has made a strong case for the presence in Rabelais's *Gargantua* and *Pantagruel* of a Purim sensibility, suggesting an immanent and not just a generic connection between the Rabelaisian chronotope and the *Purimshpiel*. It becomes a "writing against fear"—in the case of Rabelais, the fear of censorship. "Rabelais among the Censors," *Representations*, no. 32 (fall 1990): 21.

62. The letter from Sholem Aleichem to Bialik is quoted in Shmeruk, "Sipurei Motl," p. 313. The statement appears slightly altered in *Motl* (E 258; Y 2:76).

63. Miron attributes these and other inconsistencies in the story of this Jewish Peter Pan to what may be the most "elaborate stylistic paradox" in Sholem Aleichem's works—namely, that we have neither the language of a "genuine child nor . . . the sustained style of an adult narrator recapitulating his childhood" ("Sholem Aleykhem's *Motl Peyse dem khazns*," pp. 136–37). This is hardly a paradox, however, but rather a rhetorical tension not uncommon in European literature. Elsewhere Miron suggests that the absence of "Sholem Aleichem" as either narrator or interlocutor implies that he has become a "ghost writer" for Motl, since the "writings" of an illiterate boy would demand such mediation. *Sholem Aleykhem: Person, Persona, Presence* (New York: Yivo Institute for Jewish Research, 1972), pp. 24–25. Sokoloff argues that the absence of growth makes the novel more of a picaresque narrative than a bildungsroman (*Imagining the Child*, pp. 60–63). Roskies claims that the child's voice recovers the "unadulterated experience" (*A Bridge of Longing*, p. 172). And Shmeruk extends the discussion to consider the *reader* as child, arguing that although the targeted reader in the Yiddish original was not meant to be a child, since children's literature in Yiddish hardly existed at the time, the author talked to Bialik and Ravnitzky about making it a series for children when negotiating the translation of the stories into Hebrew ("Sipurei Motl," p. 319). So it remains until this day; the paratext in both the Hebrew and the English translations, as well as the illustrations and cover graphics, clearly designates it for the children's shelf. On the issue of translations and targeted audiences, see also Shandler, "Reading Sholem Aleichem from Left to Right," and Rhoda S. Kachuck, "Sholom Aleichem's Humor in English Translation," *YIVO Annual of Jewish Social Science* 11 (1956–57): 39–81.

All of these discussions acknowledge that the child is a pivotal figure in this moment of transition from traditional to more modern forms of Jewish life. Mine goes beyond the intratextual in the direction of the *con*textual by incorporating the contradictory narrative signs into a grammar of socialization.

64. Sholem Aleichem, "Di Khaliastre oyf der arbeit" (E 266–67; Y 2:86–87). I have modified the translation somewhat.

65. Philip Fisher, *Hard Facts: Setting and Form in the American Novel* (Oxford: Oxford University Press, 1987), pp. 134–35. He adds: "For a man inside the city his self is not inside his body but around him, outside the body" (p. 134).

66. As Stephen Kern points out, "'profane' means 'outside the temple,'" and many artists and intellectuals of this century found themselves not only outside

but without a temple, facing a post-Nietzschean void; yet many "learned to love their fate in the face of the void. If there are no holy temples, any place can become sacred; if there are no consecrated materials, then ordinary sticks and stones must do." *The Culture of Time and Space, 1880–1918* (Cambridge, Mass.: Harvard University Press, 1983), p. 179. On the loss of the sense of eternity that goes along with the modernist enactment of life's scenarios in the spatial plane, see also Frederick Hoffman, *The Mortal No: Death and the Modern Imagination* (Princeton: Princeton University Press, 1964).

67. Here I am suggesting a different emphasis from that of Sokoloff, who argues on the basis of the polyphonic nature of the novel that Motl is, "finally, a narrative construct that gauges changing collective values, not a complex individual in his own right [and that] in 'stealing across the border' [the title of one of the chapters], the family continually puts into relief the borders of their own discourse as it comes in contact with others" (*Imagining the Child*, pp. 60, 62). Although that is largely true of Motl's family, who are more instances of language 'talking,' I am arguing that the fact that Motl is not a 'complex individual' does not make him a 'narrative construct'—at least not once he arrives in America.

68. Miron, afterword to Sholem Aleichem, *Sipurei rakevet*, pp. 292–94.

69. Examples include "In new-york oyf der *street*" (In the streets of New York), "Mir zukhn a *djob*" (We look for a job), "Mir *straykn!*" (We strike), "Mir *kolektn*" (We collect), "Mir geyen in *biznes*" (We open a business), "Mir *mufn*" (We move); emphases mine.

70. On democratic aesthetics, see Yaron Ezrahi, *The Descent of Icarus*, p. 290. This is an American sensibility that is shared, conceptually at least, with a number of European modernisms, including those adapted by Jewish writers. See Chana Kronfeld, *On the Margins of Modernism: Decentering Literary Dynamics* (Berkeley: University of California Press, 1996).

71. Berkovitz, "Tuvye ha-holev nose'a le-eretz Yisrael," p. 192.

72. I have substantially altered the English translation (E 245).

73. "More than eighteen hundred years we have been dragging around as tenants from one house to another. Have we ever tried thinking seriously—how long? How much longer? What will be the end of it?" Sholem Aleichem, "Why Do the Jews Need a Land of Their Own?" the title essay in a collection of his writings on Zionism (1890–1913), edited and translated by Joseph Leftwich and Mordecai S. Chertoff ([New York: Herzl Press, 1984], p. 49). This is a populist interpretation of well-defined Zionist ideas.

74. All of the eulogies at the funeral presented Sholem Aleichem as the quintessential "goles Jew"; the funeral itself was described by one contemporary journalist as "the ingathering of the exiles, like a meeting-place of the children of the entire Diaspora." "Traversing the Jewish turf of their adopted city," Kellman writes, "they mourned the Yiddish writer as one vast community of the uprooted" ("Sholem Aleichem's Funeral," pp. 291–97). Shandler cites the Smithsonian Institution's 1979 exhibition titled *Abroad in America: Visitors to the New Nation, 1776–1914*, which included portraits of prominent visitors to America from Alexis de Tocqueville to . . . Sholem Rabinowitz. He justifies the definition of Sholem Aleichem's status as that of sojourner rather than immigrant to America, even though he died there ("Reading Sholem Aleichem from Left to Right," p. 305).

75. Reprinted in Sholem Aleichem, *Geklibene verk* [Selected Work] (New York: Dos yidishes tageblat, 1912), vol. 1, unpaginated preface; quoted in Kellman, "Sholem Aleichem's Funeral," pp. 280–81.

76. What is important is that for all intents and purposes, Kasrilevke has already moved to New York: "All Kasrilovka has moved to America. They tell us that after we had left the old country, a commotion started there, a real exodus. They tell us that a terrible pogrom broke out—slaughter and fire. The whole town went up in flames" (E 293; Y 2:129). Yet no one from the "known world" died in the pogrom; the others made it to New York, and the moral and human *communitas* of the shtetl was preserved.

77. See again Bernstein, *Foregone Conclusions*, and the discussion of its implications for post-Holocaust representations in chapter 7 of this volume.

Discussing the image of the shtetl in classical Yiddish and Hebrew fiction, Dan Miron argues that in editing his collected works late in life, Sholem Aleichem accentuated the "Kasrilevke" factor, making it appear even more ubiquitous in an ongoing sequence of narratives that underscored its hermetic, economically nonviable (feudal), but socially intimate character. As historical anachronism and as the personal point of reference relegated to the sphere of childhood—i.e., ephemeral—memories, it becomes a candidate for extinction and nostalgia, according to this reading. The shtetl's destruction by conflagration or pogrom in the writing of Sholem Aleichem, Abramovitsh, and others takes on the mythical status of a *hurbn*, complementing myths of origin. Miron, "The Literary Image of the Shtetl," *Jewish Social Studies* 1, no. 3 (spring 1995): 1–43 (originally published in Hebrew as a five-part article, "Ha-dimui ha-sifruti ha-klasi shel ha-'ayara," *Hadoar* 55 [1976] and 56 [1977], and in Yiddish as *Der imazh fun Shtetl: dray literatishe shtudiye* [Tel Aviv: Y. L. Peretz, 1981]). And see above, chapter 2.

78. Maurice Samuel, *The World of Sholem Aleichem* (1943; reprint, New York: Schocken Books, 1965), p. 3.

79. Natan Alterman, "Mikhtav shel Menakhem Mendl" [Letter from Menakhem Mendl], *Davar*, March 9, 1945; reprinted in *Ha-tur ha-shvi'i* [The Seventh Column] (Tel Aviv: Ha-kibbutz ha-me'uhad, 1977), vol. 1, pp. 12–14; discussed more fully in chapter 8.

80. Walter Benjamin, "The Storyteller," in *Illuminations*, ed. Hannah Arendt, tr. Harry Zohn (New York: Schocken Books, 1969), p. 84.

81. See David Grossman, *See Under: Love*, tr. Betsy Rosenberg (New York: Farrar Straus, and Giroux, 1989). "When I was eight years old," writes Grossman in an essay,

my father gave me the stories of *Mottel, the Son of Peyse the Cantor* to read. . . . That was my Sholem Aleichem year. Incessantly I dug my tunnel to the Diaspora. . . . The strange thing about it was that all that time (about a year and a half) I believed that the other world existed parallel to mine . . . carrying on somewhere according to its laws and its mystery and its various institutions and its special language. When I was about nine and a half, in the middle of the Holocaust Day ceremony . . . suddenly, it pierced me: the six million, the slain martyrs . . . they were my people. They were my secret world. The six million were Mottel and Tevye and . . . Chava . . . and Stempenyu. . . . On the blazing asphalt of the Beit Hakerem schoolyard, I felt as if I was literally disappearing, shriveling and dissolving. . . . Where had their army been? Why didn't their air force or their paratroopers fight? Above all, I was panic-stricken because I imagined that I might now be the only child . . . whose responsibility it was to remember all those people. . . . The first part of *See Under: Love* is about a child called Momik . . . who tries to understand the Diaspora in Israeli terms [or, as I have been arguing, Israel in diasporic terms].

> "My Sholem Aleichem," *Modern Hebrew Literature*, no. 14 (spring/summer 1995): pp. 4–5.

PART TWO.   JEWISH GEOGRAPHIES

1. Paul Celan, "Conversation in the Mountain," in *Collected Prose*, ed. and tr. Rosemarie Waldrop (New York: Sheep Meadow Press, 1986), p. 17.

2. While language may be the lightest and most inalienable of chattel, German under the sign of the swastika was, of course, anything but an uncontested Jewish birthright. There are many who claim, like Jean Améry, that German-speaking Jews were dispossessed of their language even before being divested of other belongings. See *At the Mind's Limits: Contemplations by a Survivor on Auschwitz and Its Realities*, tr. Sidney Rosenfeld and Stella P. Rosenfeld (Bloomington: Indiana University Press, 1980), pp. 42–54. For Celan, as we will see, "only one thing remained reachable, close and secure amid all losses: language. Yes, language. In spite of everything, it remained secure against loss. But it had to go through its own lack of answers, through terrifying silence, through the thousand darknesses of murderous speech." Celan, "Speech on the Occasion of Receiving the Literature Prize of the Free Hanseatic City of Bremen," in *Collected Prose*, p. 34.

3. Aharon Appelfeld, *The Age of Wonders*, tr. Dalya Bilu (New York: Washington Square Press, 1981), p. 166.

4. Naomi Seidman, *A Marriage Made in Heaven: The Sexual Politics of Hebrew and Yiddish* (Berkeley: University of California Press, 1997), p. 135.

5.   WRITING POETRY AFTER AUSCHWITZ: PAUL CELAN AS THE LAST BARBARIAN

1. For a discussion of the evolution of the anagram *Celan* in postwar Bucharest, see Israel Chalfen, *Paul Celan: A Biography of His Youth*, tr. Maximilian Bleyleben (New York: Persea Books, 1991), pp. 182–84.

2. Paul Celan, "Todesfuge," from *Mohn und Gedächtnis* (1952), translated by John Felstiner in *Paul Celan: Poet, Survivor, Jew* (New Haven: Yale University Press, 1995), p. 31. For a more detailed discussion of some of the issues raised in this chapter, especially of the reception of "Todesfuge" in Germany, see also my "'The Grave in the Air': Unbound Metaphors in Post-Holocaust Poetry," in *Probing the Limits of Representation: Nazism and the "Final Solution,"* ed. Saul Friedländer (Cambridge, Mass.: Harvard University Press, 1992), pp. 253–84.

3. T. W. Adorno, "Cultural Criticism and Society," in *Prisms*, tr. Samuel and Shierry Weber (London: Neville Spearman, 1967), p. 34.

4. Ernst Bloch, Georg Lukács, Bertold Brecht, Walter Benjamin, and Theodor Adorno, *Aesthetics and Politics*, ed. and tr. Ronald Taylor (London: NLB, 1977), p. 188; the "most important artists of the age" include such modernists as Kafka, Beckett . . . and Celan. See T. W. Adorno, *Aesthetic Theory*, tr. C. Lenhardt (Lon-

don: Routledge and Kegan Paul, 1970), pp. 352–54, 443–44; Adorno, *Prisms*, pp. 245–71.

5. On the seductive appeal of "silence," see my "Representing Auschwitz," *History and Memory* 7, no. 2 (winter 1996): 121–54.

6. Celan, "In der Luft," from *Die Niemandsrose* (1963), tr. in Felstiner, *Paul Celan*, pp. 197–98. For a discussion of these tropes of displacement, see also Amy Colin, *Paul Celan: Holograms of Darkness* (Bloomington: Indiana University Press, 1991), pp. 133–40.

7. The differend is the unstable state and instant of language wherein something which must be able to be put into phrases cannot yet be. . . . The silence that surrounds the phrase, *Auschwitz was the extermination camp* is . . . the sign that something remains to be phrased which is not, something which is not determined. . . . The indetermination of meanings left in abeyance [*en souffrance*], the extermination of what would allow them to be determined, the shadow of negation hollowing out reality to the point of making it dissipate, in a word, the wrong done to the victims that condemns them to silence—it is this . . . which calls upon unknown phrases to link onto the name of Auschwitz.

> Jean-François Lyotard, *The Differend: Phrases in Dispute*, tr. Georges Van Den Abbeele, Theory and History of Literature 46 (Minneapolis: University of Minnesota Press, 1988), pp. 13, 56–57.

In suggesting incommensurability or inarticulability or excess—the "dissipation" that comes of extermination—"le différend" may actually reinforce the idea of the propriety or the limits of symbolic as well as referential language.

8. Leo Bersani, *The Culture of Redemption* (Cambridge, Mass.: Harvard University Press, 1990), pp. 1–2.

9. The photograph, taken during the Warsaw Ghetto uprising, is prominently displayed in an enormous blowup in the Yad Vashem Holocaust museum in Jerusalem. See Jurgen Stroop, *The Stroop Report* (Nuremberg Documents P.S. 1061), tr. Sybil Milton (New York: Pantheon Books, 1979).

10. The accusation, launched by the widow of Franco-German modernist poet Yvan Goll, that Celan borrowed his black milk from her husband's poetry, is not very significant in itself—Goll's influence on Yiddish and Hebrew modernism can be documented in many ways, and prominent poets are not infrequently beset by claims that would impugn their originality (like many of Celan's poems, "Todesfuge" is replete with citations and allusions); what matters is the receptivity of sectors of the German public to such insinuations and the defensiveness of Celan's own response. On this charge and other questions of "literary provenance," see John Felstiner, "Translating Paul Celan's 'Todesfuge,'" in Friedländer, *Probing the Limits of Representation*, pp. 243–44; and Felstiner, *Paul Celan*, p. 34. See also the works of other poets, such as Rose Auslander and Immanuel Weissglas, which raise similar questions of poetic affinity; on the poets from Bukovina and their connections—personal, intertextual—see Colin, *Paul Celan*, chap. 1.

11. Celan is quoted in Felstiner, "Translating Celan's 'Todesfuge,'" p. 250.

12. See Mark Rosenthal, *Anselm Kiefer*, exhibition catalogue (Chicago: Art Institute of Chicago; Philadelphia: Museum of Art, 1987), p. 95; and Paul Taylor, "Painter of the Apocalypse," *New York Times Magazine*, October 16, 1988, p. 49.

13. For a discussion of the "black hole" and the concentric circles emanat-

ing from it in the cultural perception of post-Holocaust writers and readers, see my "Representing Auschwitz."

14. "Attention," Celan wrote, quoting Malebranche, is the "natural prayer of the soul." Cited in Michael Hamburger's introduction to *Poems of Paul Celan*, tr. Michael Hamburger (New York: Persea Books, 1988), p. 31. Hamburger belongs to that primary group of readers and translators who claim what he calls a "special kind of attention and perhaps a special kind of faith in the authenticity of what [such poetry] enacts. Without the same attention, it could not have been written, for the risk is shared by writer and reader." See also the debate between Hans-Georg Gadamer and Peter Szondi on the issue of access and interpretation, summarized by Colin in *Paul Celan*, p. xxiv.

15. Paul Celan, "Engführung" [Stretto], from *Sprachgitter* (1959), tr. in Felstiner, *Paul Celan*, p. 119.

16. Paul Celan, "Speech on the Occasion of Receiving the Literature Prize of the Free Hanseatic City of Bremen," in *Collected Prose*, ed. and trans. Rosemarie Waldrop (New York: Sheep Meadow Press, 1986), p. 35. See also his poem "Inselhin," from *Von Schwelle zu Schwelle* (1955), tr. in *Poems of Paul Celan*, pp. 100–101.

17. For example, Felstiner's monumental attempt in *Paul Celan: Poet, Survivor, Jew* to uncover not only the references but all possible allusions in the poetry is, I believe, a way of reincorporating Celan into the world he lost. See his discussion of "Engführung," which he views as Celan's response to aestheticized readings of "Todesfuge"; Felstiner argues that the poet attempted in his later poetry to concretize images that might otherwise be again unmoored, as it were, from their referential base by complicit structuralist, decontextualized readings (pp. 118–25).

18. Unpublished manuscript from a private collection, quoted in Colin, *Paul Celan*, p. 68.

19. Robert Musil is quoted in James E. Young, *The Texture of Memory: Holocaust Memorials and Meaning* (New Haven: Yale University Press, 1993), p. 13.

20. Adorno, who described the "hermetic procedure" that allows art to "maintain its integrity only by refusing to go along with communication," was, of course, not the only critic to characterize Celan's poetry as hermetic (*Aesthetic Theory*, appendix 1, p. 443). See also Amy D. Colin, "Paul Celan's Poetics of Destruction," in *Argumentum e Silentio: International Paul Celan Symposium,* ed. Amy D. Colin (Berlin: Walter de Gruyter, 1987), pp. 177–78; and Alan Udoff, "On Poetic Dwelling: Situating Celan and the Holocaust," in ibid., pp. 321–51.

21. Although others such as Rose Auslander and Nelly Sachs continued to write in German, and a number of postwar German writers have emerged, Celan belongs to the last of the great German-Jewish diasporic writers with roots in the prewar world.

22. Quoted from a statement made by Celan to his translator Michael Hamburger, in Katharine Washburn's introduction to Paul Celan, *Last Poems*, ed. and trans. Katharine Washburn and Margret Guillemin (San Francisco: North Point Press, 1986), p. vi.

23. Paul Celan, "In Eins," from *Die Niemandsrose* (1963), in *Sprachgitter;*

Die Niemandsrose: Gedichte (Frankfurt am Main: S. Fischer Verlag, 1986), p. 132.

24. Jacques Derrida, "Schibboleth," in Colin, *Argumentum e Silentio*, pp. 22, 24. In Derrida's analysis of the poem "In Eins," the incomplete dating (February 13 without a specific year) seems to establish historicity not as a limiting fact but as the status and symbolic complexity of reality, both past and future. The multiplicity of possible witnesses and the indeterminate nature of this hour or this appointed time—which can encapsulate the Spanish Civil War, the French-Algerian War, and of course the *unmentioned* war—make this both an urgent and an open-ended poem.

25. What such polyphony suggests is that the poem is bound by no single linguistic code or convention, place or situation. See Evan Watkin, "Lyric Poetry as Social Language," in Colin, *Argumentum e Silentio*, p. 270. Celan's poetic transactions included translations from English, Hebrew, Russian, and German.

26. Paul Celan, "The Meridian," in *Collected Prose*, p. 50.

27. Stéphane Mosès, "Quand le langage se fait voix: Paul Celan: Entretien dans la montagne," in *Contre-Jour: Etudes sur Paul Celan: Colloque de Cerisy*, ed. Martine Broda (Paris: Cerf, 1986), pp. 125–26.

One of the most enlightening discussions of the dialogic—or failed dialogic—nature of Celan's poetry, his "interrupted discourse" as evidence of his "dispersed cosmos," can be found in Shira Wolosky, *Language Mysticism: The Negative Way of Language in Eliot, Beckett, and Celan* (Stanford: Stanford University Press, 1995), pp. 173–98.

28. Paul Celan, "Espenbaum," from *Mohn und Gedachtnis* (1952); tr. as "Aspen Tree," in *Poems of Paul Celan*, p. 39.

29. "The region from which I come to you—with what detours!" Celan said in a 1958 speech, "will be unfamiliar to most of you. It is the home of many of the Hassidic stories which Martin Buber has retold in German. It was—if I may flesh out this topographical sketch with a few details which are coming back to me from a great distance—it was a landscape where both people and books lived"("On the Occasion of Receiving the Literature Prize of Bremen," in *Collected Prose*, p. 33).

30. Hebrew is referred to as the "wahr gebliebene, wahr gewordene," the language that has remained true, that has therefore become true. John Felstiner, "'Ziv, that light': Translation and Tradition in Paul Celan," *New Literary History* 18, no. 3 (1987): 630.

31. Paul Celan, "Hüttenfenster," from *Die Niemandsrose* (1963); tr. as "Tabernacle Window," in *Poems of Paul Celan*, pp. 213–15.

32. Benjamin Harshav argues forcefully that it is Yiddish that is the model for Chagall's articulation of the polyphonic collage; see "The Role of Language in Modern Art: On Texts and Subtexts in Chagall's Paintings," *Modernism and Modernity* 1, no. 2 (April 1994): 51–87. Chana Kronfeld adds that Celan's Yiddish allusions are the ultimate way to "deracinate German from within," noting that read from within Yiddish idiom and syntax, much of the "hermeticism" of Celan's poetry is dissipated (private communication).

33. Jorge Borges, "The Aleph," in *The Aleph and Other Stories, 1933–1969: Together with Commentaries and an Autobiographical Essay*, ed. and tr. Nor-

man Thomas Di Giovanni in collaboration with the author (New York: E. P. Dutton, 1970), p. 23.

34. "Und ich finde hier, in dieser äusseren und inneren Landschaft, viel von den Wahrheitszwängen, der Selbstevidenz und der weltoffenen Einmaligkeit grosser Poesie." Paul Celan, "Ansprache vor dem hebraïschen schriftstellerverband," Tel Aviv, October 14, 1969, in *Gesammelte Werke* (Frankfurt am Main: Suhrkamp Verlag, 1983), vol. 3, p. 203. tr. in *Collected Prose*, p. 57.

35. Ibid.

36. Peter Szondi, a close friend whose own suicide followed hard on Celan's, went further in his claim that poetry is a form of substantiation, writing that Celan's poetry "ceases to be *mimesis*, representation: it becomes reality." See "Lecture de Strette," in *Poésies et Poétiques de la Modernité*, ed. Mayotte Bollack ([Lille]: Presses Universitaires de Lille, 1981), p. 169. I am arguing that mimesis has its own integrity as *the* mandate of the diasporic imagination.

37. Primo Levi, "On Obscure Writing," in *Other People's Trades*, tr. Raymond Rosenthal (New York: Summit Books, 1989), pp. 173–74.

38. Celan, "The Meridian," p. 51.

39. Ibid., pp. 49, 53–55.

40. Paul Celan, "Heimkehr" (in *Sprachgitter*, 1959) and "Was Geschah?" (in *Atemwende*, 1967), tr. in *Poems of Paul Celan*, pp. 108, 204. Here we may see a possible example of the syntactic/morphological "Yiddishization" of the German.

41. George Steiner, *After Babel: Aspects of Language and Translation* (London: Oxford University Press, 1975), p. 389; quoted in Colin, "Paul Celan's Poetics of Destruction," p. 172.

42. Colin, "Paul Celan's Poetics of Destruction," p. 172.

43. Washburn, introduction to Celan, *Last Poems*, p. xxxv.

6. RECLAIMING A PLOT IN RADAUTZ:
DAN PAGIS AND THE PROSAICS OF MEMORY

1. Dan Pagis, "Point of Departure," in *Dan Pagis: Points of Departure*, tr. Stephen Mitchell (Philadelphia: Jewish Publication Society, 1981), pp. 40–41. Published originally as "Nekudat ha-motza" in *Moah*, and reprinted in *Kol ha-shirim; 'Abba' (pirkei proza)* [Collected Poems and 'Father' (prose passages)], ed. Hanan Hever and T. Carmi (Jerusalem: Ha-kibbutz ha-me'uhad and Bialik Institute, 1991), p. 173. All translations of Pagis's poetry are by Stephen Mitchell unless otherwise specified. For a more detailed discussion of some of the issues raised in the first part of this chapter, see my "Dan Pagis—Out of Line: A Poetics of Decomposition," *Prooftexts* 10, no. 2 (May 1990): 335–63.

2. Dan Pagis, "Ready for Parting," in *Points of Departure*, p. 97; "Mukhan li-preida" from *Shehut Me'uheret* [A Late Sojourn], in *Kol ha-shirim*, p. 84. See Rilke's response to the visitation from a dead friend: "Requiem für eine Freundin" (1909).

3. Dan Pagis, "Honi," from *Shehut me'uheret*, in *Kol ha-shirim*, p. 74 (translation mine). Pagis defined the midrashic figure Honi ha-ma'agel in an essay as one of those immortal mythical characters, like the phoenix, who live forever. "Of ha-almavet: motiv ha-feniks ba-sifrut ha-midrash ve-ha-aggadah" [The Im-

mortal Bird: Motif of the Phoenix in Midrashic and Aggadic Literature], in *Sefer Ha-yovel* [Jubilee Volume], ed. H. Merhavia (Jerusalem: Hebrew High School of Jerusalem, 1962), p. 74.

4. See, for example, the fiction of Aharon Appelfeld, discussed in chapter 7.

5. Paul Ricoeur, *Time and Narrative*, tr. Kathleen McLaughlin and David Pellauer (Chicago: University of Chicago Press, 1984) vol. 1, p. 3.

6. Pagis, "Honi," p. 74.

7. See, for example, Haim Gouri's poem "Odysses" [Odysseus], in *Shoshanat ruhot* [Phantom Flower] (Tel Aviv: Ha-kibbutz ha-me'uhad, 1960), pp. 115–16; and Chana Kronfeld on the wider implications of the figure of the wanderer in modernist Hebrew and Yiddish poetry, *On the Margins of Modernism: Decentering Literary Dynamics* (Berkeley: University of California Press, 1996), pp. 71, 205–6.

8. Dan Pagis, "Brain" and "The Readiness," in *Points of Departure*, pp. 111, 13; "Moah" from *Moah* [Brain] and "Likrat" [Toward] from *Gilgul* [Metamorphosis], in *Kol ha-shirim*, pp. 199, 127. "Likrat" is also the name of the modernist group with which Pagis was marginally affiliated.

9. Dan Pagis, "Information," in *Variable Directions: The Selected Poetry of Dan Pagis*, tr. Stephen Mitchell (San Francisco: North Point Press, 1989), p. 55; "Meida," from *Milim nirdafot* [Synonyms], in *Kol ha-shirim*, p. 233.

10. Dan Pagis, "Written in Pencil in a Sealed Railway Car," in *Points of Departure*, p. 23; "Katuv be-'iparon ba-karon he-hatum," from *Gilgul*, in *Kol ha-shirim*, p. 135.

11. The "you" who appears in an occasional poem tends to be an impersonal pronominal stand-in for the integrity of both the self and a significant other. See, for example, Dan Pagis, "How To," in *Variable Directions*, p. 117; "Hahatkanah," in *Kol ha-shirim*, p. 232.

12. Educators at Yad Vashem and elsewhere suggest to their students that the poem be read cyclically, implicitly insisting on providing some closure—if only structural—to this intolerably open-ended poem.

13. See Don Handelman, *Models and Mirrors: Towards an Anthropology of Public Events* (Cambridge: Cambridge University Press, 1990); and James E. Young, *The Texture of Memory: Holocaust Memorials and Meaning* (New Haven: Yale University Press, 1993).

14. Dan Pagis, "Ahim" [Brothers], in *Kol ha-shirim*, p. 163. The translation I have given here is more literal than Mitchell's in *Points of Departure*, p. 5. "Autobiography," in *Points of Departure*, p. 3.

15. See the biographical/autobiographical volume by Pagis's wife, Ada Pagis, *Lev Pitomi* [Sudden Heart] (Tel Aviv: Am Oved, 1995). This courageous and troubling text both resolves some of the riddles and demonstrates how deep-seated was Pagis's strategy of concealment. "His friend the poet T. Carmi told me how he once succeeded in extracting from Dan's very depths (*mi-ma'amakav shel Dan*) the fundamental repressed experience in one of his poems." The sign that the repressed experience has resurfaced is the cold sweat on Dan's forehead; the experience itself remains untold, even to his best friends and his wife (pp. 38–39).

16. See, respectively, Ada Kuntsler, "Kisuyim shkufim ve-shikufim mekhusim" [Transparent Opacities and Opaque Transparencies], *Moznayim* 55 (August

1982): 11; Ariel Hirshfeld, "Ketivat sod 'al derekh ha-emet: 'al tzura u-masma'ut be-'Shneym-'asar panim shel esmergad' le-Dan Pagis" [Writing Secrets As If They Were True: On Form and Meaning in "Twelve Faces of the Emerald" by Dan Pagis], *Mehkerei Yerushalayim ba-sifrut ha-'ivrit* [Jerusalem Studies in Hebrew Literature] 10–11 (1987–88): 151; Ruth Kartun-Blum, "Ha-mavet ke-meshamer ha-hayyim: 'iyun be-shirav shel Dan Pagis 'Hasifa' ve-'Ha-hatkana'" [Death as Life's Preserver: A Study of Dan Pagis's Poems "Exposure" and "How To"], in ibid., p. 122.

17. Gershon Shaked, "Gavish" [Crystal], *Yediot Ahronot*, July 7, 1986, p. 21.

18. For English translations of poems by Avot Yeshurun, whose real name was Yehiel Perlmutter, see Avot Yeshurun, *The Syrian-African Rift and Other Poems*, a bilingual edition, tr. Harold Schimmel (Philadelphia: Jewish Publication Society, 1980). For a discussion of him as a "shmatte peddlar," see Schimmel's introduction. Avot Yeshurun's writing is one of the landmarks of a discourse of the displaced that also foregrounds the voices of the native Arab population dislocated by the immigrant Jewish population.

19. For a discussion of the ambiguous position of those Hebrew and Yiddish poets "marginal" to a modernism that is defined by its marginality, see Kronfeld, *On the Margins of Modernism*.

20. Dan Pagis, "Art of Contraction," in *Variable Directions*, p. 87; "Omanut ha-tzimtzum," from *Shirim ahronim* [Final Poems], in *Kol ha-shirim*, p. 306. Pagis's image—and his minimalistic aesthetics—are an ironic amalgam of Platonic and Kabbalistic notions of "contraction," limitation, and derivative form.

21. Dan Pagis, "Souvenir," in *Variable Directions*, p. 9; "Hamazkeret," from *Milim nirdafot*, in *Kol ha-shirim*, p. 262.

22. See Leonard Barkan, "Rome's Other Population," *Raritan* 11, no. 2 (fall 1991): 47: "Thus statues *emerge* from the ground in a one-way pattern of travel. Suddenly the space of Rome is both real and symbolic; the past is both an idea and a buried physical reality." See also chapter 1, above. Archaeological metaphors have, of course, enormously enriched the psychoanalytic and poetic exploration of memory in late nineteenth and twentieth centuries. See Marianna Torgovnick, *Gone Primitive: Savage Intellects, Modern Lives* (Chicago: University of Chicago Press, 1990), and Carl Schorske, "Freud: The Psycho-archaeology of Civilizations," in *The Cambridge Companion to Freud*, ed. Jerome Neu (Cambridge: Cambridge University Press, 1991), pp. 8–24.

23. On childhood as a "nature preserve" or protected area that can provide a base for a posttraumatic future, see my "Representing Auschwitz," *History and Memory* 7, no. 2 (winter 1996): 138–42. And on photographs of the pre-Holocaust world furnishing the absent memories for the children of survivors, see Marianne Hirsch, "Past Lives: Postmemories in Exile," *Poetics Today* 17, no. 4 (winter 1996): 659–86, and *Family Frames: Photography, Narrative, and Postmemory* (Cambridge, Mass.: Harvard University Press, 1997).

24. Vladimir Nabokov, *Speak, Memory: An Autobiography Revisited* (New York: G. P. Putnam's Sons, 1966), p. 20.

25. Gaston Bachelard, *The Poetics of Space*, tr. Maria Jolas (Boston: Beacon Press, 1964), p. 7.

26. See, for example, "'Akevot" [Footprints] and "Ha-misdar" [The Roll-call], both published in *Gilgul* in 1970; *Kol ha-shirim*, pp. 141–46, 136.

27. "Beka' be-homat ha-shikheha" is the way Pagis phrased it in Hebrew to Yaira Genossar. Genossar, "Dan Pagis—Likro bishem, linkot 'emda" [Dan Pagis—Calling It by Its Name, Taking a Stand], '*Iton 77*, no. 38 (February 1983): 33.

28. Pierre Nora, "Between Memory and History: Les Lieux de Mémoire," *Representations*, no. 26 (spring 1989): 7, 9 (translated from "Entre Mémoire et Histoire," the introduction to his multivolume study, *Les lieux de mémoire* [Paris: Gallimard, 1984], pp. xvii, xix).

29. Dan Pagis, "Footprints," in *Points of Departure*, pp. 35, 37; "'Akevot," in *Kol ha-shirim*, p. 142.

30. Pagis, "Footprints," pp. 30–31.

31. Genossar, "Dan Pagis," p. 33.

32. Ibid.

33. Roland Barthes, *Camera Lucida: Reflections on Photography* (New York: Hill and Wang, 1981), p. 76.

34. Susan Sontag, *On Photography* (New York: Farrar, Straus, and Giroux, 1977), p. 154. Footprints, as we have seen, and death masks are two of the primary trace elements in Pagis's universe.

35. Barthes, *Camera Lucida*, p. 6.

36. For extreme and perhaps oversimplified statements of this thesis about Barthes, see Paul John Eakin, *Touching the World: Reference in Autobiography* (Princeton: Princeton University Press, 1992), pp. 4, 18; and J. Gerald Kennedy, "Roland Barthes, Autobiography, and the End of Writing," *Georgia Review* 35, no. 2 (summer 1981): 390.

37. See Pagis's poem "Gravity" ("Koah meshiha" in Hebrew) in *Kol ha-shirim*, p. 257.

38. "Lines in a poem, long ones, short ones: each bound to its allotted end. But we, out of line, fly about in space, return, ignite at the air's edge, burn out, spread darkness all around us." Dan Pagis, "Out of Line," in *Variable Directions*, p. 100; "Mi-hutz la-shura," from *Milim nirdafot*, in *Kol ha-shirim*, p. 256.

39. See Dan Pagis, "Misped le-ba'al signon" [Eulogy for a Stylist], in *Kol ha-shirim*, p. 259.

40. Dan Pagis, "For a Literary Survey," in *Variable Directions*, p. 85; "Le-mish'al sifruti," in *Kol ha-shirim*, p.308. I have added the words in italics, which were, for some reason, left untranslated in the English text. I am grateful to Oren Stier for calling my attention to this omission.

41. Dan Pagis, "The Story." See also "A Small Poetics" ("obey / the voice of / the empty page"), in *Points of Departure*, p. 45, and *Variable Directions*, p. 81; "Ha-sipur" and "Poetika ketana," both from *Milim nirdafot*, in *Kol ha-shirim*, pp. 243, 228.

42. My judgment that the poem was unfinished is based both on the evidence of the text itself (with marginalia that clearly indicate work-in-progress) and on the personal testimony of Hanan Hever and T. Carmi, who worked closely with Pagis during his lifetime and co-edited the posthumous volume of his collected works. I am indebted to Ada Pagis for allowing me to look at this material, even

before it was published, and to Carmi for his unstinting sharing of ideas and material in our long conversations regarding the man who was not only a fellow poet but a dear friend as well. Carmi's own poem in memory of Pagis—"Lezekher Dan Pagis" [In Memory of Dan Pagis] (1986), in *Shirim min ha-'azuva* [Monologues and Other Poems] (Tel Aviv: Dvir, 1988)—so accommodates the rhetoric of his friend that the two voices merge inextricably into what, after Carmi's own death, becomes a poetic tribute and eulogy to both poets. See also Carmi's "Dan Pagis: Words of Farewell," *Orim* 2, no. 2 (spring 1987): 76–78.

43. See Celan, "Gespräch im Gebirg," and the discussion of it in chapter 5, above.

44. The prosaic, practical nature of the encounter acknowledges the mechanical problems entailed in a dialogue between the living and the dead: "If I were still alive," says the father, "you could even have done a comparative blood test [to establish paternity beyond a shadow of a doubt]" ("Abba," p. 364).

45. John Freccero, "Autobiography and Narrative," in *Reconstructing Individualism: Autonomy, Individuality, and the Self in Western Thought*, ed. Thomas C. Heller (Stanford: Stanford University Press, 1986), p. 17. Freccero's argument, that the modern autobiographical narrative traces its genealogy to the confessions of the saints, posits a conversion experience as the inception of the confessional/autobiographical mode. That the story of a conversion is not necessarily synonymous with conversion *as story* is, I think, demonstrated in the radical but nonreligious transformation that Pagis undergoes as he moves into a confessional prose.

46. Pagis, "Abba," p. 341.

47. Don Pagis, "Parvot" [Furs], in *Kol ha-shirim*, p. 333.

48. Don Pagis, "She'ela matzhikah" [A Funny Question], from *Shirim ahronim*, in *Kol ha-shirim*, p. 290.

49. Shuli Barzilai, "Borders of Language: Kristeva's Critique of Lacan," *PMLA* 106, no. 2 (March 1991): 295–96.

50. Don Pagis, "Ha-shem shelkha" [Your Name] (in "Abba"), in *Kol ha-shirim*, p. 366. In a public address after the appearance of her biography of her husband, Ada Pagis admitted that a distant relative had called to reveal to her Dan's real (i.e., diasporic) name; that information, which she had not gleaned from Dan himself, she preferred not to share with the audience.

51. Pagis, "Abba," p. 347.

52. Don Pagis, "Ein Leben" [A Life], tr. Stephen Mitchell, *New Yorker*, April 3, 1989, p. 85; from *Shirim ahronim*, in *Kol ha-shirim*, p. 277.

53. Barthes, *Camera Lucida*, p. 73.

54. Ibid., p. 40.

55. Pagis, "Ein Leben," p. 85.

56. See, for example, Pagis's marginalia on the passage in which a bottle of Cherry Herring breaks in the airport just after the narrator receives word that his father has died: "Take out? If not, it can be less symbolic, even if the whole thing is *true*." In *Kol ha-shirim*, p. 380.

57. Dan Pagis, "Central Park, Twilight," tr. Stephen Mitchell, *Orim* 2, no. 2 (spring 1987): 79; "Central Park, dimdumim," from *Milim nirdafot*, in *Kol ha-shirim*, p. 246.

58. For a discussion of "repatriation" through narrative form, see Michael Seidel, *Exile and the Narrative Imagination* (New Haven: Yale University Press, 1986), p. 198.

59. Pagis, "Honi," p. 74. See also the early poem "Shiva meyuteret" [Gratuitous Return], from *Shehut me'uheret* (collectively a pun on the Zionist call to a [belated] homecoming or *shiva me'uheret*), in *Kol ha-shirim*, p. 95.

60. In an article on "Abba," Hanan Hever argues that this autobiographical text stands diametrically opposed to the standard Zionist-oedipal story, for it is the *father* who abandons the son to go to Palestine, in effect leaving the son to die. "She-harei kvar higa'nu, nakhon?" [For We Have Already Arrived, Right?], *Davar*, February 21, 1992, p. 26. Yet even as a parody or rewrite of the Zionist story, the text still engages the epic terms of the story.

61. For a theory of the "prosaic," see Gary Saul Morson and Caryl Emerson on Tolstoy and Bakhtin in *Mikhail Bakhtin: Creation of a Prosaics* (Stanford: Stanford University Press, 1990).

62. On "backshadowing," and Michael André Bernstein's application of the term to the writing of Aharon Appelfeld, see chapter 7.

7. BETWEEN BUKOVINA AND JERUSALEM: AHARON APPELFELD AND PILGRIMAGE TO THE RUINED SHRINE

1. For a more detailed discussion of *Mikhvat ha-or* and *Tor ha-pla'ot*, see my "Aharon Appelfeld: The Search for a Language," *Studies in Contemporary Jewry* 1 (1984): 366–80. *Mikhvat ha-or* has not yet appeared in English translation. This omission could betray the author's own ambivalence, born of his present distance from the stark judgments represented in that narrative.

2. These stories by Aharon Appelfeld appear in such collections as *'Ashan* [Smoke] (Jerusalem: Akhshav, 1962), *Ba-gai ha-poreh* [In the Fertile Valley] (Jerusalem: Schocken, 1964), *Kfor 'al ha-aretz* [Frozen Ground] (Ramat Gan: Massada, 1965), and *Adanai ha-nahar* [Sills of the River] (Tel Aviv: Ha-kibbutz ha-me'uhad, 1971). For a further discussion of this subject, see Yigal Schwartz, *Kinat ha-yahid ve-netzah ha-shevet: Aharon Appelfeld: tmunat 'olam* [Individual Lament and Tribal Eternity: Aharon Appelfeld, the Picture of His World] (Jerusalem: Keter, 1996). For a taxonomy of the travel narratives, see Lily Rattok, *Bayit 'al blimah: omanut ha-sipur shel A. Appelfeld* [A Precarious House: The Narrative Art of A. Appelfeld] (Tel Aviv: Heker, 1989), pp. 119–36.

3. The reference to the "little sister" is from Abba Kovnar's long poem *Ahoti ketanah: poema* [My Little Sister] (Merhavia: Sifriyat po'alim, 1967).

4. Abba Kovner, "It's Late," "A Canopy in the Desert" no. 96, in *A Canopy in the Desert: Selected Poems*, tr. Shirley Kaufman (Pittsburgh: University of Pittsburgh Press, 1973), pp. 202–3; *Hupa ba-midbar* (Merhavia: Sifriat po'alim, 1970).

See also Yehuda Amichai's long, digressive novel *Not of This Time, Not of This Place*, which traces the schizophrenic path of a Jewish immigrant who had come to Palestine as a child from Nazi Germany. The "Joel" who goes back to Weinburg and confronts the remnants of his childhood is rewarded by a profound sense of finally returning to a center sacralized by pilgrimage to his native home ("I knew where I was returning. To my home. To Jerusalem . . . "), while the "Joel" who stays in Jerusalem and refuses to take the risk of going back is blown up on Mt. Scopus, the unvisited past exploding within him in the form of an old mine from "another war, another time and place." *Lo me-'akhshav lo mi-kan* (Jerusalem: Schocken, 1963), p. 611. There is also an abbreviated English version of this novel. Unlike the other Hebrew writers cited here, Amichai, who emigrated to Jerusalem in 1936, is a survivor not of the Holocaust but of European Jewish civilization on the eve of its collapse.

5. Shulamith Hareven, "Twilight," tr. Miriam Arad, in *Facing the Holocaust: Selected Israeli Fiction*, ed. Gila Ramras-Rauch and Joseph Michman-Melkman (Philadelphia: Jewish Publication Society, 1985), pp. 169–70; originally published in Hebrew in *Bididut* [Loneliness] (Tel Aviv: Am Oved, 1980).

6. Itamar Yaoz-Kest, "The Phosphorus Line," tr. Dalya Bilu, in Ramras-Rauch and Michman-Melkman, *Facing the Holocaust*, p. 110; "Ha-kav ha-zarhani" is the second part of a Hebrew novella published in 1972 (in *Vakum ha-'olam: mivhar pirkei shira ve-prosa mi-thum ha-shoah, 1958–1978* [The World's Vacuum: Selected Poetry and Prose from the Holocaust, 1958–1978] [Tel Aviv: Eked, 1978]).

7. Dan Miron, "El mul ha-av: hithadshut be-yitzirat Aharon Appelfeld" [Facing the Father: Renewal and Power in the Work of Aharon Appelfeld], *Yediot Ahronot*, Literary Supplement, June 2, 1978, p. 1. See also Schwartz, *Kinat ha-yahid*.

8. Aharon Appelfeld, *The Age of Wonders*, tr. Dalya Bilu (New York: Washington Square Press, 1981), p. 166.

9. Frederick Hoffman, *The Mortal No: Death and the Modern Imagination* (Princeton: Princeton University Press, 1964), pp. 463–64. Hoffman is referring to Samuel Beckett.

10. Appelfeld, *The Age of Wonders*, p. 138.

11. Walter Benjamin, "The Work of Art in the Age of Mechanical Reproduction," in *Illuminations*, ed. Hannah Arendt, tr. Harry Zohn (New York: Schocken Books, 1969), p. 220. See also Jean Baudrillard, "Simulacra and Simulations," in *Selected Writings*, ed. Mark Poster (Stanford: Stanford University Press, 1988), pp. 166–84.

12. Aharon Appelfeld, "Bertha," tr. Tirza Zandbank in Ramras-Rauch and Michman-Melkman, *Facing the Holocaust*, p. 148. The story appeared originally in *'Ashan*.

13. Ibid., p. 145.

14. Gershon Shaked was one of the first readers to point out that "Appelfeld's characters are not capable of disengaging from their Berthas; they constitute a real part of their lives . . . from which they will never be able to separate. They carry the 'retarded child' of their lost childhood with them. The Holocaust is not a memory of childhood but nailed into their daily lives." *Gal hadash ba-siporet ha-'ivrit* [New Wave in Hebrew Fiction] (Tel Aviv: Sifriat Po'alim, 1974), p. 80.

15. Aharon Appelfeld, *The Immortal Bartfuss*, tr. Jeffrey M. Green (New York: Weidenfeld and Nicolson, 1988). The novella "Bartfuss ben almavet" was collected in *Ha-kutonet ve-ha-pasim* [The Coat and the Stripes] (Tel Aviv: Ha-kibbutz ha-me'uhad, 1983).

16. Aharon Appelfeld, *Katerina*, tr. Jeffrey M. Green (New York: Random House, 1992).

17. Yehuda Amichai, *Zman* (Tel Aviv: Schocken, 1977), p. 7, translation mine (an English translation by the author appeared in *Time: Poems* [New York: Harper and Row, 1979]).

18. In their study of Jewish exiles living in Paris, who hail from former Jewish communities in both North Africa and Europe, Lucette Valensi and Nathan Wachtel observe the ubiquity of childhood as a protected sphere: an environment "composed of concentric circles [nature, family, community] formed a totality in which individuals, as they remember it, were harmoniously integrated. . . . It is this early refuge of peace and affection that appears in memory as the ideal of all joy. The rest of life will preserve a longing for it." *Jewish Memories*, tr. Barbara Harshav (Berkeley: University of California Press, 1991), pp. 89–92.

See Richard N. Coe's discussion in *When the Grass Was Taller: Autobiography and the Experience of Childhood* (New Haven: Yale University Press, 1984) of childhood's paradise lost as a closed or protected world, an "alternative dimension" that becomes particularly compelling when something in the present intensifies the normal sense of loss and nostalgia.

19. In the course of a five-hour interview conducted by Yigal Schwartz, Appelfeld expanded on his attachment to the natural world that provided him shelter during the war—its waterfalls, its fruit, its forests. Because it coincided with the war that killed his world, this place and time cannot, of course, retain the prelapsarian innocence of the crèche. Aharon Appelfeld, interview, in "Milim u-demuyot: proyekt ha-sifrut shel Yerushalayim" [Words and Images: Jerusalem Literary Project], oral history archived in the National Library, Hebrew University of Jerusalem, dir. Nathan Beyrack and Eleonora Lev, Jerusalem, December 1992). And see Schwartz, *Kinat ha-yahid*.

20. Michael André Bernstein, *Foregone Conclusions: Against Apocalyptic History* (Berkeley: University of California Press, 1994), p. 58. Bernstein brings as his primary example Appelfeld's two-part novella *Badenheim, 1939*. Book 1 of *The Age of Wonders* is an equally good example.

In his analysis of the early stories of Appelfeld, many of which remain unavailable in English translation, Alan Mintz notes that "Appelfeld intentionally and systematically commits the fallacy of projecting onto the past a knowledge of later events," relating that technique to the author's mythic imagination in which "the ancestral order, as a world suffused with despair, entropy, and disintegration, was always already under the star of the Holocaust." *Hurban: Responses to Catastrophe in Hebrew Literature* (New York: Columbia University Press, 1984), p. 215.

21. Aharon Appelfeld, *Beyond Despair: Three Lectures and a Conversation with Philip Roth* (New York: Fromm International Publishing, 1994), p. 70.

22. For an elaboration of this thesis and a more detailed discussion of the issues it raises, see my "Representing Auschwitz," *History and Memory* 7, no. 2 (winter 1996): 121–54.

23. Mintz's reading of "Hishtanut" suggests a "parody of evolution, in which the gradually acquired adaptive traits in the long struggle for survival are com-

pressed into a few moments" (*Hurban*, p. 221). Though the obvious affinity between this story and Kafka's "Metamorphosis," which Mintz elucidates, renders this story more patently absurd than most of the others, it is not so much a parody of evolution as the substitution of evolution for other paradigms. The story originally appeared in *Be-komat ha-karka'* [On the Ground Floor] (Tel Aviv: Daga, 1968).

24. Aharon Appelfeld, *Masot be-guf rishon* [Essays in the First Person] (Jerusalem: Ha-sifria ha-tzionit, 1979) p. 12. Many of the passages or phrases in *Beyond Despair* are variations on passages that appeared some fifteen years earlier in *Masot be-guf rishon*; I prefer to use my own translations except where otherwise noted.

25. Ibid., p. 36.

26. There is, of course, a sensory-auditory quality to the verbal mechanism, to memory that is almost invariably triggered by the *spoken* word; nevertheless, the process of recovery and the mode of retrieval focus on the associative content of language as *primary* medium. The father in both *Mikhvat ha-or* and *The Age of Wonders* is a writer whose identity is embodied in his language, and it is through language that the struggle of the son manifests itself.

27. Aharon Appelfeld, *Mikhvat ha-or* (Tel Aviv: Ha-kibbutz ha-me'uhad, 1980), p. 30.

28. "I am exercising all the powers of memory but I cannot summon up a thing" (ibid., p. 117).

29. Ibid., p. 31.

30. Appelfeld, *Masot be-guf rishon*, pp. 79–86.

31. Ibid., p. 10. Yiddish was, by Appelfeld's own account, a familiar language in the environment of his childhood, but neither he nor the members of his family were literate in Yiddish (see Appelfeld, interview by Schwartz). Nonetheless, the continued postwar prestige of German over Yiddish may account for Appelfeld's reluctance in essays and fiction to reveal whether his primary spoken language or mother tongue was German or Yiddish.

32. Appelfeld, *Masot be-guf rishon*, p. 63. German is the language of both the killed and the killers, of the mother and her murderers.

33. Appelfeld, *Mikhvat ha-or*, p. 33.

34. Ibid., p. 98.

35. To the extent that childhood memories resonate with the language of sacred texts, Hebrew could also become the avenue of retrieval of the writer's personal past. For Abba Kovner, who had had a traditional religious education before the war, and who survived as leader of the Vilna partisans to become a major postwar Israeli poet, biblical and medieval Hebrew provides the avenue to the most primordial memories. Kovner illuminates this process in describing his own agonized search for a bridge to the dead; he states that as he was completing the fortieth chapter of his long poem *Ahoti ktanah* [My Little Sister], a chasm suddenly opened up before him and, without a rope to pull him across, he could not proceed:

> She stands on the other side and does not hear me, does not understand my language. My God! There must be a language which will make a bridge between us. A language of the living which the dead will also hear and understand.

And then I hear the voice of the syllables like drops of rain which fall on a hot tin roof:
ridudi . . . midadi . . . gdudi . . . kitvi . . . metfi . . . dodi . . . litsvi . . .

li . . . bemarli . . .

I didn't know how they came to me. And I didn't ask at this time or this hour about their origins. Like a woman beaten by a dry season who comes hesitantly toward the first rain, I collected the drops in a small bowl. Still I remember the magic sound of the words while they fell. Like the weeping of many violins.

In *A Canopy in the Desert*, pp. 214–15.

The language of the medieval *piyyut* or liturgical poem, erupting like grace from the depths of the collective unconscious, is a bridge to the poet's private as well as public memory. As Chana Kronfeld has pointed out, for the Zionist kibbutznik that Kovner had become, Yiddish was not an option, despite its being the language of his *sister* (private communication).

36. Appelfeld, *The Age of Wonders*, pp. 146, 152.

37. Ibid., p. 138. I have altered the English translation somewhat to bring it closer to the Hebrew original.

38. Ibid., p. 204.

39. See Y. H. Brenner, "Nerves" ['Atzabim] (1909), tr. Hillel Halkin, in *Eight Great Hebrew Short Novels*, ed. Alan Lelchuk and Gershon Shaked (New York: New American Library, 1983), pp. 31, 32.

40. Leah Goldberg, "Tel Aviv, 1935," in *The Penguin Book of Hebrew Verse*, ed. T. Carmi (Harmondsworth: Penguin, 1981), pp. 553–54.

41. The poem appears in English translation in *The Syrian-African Rift and Other Poems*, a bilingual edition, tr. Harold Schimmel (Philadelphia: Jewish Publication Society, 1980), p. 55; the quote is from an interview with Nissim Calderon that was broadcast on Israeli television (April 12, 1992).

Aharon Appelfeld has invoked the same distinction between *mehagrim* and *'olim*; see "Aharon Appelfeld: kol ha-starim geluyim" [All the Mysteries Are Revealed], interview by Shulamit Gingold-Gilboa, *Iton 77*, no. 46 (October 1983): 28–29.

42. Appelfeld, *Beyond Despair*, p. 70.

43. Ibid., p. 66. See Mintz's description of Appelfeld's short fiction as "set in the indefinite past and evok[ing] the ancestral order of Jewish life in eastern Europe as a time of disintegration and incipient apocalypse" (*Hurban*, p. 207).

44. "Kotsk," folksong of the pilgrimage to the Kotsker rebbe (probably composed no earlier than the 1920s), in *Pearls of Yiddish Song*, comp. Eleanor Gordon Mlotek and Joseph Mlotek (New York: Workmen's Circle, 1988), p. 138 (I have emended the translation somewhat). I am grateful to David Roskies for singing the song and to Dov Noy and Eleanor Mlotek for locating it.

45. Gershon Shaked offers the Exodus from Egypt as the underlying paradigm that structures and explains the survival of Layish, Srul (who is "Israel"), and the handful of other stragglers who complete the journey through this narrative; in every exodus, he argues, it is only a precious, chosen few who arrive in the Promised Land. "Be-khol dor va-dor hayav adam lirot et 'atzmo" [In Each Generation One Must Regard Oneseif], review of *Layish*, *Ha-aretz*, Book Section, July 27, 1994, p. 8. Hanna Yaoz also sees the final destination, Jerusalem, as a kind of refinery that exalts the "new Jew" in the "Jewish state" in opposition to the degradation of the "perennial Jewish refugee." Yaoz, "Ha-mitos shel

ha-palit" [The Myth of the Refugee], 'Iton 77, no. 9 (August–September 1994): 175–76.

46. Aharon Appelfeld, Layish (Jerusalem: Keter, 1994), pp. 51, 97, 100, 147. See Avi Katz, who writes that the relationship between the "goal" or "destination" and the road to it is paradoxical, and that the "basic dynamic of the novel is in its alternating between motifs of progress and of regress [or delay]." Katz, "Ha-kol melukhlakh hutz mi-yerushalayim" [Everything Is Filthy except Jerusalem], Ha-aretz, July 22, 1994, sec. B, p. 8.

47. David Quint, Epic and Empire: Politics and Generic Form from Virgil to Milton (Princeton: Princeton University Press, 1993), p. 9. See chapter 2, above.

48. In its disenchantment, Layish resembles Agnon's brooding, disenchanted novel Tmol shilshom [Just Yesterday] more than his Bilvav yamim [In the Heart of the Seas]. See chapter 3, above.

49. Shmuel Yosef (Agnon) appears on p. 171 of Layish, Yosef Haim (Brenner) on p. 192; the intertext from Bialik's poem "'Al ha-shehita" [On the Slaughter] appears in the mouth of one agonizing woman—"'Im yesh el ba-shamayim, yofi'a miyad"—on p. 142.

50. Ibid., pp. 185, 165.

51. Ibid., p. 148.

52. Aharon Appelfeld, The Iron Tracks, tr. Jeffrey M. Green (New York: Schocken Books, 1998), pp. 4–5. Originally published as Mesilat Barzel (Jerusalem: Maxwell-Macmillan-Keter Publishing House, 1991).

53. The manifest absurdity of the proposal of Philip Roth's character "Philip Roth"—to return the Jews of Ashkenaz to their "ancestral homes" in Kiev, Warsaw, and Czernowitz—simply underscores this point. See my discussion of Operation Shylock in chapter 9.

8.   (RE)IMAGINING EUROPE:
     THE ANACHRONISTIC TALES OF I. B. SINGER

1. Isaac Bashevis Singer, "Gimpel the Fool," tr. Saul Bellow, in Gimpel the Fool and Other Stories (New York: Noonday Press, 1957), pp. 3–22. The story originally appeared in Yiddish as "Gimpl tam," Yidisher Kemfer, March 30, 1945, pp. 17–20. Hereafter these editions will be cited parenthetically in the text as E and Y. As with Sholem Aleichem's Motl, I have chosen to use the Yiddish orthography, Gimpl, instead of the English Gimpel, except when quoting directly from or referring to the English translation.

2. On the concatenation of the wedding feast and rites of mourning, a practice that in times of great upheaval yields to weddings performed in graveyards, see Chana Kronfeld, On the Margins of Modernism: Decentering Literary Dynamics (Berkeley: University of California Press, 1996), p. 218.

3. A good example of such a process is Hillel Halkin's 1987 English translation of stories from Sholem Aleichem's Tevye der milkhiker and Ayznban geshikhtes: ksovim fun a komivoyazher, in which, as we saw in chapter 4 above, untranslated phrases abound; these are, for the most part, prooftexts from Hebrew Scriptures whose unmediated presence signals a culture in the process of recovering its textual authorities. In Halkin's discussion of the sources

(mis)quoted by Sholem Aleichem's narrators, and the dilemmas they pose for the translator, he disarmingly underscores the artifactual status of the auditory by suggesting that for the reader who cannot understand the untranslated Hebrew passages, "there is no need to skip over the Hebrew quotations just because one does not understand them. Read them aloud; savor them; try saying them as Tevye did. There is no way to reproduce in print the exact sights, smells, and tastes of Tevye's world, *but a bit of the sound of it is in these pages.*" Introduction to Sholem Aleichem, *Tevye the Dairyman and the Railroad Stories,* ed. and tr. Hillel Halkin (New York: Schocken Books, 1987), p. xxxi; emphasis mine.

For a whimsical exploration of the mediating function of the translator in recovering lost cultural memory, see Cynthia Ozick's "Envy: or, Yiddish in America," in *The Pagan Rabbi and Other Stories* (New York: Knopf, 1971), pp. 39–100; on the issues of translation relevant to Bashevis Singer's special status among American readers and critics, see Anita Norich, "Isaac Bashevis Singer in America: The Translation Problem," *Judaism* 44, no. 2 (spring 1995): 209–18.

4. H. Leyvik, "Here Lives the Jewish People," in *American Yiddish Poetry,* ed. and trans. Benjamin and Barbara Harshav (Berkeley: University of California Press, 1986), pp. 694–97.

5. For a more extensive discussion of the ironies of acculturation and related issues raised in this chapter, see my "State and Real Estate: Territoriality and the Modern Jewish Imagination," in *Terms of Survival: The Jewish World Since 1945,* ed. Robert S. Wistrich (London: Routledge, 1995), pp. 428–48.

6. There is a two-line, untranslated Yiddish dialogue at the end of the prologue between Genya Shearl, who has just disembarked at Ellis Island with her young son, and her husband Albert, who has been living in America for some months. Its lonely status only underscores the absence of Yiddish in the rest of the narrative and the radical nature of the "translation" that is being enacted throughout. Henry Roth, *Call It Sleep* (1934; reprint, New York: Noonday Press, 1991), p. 16.

It would be interesting to explore the parallels and deviations between Yiddish as the presumed but absent mother tongue in *Call It Sleep* and Yiddish as unacknowledged absence in the prose of Aharon Appelfeld. See above, chapter 7.

7. Ibid., pp. 213, 227.

8. Leslie Fiedler, "Isaac Bashevis Singer; or, The American-ness of the American-Jewish Writer," in *Fiedler on the Roof: Essays on Literature and Jewish Identity* (Boston: David R. Godine, 1991), pp. 77–81. See also Isaac Bashevis Singer's *Lost in America* (New York: Doubleday, 1981), and his stories "Lost" (in *A Crown of Feathers and Other Stories* [New York: Farrar, Straus, and Giroux, 1973], pp. 181–93) and "The Key" (in *A Friend of Kafka and Other Stories* [Harmondsworth: Penguin, 1972], pp. 40–50), in which the protagonists manage to lose things—and themselves—and then to recover them through the human intervention and compassion that, as we will see, become increasingly prevalent in the "American" stories.

9. The term "kaleidoscopic" comes from the 1919 manifesto "Introspectivism," tr. Anita Norich in Benjamin and Barbara Harshav, *American Yiddish Poetry,* pp. 774–84.

10. Saul Bellow, *Herzog* (Harmondsworth: Penguin, 1964), p. 7.

11. "Gimpel the Full" is what Janet Hadda calls him. "Gimpel the Full," *Prooftexts* 10, no. 2 (May 1990): 283–95. Most of the commentators on the Yiddish text have called attention to the nuances in Gimpl's invoking, by turn, the fool as *tam* and as *nar*.

12. Ruth Wisse, *The Schlemiel as Modern Hero* (Chicago: University of Chicago Press, 1971) pp. 39, 4, 44, 54. (On *Benjamin the Third*, see chapter 2, above.) See also Sanford Pinsker, *The Schlemiel as Metaphor: Studies in the Yiddish and American Jewish Novel* (Carbondale: Southern Illinois University Press, 1972), and Ezra Greenspan, *The Schlemiel Comes to America* (Metuchen, N.J.: Scarecrow Press, 1983).

The genealogy of the shlemiel as folk hero remains a subject of some debate. Sander Gilman traces his origin to the projection of the denied self in eighteenth-century Germany that generated a "double" or "anti-image of the enlightened Jew"—an image bearing the "negative qualities" of the vilified Eastern European Jew from which enlightened German Jews could distance themselves. *Jewish Self-Hatred: Anti-Semitism and the Hidden Language of the Jews* (Baltimore: Johns Hopkins University Press, 1986), pp. 107–14. See also Daniel Boyarin, *Unheroic Conduct: The Rise of Heterosexuality and the Invention of the Jewish Man* (Berkeley: University of California, 1997).

Benjamin Harshav, elaborating on the discursive and verbal character of the Yiddish narrative as a kind of backstage version of history, writes that "what was missing in this world in terms of love affairs and murders, etc. was [made up for by] a world rich in talking and free-associating and relating any small event to a universe of collective wisdom and texts. . . . Only Yiddish was suited for this task of creating plausible fictional worlds out of conversation." *The Meaning of Yiddish* (Berkeley: University of California Press, 1990), p. 154.

13. Wisse, *The Schlemiel as Modern Hero*, pp. 125–26.

Because, as G. K. Anderson points out, Shelley could not have known *Peter Schlemihl*, which appeared almost simultaneously with *Queen Mab*, it becomes an even more curious indication of folk culture that Shelley's Ahasuerus is presented as a phantom who does not cast a shadow. *The Legend of the Wandering Jew* (Providence, R.I.: Brown University Press, 1965), p. 184.

14. Isaac Bashevis Singer, *Nobel Lecture* [in English and Yiddish] (New York: Farrar, Straus, and Giroux, 1978), pp. 6–7, 9 (English); pp. 23, 25–26 (Yiddish).

15. Dan Miron, "Passivity and Narration: the Spell of Bashevis Singer," *Judaism* 41, no. 1 (winter 1992): 14–16 (originally published as "Svilut ve-siper: le-kismo shel bashevis-singer," *Yediot ahronot*, August 2, 1991, pp. 22–23). See above, chapter 3, for a discussion of Yitzhak Kummer as Agnon's tragic version of the shlemiel.

16. Jacob Glatshteyn, "Singer's Literary Reputation," in *Recovering the Canon: Essays on Isaac Bashevis Singer*, ed. David Neal Miller (Leiden: E. J. Brill, 1986), p. 148. Glatshteyn writes (not without justification) that "a story by Singer . . . reads better in English than in the original Yiddish." But then he adds that for the "Jewish reader . . . Singer's themes are a distasteful blend of superstition and shoddy mysticism, . . . [of] horror and lust. . . . [He] dehumanizes . . .

his so-called heroes . . . by forcing them to commit the most ugly deeds" (pp. 145–46).

17. Irving Howe, "I. B. Singer," *Encounter*, March 1966, pp. 60–70. Bashevis Singer's appropriation of the "as if" philosophy is articulated as early as 1963. See "Interview with Isaac Bashevis Singer," by Joel Blocker and Richard Elman, *Commentary*, May 1963, p. 365.

18. Isaac Bashevis Singer and Richard Burgin, *Conversations with Isaac Bashevis Singer* (New York: Farrar, Straus, and Giroux, 1985), p. 10.

19. Nathan Alterman, "Mikhtav shel Menakhem-Mendl" (1945), in *Hatur ha-shvi'i* [The Seventh Column] (Tel Aviv: Ha-kibbutz ha-me'uhad, 1977), vol. 1, pp. 12–14.

20. Isaac Bashevis Singer, "The Last Demon," in *Short Friday* (New York: Noonday Press, 1964), pp. 119, 129. Originally published in Yiddish as "Mayse Tishevits," *Forverts*, March 29, 1959.

21. For a social and literary history of these groups, see Ruth Wisse, *A Little Love in Big Manhattan* (Cambridge, Mass.: Harvard University Press, 1988); Judd Teller, *Strangers and Natives: The Evolution of the American Jew from 1921 to the Present* (New York: Delacorte Press, 1968); Benjamin and Barbara Harshav, *American Yiddish Poetry*.

22. For a modern example of anachronism as literary principle, see Itzik Manger, *Medrash Itzik* [Itzik's Midrash] (Jerusalem: Hebrew University, Department of Yiddish Literature, 1969) (published originally in Paris in 1951).

23. Isaac Bashevis Singer [Isaac Varshavski, pseud.], "Problemen fun der yidisher proze in amerike," *Svive* 2 (1943): 12–13. Translated and discussed by Itamar Even Zohar and Chone Shmeruk, "Authentic Language and Authentic Reported Speech: Hebrew vs. Yiddish," *Poetics Today* 11, no. 1 (spring 1990): 162–63. See also Isaac Bashevis [Singer], "Arum der yidisher literature in polyn" [About Yiddish Literature in Poland] *Tsukunft* (1943): 468–75; and Ruth Wisse, "Singer's Paradoxical Progress," *Commentary*, February 1979, pp. 36–38. Not surprisingly, Bashevis Singer's diagnosis was far from popular when it was formulated in 1943, and it contributed to his isolation among his fellow Yiddish writers.

24. Harshav, *The Meaning of Yiddish*, pp. 190–92. Ruth Wisse writes, in a similar vein, that "before the war [Abraham] Sutzkever had been part of the dynamic literary group Yung-Vilne that joked about 'die laydn fun yunge verter' (the sorrows of young words), punning on Goethe's *The Sorrows of Young Werther*. Overnight, surviving Yiddish writers had been turned into custodians of the once-young words of a flourishing language, now pushed to the brink of extinction." Wisse, "The Jewish Writer and the Problem of Evil," in *Terms of Survival: The Jewish World Since 1945*, ed. Robert S. Wistrich (London: Routledge, 1995), pp. 416–17.

25. Jacob Glatshteyn, "I Shall Transport Myself" [Khvel zikh eingloybern] (1953), in Benjamin and Barbara Harshav, *American Yiddish Poetry*, pp. 341–43.

26. Harshav, *The Meaning of Yiddish*, p. 192. Harshav continues to trace the process by which words, which were once contained in space, came to contain all the space there was . . . until the moment when "a new pain arose, the pain of losing hold of the words themselves."

27. Glatshteyn, "I Shall Transport Myself," p. 341.

28. See my "Representing Auschwitz," *History and Memory* 7, no. 2 (winter 1996): 121–54, for a discussion of the epistemological, aesthetic, and ethical ramifications of suspending historical hindsight to construct alternative history.

29. Glatshteyn, "I Shall Transport Myself," p. 343; emphasis mine.

30. For a discussion of the ideological implications for late-twentieth-century cultural studies of "the politics of Jewish memory," see Jonathan Boyarin, *The Storm from Paradise: The Politics of Jewish Memory* (Minneapolis: University of Minnesota Press, 1992); his first chapter focuses on the vestiges of Jewish life in Manhattan's Lower East Side and argues, rather provocatively, that "more has been forgotten in and about the Jewish Lower East Side than virtually any other place or time in America" (p. 2).

31. The negotiation of place is one of the chief privileges and burdens of immigrant and first-generation native writers. See Alfred Kazin, *A Walker in the City* (New York: Harcourt and Brace, 1951), and his discussion, decades later, of the process by which the Lower East Side was appropriated as mythic space; seeking to write a very ambitious "personal epic" about the city of New York, he recalls that he "suddenly opted for a small country, my natal country"— Brownsville. "My New Yorks: Writing *A Walker in the City*," *New York Times Book Review*, August 24, 1986, p. 29.

32. The challenge of creating great fiction . . . lies . . . in the formation of a new, coherent "Social Space," an interdependent cluster of time, space, characters, ideas, and style. . . . The "shtetl" was not the real background of all Yiddish speakers . . . but it was their proverbial, mythological "space," a collective *locus* of a network of social and ideological relationships wrought in the phraseology of Yiddish folklore and literature. . . . Yiddish classical literature used the iconography of the shtetl, its mythological behavior and language, as a microcosm of Jewish nature.

Harshav, *The Meaning of Yiddish*, pp. 153–54, 94–95.

33. Teller, *Strangers and Natives*, p. 262.

34. On Chagall as literalizer of such Yiddish idioms as *a ku oyfn dakh* (cow on the roof), see Benjamin Harshav, "The Role of Language in Modern Art: On Texts and Subtexts in Chagall's Paintings," *Modernism and Modernity* 1, no. 2 (April 1994): 56–63.

35. I have dealt with the debate over the levels of hindsight or denial that inform postwar representations of prewar Jewish life earlier in this book; see chapter 7. In connection with Bashevis Singer, the issue was also raised in my book *By Words Alone: The Holocaust in Literature* (Chicago: University of Chicago Press, 1980), pp. 123–26, and has been both debated and reinforced in Hana Wirth-Nesher's *City Codes: Reading the Modern Urban Novel* (Cambridge: Cambridge University Press, 1996), pp. 30–47. Wirth-Nesher considers *The Family Moskat*, which ends in Warsaw right after Germany's invasion of Poland, to be an urban novel that contains, in its symbolic language, intimations of coming events. The question of whether the burden of consciousness rests in the author's voice or the reader's ear cannot be answered of fiction not saturated with hindsight; here, however, it not only arises but takes on different resonance in the different interpretive communities addressed in the original and in the translated versions of the novel. In English the novel ends with the ominous phrase "Death

is the Messiah," which could certainly be seen as a foreshadowing of the events of the succeeding years; the Yiddish is far more ambiguous. For the discussion of the different endings and their different constituencies, see Milton Hindus, "A Monument with a Difference," review of *The Family Moskat, New York Times Book Review*, March 14, 1965, pp. 4, 44–45; I. Saposnik, "Translating the Family Moskat: The Metamorphosis of a Novel," *Yiddish* 1, no. 2 (fall 1973): 26–37; and Susan A. Slotnick, "*The Family Moskat* and the Tradition of the Yiddish Family Saga," in Miller, *Recovering the Canon*, pp. 24–38.

36. Melvin Bukiet, *Stories of an Imaginary Childhood* (Evanston, Ill.: Northwestern University Press, 1992); Arieh Eckstein, *Doda Ester* [Auntie Esther] (Jerusalem: Keter, 1992); and Allen Hoffman, *Small Worlds* (New York: Abbeville Press, 1996).

37. Signs of the shlemiel's embattled state in the last decades of this century can be measured in Ruth Wisse's own distancing from the normative implications of his survival. With increasing suspicion she has aligned him to the liberal cause and to speech acts viewed not as a mandated response to powerlessness but as a chosen alternative to the exercise of power; she thus has increasingly come to regard the shlemiel not as the hero whom she once heralded but as the enemy of the historical renaissance of the Jewish people—casting a new, cold light on her own cultural project. The narrative device of "rendering action as speech, and . . . transforming events of which Jews were so frequently the victims into a controlled interpretation of those events, had created the illusion of cultural endurance and cohesion," she wrote in 1989;

> But my study of Yiddish literature suggested that there was another side as well to this creative affirmation. . . .
> Locked as they are within their own Jewish language, the characters bodied forth in Yiddish writing, and to a certain extent the authors who created those characters, can become so internal and self-referring as to ignore objective historical circumstances altogether and to a disastrous extent. A device for speaking comfortably about the world can become a device for solipsistically shutting out the world—which does not, in consequence, cease to exist.
>
> "Jewish Guilt and Israeli Writers," *Commentary*, January 1989, p. 27.

In her monograph on I. L. Peretz (*I. L. Peretz and the Making of Modern Jewish Culture* [Seattle: University of Washington Press, 1991]), Wisse traces the status of that fin de siècle Yiddish writer as one of the primary reshapers or reinventors of modern Jewish culture. In her analysis, many of the modern folktales by Peretz "offer . . . reassurance that the liberal ethic has taken over from the Divine imperative. . . . Through . . . manifestations of goodness, the Jews also triumph over their enemies. . . . Implicit in Peretz's tales . . . is an idea of Jewish moral potency that compensates for Jewish political impotence" (pp. 85, 86). We have here a good example of the breakdown of the tension between art and life when Auschwitz becomes the terminal referent, applied anachronistically, for modes of representation of the past. While this is implicit throughout the monograph, in the last lines Wisse's sense of the utter futility of all cultural Jewish projects not founded on a vision of a territorial polity with armed force becomes explicit: "While Peretz was shaping an earthly culture that outrivaled heaven's in its goodness, others were shaping an earthly culture that outrivaled hell's in

its venom. The schoolchildren of Vilna and of all Poland were murdered with
the words of Peretz on their lips" (p. 109).

38. Isaac Bashevis Singer, "The Little Shoemakers," tr. Isaac Rosenfeld, in
Gimpel the Fool, p. 83; "Di kleyne shusterlekh," *Tsukunft* 50, no. 4 (April 1945):
233.

39. Ibid., 95–99 (English); 238–39 (Yiddish). Like Sholem Aleichem's character, Abba appropriates Abraham's role as *wanderer*, not as *halutz*.

40. Ibid., 102 (English); 240 (Yiddish).

41. For discussions of Jewish pilgrimages, especially to memorial sites dedicated to victims of the Holocaust, see James E. Young, *The Texture of Memory:
Holocaust Memorials and Meaning* (New Haven: Yale University Press, 1993);
Jack Kugelmass, "Why We Go to Poland: Holocaust Tourism as Secular Ritual,"
in *The Art of Memory: Holocaust Memorials in History*, ed. James E. Young,
exhibition catalogue (New York: Prestel, 1994), pp. 175–84. "In the face of historical and social discontinuity, American Jewish memory culture has frozen
Poland in time and turned its inhabitants into a vast *tableau vivant*," Kugelmass
writes (p. 181).

The important distinction between American and Israeli pilgrimages to Eastern Europe has been the subject of some discussion among cultural anthropologists and sociologists. The pilgrimage to the ruins of Jewish Europe and to
the death camps by Israeli youth just before their induction into the army is constructed around myths of national solidarity. My emphasis here is on pilgrimage
as a diasporic—i.e., in this context, primarily American Jewish—phenomenon.

42. Donald Horne, *The Great Museum: The Re-Presentation of History*
(London: Pluto Press, 1984), pp. 1, 17.

43. Affirmation of the pristine in America's natural landscape was accompanied by the self-conscious preservation of a sense of the past in the European
landscape; modern American tourism to Europe is likened by Horne to a medieval pilgrimage: "As well as the intrinsic holiness of venerated objects, it also
offers cults of the dead—at the tombs, monuments and museums of secular saints"
(*The Great Museum*, p. 17). In his exhaustive study of memory and memory-
sites, *The Past is a Foreign Country* (Cambridge: Cambridge University Press,
1985), David Lowenthal quotes Henry Ward Beecher's explanation of why he
had wept at Kenilworth Castle: "I had never seen a ruin" (p. 114).

Relics become increasingly significant as the keys to the past become increasingly remote to a present-oriented culture in twentieth-century Europe and
America; "uneasiness with the present was so great that, for most of the nineteenth century, the past was nostalgically plundered to provide a modern sense
of dignity and meaning," writes Horne (p. 22). "Unwilling or unable to incorporate the legacy of the past into our own creative acts, we concentrate instead on saving its remaining vestiges," adds Lowenthal. "The less integral the
role of the past in our lives, the more imperative the urge to preserve its relics"
(p. 384).

44. Umberto Eco, *Travels in Hyperreality*, tr. William Weaver (London: Pan
Books, 1986), p. 11. Replication of the past serves, in Eco's view, an American
"philosophy of immortality as duplication. . . . For historical information to be

absorbed, it has to assume the aspect of a reincarnation." His attention to wax
museums underscores the equal status granted to historical and imaginary
figures in the American popular imagination: Mozart and Tom Sawyer, Lincoln
and Dr. Faustus (pp. 6–7, 14).

In an interesting argument against such postmodern deployments of "hyperreality" and reproduction to explain American culture, Edward M. Bruner claims
that "in the work of Baudrillard and Eco about America, despite their theoretical arguments against origins, there is an implicit original, and it is Europe, for
America is seen as essentially a satellite of Europe." Bruner, "Abraham Lincoln
as Authentic Reproduction: A Critique of Postmodernism," *American Anthropologist* 96, no. 2 (June 1994): 398. That statement, though perhaps less appli-
cable to Americans more removed from their source, is particularly true for American Jews who both are more proximate to the European "original" *and* are facing
it in its ruin. Bruner's essay is relevant to literary representations of the shtetl
that are also judged as artifacts. His study of New Salem, Illinois, and other reconstructed sites leads him to endorse Clifford Geertz's view that "'it is the copy-
ing that originates,'" and he argues further that the past is "continually being
constructed in an endless process of production and reproduction . . . [and that]
what is called the copy changes our view of the original"(p. 407). Bruner's critique of Eco offers a definition of *reproduction* that is consistent with what I
have been calling the "diasporic" mode. By comparing *American* with American *Jewish* pilgrimage to Europe, and by elevating *reproduction* to an authentic
cultural practice, I am claiming that what American Jews are doing in their pilgrimages to Eastern Europe is a profoundly Jewish as well as a profoundly American act.

9.   THE GRAPES OF ROTH: DIASPORISM
FROM PORTNOY TO SHYLOCK

1. Cynthia Ozick, "Toward a New Yiddish," in *Art and Ardor: Essays* (New
York: E. P. Dutton, 1983), pp. 173–74; originally published in *Judaism* 19, no.
3 (summer 1970): 264–82.

2. In 1970, Ozick had identified the "nineteenth century novel at its best" as
"Judaized," concerned with "History" and "Idea," with will and commandment.
What qualifies as "Jewish" for her is whatever "touches on the liturgical," as
distinguished from the sacramental or idolatrous that she identifies with the "new
novel" and with (nonliturgical) poetry generally. Identifying Exile with narrative brought Ozick close to a diasporist position, even if she did not take the next
step toward acknowledging the danger of a sacramental, idolatrous attitude toward Hebrew in Israel, where Language and Land converge. That is what makes
Ozick's disclaimer, written twelve years later, so consequential; in a few pages
appended to the reprinted essay, she admits to being "no longer so tenderly dis-
posed to the possibility of a New Yiddish—which was, anyhow, an invention, a
literary conceit calculated to dispel pessimism." In contrast, she claims, Hebrew
has the status of being the "original vessel for the revolution of human conscience," as a result of which "all languages have a Hebrew-speaking capacity"

(ibid., pp. 164, 169, 151–52). Ozick's distancing herself from her earlier diasporic position is analogous to Ruth Wisse's in ways that have political as well as cultural ramifications. See chapter 8, above.

3. The most monumental study of that shelf of good Jewish books is Irving Howe's *World of Our Fathers* (New York: Harcourt Brace Jovanovich, 1976). See also John Hollander, "The Question of American Jewish Poetry," and Robert Alter, "Jewish Dreams and Nightmares," both collected in *What Is Jewish Literature?* ed. Hana Wirth-Nesher (Philadelphia: Jewish Publication Society, 1994), pp. 36–52 and 53–66; and Harold Bloom, "Free and Broken Tablets: The Cultural Prospects of American Jewry," in *Agon: Towards a Theory of Revisionism* (New York: Oxford University Press, 1982), pp. 318–29.

4. See Philip Roth, *Portnoy's Complaint* (New York: Bantam, 1969), and his subsequent essays defending his idea of the Jewish character in contemporary fiction, especially "Imagining Jews" and "Writing about Jews," collected in *Reading Myself and Others* (New York: Bantam, 1977), pp. 215–24, 149–70.

5. Philip Roth, *Operation Shylock: A Confession* (New York: Simon and Schuster, 1993), p. 359. Subsequent references to this edition will be made parenthetically in the text.

6. See Hillel Halkin, "How to Read Philip Roth," *Commentary*, February 1994, p. 46.

7. Philip Roth, *The Counterlife* (New York: Farrar, Straus, and Giroux, 1986), pp. 319–20.

8. Halkin, "How to Read Philip Roth," p. 48.

9. Philip Roth, *The Ghost Writer*, in *Zuckerman Bound: A Trilogy and Epilogue* (New York: Farrar, Straus, and Giroux, 1985), p. 158. In *The Anatomy Lesson*, Nathan feels guilty for the popularity of *Carnovsky* [= *Portnoy*], "for the family portrait the whole country had assumed to be his, for the tastelessness that had affronted millions and the shamelessness that had enraged his tribe." In ibid., p. 440.

10. Roth, *Portnoy's Complaint*, pp. 271, 268, 265, 124, 269.

11. Paul Breines, *Tough Jews: Political Fantasies and the Moral Dilemma of American Jewry* (New York: Basic Books, 1990), p. 3. For a recent discussion of the shlemiel and sexual impotence as related to works of American Jewish writers, entertainers, and filmmakers such as Philip Roth and Woody Allen, see David Biale, *Eros and the Jews: From Biblical Israel to Contemporary America* (Berkeley: University of California Press, 1997), pp. 204–30. Ruth Wisse's *Schlemiel as Modern Hero* (Chicago: University of Chicago Press, 1971) and the discourse that it generated define not only the place of a major Yiddish trope, but also the centrality of the shlemiel as radical diasporic alternative to the cultures of power in which Jews have lived. See chapter 8, above.

12. Compare, for example, the protagonist's heroic fantasy of killing the czar at the end of *The Fixer* and Herzog's vengeful fantasy of killing Gersbach in *Herzog* with the actual, gratuitous violence in such Hebrew narratives as A. B. Yehoshua's "Evening in Yatir Village" and Amos Oz's "Nomad and Viper" and *My Michael*.

13. The review was by D. M. Thomas and illustrated by Raul Colon; see "Face to Face with His Double," *New York Times Book Review*, March 7, 1993, p. 1.

14. Philip Roth, "The Prague Orgy," in *Zuckerman Bound*, pp. 761–62.

15. See Roth, "The Prague Orgy"; "I Always Wanted You to Admire My Fasting; Or, Looking at Kafka," in *Reading Myself and Others*; and *The Ghost Writer*. Hana Wirth-Nesher discusses Roth's search for "literary fathers" and for a connection, on his own terms, with the "more compelling drama of his fellow Jews in Europe." Wirth-Nesher, "From Newark to Prague: Roth's Place in the American Jewish Literary Tradition," in Wirth-Nesher, *What Is Jewish Literature?* pp. 216–29. Norman Finkelstein enlarges the discussion to delineate a "post-Enlightenment metanarrative of nostalgia" that Roth both endorses and parodies. See his *Ritual of New Creation: Jewish Tradition and Contemporary Literature* (Albany: State University of New York Press, 1992), p. 135.

16. That slander can kill has been amply demonstrated in Israel at the end of our century. The Aramaic curse (*pulsa de nura*) that had been declared in certain rabbinic circles in the fall of 1995 was understood by the literalizers as a contract for Itzhak Rabin's head—effectively overriding the disclaimer that accompanies extreme halakhic rulings to the effect that they are to be understood as only theoretically binding (*le-halakha ve-lo le-ma'aseh*). The delicate balance between theory and practice (or between "legal fictions" and praxis) that has been violated in orthodox and ultra-orthodox circles has produced monstrous forms of life in "sacred" time and place.

17. Thomas G. Pavel, *Fictional Worlds* (Cambridge, Mass.: Harvard University Press, 1986), p. 16.

18. Ibid., pp. 64, 143.

19. One of the most persuasive discussions of the "wandering meanings and textual homelands" that form a postmodern "culture of exile" in America is Finkelstein, *The Ritual of New Creation*, pp. 138–40.

20. Roth figures prominently in R. B. Kitaj's *First Diasporist Manifesto* (London: Thames and Hudson, 1989). Roth's portrait is accompanied by a quote from *The Counterlife* that serves as the epigraph for the prologue: "The poor bastard had Jew on the brain." Later in the essay, Kitaj refers to "my buddy Philip Roth" (pp. 8–9, 79).

21. R. B. Kitaj, "Kitaj Interviewed by Richard Morphet," in *R. B. Kitaj: A Retrospective*, ed. Richard Morphet (London: Rizzoli, 1994), p. 53. I must stress here that Kitaj's verbal articulation of his theories, especially in the *First Diasporist Manifesto*, does not have the immediacy and evocative power of his paintings.

22. Kitaj's quoted sources include Nietzsche and Gershom Scholem. See also the epigraph on the Jews quoted from Charles Peguy: "Being elsewhere, the great vice of this race, the great secret virtue, the great vocation of this people" (*First Diaspora Manifesto*, pp. 73, 117, 113).

23. Ibid., pp. 27, 75; and Kitaj, "Kitaj Interviewed by Richard Morphet," p. 54.

24. Kitaj, *First Diasporist Manifesto*, pp. 29, 33, 35.

25. Elliott Horowitz, "The Rite to Be Reckless: On the Perpetration and Interpretation of Purim Violence," *Poetics Today* 15, no. 1 (spring 1994): 9–54; see above, chapter 4.

26. See Zali Gurevitch and Gideon Aran, " 'Al ha-makom" [On Place], *Alpayim* 4 (1991): 9–45; the English version appeared as "The Land of Israel: Myth

and Phenomenon," in *Reshaping the Past: Jewish History and the Historians*, ed. Jonathan Frankel, Studies in Contemporary Jewry 10 (New York: Oxford University Press, 1994), pp. 195–210. And see the introduction to this volume.

27. Amnon Raz-Karkotzkin, "Galut be-tokh ribonut: le-bikorit 'shlilat ha-galut' ba-tarbut ha-yisraelit" [Exile within a Sovereign State: A Critique of the "Negated Exile" in Israeli Culture], *Teoria u-vikoret*, no. 4 (fall 1993): 34–38.

CONCLUSION: THE IMAGINATION OF RETURN AND THE RETURN OF IMAGINATION

1. As an attempt to chart the Jewish poetics of exile and homecoming, my own agenda is, admittedly, no less ideologically charged than that of those who argue (from the precincts of postcolonialist dogma) that "liberation as an intellectual mission . . . has now shifted from the settled, established, and domesticated dynamics of culture to its unhoused, decentered, and exilic energies," that "it is from those who have suffered the sentence of history—subjugation, domination, diaspora, displacement—that we learn our most enduring lessons for living and thinking." See, respectively, Edward Said, *Culture and Imperialism* (New York: Knopf, 1993), p. 332; and Homi Bhabha, "Postcolonial Criticism," in *Redrawing the Boundaries: The Transformation of English and American Literary Studies*, ed. Stephen Greenblatt and Giles Gunn (New York: Modern Language Association of America, 1992), p. 438. See also Jean-François Lyotard, *Heidegger and the "jews,"* tr. Andreas Michel and Marc Roberts (Minneapolis: University of Minnesota Press, 1990); Daniel and Jonathan Boyarin's discussion of the "allegorical Jew" in "Diaspora: Generation and the Ground of Jewish Identity," *Critical Inquiry* 19, no. 4 (summer 1993): 697–701, and their edited volume *Jews and Other Differences: The New Jewish Cultural Studies* (Minneapolis: University of Minnesota Press, 1997); David Biale, Michael Galchinsky, and Susannah Heschel, eds., *Insider/Outsider: American Jews and Multiculturalism* (Berkeley: University of California Press, 1998), especially the essay by Michael Gluzman, "Modernism and Exile: A View from the Margins," pp. 231–53; and Bryan Cheyette and Laura Marcus, eds., *Modernity, Culture and "the Jew"* (Stanford: Stanford University Press, 1998).

In the 1950s the voice of "Diasporism" was most whimsically heard in Grace Paley's short stories. "I believe in the Diaspora, not only as a fact but as a tenet," says the narrator of "The Used-Boy Raiser":

> I'm against Israel on technical grounds. I'm very disappointed that they decided to become a nation in my lifetime. I believe in the Diaspora. After all, they are the chosen people. Don't laugh. They really are. But once they're huddled in one little corner of a desert, they're like anyone else: Frenchies, Italians, temporal nationalities. Jews have one hope only—to remain a remnant in the basement of world affairs—no, I mean something else—a splinter in the toe of civilizations, a victim to aggravate the conscience. . . . I sighed. My needle was now deep in the clouds which were pearl gray and late afternoon. I am only trying to say that they aren't meant for geographies but for history. They are not supposed to take up space but to continue in time.

> In *The Little Disturbances of Man* (New York: Viking Press, 1959), pp. 132–32.

2. *Hurva*, or ruin, is cognate with the designation for the destruction of the Temple of Solomon (*hurban*); it is also the Yiddish word (*hurbn*) for the Holo-

caust, and enters in its Arabic form into the Israeli dialogue on the expulsion and occupation of the Arabs: "*Hirbet* Hiz'ah" is the title of a 1949 story by S. Yizhar.

3. Pinkhes Kohn, "Oysterlishe minhogim fun yidn in Samarkand" [Outlandish Practices of the Jews of Samarkand], *Der Moment*, no. 144 (June 22, 1928): 6. I am grateful to Vera Solomon for this reference. For analogous practices elsewhere in Europe, see Sylvie-Anne Goldberg, *Crossing the Yabok: Illness and Death in Ashkenazi Judaism in Sixteenth- through Nineteenth-Century Prague*, tr. Carol Cosman (Berkeley: University of California Press, 1996).

4. S. Y. Agnon, "Tehila," tr. Walter Lever, in *Firstfruits: A Harvest of 25 Years of Israeli Writing*, ed. James A. Michener (Philadelphia: Jewish Publication Society, 1973), p. 39.

5. No matter where we start our investigation—with the Jebusites, the Hebrews, the Romans, the Saracens, the Crusaders—one group's claim comes at the expense of every other's. Jerusalem remembers them all and in her own way contains them all. It is we who insist on exclusive rights, erasing the graffiti of our predecessors in order to cover the walls with our own name and our own story. The most dramatic recent signs of that mutual effacement are the graffiti-covered walls of the Intifada.

6. See Yaron Ezrahi, *Rubber Bullets: Power and Conscience in Modern Israel* (New York: Farrar, Straus, and Giroux, 1997).

The tension between these two aesthetics is nowhere more dramatically enacted than at the scene of a suicide bombing in Israel. The cameras that focus on body parts strewn all over the streets and on the blood in the intersections are not only engaged in reportage; they allow for an aesthetics of fragmentation, of horror. At the same time, however, members of the Jewish Burial Society in bright yellow vests are collecting body parts that must be buried with the mutilated corpses in order to ensure the aesthetics of the whole that is associated with the sacrificial representation of death and the resurrection of the body.

7. Thomas G. Pavel, *Fictional Worlds* (Cambridge, Mass.: Harvard University Press, 1986), p. 81.

8. Kendall Walton is quoted in ibid., p. 86.

9. See Georges Van Den Abbeele, *Travel as Metaphor: From Montaigne to Rousseau* (Minneapolis: University of Minnesota Press, 1992), discussed in chapter 3, above.

10. Good illustrations of the ripple effect can be found in revisionist readings of major canonic poems such as "Ve-ulai" by the poet Rahel and "Magash ha-kesef" [The Silver Platter] by Natan Alterman. Rahel, the official "pioneer poet" of the 1920s, looking back on (not at) her beloved Lake Kinneret, asked "were you there or did I dream a dream?" Rachel Bluvstein, *Shirat Rahel* [The Poetry of Rachel], 27th ed. (Tel Aviv: Davar, 1978–79), p. 79. For a highly idiosyncratic but interesting interpretation of this poem, see "Was It Only a Dream?" in *Flowers of Perhaps: Selected Poems of Ra'hel*, tr. Robert Friend (London: Menard Press, 1995), p. 31. Her recall, I believe, was not merely dimmed by time but also subverted by the profound skepticism that relativized even as it romanticized the reclaimed Sea of Galilee. But over the years, this poem, set to music, became so embalmed in the sentimental culture in Israel that its subversive implications were vitiated. For a survey and critique of the discussion on the role

of women poets in the canon formation of Hebrew literature, see Michael Gluzman, "The Exclusion of Women from Hebrew Literary History," *Prooftexts* 11,
no. 3 (September 1991): 259–78.

Alterman's "Magash ha-kesef," written in the very heat of the Israeli War
of Independence and published on December 19, 1947, bears as its motto a
quote from Chaim Weizman—that no people receives a state on a silver platter. The entire Nation, personified (and feminized) as *ha-uma*, stands dressed
in its finery awaiting the ceremony that will consecrate its victory and its
sacrifice. But the liturgical status of this poem in the official commemorative
rituals and curricula of the State of Israel over the decades since the war is tied
to the ceremony that *never* took place within the confines of the poem; and it
is this performative function that has safeguarded its subversive subtext from
scrutiny for nearly half a century. Like Rahel's "Ve-ulai," it is a poem declaimed,
recited, intoned by generations of Israelis—and *never really heard*. The penultimate lines of the poem are spoken by the anonymous girl and boy (*na'ara va-
na'ar*) who stumble to the podium weary, wounded, and filthy in their tattered
uniforms to answer the Nation's question, "Who are you?" With their final
breath they declare, "we are the silver platter on which is given to you the Jewish State." "Magash ha-kesef" appeared in Alterman's column, "Ha-tur ha-
shivi'i" [The Seventh Column], in *Davar*, December 19, 1947, and is collected
in *Ha-tur ha-shivi'i* (Tel Aviv: Ha-kibbutz ha-me'uhad, 1977), vol. 1, pp.
154–55. For a revisionist reading of this poem, see Dan Miron, *Mul ha-ah ha-
shotek* [Facing the Silent Brother] (Jerusalem: Keter, 1992), pp. 63–88. And
see the resounding critique of Miron's readings in Itzhak Laor, *Anu kotvim
otakh, moledet* [Narratives with No Natives] (Tel Aviv: Ha-kibbutz ha-
me'uhad, 1995), pp. 199–215.

As major sites in the narrative of Israel's homecoming, the lake and the silver platter become, over time, rippled or tarnished reflections of the static nar-
cissism of an earlier epoch/epic.

11. Homi K. Bhabha, "DissemiNation: Time, Narrative, and the Margins of
the Modern Nation," in *Nation and Narration*, ed. Homi K. Bhabha (London:
Routledge, 1990), p. 316.

12. See Anton Shammas's Hebrew novel, *Arabeskot* (1986), tr. as *Arabesques*
by Vivian Eden (New York: Harper and Row, 1988), and its reception in Israel.
For a discussion of Shammas's writing as exemplifying a "littérature mineure"
in Hebrew, see Hanan Hever, "Hebrew in an Israeli Arab Hand: Six Miniatures
on Anton Shammas's *Arabesques*," in *The Nature and Context of Minority Discourse*, ed. Abdul R. JanMohamed and David Lloyd (Oxford: Oxford University Press: 1990), pp. 264–93; and Rivka Feldhai-Brenner, "In Search of Identity: the Israeli-Arab Artist in Anton Shammas's *Arabesques*," *PMLA* 108, no.
3 (May 1993): 431–45.

13. "The poet in Avot Yeshurun is a *weltmensch*," writes Harold Schimmel
in his introduction to a collection of Avot Yeshurun's poems;

> the poet as poor, wandering Jew, ragman, collector of assorted junk (*alte sachen*). . . .
> The pungent thingness of objects in Avot Yeshurun's poetry keeps its loyalty to Yiddish.
> Hebrew seems not nearly so weighted in the naming of objects. A clearer, sharper, harsher
> light lent *things* in the world of biblical literature their proper perspective. They were dis-

posed in a real and native landscape, they held shadow potential, and their colors blurred into the soft full spectrum of gray as the light from above of the great luminary descended. There, objects were tools or incidents in the lives and hands of the heroes.

> Introduction to Avot Yeshurun, *The Syrian-African Rift and Other Poems*, tr. Harold Schimmel, bilingual edition (Philadelphia: Jewish Publication Society, 1980), pp. xvii, xii.

The loyalty to Yiddish, preserved through its objects, and the perspectival thingness of biblical Hebrew are supplemented by the palpability and pathos of Arabic in Avot Yeshurun's poetry.

14. Pavel, *Fictional Worlds*, pp. 84–85.

Bibliography

Abbeele, Georges Van Den. *Travel as Metaphor: From Montaigne to Rousseau.* Minneapolis: University of Minnesota Press, 1992.

Aberbach, David. "Homosexual Fantasies in Mendele and Agnon." In *Tradition and Trauma: Studies in the Fiction of S. Y. Agnon,* ed. David Patterson and Glenda Abramson. Boulder, Colo.: Westview Press, 1994.

———. *Realism, Caricature, and Bias: The Fiction of Mendele Mocher Sefarim.* London: Littman Library of Jewish Civilization, 1993.

Abramovitsh, S. Y. [Mendele Mokher Sfarim]. *Ale verk fun Mendele moykher sforim (S. Y. Abramovitsh)* [The Complete Works of Mendele Moykher Sforim (S. Y. Abramovitsh); Yiddish]. Cracow: Farlag Mendele, 1911.

———. *Kol kitvei Mendele mokher sfarim* [The Complete Works of Mendele Mokher Sfarim]. Tel Aviv: Dvir, 1957.

———. *Mas'ot Benyamin ha-shlishi* [The Travels of Benjamin the Third]. Tel Aviv: Dvir, 1950.

———. "Of Bygone Days." In *A Shtetl and Other Yiddish Novellas,* ed. Ruth Wisse. New York: Behrman House, 1973.

———. *Tales of Mendele the Book Peddler: Fishke the Lame and Benjamin the Third.* Ed. Dan Miron and Ken Frieden, tr. Ted Gorelick and Hillel Halkin. New York: Schocken Books, 1996.

———. "The Travels of Benjamin the Third." In *The Shtetl.* Ed. and tr. Joachim Neugroschel. New York: Richard Marek, 1979.

Adams, Percy G. *Travel Literature and the Evolution of the Novel.* Lexington: University Press of Kentucky, 1983.

Adorno, T. W. *Aesthetic Theory.* Tr. C. Lenhardt. London: Routledge and Kegan Paul, 1970.

———. *Minima Moralia: Reflections from Damaged Life.* Tr. E. F. N. Jephcott. London: New Left Books, 1974.

———. *Prisms*. Tr. Samuel and Shierry Weber. London: Neville Spearman, 1967.

Agnon, S. Y. *'Ad hena* [This Far]. Jerusalem: Schocken, 1974.

———. *Bilvav yamim: sippur aggadah shel S. Y. Agnon* [In the Heart of the Seas: A Legend by S. Y. Agnon]. From Sippurim shel Eretz Yisrael [Stories from the Land of Israel]. In *Elu ve-elu* [These and Those]. Jerusalem: Schocken, 1971.

———. *A Book That Was Lost and Other Stories*. Ed. with intro. by Alan Mintz and Anne Golomb Hoffman. New York: Schocken Books, 1995.

———. *Bridal Canopy*. [Hakhnasat kallah]. Tr. I. M. Lask. New York: Literary Guild of America, 1937.

———. *Hakhnasat kallah* [Bridal Canopy]. Jerusalem: Schocken, 1974.

———. *In the Heart of the Seas: A Story of a Journey to the Land of Israel*. Tr. I. M. Lask. New York: Schocken Books, 1947.

———. *Ir u-melo'ah* [An Entire City]. Tel Aviv: Schocken, 1973.

———. *Oreah nata la-lun* [A Guest for the Night]. Jerusalem: Schocken, 1939.

———. "Tehila." Tr. Walter Lever. In *Firstfruits: A Harvest of 25 Years of Israeli Writing*. Ed. James A. Michener. Greenwich, Conn.: Fawcett, 1973.

———. *Tmol shilshom* [Just Yesterday]. Jerusalem: Schocken, 1971.

———. *Twenty-One Stories*. Ed. Nahum Glatzer. New York: Schocken Books, 1970.

Albright, Daniel. *Representation and the Imagination: Beckett, Kafka, Nabokov, and Schoenberg*. Chicago: University of Chicago Press, 1981.

Alcalay, Amiel. *After Jews and Arabs: Remaking Levantine Culture*. Minneapolis: University of Minnesota Press, 1993.

Alter, Robert. *Hebrew and Modernity*. Bloomington: Indiana University Press, 1994.

———. "How Important Are the Dead Sea Scrolls?" *Commentary*, February 1992, pp. 34–41.

———. *The Invention of Hebrew Prose: Modern Fiction and the Language of Realism*. Seattle: University of Washington Press, 1988.

———. "Jewish Dreams and Nightmares." In *What Is Jewish Literature?* ed. Hana Wirth-Nesher. Philadelphia: Jewish Publication Society, 1994.

———. "A Problem of Horizons." In *Contemporary Israeli Literature*, ed. Elliott Anderson. Philadelphia: Jewish Publication Society, 1977.

———, ed. *Modern Hebrew Literature*. New York: Berman House, 1975.

Alterman, Natan. "Magash ha-kesef" [The Silver Platter]. *Davar*, December 19, 1947. Reprinted in *Ha-tur ha-shivi'i* [The Seventh Column], vol. 1 (Tel Aviv: Ha-kibbutz ha-me'uhad, 1977).

———. "Mikhtav shel Menakhem-Mendl" [Letter from Menakhem Mendl]. *Davar*, March 9, 1945. Reprinted in *Ha-tur ha-shivi'i* [The Seventh Column], vol. 1 (Tel Aviv: Ha-kibbutz ha-me'uhad, 1977).

Altmann, Alexander, ed. *Biblical and Other Studies*. Cambridge, Mass.: Harvard University Press, 1963.

Améry, Jean. *At the Mind's Limits: Contemplations by a Survivor on Auschwitz and Its Realities*. Tr. Sidney Rosenfeld and Stella P. Rosenfeld. Bloomington: Indiana University Press, 1980.

Amichai, Yehuda. *Lo me-akhshav lo mi-kan* [Not of This Time, Not of This Place]. Jerusalem: Schocken, 1963.

———. *Poems of Jerusalem and Love Poems.* Bilingual edition. New York: Sheep Meadow Press, 1996.

———. *Selected Poetry of Yehuda Amichai.* Ed. and tr. Chana Bloch and Stephen Mitchell. New York: Harper and Row, 1986.

———. *Songs of Jerusalem.* Bilingual edition. Jerusalem: Schocken, 1987.

———. *Time: Poems.* New York: Harper and Row, 1979.

———. *Zman* [Time]. Tel Aviv: Schocken, 1977.

Anderson, Benedict. *Imagined Communities: Reflections on the Origin and Spread of Nationalism.* Rev. ed. London: Verso, 1991.

Anderson, Elliott, ed. *Contemporary Israeli Literature.* Philadelphia: Jewish Publication Society, 1977.

Anderson, George K. *The Legend of the Wandering Jew.* Providence, R.I.: Brown University Press, 1965.

Antin, Mary. *From Plonsk to Boston.* 1899. Reprint, New York: M. Wiener, 1986.

Appelfeld, Aharon. *Adanai ha-nahar* [Sills of the River]. Tel Aviv: Ha-kibbutz ha-me'uhad, 1971.

———. *The Age of Wonders.* Tr. Dalya Bilu. New York: Washington Square Press, 1981.

———. "Aharon Appelfeld: kol ha-starim geluyim" [All the Mysteries Are Revealed]. Interview by Shulamit Gingold-Gilboa. *Iton 77,* no. 46 (October 1983): 28–29.

———. *'Ashan* [Smoke]. Jerusalem: Akhshav, 1962.

———. *Ba-gai ha-poreh* [In the Fertile Valley]. Jerusalem: Schocken, 1964.

———. *Beyond Despair: Three Lectures and a Conversation with Philip Roth.* New York: Fromm International Publishing, 1994.

———. *Ha-kutonet ve-ha-pasim* [The Coat and the Stripes]. Tel Aviv: Ha-kibbutz ha-me'uhad, 1983.

———. *The Immortal Bartfuss.* Tr. Jeffrey M. Green. New York: Weidenfeld and Nicolson, 1988.

———. Interview by Yigal Schwartz. In "Milim u-demuyot: proyekt ha-sifrut shel Yerushalayim" [Words and Images: Jerusalem Literary Project]. Oral history archived in the National Library, Hebrew University of Jerusalem. Dir. Nathan Beyrack and Eleonora Lev. Jerusalem, December 1992.

———. *The Iron Tracks.* Tr. Jeffrey M. Green. New York: Schocken Books, 1998.

———. *Katerina.* Tr. Jeffrey M. Green. New York: Random House, 1992.

———. *Kfor 'al ha-aretz* [Frozen Ground]. Ramat Gan: Massada, 1965.

———. *Layish* [Layish]. Jerusalem: Keter, 1994.

———. *Masot be-guf rishon* [Essays in the First Person]. Jerusalem: Hasifria hatzionit, 1979.

———. *Mesilat Barzel* [Iron Tracks]. Jerusalem: Maxwell-Macmillan-Keter, 1991.

———. *Mikhvat ha-or* [Searing Light]. Tel Aviv: Ha-kibbutz ha-me'uhad, 1980.

Avishai, Bernard. *The Tragedy of Zionism: Revolution and Democracy in the Land of Israel.* New York: Farrar, Straus, and Giroux, 1985.

Avot Yeshurun. *The Syrian-African Rift and Other Poems.* Tr. Harold Schimmel. Bilingual edition. Philadelphia: Jewish Publication Society, 1980.

Ba'al-Makhshoves [Israel Isidor Elyshev]. "One Literature in Two Languages"

[Tsvey shprakhn—eyneyntsige literatur] (1918). In *What Is Jewish Literature?* ed. Hana Wirth-Nesher. Philadelphia: Jewish Publication Society, 1994.

Babel, Isaac. 1955. *Collected Stories*. Ed. and tr. Walter Morison. New York: Meridian Books.

Bachelard, Gaston. *The Poetics of Space*. Tr. Maria Jolas. Foreword Etienne Gilson. Boston: Beacon Press, 1964.

Baer, Yitzhak. *Galut*. [Tr. Robert Warshow.] New York: Schocken Books, 1947.

Bakhtin, M. M. *The Dialogic Imagination: Four Essays*. Ed. Michael Holquist, tr. Caryl Emerson and Michael Holquist. Austin: University of Texas Press, 1981.

Bal, Miecke. "Lots of Writing." *Poetics Today* 15, no. 1 (spring 1994): 89–114.

Band, Arnold. *Nostalgia and Nightmare: A Study in the Fiction of S. Y. Agnon*. Berkeley: University of California Press, 1968.

Barkan, Leonard. "Rome's Other Population." *Raritan* 11, no. 2 (fall 1991): 66–81.

Barthes, Roland. *Camera Lucida: Reflections on Photography*. New York: Hill and Wang, 1981.

Barzel, Hillel, ed. *Shmuel Yosef Agnon: Mivhar ma'amarim 'al yetzirato* [Selected Essays on the Work of Shmuel Yosef Agnon]. Tel Aviv: Am Oved, 1982.

Barzilai, Shuli. "Borders of Language: Kristeva's Critique of Lacan." *PMLA* 106, no. 2 (March 1991): 294–305.

Baskin, Judith R., ed. *Women of the Word: Jewish Women and Jewish Writing*. Detroit: Wayne State University Press, 1994.

Baudrillard, Jean. *Selected Writings*. Ed. with intro. by Mark Poster. Stanford: Stanford University Press, 1988.

———. *Simulations*. Tr. Paul Foss, Paul Patton, and Philip Beitchman. New York: Semiotext(e), 1983.

Be'er, Haim. *Gam ahavatam, gam sinatam: Bialik, Brenner, Agnon, ma'arekhet yahasim* [Their Love and Their Hate: H. N. Bialik, Y. H. Brenner, S. Y. Agnon]. Tel Aviv: Am Oved, 1992.

Bellow, Saul. *The Adventures of Augie March*. New York: Viking, 1953.

———. *Herzog*. Harmondsworth: Penguin, 1964.

Ben-Ari, Eyal, and Yoram Bilu, eds. 1997. *Grasping Land: Space and Place in Contemporary Israeli Discourse and Experience*. Albany: State University of New York Press.

Ben-Arieh, Yehoshua. "Perceptions and Images of the Holy Land." In *The Land That Became Israel: Studies in Historical Geography*, ed. Ruth Kark. New Haven: Yale University Press, 1989.

———. *The Rediscovery of the Holy Land in the Nineteenth Century*. Jerusalem: Magnes Press, Hebrew University; Detroit: Wayne State University Press, 1979.

Ben Dov, Nitza. *Agnon's Art of Indirection: Uncovering Latent Content in the Fiction of S. Y. Agnon*. Leiden: E. J. Brill, 1993.

Benjamin of Tudela. *The Itinerary of Rabbi Benjamin of Tudela*. Ed. and tr. A. Asher. 2 vols. New York: Hakeshet Publishing, 1841.

Benjamin, Walter. *Illuminations*. Ed. Hannah Arendt, tr. Harry Zohn. New York: Schocken Books, 1969.

Ben-Sasson, Haim Hillel, ed. *A History of the Jewish People*. London: Weidenfeld and Nicolson, 1977.

Bercovitch, Sacvan, and Myra Jehlen, eds. 1986. *Ideology and Classic American
Literature*. Cambridge: Cambridge University Press.

Berger, Peter, Brigitte Berger, and Hansfried Kellner. *The Homeless Mind: Modernization and Consciousness*. New York: Random House, 1973.

Berkovitz, Y. D. *Kitvei Y. D. Berkovitz* [The Writing of Y. D. Berkovitz]. 2 vols.
Tel Aviv: Dvir, 1959.

Bernstein, Michael André. *Foregone Conclusions: Against Apocalyptic History*.
Berkeley: University of California Press, 1994.

Bersani, Leo. *The Culture of Redemption*. Cambridge, Mass.: Harvard University Press, 1990.

Beyrack, Nathan, and Eleonora Lev, dirs. "Milim u-demuyot: proyekt ha-sifrut
shel Yerushalayim" [Words and Images: Jerusalem Literary Project]. Oral history archived in the National Library, Hebrew University of Jerusalem, 1992.

Bhabha, Homi K. "DissemiNation: Time, Narrative, and the Margins of the Modern Nation." In *Nation and Narration*, ed. Homi K. Bhabha. London: Routledge, 1990.

———. "Postcolonial Criticism." In *Redrawing the Boundaries: The Transformation of English and American Literary Studies*, ed. Stephen Greenblatt and
Giles Gunn. New York: Modern Language Association of America, 1992.

———, ed. *Nation and Narration*. London: Routledge, 1990.

Biale, David. *Eros and the Jews: From Biblical Israel to Contemporary America*.
Berkeley: University of California Press, 1997.

Biale, David, Michael Galchinsky, and Susannah Heschel, eds. *Insider/Outsider:
American Jews and Multiculturalism*. Berkeley: University of California
Press, 1988.

Bialik, Haim Nahman. *Ha-sefer ha-'ivri* [On the Hebrew Book]. Jerusalem: Goldberg, 1913.

Blanchot, Maurice. *The Space of Literature*. Tr. Ann Smock. Lincoln: University
of Nebraska Press, 1982.

Bland, Kalman. *The Artless Jew: Medieval and Modern Affirmations and Denials of the Visual*. Princeton: Princeton University Press, forthcoming.

———. "Medieval Jewish Aesthetics: Maimonides, Body, and Scripture in
Profiat Duran." *Journal of the History of Ideas* 54, no. 4 (October 1993):
533–59.

Bloch, Ernst. *The Utopian Function of Art and Literature: Selected Essays*. Tr.
Jack Zipes and Frank Mecklenburg. Cambridge, Mass.: MIT Press, 1988.

Bloch, Ernst, Georg Lukács, Bertold Brecht, Walter Benjamin, and Theodor
Adorno. *Aesthetics and Politics*. Ed. and tr. Ronald Taylor. Afterword by
Fredric Jameson. London: NLB, 1977.

Bloom, Harold. *Agon: Towards Theory of Revisionism*. New York: Oxford University Press, 1982.

Bollack, Mayotte, ed. *Poésies et Poétiques de la Modernité*. [Lille]: Presses Universitaires de Lille, 1981.

Borges, Jorge. *The Aleph and Other Stories, 1933–1969: Together with Com-

mentaries and an Autobiographical Essay. Ed. and tr. Norman Thomas Di Giovanni in collaboration with the author. New York: E. P. Dutton, 1970.

Boyarin, Daniel. "Epater L'embourgeoisement: Freud, Gender, and the (De)colonized Psyche." *Diacritics* 24, no. 1 (spring 1994): 17–41.

———. *Unheroic Conduct: The Rise of Heterosexuality and the Invention of the Jewish Man*. Berkeley: University of California Press, 1997.

Boyarin, Daniel, and Jonathan Boyarin. "Diaspora: Generation and the Ground of Jewish Identity." *Critical Inquiry* 19, no. 4 (summer 1993): 697–701.

———, eds. *Jews and Other Differences: The New Jewish Cultural Studies*. Minneapolis: University of Minnesota Press, 1997.

Boyarin, Jonathan. *The Storm from Paradise: The Politics of Jewish Memory*. Minneapolis: University of Minnesota Press, 1992.

Boyers, Robert. *Atrocity and Amnesia: The Political Novel Since 1945*. New York: Oxford University Press, 1985.

———, ed. *The Legacy of the German Refugee Intellectuals*. New York: Schocken Books, 1969.

Brann, Ross. *The Compunctious Poet: Cultural Ambiguity and Hebrew Poetry in Muslim Spain*. Baltimore: Johns Hopkins University Press, 1991.

———. "Judah Halevi: The Compunctious Poet." *Prooftexts* 7, no. 2 (May 1987): 123–43.

Breines, Paul. *Tough Jews: Political Fantasies and the Moral Dilemma of American Jewry*. New York: Basic Books, 1990.

Brenner, Y. H. "Nerves" ['Atzabim]. Tr. Hillel Halkin. In *Eight Great Hebrew Short Novels*, ed. Alan Lelchuk and Gershon Shaked. New York: New American Library, 1983.

Brinker, Menahem. *'Ad ha-simtah ha-teveriyanit* [Narrative Art and Social Thought in Y. H. Brenner's Work]. Tel Aviv: Am Oved, 1990.

Bruner, Edward M. "Abraham Lincoln as Authentic Reproduction: A Critique of Postmodernism." *American Anthropologist* 96, no. 2 (June 1994): 397–415.

Buber, Martin. *The Tales of Rabbi Nachman*. Tr. Maurice Friedman and Stanley Goodman. Intro. by Paul Mendes-Flohr and Ze'ev Gries. Atlantic Highlands, N.J.: Humanities Press International, 1988.

Budick, Sanford. "Rembrandt's and Freud's 'Gerusalemme Liberata.'" In *Home: A Place in the World*. Special issue of *Social Research* 58, no. 1 (spring 1991): 189–207.

Bukiet, Melvin. *Stories of an Imaginary Childhood*. Evanston, Ill.: Northwestern University Press, 1992.

Butor, Michel. "Travel and Writing." *Mosaic* 8, nos. 1–2 (fall 1974): 1–16.

Calvino, Italo. "The Adventure of a Soldier." In *Difficult Loves*. Tr. William Weaver, Archibald Colquhoun, and Peggy Wright. London: Picador, 1983.

Carmel, Y. "Shirat ha-historia shelanu" [The Poetry of Our History]. *Gilyonot* 1 (1934): 32–42.

Carmi, T. "Dan Pagis: Words of Farewell." *Orim* 2, no. 2 (spring 1987): 76–78.

———. *Shirim min ha-'azuva* [Monologues and Other Poems]. Tel Aviv: Dvir, 1988.

———, ed. *The Penguin Book of Hebrew Verse*. Harmondsworth: Penguin, 1981.

Casson, Lionel. *Travel in the Ancient World*. Toronto: Hakkert, 1974.

Cavafy, C. P. *Collected Poems*. Ed. George Savadis, tr. Edmund Keely and Philip Sherrard. Princeton: Princeton University Press, 1975.

Celan, Paul. *Collected Prose*. Ed. and tr. Rosemarie Waldrop. New York: Sheep Meadow Press, 1986.

———. *Gesammelte Werke*. 5 vols. Frankfurt am Main: Suhrkamp Verlag, 1983.

———. *Last Poems*. Ed. and tr. Katharine Washburn and Margret Guillemin. San Francisco: North Point Press, 1986.

———. *Poems of Paul Celan*. Tr. with intro. by Michael Hamburger. New York: Persea Books, 1988.

———. *Sprachgitter; Die Niemandsrose: Gedichte*. Frankfurt am Main: S. Fischer Verlag, 1986.

Certeau, Michel de. *The Practice of Everyday Life*. Tr. Steven F. Rendall. Berkeley: University of California Press, 1984.

Cervantes Saavedra, Miguel de. *Adventures of Don Quixote*. Tr. J. M. Cohen. Harmondsworth: Penguin, 1950.

Chalfen, Israel. *Paul Celan: A Biography of His Youth*. Tr. Maximilian Bleyleben. Intro. by John Felstiner. New York: Persea Books, 1991.

Cheyette, Bryan, and Laura Marcus. *Modernity, Culture, and "the Jew."* Stanford: Stanford University Press, 1998.

Coe, Richard N. *When the Grass Was Taller: Autobiography and the Experience of Childhood*. New Haven: Yale University Press, 1984.

Cohen, Gerson. "Abraham Ibn Daud's Universe of Discourse." Introduction to Abraham Ibn Daud, *The Book of Tradition* [Sefer Ha-Qabbalah]. Philadelphia: Jewish Publication Society, 1967.

Cohen, Richard. *Jewish Icons: Art and Society in Modern Europe*. Berkeley: University of California Press, 1998.

Colin, Amy D. *Paul Celan: Holograms of Darkness*. Bloomington: Indiana University Press, 1991.

———. "Paul Celan's Poetics of Destruction." In *Argumentum e Silentio: International Paul Celan Symposium*, ed. Amy D. Colin. Berlin: Walter de Gruyter, 1987.

———, ed. *Argumentum e Silentio: International Paul Celan Symposium*. Berlin: Walter de Gruyter, 1987.

Curtius, E. R. *European Literature and the Latin Middle Ages*. Tr. Willard R. Trask. New York: Pantheon Books, 1953.

Davies, W. D. *The Territorial Dimension of Judaism*. Berkeley: University of California Press, 1982.

Davis, Natalie Zemon. "Rabelais among the Censors." *Representations*, no. 32 (fall 1990): 1–32.

Deleuze, Gilles, and Félix Guattari. *Kafka: Toward a Minor Literature*. Tr. Dana Polan. Minneapolis: University of Minnesota Press, 1986.

Derrida, Jacques. *Of Grammatology*. Tr. Gayatri Chakravorty Spivak. Baltimore: Johns Hopkins University Press, 1976.

———. "Schibboleth." In *Argumentum e Silentio: International Paul Celan Symposium*, ed. Amy D. Colin. Berlin: Walter de Gruyter, 1987.

Don-Yehiya, Eliezer. "'Galut' in Zionist Ideology and in Israeli Society." In *Is-*

rael and Diaspora Jewry: Ideological and Political Perspectives, ed. Eliezer
    Don-Yehiya. Tel Aviv: Bar Ilan University Press, 1991.

————, ed. 1991. *Israel and Diaspora Jewry: Ideological and Political Perspec-*
    tives. Tel Aviv: Bar Ilan University Press.

Drori, Rina. "'Al tafkida shel ha-sifrut ha-karait be-toldot ha-sifrut ha-yehudit
    ba-mea ha-'asirit" [On the Role of Karaite Literature in Jewish Literature of
    the Tenth Century]. *Dapim le-mehkar be-sifrut* [Pages in Literary Research]
    9 (1993–94): 101–10.

Eade, John, and Michael J. Sallnow, eds. *Contesting the Sacred: The Anthropology*
    of Christian Pilgrimage. London: Routledge, 1991.

Eakin, Paul John. *Touching the World: Reference in Autobiography.* Princeton:
    Princeton University Press, 1992.

Eckstein, Arieh. *Doda Ester* [Auntie Esther]. Jerusalem: Keter, 1992.

Eco, Umberto. *Travels in Hyperreality.* Tr. William Weaver. London: Pan Books,
    1986.

Eisen, Arnold. *Galut: Modern Jewish Reflection on Homelessness and Home-*
    coming. Bloomington: Indiana University Press, 1986.

Eisenzweig, Uri. *Territoires occupés de l'imaginaire juif: Essai sur l'espace sion-*
    iste. Paris: Christian Bourgois, 1980.

Elboim-Dror, Rahel. "Gender in Utopianism: The Zionist Case." *History Work-*
    shop Journal, no. 37 (1994): 99–116.

————. *Ha-mahar shel ha-etmol* [Yesterday's Tomorrow]. 2 vols. Jerusalem: Ben-
    Zvi and Mossad Bialik, 1993.

Eliade, Mircea. *The Sacred and the Profane: The Nature of Religion.* Tr. Willard
    Trask. New York: Harcourt Brace and World, 1959.

Elon, Amos. *The Israelis.* London: Weidenfeld and Nicolson, 1971.

Erik, Max. "Menakhem-Mendl" (1935). Translated in *Prooftexts* 6, no. 1 (Jan-
    uary 1986): 23–39.

Eshkoli, A. Z. "Yehudei habash ba-sifrut ha-'ivrit" [Jews of Ethiopia in Hebrew
    Literature]. *Zion* 1 (1936): 316–36.

Even Zohar, Itamar, and Chone Shmeruk. "Authentic Language and Authentic
    Reported Speech: Hebrew vs. Yiddish." *Poetics Today* 11, no. 1 (spring 1990):
    155–63. Translation and discussion of Isaac Bashevis Singer [Isaac Varshavski,
    pseud.], "Problemen fun der yidisher proze in amerike," *Svive* 2 (1943):
    12–13.

Ezrahi, Sidra DeKoven. "Agnon Before and After." *Prooftexts* 2, no. 1 (January
    1982): 78–94.

————. "Aharon Appelfeld: The Search for a Language." *Studies in Contem-*
    porary Jewry 1 (1984): 366–80.

————. *By Words Alone: The Holocaust in Literature.* Chicago: University of
    Chicago Press, 1980.

————. "Dan Pagis—Out of Line: A Poetics of Decomposition." *Prooftexts* 10,
    no. 2 (May 1990): 335–63.

————. "'The Grave in the Air': Unbound Metaphors in Post-Holocaust Poetry."
    In *Probing the Limits of Representation: Nazism and the "Final Solution,"*
    ed. Saul Friedländer. Cambridge, Mass.: Harvard University Press, 1992.

————. "Representing Auschwitz." *History and Memory* 7, no. 2 (winter 1996): 121–54.

————. "State and Real Estate: Territoriality and the Modern Jewish Imagination." In *Terms of Survival: The Jewish World Since 1945*, ed. Robert Wistrich. London: Routledge, 1995.

Ezrahi, Yaron. *The Descent of Icarus: Science and the Transformation of Contemporary Democracy*. Cambridge: Mass.: Harvard University Press, 1990.

————. *Rubber Bullets: Power and Conscience in Modern Israel*. New York: Farrar, Straus, and Giroux, 1997.

Feldhai-Brenner, Rivka. "In Search of Identity: The Israeli-Arab Artist in Anton Shammas's *Arabesques*." *PMLA* 108, no. 3 (May 1993): 431–45.

Feldman, Jackie. "The Pull of the Center and the Experience of Communitas in Pilgrimage to the Second Temple." M.A. thesis, Hebrew University of Jerusalem, 1988.

Feldman, Yael. *Modernism and Cultural Transfer: Gabriel Preil and the Tradition of Jewish Literary Bilingualism*. Cincinnati: Hebrew Union College Press, 1986.

Felstiner, John. *Paul Celan: Poet, Survivor, Jew*. New Haven: Yale University Press, 1995.

————. "Translating Paul Celan's 'Todesfuge.'" In *Probing the Limits of Representation: Nazism and the "Final Solution,"* ed. Saul Friedländer. Cambridge, Mass.: Harvard University Press, 1992.

————. "'Ziv, that light': Translation and Tradition in Paul Celan." *New Literary History* 18, no. 3 (1987): 611–31.

Fernandez, James D. "The Bonds of Patrimony: Cervantes and the New World." *PMLA* 109, no. 5 (October 1994): 969–81.

Fiedler, Leslie. *Fiedler on the Roof: Essays on Literature and Jewish Identity*. Boston: David R. Godine, 1991.

Finkelstein, Norman. *The Ritual of New Creation: Jewish Tradition and Contemporary Literature*. Albany: State University of New York Press, 1992.

Fisch, Harold. "Reading and Carnival: On the Semiotics of Purim." *Poetics Today* 15, no. 1 (spring 1994): 55–74.

Fishbane, Michael. "The Aggadah: Fragments of Delight." *Prooftexts* 13, no. 2 (March 1993): 181–90.

————. *The Kiss of God: Spiritual and Mystical Death in Judaism*. Seattle: University of Washington Press, 1994.

Fisher, Philip. *Hard Facts: Setting and Form in the American Novel*. Oxford: Oxford University Press, 1987.

Fleck, Jeffrey. "Mendele in Pieces." *Prooftexts* 3, no. 2 (May 1983): 169–88.

Foucault, Michel. *The Order of Things: An Archaeology of the Human Sciences*. New York: Vintage Books, 1973.

Frank, Joseph. "Spatial Form in Modern Literature" (1945). In *The Idea of Spatial Form*. New Brunswick, N.J.: Rutgers University Press, 1991.

Frankel, Jonathan, ed. *Jews and Messianism in the Modern Era: Metaphor and Meaning*. Studies in Contemporary Jewry 7. New York: Oxford University Press, 1991.

————, ed. *Reshaping the Past: Jewish History and the Historians*. Studies in Contemporary Jewry 10. New York: Oxford University Press, 1994.

Franklin, Walker. *Irreverent Pilgrims: Melville, Browne, and Mark Twain in the Holy Land*. Seattle: University of Washington Press, 1974.

Freccero, John. "Autobiography and Narrative." In *Reconstructing Individualism: Autonomy, Individuality, and the Self in Western Thought*, ed. Thomas C. Heller. Stanford: Stanford University Press, 1986.

Friedländer, Saul, ed. *Probing the Limits of Representation: Nazism and the "Final Solution."* Cambridge, Mass.: Harvard University Press, 1992.

Friedländer, Saul, Gerald Holton, Leo Marx, and Eugene Skolnikoff, eds. 1985. *Visions of Apocalypse: End or Rebirth?* New York: Holmes and Meier.

Friedman, S. *Land of Dust: Palestine at the Turn of the Century*. Lanham, Md.: University Press of America, 1982.

Frymer-Kensky, Tikva. 1992. *In the Wake of the Goddesses: Women, Culture, and the Biblical Transformation of Pagan Myth*. New York: Fawcett Columbine.

Gellrich, Jesse M. 1985. *The Idea of the Book in the Middle Ages*. Ithaca: Cornell University Press.

Genette, Gérard. "Fictional Narrative, Factual Narrative." *Poetics Today* 11, no. 4 (winter 1990): 755–74.

Genossar, Yaira. "Dan Pagis—Likro bishem, linkot 'emda" [Calling It by Its Name, Taking a Stand]. *'Iton 77*, no. 38 (February 1983): 32–33.

Gibbs, Robert. *Correlations in Rosenzweig and Levinas*. Princeton: Princeton University Press, 1992.

Gil, Moshe. "'Aliya ve-'aliya la-regel bi-tekufat ha-kibbush ha-muslemi ha-rishon (634–1099)" [Pilgrimage and Settlement in the Time of the First Moslem Conquest]. *Katedra* 8 (1978): 124–33.

Gilman, Sander L. *Jewish Self-Hatred: Anti-Semitism and the Hidden Language of the Jews*. Baltimore: Johns Hopkins University Press, 1986.

————. "To Quote Primo Levi: 'Redest Keyn Jiddisch, bist nit kejn jid" [If you don't speak Yiddish, you're not a Jew]." *Prooftexts* 9, no. 2 (May 1989): 139–60.

Ginsburg, Elliot K. *The Sabbath in the Classical Kabbalah*. Albany: State University of New York Press, 1989.

Glatshteyn, Jacob. "I Shall Transport Myself" [Khvel zikh eingloybern] (1953). In *American Yiddish Poetry*, ed. and tr. Benjamin and Barbara Harshav. Berkeley: University of California Press, 1986.

———— "Singer's Literary Reputation." In *Recovering the Canon: Essays on Isaac Bashevis Singer*, ed. David Neal Miller. Leiden: E. J. Brill, 1986.

Gluzman, Michael. "The Exclusion of Women from Hebrew Literary History." *Prooftexts* 11, no. 3 (September 1991): 259–78.

————. "Modernism and Exile: A View from the Margins." In *Insider/Outsider: American Jews and Multiculturalism*, ed. David Biale, Michael Galchinsky, and Susannah Heschel. Berkeley: University of California Press, 1998.

Goitein, Shelomo Dov. "The Biography of Rabbi Yehudah Ha Levi in the Light of the Cairo Geniza Documents." *Proceedings of the American Academy for Jewish Research* 78 (1959): 41–56.

————. "Ha-im higia' rav yehuda halevi el hof eretz-yisrael?" [Did R. Yehuda Halevi Ever Reach the Land of Israel?]. *Tarbiz* 46, nos. 3–4 (autumn 1977): 245–50.

————. "'Meeting in Jerusalem': Messianic Expectations in the Letters of the Cairo Geniza." *AJS Review* 4 (1979): 43–57.

Goldberg, Harvey, ed. *Judaism Viewed from Within and from Without: Anthropological Studies.* Albany: State University of New York Press, 1987.

Goldberg, Leah. *Shirim* [Poems]. 3 vols. Tel Aviv: Sifriat po'alim, 1986.

Goldberg, Sylvie-Anne. *Crossing the Jabbok: Illness and Death in Ashkenazi Judaism in Sixteenth- through Nineteenth-Century Prague.* Tr. Carol Cosman. Berkeley: University of California Press, 1996.

Goldner, Martin, ed. *Die Gabe: For Franz Rosenzweig on His 40th Birthday, 12/25/26.* New York: Leo Baeck Institute, 1987.

Gouri, Haim. *Shoshanat ruhot* [Phantom Flower]. Tel Aviv: Ha-kibbutz ha-me'uhad, 1960.

Grafton, Anthony. *New Worlds, Ancient Texts: The Power of Tradition and the Shock of Discovery.* Cambridge, Mass.: Harvard University Press, 1992.

Greenberg, Uri Zvi. "Bizkhut em u-vena viyirushalayim" [For the Sake of a Mother and Her Son and Jerusalem]. In *Kol Ketavav* [Collected Work], vol. 7. Jerusalem: Mossad Bialik, 1994.

Greenblatt, Stephen. *Marvelous Possessions: The Wonder of the New World.* Chicago: University of Chicago Press, 1991.

Greenblatt, Stephen, and Giles Gunn, eds. *Redrawing the Boundaries: The Transformation of English and American Literary Studies.* New York: Modern Language Association of America, 1992.

Greenspan, Ezra. *The Schlemiel Comes to America.* Metuchen, N.J.: Scarecrow Press, 1983.

Grossman, David. "My Sholem Aleichem." *Modern Hebrew Literature*, no. 14 (spring/summer 1995): pp. 4–5.

————. *See Under: Love.* Tr. Betsy Rosenberg. New York: Farrar, Straus, and Giroux, 1989.

Gurevitch, Zali. "The Double Site of Israel." In *Grasping Land: Space and Place in Contemporary Israeli Discourse and Experience*, ed. Eyal Ben-Ari and Yoram Bilu. Albany: State University of New York Press, 1997.

Gurevitch, Zali, and Gideon Aran. "'Al ha-makom" [On Place]. *Alpayim* 4 (1991): 9–45.

————. "The Land of Israel: Myth and Phenomenon." In *Reshaping the Past: Jewish History and the Historians*, ed. Jonathan Frankel. Studies in Contemporary Jewry 10. New York: Oxford University Press, 1994.

Hadani, Eldad. *Eldad Ha-dani: sipurav ve-hilkhotav be-mahadurot shonot 'al pi kitvei-yad ve-defusim 'atikim 'im mevo ve-he'arot* [Eldad the Danite: Editions of His Story and Precepts, Based on Ancient Manuscripts, with Introduction and Annotations]. Ed. Avraham Epstein. Pressburg: Druck von Adolf Alkalay, 1981.

Hadda, Janet. "Gimpel the Full." *Prooftexts* 10, no. 2 (May 1990): 283–95.

Halbwachs, Maurice. *On Collective Memory.* Ed., trans., and with intro. by Lewis A. Coser. Chicago: University of Chicago Press, 1992.

Halevi, Shimshon Block. *Shvilei 'Olam* [Pathways through the World]. Warsaw: n.p., 1855.

Halevi, Yehuda. *Book of Kuzari*. Tr. with intro. by Hartwig Hirschfeld. London: George Routledge and Son, 1969.

———. *On the Sea* [Shirei yam]. Tr. with intro. by Gabriel Levin. Jerusalem: Ibis Editions, 1997.

———. "Sea Poems." Tr. Gabriel Levin. *Jerusalem Post*, November 21, 1986, 18.

———. *Selected Poems of Jehudah Halevi*. Tr. Nina Salaman. Philadelphia: Jewish Publication Society, 1928.

———. *Shirei ha-kodesh le-rebbe Yehuda Halevi* [The Liturgical Poetry of R. Yehudah Halevi]. Ed. and tr. D. Yarden. 4 vols. Jerusalem: Kiryat no'ar, 1978–85.

Halkin, A. S. "The Medieval Jewish Attitude toward Hebrew." In *Biblical and Other Studies*, ed. Alexander Altmann. Cambridge, Mass.: Harvard University Press, 1963.

———, ed. *Kitab al-Muhadara wal-Mudhakara: Liber Discussionis et Commemorationis (Poetica Hebraica)*. Bilingual edition. Jerusalem: Mikitzei nirdamim, 1975.

Halkin, Hillel. "How to Read Philip Roth." *Commentary*, February 1994, pp. 43–48.

Hamburger, Michael. *The Truth of Poetry: Tensions in Modern Poetry from Baudelaire to the 1960s*. London: Methuen, 1982.

Hamori, Andras. "Lights in the Heart of the Sea: Some Images of Judah Halevi's." *Journal of Semitic Studies* 30, no. 1 (spring 1985): 75–83.

Handelman, Don. *Models and Mirrors: Towards an Anthropology of Public Events*. Cambridge: Cambridge University Press, 1990.

Handelman, Don, and Lea Shamgar-Handelman. "The Presence of Absence: The Memorialism of National Death in Israel." In *Grasping Land: Space and Place in Contemporary Israeli Discourse and Experience*, ed. Eyal Ben-Ari and Yoram Bilu. Albany: State University of New York Press, 1997.

Hareven, Shulamit. *Bididut* [Loneliness]. Tel Aviv: Am Oved, 1980.

———. "Twilight." Tr. Miriam Arad. In *Facing the Holocaust: Selected Israeli Fiction*, ed. Gila Ramras-Rauch and Joseph Michman-Melkman. Philadelphia: Jewish Publication Society, 1985.

Harshav, Benjamin. 1993. *Language in Time of Revolution*. Berkeley: University of California Press.

———. "Masa 'al tehiyat ha-lashon ha-'ivrit" [Essay on the Revival of the Hebrew Language]. *Alpayim* 2 (1990): 9–54.

———. *The Meaning of Yiddish*. Berkeley: University of California Press, 1990.

———. "Note on the Systems of Hebrew Versification." In *The Penguin Book of Hebrew Verse*, ed. T. Carmi. Harmondsworth: Penguin, 1981.

———. "The Role of Language in Modern Art: On Texts and Subtexts in Chagall's Paintings." *Modernism and Modernity* 1, no. 2 (April 1994): 51–87.

Harshav, Benjamin, and Barbara Harshav, eds. and trs. *American Yiddish Poetry*. Berkeley: University of California Press, 1986.

Hassan-Rokem, Galit, and Alan Dundes, eds. *The Wandering Jew: Essays in the*

Interpretation of a Christian Legend. Bloomington: Indiana University Press, 1985.

Heine, Heinrich. "Romanzero," *Hebraische Melodien.* In *Heinrich Heine Werke,* vol. 1. Frankfurt am Main: Insel Verlag, 1968.

Herzl, Theodor. *Altneuland, Roman.* Leipzig: Hermann Seemann Nachfolger, 1902.

———. *Altneuland* (in Yiddish). Tr. Isidor Elyshev. Warsaw: Hatzefirah, 1902.

———. *Old-Newland ("Altneuland").* Tr. with revised notes by Lotta Levensohn. New York: Bloch Publishing Company and Herzl Press, 1960.

———. *Tel Aviv, Sipur* [Altneuland, Roman; in Hebrew]. Tr. Nahum Sokolov. Warsaw: Hatzefirah, 1902.

Hever, Hanan. "Hebrew in an Israeli Arab Hand: Six Miniatures on Anton Shammas's Arabesques." In *The Nature and Context of Minority Discourse,* ed. Abdul R. JanMohamed and David Lloyd. Oxford: Oxford University Press, 1990.

———. "She-harei kvar higa'nu, nakhon?" [For We Have Already Arrived, Right?]. *Davar,* February 21, 1992, p. 26.

Hindus, Milton. "A Monument with a Difference." Review of *The Family Moskat* by I. B. Singer. *New York Times Book Review,* March 14, 1965, pp. 4, 44–45.

Hirsch, Marianne. *Family Frames: Photography, Narrative, and Postmemory.* Cambridge, Mass.: Harvard University Press, 1997.

———. "Past Lives: Postmemories in Exile." *Poetics Today* 17, no. 4 (winter 1996): 659–86.

Hirshfeld, Ariel. "Ketivat sod 'al derekh ha-emet: 'al tzura u-masma'ut be-'Shneim-'asar panim shel esmargad' le-Dan Pagis" [Writing Secrets As If They Were True: On Form and Meaning in "Twelve Faces of the Emerald" by Dan Pagis]. *Mehkerei Yerushalayim ba-sifrut ha-'ivrit* [Jerusalem Studies in Hebrew Literature] 10–11 (1987–88): 137–52.

Hoffman, Allen. *Small Worlds.* New York: Abbeville Press, 1996.

Hoffman, Anne Golomb. *Between Exile and Return: S. Y. Agnon and the Drama of Writing.* Albany: State University of New York Press, 1991.

Hoffman, Eva. *Lost in Translation: A Life in a New Language.* London: Heinemann, 1989.

Hoffman, Frederick. *The Mortal No: Death and the Modern Imagination.* Princeton: Princeton University Press, 1964.

Hoffman, Lawrence, ed. 1986. The Land of Israel: Jewish Perspectives. Notre Dame, Ind.: University of Notre Dame Press.

Hollander, John. "It All Depends." In *Home: A Place in the World.* Special issue of *Social Research* 58, no. 1 (January 1991): 31–49.

———. "The Question of American Jewish Poetry." In *What Is Jewish Literature?* ed. Hana Wirth-Nesher. Philadelphia: Jewish Publication Society, 1994.

Horne, Donald. *The Great Museum: The Re-Presentation of History.* London: Pluto Press, 1984.

Horowitz, Elliott. "The Rite to Be Reckless: On the Perpetration and Interpretation of Purim Violence." *Poetics Today* 15, no. 1 (spring 1994): 9–54.

Howe, Irving. "I. B. Singer." *Encounter,* March 1966, pp. 60–70.

———. *World of Our Fathers.* New York: Harcourt Brace Jovanovich, 1976.

Howe, Irving, and Eliezer Greenberg, eds. *A Treasury of Yiddish Stories*. New York: Viking, 1953.

Huizinga, Johan. *The Waning of the Middle Ages: A Study of the Forms of Life, Thought, and Art in France and the Netherlands in the XIVth and XVth Centuries*. New York: Doubleday, 1954.

Huston, Nancy. "Novels and Navels." *Critical Inquiry* 21, no. 4 (summer 1995): 708–21.

Hutchinson, Steven. *Cervantine Journeys*. Madison: University of Wisconsin Press, 1992.

Ibn Daud, Abraham. *The Book of Tradition* [Sefer Ha-Kabbalah]. Philadelphia: Jewish Publication Society, 1967.

Idel, Moshe. "The Land of Israel in Medieval Kabbalah." In *The Land of Israel: Jewish Perspectives*, ed. Lawrence Hoffman. Notre Dame, Ind.: University of Notre Dame Press, 1986.

Jabès, Edmond. *From the Book to the Book: An Edmond Jabès Reader*. Tr. Rosemarie Waldrop. Middletown, Conn.: Wesleyan University Press, 1991.

———. "This Is the Desert: Nothing Strikes Root Here." Interview by Bracha Ettinger Lichtenberg. In *Routes of Wandering: Nomadism, Voyages, and Transitions in Contemporary Israeli Art*, ed. Sarit Shapira. Exhibition catalogue. Bilingual edition. Jerusalem: Israel Museum, 1991.

Jusdanis, Gregory. *Belated Modernity and Aesthetic Culture: Inventing National Literature*. Minneapolis: University of Minnesota Press, 1991.

Kachuck, Rhoda S. "Sholom Aleichem's Humor in English Translation." *YIVO Annual of Jewish Social Science* 11 (1956–57): 39–81.

Kafka, Franz. *The Penguin Complete Novels of Franz Kafka*. Tr. Willa and Edwin Muir. Harmondsworth: Penguin, 1983.

Kark, Ruth, ed. *The Land That Became Israel: Studies in Historical Geography*. New Haven: Yale University Press, 1989.

Kartun-Blum, Ruth. "Ha-mavet ke-meshamer ha-hayyim: 'iyun be-shirav shel Dan Pagis 'Hasifa' ve-'ha-hatkana'" [Death as Life's Preserver: A Study of Dan Pagis's Poems "Exposure" and "How To"]. In *Mehkerei yerushalayim ba-sifrut ha-'ivrit* [Jerusalem Studies in Hebrew Literature] 10–11 (1988): 113–22.

Katz, Avi. "Ha-kol melukhlakh hutz mi-yerushalayim" [Everything Is Filthy except Jerusalem]. *Ha-aretz*, July 22, 1994, sec. B, p. 8.

Kaufmann, Walter. "The Reception of Existentialism in the United States." In *The Legacy of the German Refugee Intellectuals*, ed. Robert Boyers. New York: Schocken Books, 1969.

Kaufmann, Yehezkel. *Golah ve-nekhar* [Exile and Foreignness]. 2 vols. Tel Aviv: Dvir, 1962.

Kazin, Alfred. *God and the American Writer*. New York: Knopf, 1997.

———. "My New Yorks: Writing *A Walker in the City*." *New York Times Book Review*, August 24, 1986, pp. 1, 29–30.

———. *A Walker in the City*. New York: Harcourt and Brace, 1951.

Kellman, Ellen D. "Sholem Aleichem's Funeral (New York, 1916): The Making of a National Pageant." *YIVO Annual* 20 (1991): 277–304.

Kennedy, J. Gerald. "Roland Barthes, Autobiography, and the End of Writing." *Georgia Review* 35, no. 2 (summer 1981): 381–400.

Kermode, Frank. "Apocalypse and the Modern." In *Visions of Apocalypse: End or Rebirth?* ed. Saul Friedländer, Gerald Holton, Leo Marx, and Eugene Skolnikoff. New York: Holmes and Meier, 1985.

———. *The Sense of an Ending: Studies in the Theory of Fiction.* New York: Oxford University Press, 1967.

Kern, Stephen. *The Culture of Time and Space, 1880–1918.* Cambridge, Mass.: Harvard University Press, 1983.

Kitaj, R. B. *First Diasporist Manifesto.* London: Thames and Hudson, 1989.

———. "Kitaj Interviewed by Richard Morphet." In *R. B. Kitaj: A Retrospective,* ed. Richard Morphet. London: Rizzoli, 1994.

Knoepflmacher, U. C. "Hardy Ruins: Female Spaces and Male Designs." *PMLA* 105, no. 5 (October 1990): 1055–70.

Kohn, Pinkhes. "Oysterlishe minhogim fun yidn in Samarkand" [Outlandish Practices of the Jews of Samarkand]. *Der Moment,* no.144 (June 22, 1928): 6.

Kovner, Abba. *Ahoti ketanah: poema* [My Little Sister: A Poem]. Merhavia: Sifriat po'alim, 1967. Translated in *My Little Sister and Selected Poems, 1965–1985,* tr. Shirley Kaufman (Oberlin, Ohio: Oberlin College, 1986).

———. *A Canopy in the Desert: Selected Poems.* Tr. Shirley Kaufman. Pittsburgh: University of Pittsburgh Press, 1973.

———. *Hupa ba-midbar* [A Canopy in the Desert]. Merhavia: Sifriyat po'alim, 1970.

Krojanker, Gustav. 1991. *Yetzirato shel Shai Agnon* [The Work of S. Y. Agnon]. Tr. Jacob Gotschalk. Intro. by Dan Laor. Jerusalem: Mosad Bialik, 1991.

Kronfeld, Chana. *On the Margins of Modernism: Decentering Literary Dynamics.* Berkeley: University of California Press, 1996.

Kuntsler, Ada. "Kisuyim shkufim ve-shikufim mekhusim" [Transparent Opacities and Opaque Transparencies]. *Moznayim* 55 (August 1982): 10–15.

Laor, Itzhak. *Anu kotvim otakh, moledet* [Narratives with No Natives]. Tel Aviv: Ha-kibbutz ha-me'uhad, 1995.

Lelchuk, Alan, and Gershon Shaked, eds. *Eight Great Hebrew Short Novels.* New York: New American Library, 1983.

Levi, Primo. *If Not Now, When?* Tr. William Weaver. New York: Summit Books, 1985.

———. *Other People's Trades.* Tr. Raymond Rosenthal. New York: Summit Books, 1989.

———. *Survival in Auschwitz: The Nazi Assault on Humanity.* Tr. Stuart Woolf. New York: Collier, 1959.

Levine, Yisrael. "Masa'o shel Rabi Yehuda Halevi le-eretz yisrael—siyumo shel tahalikh ruhani" [R. Yehuda Halevi's Voyage to the Land of Israel—the Conclusion of a Spiritual Process]. *Apiryon,* nos. 26–27 (spring 1993): 7–13.

Leyvik, H. "Here Lives the Jewish People." In *American Yiddish Poetry,* ed. and trans. Benjamin and Barbara Harshav. Berkeley: University of California Press, 1986.

Lloyd, David. *Nationalism and Minor Literature: James Clarence Mangan and the Emergence of Irish Cultural Nationalism.* Berkeley: University of California Press, 1987.

Lowenthal, David. *The Past Is a Foreign Country.* Cambridge: Cambridge University Press, 1985.

Löwy, Michael. *Redemption and Utopia: Jewish Libertarian Thought in Central Europe, a Study in Elective Affinity.* Tr. Hope Heaney. London: Athlone Press, 1992.

Lyotard, Jean-François. *The Differend: Phrases in Dispute.* Tr. Georges Van Den Abbeele. Theory and History of Literature 46. Minneapolis: University of Minnesota Press, 1988.

———. *Heidegger and the "jews."* Tr. Andreas Michel and Marc Roberts. Minneapolis: University of Minnesota Press, 1990.

Maccoby, Hyam. "The Wandering Jew as Sacred Executioner." In *The Wandering Jew: Essays in the Interpretation of a Christian Legend,* ed. Galit Hassan-Rokem and Alan Dundes. Bloomington: Indiana University Press, 1985.

Manger, Itzik. *Medrash Itzik* [Itzik's Midrash]. Jerusalem: Hebrew University, Department of Yiddish Literature, 1969.

Mann, Thomas. "Voyage with Don Quixote" (1934). In *Essays by Thomas Mann.* Tr. H. T. Lowe-Porter. New York: Vintage Books, 1957.

Marx, Leo. *The Machine in the Garden: Technology and the Pastoral Ideal in America.* London: Oxford University Press, 1964.

———. "Pastoralism in America." In *Ideology and Classic American Literature,* ed. Sacvan Bercovitch and Myra Jehlen. Cambridge: Cambridge University Press, 1986.

Mendelsohn, Ezra, ed. *Jews and Messianism in the Modern Era: Metaphor and Meaning.* Studies in Contemporary Jewry 7. New York: Oxford University Press, 1991.

Michael, John. "History and Romance, Sympathy and Uncertainty: The Moral of the Stones in Hawthorne's *Marble Faun.*" *PMLA* 103, no. 2 (March 1988): 150–61.

Mignolo, Walter. "Colonial Situations." In *Colonial Discourse.* Special issue of *Dispositio* 14, nos. 36–38 (1989): 93–140.

Miller, David Neal. "Don't Force Me to Tell You the Ending: Closure in the Short Fiction of Sh. Rabinovitsch (Sholem-Aleykhem)." *Neophilologus* 66 (1982): 102–10.

———, ed. *Recovering the Canon: Essays on Isaac Bashevis Singer.* Leiden: E. J. Brill, 1986.

Mintz, Alan. *Hurban: Responses to Catastrophe in Hebrew Literature.* New York: Columbia University Press, 1984.

Miron, Dan. "Agnon's Transactions with the Novel." *Prooftexts* 7, no. 1 (January 1987): 1–27.

———. *Bo'ah, laylah: ha-sifrut ha-'ivrit bein higayon le-i-higayon be-mifne ha-mea ha-'esrim* [Come, Night: Hebrew Literature between the Rational and the Irrational at the Turn of the Twentieth Century]. Tel Aviv: Dvir, 1987.

———. *Bodedim be-mo'adam: le-diyukana shel ha-republika ha-sifrutit ha-'ivrit be-tehilat ha-mea ha-'esrim* [When Loners Come Together: A Portrait of He-brew Literature at the Turn of the Twentieth Century]. Tel Aviv: Am Oved, 1987.

———. "Bouncing Back: Destruction and Recovery in Sholem Aleykhem's *Motl Peyse dem khazns.*" *YIVO Annual of Jewish Social Science* 17 (1978): 119–84.

———. "El mul ha-av: hithadshut be-yitzirat Aharon Appelfeld" [Facing the Fa-ther: Renewal and Power in the Work of Aharon Appelfeld]. *Yediot Ahronot*, Literary Supplement, June 2, 1978, p. 1.

———. *Histaklut be-ravnekher: 'al Hakhnasat kala me-et Shai Agnon ve-sviva* [Under the Motley Canopy: A Study of S. Y. Agnon's Narrative Art in *The Bridal Canopy*]. Tel Aviv: Ha-kibbutz ha-me'uhad, 1996.

———. "The Literary Image of the Shtetl." *Jewish Social Studies* 1, no. 3 (spring 1995): 1–43. Originally published in Hebrew as a five-part article, "Ha-dimui ha-sifruti ha-klasi shel ha-'ayara," *Ha-do'ar* 55 (1976) and 56 (1977), and then in Yiddish as *Der imazh fun Shtetl: dray literatishe shtudiyes* (Tel Aviv: I. L. Peretz, 1981).

———. *Mul ha-ah ha-shotek* [Facing the Silent Brother]. Jerusalem: Keter, 1992.

———. "Passivity and Narration: The Spell of Bashevis Singer." *Judaism* 41, no. 1 (winter 1992): 14–16. Originally published in Hebrew as "Svilut ve-siper: le-kismo shel bashevis-Singer," *Yediot ahronot*, August 2, 1991, pp. 22–23.

———. *Sholem Aleykhem: Person, Persona, Presence.* New York: Yivo Institute for Jewish Research, 1972.

———. *A Traveler Disguised: A Study in the Rise of Modern Yiddish Fiction in the Nineteenth Century.* New York: Schocken Books, 1973.

Miron, Dan, and Anita Norich. "The Politics of Benjamin III: Intellectual Sig-nificance and Its Formal Correlatives in Sh. Y. Abramovitsh's *Masoes ben-yomin hashlishi.*" In *The Field of Yiddish: Studies in Language, Folklore, and Literature; Fourth Collection*, ed. Marvin I. Herzog et al. Philadelphia: In-stitute for the Study of Human Issues, 1980.

Mlotek, Eleanor Gordon, and Joseph Mlotek, comps. *Pearls of Yiddish Song.* New York: Workmen's Circle, 1988.

Mor, Menachem, ed. *Eretz Israel, Israel, and the Jewish Diaspora: Mutual Re-lations.* Studies in Jewish Civilization 1. Lanham, Md.: University Press of America; Omaha, Neb.: Center for the Study of Religion and Society, Creighton University, 1991.

Morphet, Richard, ed. *R. B. Kitaj: A Retrospective.* New York: Rizzoli, 1994.

Morson, Gary Saul, and Caryl Emerson. *Mikhail Bakhtin: Creation of a Pro-saics.* Stanford: Stanford University Press, 1990.

Mosès, Stéphane. "Quand le langage se fait voix: Paul Celan: Entretien dans la montagne." In *Contre-Jour: Etudes sur Paul Celan: Colloque de Cerisy*, ed. Martine Broda. Paris: Cerf, 1986.

Nabokov, Vladimir. *The Real Life of Sebastian Knight.* London: Weidenfeld and Nicolson, 1960.

———. *Speak, Memory: An Autobiography Revisited.* New York: G. P. Putnam's Sons, 1966.

Nemoy, Leon, tr. and ed. *Karaite Anthology: Excerpts from the Early Literature.* New Haven: Yale University Press, 1952.

————, tr. "The Pseudo-Qumisian Sermon to the Karaites" [bilingual text]. *Proceedings of the American Academy for Jewish Research* 43 (1976): 64–74.

Neusner, Jacob. *Judaism: The Evidence of the Mishnah*. Chicago: University of Chicago Press, 1981.

Niger, Shmuel. *Vegn Yidishe shrayber* [On Yiddish Writers]. Vol. 1. Vilna: S. Shrabark, 1912.

————. "Di Yidishe literatur un di lezerin" (1912). In *Bleter geshikhte fun der yidisher literatur* [The History of Yiddish Literature]. New York: World Yiddish Cultural Congress, 1959. For an abridged translation, see "Yiddish Literature and the Female Reader," tr. Sheva Zucker in *Women of the Word: Jewish Women and Jewish Writing*, ed. Judith R. Baskin (Detroit: Wayne State University Press, 1994).

Nora, Pierre. "Between Memory and History: Les Lieux de Mémoire." *Representations*, no. 26 (spring 1989): 7–25.

Norich, Anita. *The Homeless Imagination in the Fiction of Israel Joshua Singer*. Bloomington: Indiana University Press, 1991.

————. Introduction to *Gender and Text in Modern Hebrew and Yiddish Literature*, ed. Naomi B. Sokoloff, Anne Lapidus Lerner, and Anita Norich. New York: Jewish Theological Seminary of America, 1992.

————. "Isaac Bashevis Singer in America: The Translation Problem." *Judaism* 44, no. 2 (spring 1995): 209–18.

Ormian, Haim. 1950. "Israeli Students and Mendele." *YIVO Annual of Jewish Social Science* 5 (1950): 292–312.

Oz, Amos. *Shtikat ha-shamayim: Agnon mishtomem 'al elohim* [The Silence of Heaven: Agnon's Fear of God]. Jerusalem: Keter, 1993.

Ozick, Cynthia. *Art and Ardor: Essays*. New York: E. P. Dutton, 1983.

————. *The Pagan Rabbi and Other Stories*. New York: Knopf, 1971.

Pachter, Henry. "On Being an Exile." In *The Legacy of the German Refugee Intellectuals*, ed. Robert Boyers. New York: Schocken Books, 1969.

Pagis, Ada. *Lev Pitomi* [Sudden Heart]. Tel Aviv: Am Oved, 1995.

Pagis, Dan. "Central Park, Twilight." *Orim* 2, no. 2 (spring 1987): 79.

————. *Hebrew Poetry of the Middle Ages and the Renaissance*. Foreword by Robert Alter. Berkeley: University of California Press, 1991.

————. *Kol ha-shirim; 'Abba' (pirkei proza)* [Collected Poems and "Father" (prose passages)]. Ed. Hanan Hever and T. Carmi. Jerusalem: Ha-kibbutz ha-me'uhad and Bialik Institute, 1991.

————. "Ein Leben" [A Life]. Tr. Stephen Mitchell. *New Yorker*, April 3, 1989, p. 85.

————. "Of ha-almavet: motiv ha-feniks ba-sifrut ha-midrash ve-ha-aggadah" [The Immortal Bird: Motif of the Phoenix in Midrashic and Aggadic Literature]. In *Sefer Ha-yovel* [Jubilee Volume], ed. H. Merhavia. Jerusalem: Hebrew High School of Jerusalem, 1962.

————. *Points of Departure*. Tr. Stephen Mitchell. Intro. by Robert Alter. Philadelphia: Jewish Publication Society, 1981.

————. *Variable Directions: The Selected Poetry of Dan Pagis*. Tr. Stephen Mitchell. San Francisco: North Point Press, 1989.

Paley, Grace. "The Used-Boy Raisers." In *The Little Disturbances of Man*. New York: Viking Press, 1959.

Pardes, Ilana. "Imagining the Promised Land: The Spies in the Land of the Giants." *History and Memory* 6, no. 2 (fall/winter 1994): 5–23.

Patterson, David, and Glenda Abramson, eds. *Tradition and Trauma: Studies in the Fiction of S. Y. Agnon*. Boulder, Colo.: Westview Press, 1994.

Pavel, Thomas G. *Fictional Worlds*. Cambridge, Mass.: Harvard University Press, 1986.

Pawel, Ernst. *Nightmare of Reason: A Life of Franz Kafka*. New York: Farrar, Straus, and Giroux, 1984.

Perry, Menakhem. "Ha-analogia u-mekomah be-mivneh ha-roman shel Mendele mokher sfarim" [The Place of Analogy in the Structure of the Novels of Mendele Mokher Sefarim]. *Ha-sifrut* 1, no. 1 (spring 1968): 65–100.

———. "Thematic and Structural Shifts in Autotranslations by Bilingual Hebrew-Yiddish Writers: The Case of Mendele Mokher Sforim." *Poetics Today* 2, no. 4 (summer/autumn 1981): 181–92.

Pinsker, Sanford. *The Schlemiel as Metaphor: Studies in the Yiddish and American Jewish Novel*. Carbondale: Southern Illinois University Press, 1972.

Pinsky, David. "Der Eybiker Yid: Tragedya in eyn akt" [The Eternal Jew: Tragedy in One Act]. In *Meshihim*. Warsaw: Farlag Ch. Brzoza, 1906.

Pocock, J. G. A. "Deconstructing Europe." *London Review of Books*, December 19, 1991, pp. 6–10.

Preil, Gabriel. *Sunset Possibilities and Other Poems*. Tr. and intro. Robert Friend. Preface by T. Carmi. Philadelphia: Jewish Publication Society, 1985.

Quint, David. *Epic and Empire: Politics and Generic Form from Virgil to Milton*. Princeton: Princeton University Press, 1993.

Raczymow, Henri. *Writing the Book of Esther*. Tr. Dori Katz. London: Holmes and Meier, 1995.

Rahel [Rachel Bluvstein]. *Flowers of Perhaps: Selected Poems of Ra'hel*. Tr. Robert Friend. London: Menard Press, 1995.

———. *Shirat Rahel* [The Poetry of Rachel]. 27th ed. Tel Aviv: Davar, 1978–79.

Ramras-Rauch, Gila, and Joseph Michman-Melkman, eds. 1985. *Facing the Holocaust: Selected Israeli Fiction*. Philadelphia: Jewish Publication Society.

Ratosh, Yonatan. *Sifrut yehudit bilshon ha-'ivrit* [Jewish Literature in the Hebrew Language]. Tel Aviv: Hadar, 1982.

Rattok, Lily. *Bayit 'al blimah: omanut ha-sipur shel A. Appelfeld* [A Precarious House: The Narrative Art of A. Appelfeld]. Tel Aviv: Heker, 1989.

Raz-Karkotzkin, Amnon. "Galut be-tokh ribonut: le-bikorit 'shlilat ha-galut' ba-tarbut ha-yisraelit" [Exile within a Sovereign State: A Critique of the "Negated Exile" in Israeli Culture]. *Teoria u-vikoret* [Theory and Criticism], no. 4 (fall 1993): 23–55.

Renan, Ernst. "What Is a Nation?" Tr. Martin Thom. In *Nation and Narration*, ed. Homi K. Bhabha. London: Routledge, 1990.

Ricoeur, Paul. *Time and Narrative*. Tr. Kathleen McLaughlin and David Pellauer. 3 vols. Chicago: University of Chicago Press, 1984–88.

Robbins, Jill. *Prodigal Son—Elder Brother: Interpretations of Alterity in Au-

gustine, Petrarch, Kafka, and Levinas. Chicago: University of Chicago Press, 1991.

Rosenthal, Mark. *Anselm Kiefer.* Exhibition catalogue. Chicago: Art Institute of Chicago; Philadelphia: Museum of Art, 1987.

Rosenzweig, Franz. *The Star of Redemption.* Notre Dame, Ind.: University of Notre Dame Press, 1985.

Roskies, David. *A Bridge of Longing: The Lost Art of Yiddish Storytelling.* Cambridge, Mass.: Harvard University Press, 1995.

———. "Sholem Aleichem and Others: Laughing Off the Trauma of History." *Prooftexts* 2, no. 1 (January 1982): 53–77.

Roth, Henry. *Call It Sleep* (1934). Intro. by Alfred Kazin. Afterword by Hana Wirth-Nesher. New York: Noonday Press, 1991.

Roth, Philip. *The Counterlife.* New York: Farrar, Straus, and Giroux, 1986.

———. *Operation Shylock: A Confession.* New York: Simon and Schuster, 1993.

———. *Portnoy's Complaint.* New York: Bantam, 1969.

———. *Reading Myself and Others.* New York: Bantam, 1977.

———. *Zuckerman Bound: A Trilogy and Epilogue.* New York: Fawcett Crest, 1985.

Sadan, Dov. *'Al Shai Agnon* [On S. Y. Agnon]. Tel Aviv: Ha-kibbutz ha-me'uhad, 1959.

———. *Avnei bedek* [Foundation Stones]. Tel Aviv: Ha-kibbutz ha-me'uhad, 1962.

———. *Avnei miftan: masot 'al sofrei yidish* [Corner Stones: Essays on Yiddish Writers]. 3 vols. Tel Aviv: Y. L. Peretz, 1961.

———. "Three Foundations: Sholem Aleichem and the Yiddish Literary Tradition" (1959), tr. David G. Roskies. *Prooftexts* 6, no. 1 (January 1986): 55–64.

Said, Edward. *Culture and Imperialism.* New York: Knopf, 1993.

———. *The World, the Text, and the Critic.* Cambridge, Mass.: Harvard University Press, 1983.

Samuel, Maurice. *The World of Sholem Aleichem.* 1943. Reprint, New York: Schocken Books, 1965.

Saperstein, Marc. "Halevi's West Wind." *Prooftexts* 1, no. 3 (September 1981): 306–11.

Saposnik, I. "Translating the Family Moskat: The Metamorphosis of a Novel." *Yiddish* 1, no. 2 (fall 1973): 26–37.

Schechner, Mark. *After the Revolution: Studies in the Contemporary Jewish-American Imagination.* Bloomington: Indiana University Press, 1987.

Scholem, Gershom. *The Messianic Idea in Judaism.* New York: Schocken Books, 1971.

Schorske, Carl. "Freud: The Psycho-archaeology of Civilizations." In *The Cambridge Companion to Freud,* ed. Jerome Neu. Cambridge: Cambridge University Press, 1991.

Schwartz, Regina M. *The Curse of Cain: The Violent Legacy of Monotheism.* Chicago: University of Chicago Press, 1997.

———. "Joseph's Bones and the Resurrection of the Text: Remembering in the Bible." *PMLA* 103, no. 2 (March 1988): 114–24.

Schwartz, Yigal. *Kinat ha-yahid ve-netzah ha-shevet: Aharon Appelfeld: tmunat* 'olam [Individual Lament and Tribal Eternity: Aharon Appelfeld, the Picture of His World]. Jerusalem: Keter, 1996.

Schweid, Eliezer. *The Land of Israel: A Homeland or Land of Destiny?* Tr. Deborah Greniman. New York: Herzl Press/Associated Universities Press, 1985.

Seidel, Michael. *Exile and the Narrative Imagination.* New Haven: Yale University Press, 1986.

Seidman, Naomi. *A Marriage Made in Heaven: The Sexual Politics of Hebrew and Yiddish.* Berkeley: University of California Press, 1997.

Shabtai, Edna. "Tel Aviv as 'Place' in the Fiction of Ya'acov Shabtai." *'Akhshav,* no. 56 (spring/summer 1991): 54–78.

Shai, Eli. "Kemiha mistit le-negi'a ba-kame'a" [Mystical Yearnings to Touch the Sublime]. Review of *Be-hazara la-'ayara* [Back to the Shtetl], by Sh. Ansky, at the Israeli Museum. *Ha-aretz,* Book Section, July 13, 1994, p. 8.

Shaked, Gershon. *Bein s'hok le-dema': 'iyunim bi-yetzirato shel Mendele mokher sefarim* [Between Laughter and Tears: Studies in the Work of Mendele Mokher-Sefarim]. Ramat Gan: Massada, 1965.

———. "Be-khol dor va-dor hayav adam lirot et 'atzmo" [In Each Generation One Must Regard Oneself]. Review of *Layish* by Aharon Appelfeld. *Ha-aretz,* Book Section, July 27, 1994, p. 8.

———. *Gal hadash ba-siporet ha-'ivrit* [New Wave in Hebrew Fiction]. Tel Aviv: Sifriat Po'alim, 1974.

———. "Gavish" [Crystal]. *Yediot Ahronot,* July 7, 1986, p. 21.

———. *The Shadows Within: Essays on Modern Jewish Writers.* Philadelphia: Jewish Publication Society, 1987.

Shammas, Anton. "Amérka, Amérka: A Palestinian Abroad in the Land of the Free." *Harper's Magazine,* February 1991, pp. 55–61.

———. *Arabesques* [Arabeskot]. Tr. Vivian Eden. New York: Harper and Row, 1988.

Shandler, Jeffrey. "Reading Sholem Aleichem from Left to Right." *YIVO Annual* 20 (1991): 305–32.

Shapira, Sarit. "Vehicles." In *Routes of Wandering: Nomadism, Voyages, and Transitions in Contemporary Israeli Art,* ed. Sarit Shapira. Exhibition catalogue. Bilingual edition. Jerusalem: Israel Museum, 1991.

———, ed. *Routes of Wandering: Nomadism, Voyages and Transitions in Contemporary Israeli Art.* Exhibition catalogue. Bilingual edition. Jerusalem: Israel Museum, 1991.

Shmeruk, Chone. "Nokhvort." In Sholem-Aleykhem, *Motl Peyse dem Khazns* [Motl the Cantor Peyse's Son], vol. 2. Jerusalem: Magnes Press, 1996.

———. "Sholem-Aleykhem un Amerike" [Sholem Aleichem and America]. *Di Goldene Keyt,* no. 121 (1987): 55–77.

———. "Sipurei Motl ben he-hazan le-Shalom Aleichem: ha-situatzia ha-epit ve-toldotav shel ha-sefer" [The Tales of Motl the Cantor's Son by Sholem Aleichem: The Epic Situation and the History of the Text]. *Siman Kria,* nos. 12/13 (February 1981): 310–26.

———. "Tevye der milkhiker—toldoteha shel yetzira" [The History of "Tevye the Dairyman"]. *Ha-sifrut* 7, no. 26 (April 1978): 26–38.

Sholem Aleichem. *Adventures of Mottel the Cantor's Son.* Tr. Tamara Kahana, illustr. Ilya Schor. New York: Henry Schuman, 1953.

———. *Ale verk fun Sholem Aleykhem* [Sholem Aleichem: The Collected Work]. 28 vols. New York: Sholem-Aleykhem Folksfond oysgabe, 1927.

———. "Don-Kishot mi-mazepfke ve-simha-pinhas re'ehu" [Don Quixote of Mazepfke and His Friend Simha Pinhas]. *Pardes: osef sifruti* 1, ed. Y. H. Ravnitzky (Odessa, 1892): 267–73.

———. *Funem Yarid* [From the Fair]. New York: Warheit, 1917.

———. *Sholem Aleykhem-Bukh* [Sholem Aleichem Book]. Ed. Y. D. Berkovitz. New York: n.p., 1926.

———. *Sipurei rakevet* [The Railroad Stories]. Ed. and tr. Dan Miron. Tel Aviv: Zmora Bitan, 1989.

———. *Tevye the Dairyman and the Railroad Stories.* Ed. and tr. Hillel Halkin. New York: Schocken Books, 1987.

———. *Why Do the Jews Need a Land of Their Own?* Ed. and tr. Joseph Leftwich and Mordecai S. Chertoff. New York: Herzl Press, 1984.

Sholem-Aleykhem [Sholem Aleichem]. *Motl Peyse dem Khazns* [Motl the Cantor Peyse's Son]. 2 vols. New York: Sholem Aleichem Folksfand Oysgabe, 1927.

Singer, Isaac Bashevis [Isaac Bashevis, pseud.]. "Arum der yidisher literature in polyn" [About Yiddish Literature in Poland]. *Tsukunft* (1943): 468–75.

———. *A Crown of Feathers and Other Stories.* New York: Farrar, Straus, and Giroux, 1973.

———. *A Friend of Kafka and Other Stories.* Harmondsworth: Penguin, 1972.

———. *Gimpel the Fool and Other Stories.* New York: Noonday Press, 1957.

———. "Gimpl tam" [Gimpel the Fool]. *Yidisher Kemfer* 36, no. 593 (March 30, 1945): 364–72.

———. "Interview with Isaac Bashevis Singer." By Joel Blocker and Richard Elman. *Commentary,* May 1963, pp. 364–72.

———. "Di kleyne shusterlekh" [The Little Shoemakers]. *Tsukunft* 50, no. 4 (April 1945): 232–41.

———. "The Last Demon." In *Short Friday.* New York: Noonday Press, 1964. Originally published in Yiddish as "Mayse Tishevits," *Forverts,* March 29, 1959, p. 6.

———. *Lost in America.* Illustr. Raphael Soyer. Garden City, N.Y.: Doubleday, 1981.

———. *Nobel Lecture.* [In English and Yiddish.] New York: Farrar, Straus, and Giroux, 1978.

——— [Isaac Varshavski, pseud.]. "Problemen fun der yidisher proze in amerike," *Svive* 2 (March–April 1943): 2–13.

Singer, Isaac Bashevis, and Richard Burgin. *Conversations with Isaac Bashevis Singer.* New York: Farrar, Straus, and Giroux, 1985.

Slotnick, Susan A. "*The Family Moskat* and the Tradition of the Yiddish Family Saga." In *Recovering the Canon: Essays on Isaac Bashevis Singer,* ed. David Neal Miller. Leiden: E. J. Brill, 1986.

Smith, Henry Nash. "Symbol and Idea in *Virgin Land.*" In *Ideology and Classic American Literature,* ed. Sacvan Bercovitch and Myra Jehlen. Cambridge: Cambridge University Press, 1986.

Smith, Jonathan Z. *Map Is Not Territory: Studies in the History of Religions*. Leiden: E. J. Brill, 1978.

———. *To Take Place: Toward Theory in Ritual*. Chicago: University of Chicago Press, 1987.

Sokoloff, Naomi B. 1992. *Imagining the Child in Modern Jewish Fiction*. Baltimore: Johns Hopkins University Press.

Sokoloff, Naomi B., Anne Lapidus Lerner, and Anita Norich, eds. 1992. *Gender and Text in Modern Hebrew and Yiddish Literature*. New York: Jewish Theological Seminary of America.

Sollors, Werner. "Immigrants and Other Americans." In *Columbia Literary History of the United States*, general ed. Emory Elliott. New York: Columbia University Press, 1988.

Sontag, Susan. *On Photography*. New York: Farrar, Straus, and Giroux, 1977.

Spence, Jonathan. *The Memory Palace of Matteo Ricci*. New York: Viking, 1984.

Steiner, George. *After Babel: Aspects of Language and Translation*. London: Oxford University Press, 1975.

———. "Our Homeland, the Text." *Salmagundi*, no. 66 (winter–spring 1985): 4–25.

Stern, Michael. "Tevye's Art of Quotation." *Prooftexts* 6, no. 1 (January 1986): 79–96.

Stroop, Juergen. *The Stroop Report*. Tr. Sybil Milton. New York: Pantheon Books, 1979.

Swissa, Albert. 'Akud [The Bound]. Tel Aviv: Ha-kibbutz ha-me'uhad, 1990.

Szondi, Peter. "Lecture de Strette." In *Poésies et Poétiques de la Modernité*, ed. Mayotte Bollack. [Lille]: Presses Universitaires de Lille, 1981.

Taylor, Mark. *Erring: A Postmodern A/theology*. Chicago: University of Chicago Press, 1984.

Taylor, Paul. "Painter of the Apocalypse." *New York Times Magazine*, October 16, 1988, p. 49.

Teller, Judd. *Strangers and Natives: The Evolution of the American Jew from 1921 to the Present*. New York: Delacorte Press, 1968.

Thomas, D. M. "Face to Face with His Double." Review of *Operation Shylock*, by Philip Roth. *New York Times Book Review*, March 7, 1993, p. 1.

Torgovnik, Marianna. *Gone Primitive: Savage Intellects, Modern Lives*. Chicago: University of Chicago Press, 1990.

Trunk, Y. Y. *Sholem Aleykhem: zein vezen un zeine verk* [Sholem Aleichem: His Being and His Work]. Warsaw: Kulturlige, 1937.

Udoff, Alan. "On Poetic Dwelling: Situating Celan and the Holocaust." In *Argumentum e Silentio: International Paul Celan Symposium*, ed. Amy D. Colin. Berlin: Walter de Gruyter, 1987.

Vakum ha-'olam: mivhar pirkei shira ve-prosa mi-thum ha-shoah, 1958–1978 [The World's Vacuum: Selected Poetry and Prose from the Holocaust, 1958–1978]. Tel Aviv: 'Eked, 1978.

Valensi, Lucette, and Nathan Wachtel. *Jewish Memories*. Tr. Barbara Harshav. Berkeley: University of California Press, 1991.

Vidal-Naquet, Pierre. "Atlantis and the Nations." *Critical Inquiry* 18, no. 2 (winter 1992): 300–326.

Walfish, Barry. "The Mourners of Zion (Avelei Siyyon): Karaite Aliyah Movement of the Early Arab Period." In *Eretz Israel, Israel, and the Jewish Diaspora: Mutual Relations*, ed. Menachem Mor. Studies in Jewish Civilization 1. Lanham, Md.: University Press of America, 1991.

Watkin, Evan. "Lyric Poetry as Social Language." In *Argumentum e Silentio: International Paul Celan Symposium*, ed. Amy D. Colin. Berlin: Walter de Gruyter, 1987.

Weinreich, Max. *History of the Yiddish Language*. Chicago: University of Chicago Press, 1980.

Welsh, Alexander. *Reflections on the Hero as Quixote*. Princeton: Princeton University Press, 1981.

Werses, Shmuel. "'Olam ha-folklor beyetzirat Mendele" [Folklore in the Works of Mendele]. *Dapim le-mehkar be-sifrut* [Pages in Literary Research] 9 (1994): 7–27.

————. *Sipur ve-shorsho: 'iyunim be-hitpathut ha-prosa ha-'ivrit* [Story and Source: Studies in the Development of Hebrew Prose]. Ramat Gan: Massada, 1971.

Wirth-Nesher, Hana. *City Codes: Reading the Modern Urban Novel*. Cambridge: Cambridge University Press, 1996.

————. "From Newark to Prague: Roth's Place in the American Jewish Literary Tradition." In *What Is Jewish Literature?* ed. Hana Wirth-Nesher. Philadelphia: Jewish Publication Society, 1994.

————, ed. *What Is Jewish Literature?* Philadelphia: Jewish Publication Society, 1994.

Wisse, Ruth. *I. L. Peretz and the Making of Modern Jewish Culture*. Seattle: University of Washington Press, 1991.

————. "Jewish Guilt and Israeli Writers." *Commentary*, January 1989, pp. 25–31.

————. "The Jewish Writer and the Problem of Evil." In *Terms of Survival: The Jewish World Since 1945*, ed. Robert S. Wistrich. London: Routledge, 1995.

————. *A Little Love in Big Manhattan*. Cambridge, Mass.: Harvard University Press, 1988.

————. *The Schlemiel as Modern Hero*. Chicago: University of Chicago Press, 1971.

————. "Singer's Paradoxical Progress." *Commentary*, February 1979, pp. 33–38.

————, ed. *A Shtetl and Other Yiddish Novellas*. New York: Behrman House, 1973.

Wolosky, Shira. *Language Mysticism: The Negative Way of Language in Eliot, Beckett, and Celan*. Stanford: Stanford University Press, 1995.

Yadin, Yigal. *The Message of the Scrolls*. Ed. James H. Charlesworth. New York: Christian Origins Library, 1992.

Yaoz, Hannah. "Ha-mitos shel ha-palit" [The Myth of the Refugee]. *'Iton 77*, no. 9 (August–September 1994): 175–76.

Yaoz-Kest, Itamar. "The Phosphorus Line." Tr. Dalya Bilu. In *Facing the Holocaust: Selected Israeli Fiction*, ed. Gila Ramras-Rauch and Joseph Michman-Melkman. Philadelphia: Jewish Publication Society, 1985.

Yates, Frances Amelia. *The Art of Memory*. Harmondsworth: Penguin, 1969.

Yehoshua, A. B. *Mr. Mani*. Tr. Hillel Halkin. San Diego: Harcourt Brace, 1992.

Yerushalmi, Yosef Hayim. *Zakhor: Jewish History and Jewish Memory*. Seattle: University of Washington Press, 1982.

Young, James E. *The Texture of Memory: Holocaust Memorials and Meaning*. New Haven: Yale University Press, 1993.

————, ed. *The Art of Memory: Holocaust Memorials in History*. Exhibition catalogue. New York: Prestel, 1994.

Zerubavel, Yael. *Recovered Roots: Collective Memory and the Making of Israeli National Tradition*. Chicago: University of Chicago Press, 1995.

Zipperstein, Steven. *Elusive Prophet: Ahad Ha-am and the Origins of Zionism*. Berkeley: University of California Press, 1993.

Zunz, Leopold. "On the Geographical Literature of the Jews from the Remotest Times to the Year 1841." In vol. 2 of Benjamin of Tudela, *Itinerary of Rabbi Benjamin of Tudela*. Tr. and ed. A. Asher. New York: Hakeshet Publishing, 1841.

Index

Text:	10/13 Sabon
Display:	Sabon
Composition:	Integrated Composition Systems
Printing and binding:	Data Reproductions Corporation
Index:	Barbara Roos